Maureen Paton is a freelance journalist and broadcaster specialising in arts, media and women's issues. The author of a biography of the actor and director Alan Rickman, she is a contributor to *The Times*, the *Daily Telegraph*, the *London Evening Standard*, the *Stage*, *Radio Times* and *Woman & Home* among others. She lives in north London.

The Best of Women

The History of Women of the Year

Maureen Paton

First published by The Women's Press Ltd, 2000
A member of the Namara Group
34 Great Sutton Street, London EC1V OLQ
www.the-womens-press.com

British Library Cataloguing-in-Publication Data
A catalogue record for this book is available from the British Library.

ISBN 0 7043 4689 3

Typeset in Sabon by FiSH Books Ltd, London
Printed and bound in Great Britain by CPD (Wales) Ltd, Ebbw Vale

*To all the women whose work all over the world
upholds communities now and in the future*

Contents

List of Illustrations   ix

Prologue by Eve Pollard   xiii

1 The Shepherdess and the Solicitor   1

2 Pankhurst the Equaliser and a
    Woman Called Tony   29

3 The Best of Women:
    Odette Hallowes and Others   50

4 Pageant of Personalities   74

5 Themes of the Lunches   102

6 The Empty Chair   149

7 Could Women Change the World?   158

Epilogue by Floella Benjamin   171

Appendix A Speakers and
    Guests of Honour 1959–1999   181

Appendix B Guest lists and
    Themes 1964–1999   216

List of Illustrations

Page 1: Tony Lothian, Lady Georgina Coleridge, Odette Hallowes
Page 2: Mikki Doyle, Renée Goddard, Valentina Tereshkova, Floella Benjamin
Page 3: Emmeline Pankhurst, Coretta King, Violet Attlee, Aung San Suu Kyi
Pages 4 to 16: A panorama of guests who have attended Lunches over the years

Grateful acknowledgement for the use of these photographs is made to:
Jenny Beeston
Daily Express (photos from 1974)
Nic Dunlop (Aung San Suu Kyi)
Hulton Getty (Odette Hallowes, Violet Attlee, Emmeline Pankhurst; photos from 1966, 1981, 1987)
Charles Green (cover photos, Tony Lothian, Floella Benjamin, Coretta King, photos from 1994, 1996, 1997)
Jean Havilland (cover photos, Renée Goddard, photos from 1998)
Keystone Press Agency (photos from 1976, 1977, 1979)
Desmond O'Neill
Sound Stills Photographs (photos from 1995)
Barry Swaebe (photos from 1975)

Acknowledgements

Grateful acknowledgement is made to the following:

The Leadership Trust Foundation for their support

Eve Pollard for her Prologue

Carol Banfield

Angela Banfield

Rosalind Edwards

Geoffrey Hallowes, husband of Odette Hallowes

Georgina Coleridge

Tony Lothian OBE

Floella Benjamin

All Chairmen, Committee Members and Patrons, past, present and future

All the photographers and contributors

Elsbeth Lindner and the team at The Women's Press

Liam Maguire

Prologue
by Eve Pollard

The invitation arrives – weeks and weeks before the date. Even though many of the women attending would normally wait until closer to the event to RSVP, canny females know that for every available seat in the Savoy's Abraham Lincoln Room there are several Sarahs, Elizabeths and what-have-yous out there longing to take their place. The lunch is always over-subscribed. The invitation is prized – whether one is lucky enough to be a regular or not – because it is the culmination of a judgement by those most important to us: our peers. Put simply, this invitation means that other women have thought us worthy: that is enough.

The Women of the Year Lunch is a high-profile, unique occasion. Sometimes Fleet Street's finest journalists are sent to cover it, but they miss the point. This is not a navel-staring, dress-to-impress occasion, although without doubt there are some attendees who buy a new outfit specially. There are also lunchers who are prepared to show off their perfect grooming – just another facet of their amazing organisational abilities and brilliant career! However, many of the women attending have come straight from from the office, so clean and tidy is the order of the day.

Unlike most big lunches, this one isn't racist, ageist or

anything else – except possibly blackist – yearly the fashion colour of choice of the galaxy of females, famous and infamous, young and old, regulars or first-timers. Some are meeting friends. Some are most interested in the morning debate. Some are nervous and quite alone, braving the occasion because it is a very special one and they may have been invited for the most glorious or the most tragic of reasons.

I always wear waterproof mascara to this event. It is a rare year when, listening to the personal stories re-counted of amazing endeavour and achievement against all the odds, I don't cry. But I always laugh too – particularly when I recall one Women of the Year lunch in the eighties.

As a committee member I had been helping with the catalogue and was duly honoured by being asked to be a hostess. This involves making sure that a goodie bag (a big stiff paper bag of little gifts given by different manufacturers) is on or by each seat. These are packed by the committee and, for security, tied together and put underneath each table. On the day of the Lunch the elected table hostess arrives early in order to untie and distribute the bags.

Naturally, on the day of the Lunch, I was held up at the office and arrived late. As a result I found myself still crouched beneath one of the tables, desperately trying to untie these bags, when the ballroom started to fill with people. The more I rushed, the harder it was to separate the handles. This was, I may add, just after a well publicised television programme about mice infesting many of the kitchens of our great and famous hotels.

As I wrestled with the string and struggled to release the ten crisp, full carrier bags I felt something wet lick my cheek. Like many women I have a phobia about mice. I nearly levitated the table with me. I wanted to collapse with shock as the final knot came away. I crept out from under the table – hoping that I would be able to get to my feet notwithstanding my shocked and horrified state. Imagine my relief when I looked up to discover that one of the guests was a female shepherd – accompanied by her dog.

That was even more stressful than the year I was chosen to speak at the Women of the Year, a very special moment for me.

As usual, on the way back to the office afterwards the cab driver asked who the Woman of the Year was. I explained, as I have to every year, that we all were – even the dog!

Chapter One
The Shepherdess and the Solicitor

A unique event has captured in microcosm the lives of modern women. Held at London's Savoy Hotel every year since 1955, it has become a legend in its own lunchtime by presenting a living encyclopedia of female achievement. In bringing together key women whose deeds have helped to shape society, it has reflected nearly every major happening in the latter half of the twentieth century.

Caruso sang at the Savoy, Sir Henry Irving lived there, Monet painted the River Thames from the hotel, Pavlova danced in it and Sarah Bernhardt, always a bit of a drama queen, nearly died in it. The Savoy's very first chef, the celebrated Auguste Escoffier, created Pêche Melba in honour of the opera singer Dame Nellie Melba's visits to London; Marconi made the first wireless broadcast to America from the hotel, Guccio Gucci washed dishes in its kitchens before founding his luxury leather empire; and George Kessler, the Wall Street financier, flooded its forecourt with champagne to recreate Venice for his legendary Gondola dinner in 1905.

All this wonderfully quirky history made the Savoy the perfect dramatic setting for a gathering which has made world news on its own account year after year since its modest beginnings, when no one knew whether such an experiment could possibly last. Just as the silent-film cowboy Tom Mix caused a sensation by cantering across the Savoy ballroom on a horse called Tony, so a woman called Tony would create a similar stir and make more waves over nearly half a century than Kessler did when he floated a silk-lined gondola decorated with 12,000 carnations on his courtyard of champagne.

She created a unique event whose very decibel level sets it apart. The hundreds of voices have always reminded the author Shirley Conran of 'a convention of starlings... You would hear it as you walked towards the River Entrance of the Savoy Hotel.'

The birdsong evoked by Conran is the sound of the five hundred guests at the Women of the Year Lunch and Assembly, an occasion without precedent. Every October, five hundred women achievers from all walks of life are invited to the Savoy Hotel in the Strand in order to celebrate their success. One former Lunch chairman, Prue Penn – lady-in-waiting to the Queen Mother and a one-time collaborator with Benjamin Britten on the world-famous Aldeburgh music festival in Suffolk – cherishes the event for the way in which it brings together 'a vast number of interesting and achieving women'. What makes it so distinctive is the exhilarating, convention-defying, giddy-making mix.

Where else would you meet a woman truck driver, a shepherdess, a female Chief Constable, Britain's only woman aerobatics pilot, a cowgirl rider for Europe, a female Master of the Worshipful Company of Farmers, the UK's only female dry-stone-wall builder, the president of the National Association of Gypsy Women, solicitors, politicians, stockbrokers, writers and actresses – or hear speeches by the likes of Martin Luther King's widow, Coretta King, and Valentina Tereshkova, the first woman in space?

Every invitee is there in her own right; there are no

passengers, even by virtue of royal blood, since the royal guests must be seen to have made their mark that year in order to be invited. As for the wives of important men, they are only included if they have their own individual claim to fame.

These women are the antithesis of the mythical Ladies Who Lunch.

For many of the women who attend, lunch – except for a grabbed sandwich at work – is usually for wimps. But they make an exception for this unique occasion, which is not so much a mere Lunch as an exhilarating feast of achievement that acts as a spur to the imagination by showing exactly what women can do.

Now a national and an international symbol, the Women of the Year Lunch was born out of one woman's belief that 'when women meet, there is always more to unite than to divide'. That woman is Tony Lothian. Sinister experiences in Nazi Germany had sharpened her sense of justice. And it was her friendship with a legendary war heroine that was to concentrate her mind still further upon a radical social experiment which would mix classes, creeds, ages and colours. To bring women together in a unique gathering, Tony proposed 'an enjoyable occasion which studied serious human challenges'. The idea was to invite women at the top of their professions to meet and greet and eat, at the same time exchanging stories and raising money for charity so that none would feel guilty at travelling to London for an upmarket jolly.

The event was far ahead of its time. In the Dark Ages of 1955, it was not so easy to find five hundred famous and not-so-famous guests to fulfil the criteria; now, forty-five years on, the Women of the Year committee regretfully has to turn away thousands among those nominated. As journalist Diana Hutchinson remarked in the *Mail on Sunday*'s You magazine, 'It is a hundred times harder to get into this Lunch than to be invited to a Royal Garden Party.'

Every year at the Lunch there is an international guest of honour, whose ranks have included Petra Kelly, Jehan El-Sadat, Simone Veil, Valentina Tereshkova and Coretta King. The women who attend are jealous of their independent allegiance to a variety of beliefs, but there is one which usually unites them all: measures to advance peace. Here Coretta King personifies the ideal of peace achieved through 'non-violent social change' and on the two occasions when she spoke to the Women of the Year about this ideal all present were united to support her. 'She reminded us of how peace and civil rights were fought for and won in America and hoped the rest of the world could put the same example into practice,' says Tony Lothian.

The story of the Lunch is the story of women in the second half of the twentieth century. This 'phenomenal female hall of fame', as one female commentator called it, has included Nobel Peace Prize winner Betty Williams, Margaret Thatcher, Edwina Mountbatten, Dame Ninette de Valois, Dr Jung Chang, Queen Noor of Jordan and Germaine Greer. Themes of the Lunch have included human rights, global conservation, peace campaigns and strategies for 'making the Cold War less frozen' as well as more light-hearted subjects.

Each woman is nominated by an equally illustrious woman. The guests descend upon the welcoming reception that is held in the theatrical River Room before the Lunch begins in the cream-and-blue Lancaster Room, the rococo ballroom that has hosted so many awards ceremonies. The Assembly, established in 1998 to give Lunch guests a chance to debate the great issues of the day before the serious socialising and speech-making begin, takes place in the Beaufort Room a few hours before the reception and Lunch. In such an atmosphere, people whose paths would normally never cross discover extraordinary emotional or intellectual connections. At the centre of the hubbub is a rakish, piratical-looking figure with a cockatoo shock of dark hair, a black eyepatch and what looks suspiciously like an Irish shillelagh. Leaning on this knobbly stick with both hands, Tony Lothian surveys you with a keen, shrewd appraisal that misses nothing.

Writing in the *Guardian* back in 1982, journalist Frances Cairncross described Lady Lothian as 'an intimidating aristocrat whose black eyepatch gives her a warlike appearance'.

So who precisely is Tony Lothian OBE, founder-president of the Women of the Year Lunch? Perhaps she is best described as a contradiction in terms who has been taking delight in uniting opposites for nearly half a century. Presiding over the event like the megaphoneless director of an international, multiracial, multi-skilled film crew, Tony Lothian is a socialist who has made a very happy marriage to a Tory government minister, became mistress of Ferniehirst Castle – 'just a jumped-up farmhouse, really' – near the Border town of Jedburgh, Roxburghshire, and has been confounding prejudice and expectation ever since.

'I never thought I would ever live within the shadow of Peter Jones,' remarks a jokily doleful Tony, whose London base is her husband's flat off the King's Road in Chelsea. It is impossible not to notice that there are Christmas cards from Prince Charles and Princess Anne on one shelf, yet somehow she manages to pull off the trick of being both Establishment and anti-Establishment at the same time. Lazy assumptions are made about this highly individual character at one's peril. 'My talent', she writes in her forthcoming autobiography, 'is to be a chameleon.' Yet this woman is too distinctive, too decided, to blend in blandly with her surroundings.

She married the Chief of the Scottish Kerr clan, the 12th Marquess of Lothian, in 1943. Like Tony, Peter is an original. He also plays a mean piano – 'Bye Bye Blackbird' a speciality. 'Peter and I met in our prams,' says Tony nonchalantly. 'Our mothers knew each other. We had constant quarrels – I don't believe in marriages where you never have a cross word – but we had six children in rapid succession.' Theirs is the kind of family that can absorb political differences with a worldly tolerance, affection and mutual respect. 'The Kerrs were public servants rather than grandees, and all are involved in community work. I should say we are all idealists: we all have to have a belief, something that goes quite deep in all of us.'

Born Antonella but universally known as Tony, in 1997 the half-Italian Marchioness of Lothian was selected as one of the fifty most inspirational women in the world by *Harper's* magazine and one of the fifty most influential women in Britain by *Woman's Journal*. *Harper's* revealed that Tony tended to be in church when she wasn't working; she herself admits, 'I get strength from the quiet and peace of church as often as possible.' Yet this former journalist and TV producer, who often wears a tie characteristically wrenched askew from her neck, looks rather like a superannuated St Trinian's schoolgirl – a comparison that makes her smile.

A committed woman of peace, she reserves the right to retain a self-mocking sense of drama and mischief. 'I have always worn ties because I like Edwardian fashions like collars and ties,' she explains. 'Perhaps there's a St Trinian's schoolgirl in me still.' Despite the fact that she is an obvious force for good, she insists that she doesn't particularly like 'good' people – by which she means insufferable goody-goodies. 'I'm now comforted when I read about some saints, but saints were irritating and drove people round the bend,' she remarks in her usual disarming way. 'The key to me is that I like joking and I don't like getting serious, but behind the jokes there's quite a lot of thought – a bit like the operatic crying clown.'

Tony and her committee hammer out nominations for the Women of the Year Lunch over a series of meetings in London throughout the year. The journalist Val Hennessy sat in on one committee meeting in 1993 and recorded it in the *Sunday Express*: 'Lady Lothian... attending this meeting against doctor's orders, [says], "I may be full of pills, like a character from *The Valley of the Dolls*, but it won't prevent me from saying that this year's Luncheon will be the best ever"...'

One year, a high-achiever was placed next to her husband's mistress, while an author found herself beside the critic who had panned her book. But if that happens, don't expect Tony to lose confidence. Diplomacy aside, there are, it seems, only two rigid rules: no religion and no politics in speeches. Apart from that, no one quite knows what will happen at the Lunch. This is what has always given the gathering its edge.

'Even Royals felt they were being honoured by being invited; and I remember my disbelief, pride and joy at getting the invitation,' recalls Shirley Conran. 'Tony Lothian and her committee were in the business of talent-spotting: I was a 23-year-old fabric designer, a little unknown from Portsmouth, but Penelope Gilliatt was *Vogue* features editor in 1955 and had run an article on me. I wore a black velvet spinnaker to the Lunch and I was very nervous.'

Conran was to find herself seated next to a woman who must have been as rare as a unicorn back in the fifties: a female engineer. In those pre-feminist days, it seemed positively avant-garde, not to say freakish, to hold a high-profile Lunch at one of the world's most famous hotels in order to honour women's contribution to society. Most of the benignly condescending press coverage focused on the hats. Are we surprised? Tony Lothian responded by always wearing funny hats, an objective made possible by the royal milliner Simone Mirman who shared her sense of humour. 'When the Lunch began, it was a time when women liked celebrations where hats were worn. I hated hats so I compromised by wearing joke hats. I loved the South American film star Carmen Miranda so I copied her turban.'

Yet the Women of the Year Lunch has tracked the progress of women for nearly five decades with an unerring eye, sometimes even anticipating history and setting a world agenda with such coups as a speech for peace by the Soviet cosmonaut Valentina Tereshkova.

The twentieth century saw the greatest advancements and the greatest destruction in the history of mankind; and many of the most seismic upheavals and radical developments have been represented by a Woman of the Year. The British spy Odette led the French resistance to Nazism, while Tony Lothian and the former Hitler Youth member Renée Goddard fought valiantly against anti-Semitism and Helen Suzman against apartheid; the one-time Red Guard Dr Jung Chang chronicled the human cost of China's Cultural Revolution; space travel was embodied by Tereshkova and the astronaut Helen Sharman; the scientist Professor Margaret Gowing and the economist Barbara Ward warned of the dangers of atomic annihilation; the German Green Party MP Petra Kelly, the ecological reformer Sarah Parkin of Forum for the Future and the nutritionist Audrey Eyton addressed ecological and nutritional crises, while the feminist writer and academic Germaine Greer was a key speaker on the women's fertility revolution; and civil rights were represented by Coretta King, Mikki Doyle, the QC Helena Kennedy and Lesley Abdela.

So what was happening in the world outside the Savoy

Hotel back in 1955? Churchill, who had led Britain to victory in the Second World War and then lost the peace when the country voted for a change of government in 1945, stepped down from the Tory premiership on 5 April. Labour also elected a new leader that year when Hugh Gaitskell, whose right-of-centre philosophy would later be inherited by Tony Blair, took over from the newly ennobled Clement Attlee, beating Aneurin Bevan and Herbert Morrison into second and third place respectively. Morrison, who had been chief architect of Labour's 1945 election victory, was the deputy leader of the Labour Party and had been widely seen as the natural successor to Earl Attlee – whose wife Violet was one of the founders of the Women of the Year Lunch.

That same month of April 1955 saw Ruth Ellis sent for trial at the Old Bailey, accused of her lover's murder. Her trial lasted just two days: found guilty, she became the last woman in Britain to be executed. Such was the enormous public outcry against her hanging that her case proved to be a turning-point in the campaign for the abolition of the death penalty in the United Kingdom. Years later in her eloquent 1992 book *Eve Was Framed*, Helena Kennedy QC, a memorable speaker at the Women of the Year Lunch, was to argue that the male-dominated justice system often displayed prejudice against female transgressors, sometimes punishing them quite disproportionately by comparison with men.

On the world stage, 1955 saw the first bus boycott by black people in Montgomery, Alabama, after Rosa Parks was fined fourteen dollars for refusing to give up her seat to a white man as required by the segregationist race laws of the time. With those boycotts began the civil rights movement led by the Rev. Dr Martin Luther King, who organised the historic mass march on Washington in 1963, was awarded the Nobel Peace Prize in 1964 and was assassinated in 1968. His widow

Coretta was to be another distinguished speaker at the Women of the Year Lunch.

The year 1955 also saw an increase in the numbers of Caribbean immigrants arriving in Southampton, many of them taking up essential jobs that white people disdained. Of his human cargo in their specially fitted sixty-berth dormitories, the captain of the liner *Fairsea* commented: 'They were among the cleanest, most respectable and intelligent passengers I have ever carried.' The actress and producer Floella Benjamin, chairman of the Women of the Year Lunch and Assembly, was to recall her own passage as a child from Trinidad to the mother country three years later in her book *Coming to England*, published in 1995.

With the new vogue for working-class heroes typified by novelist Alan Sillitoe, playwright Harold Pinter, actor Albert Finney and composer Lionel Bart, Britain found itself at a cultural crossroads at the beginning of the next decade. Nineteen-sixty was the year in which a jury ruled that DH Lawrence's *Lady Chatterley's Lover*, a novel banned for thirty years for its sexual explicitness, was not obscene; one cannot help suspecting that the prosecuting counsel Mervyn Griffith-Jones's condescending question to the jury, 'Is it a book you would wish your wife or your servant to read?' might have been the turning-point. And the Lunch's committee demonstrated its ability to be ahead of its time with a prescient choice of speaker: Margaret Thatcher, who had been elected to Parliament as the Conservative Member for Finchley only the year before, one of a handful of women Members of Parliament.

Tony Lothian is indeed the talent-spotter that Shirley Conran calls her. 'We've all got a capacity – I don't want to call it a talent – for something. I'm like a water-diviner,' she acknowledges. 'I notice people who are interesting and genuine and who contribute something important. My own nature is one of intense curiosity about human beings. If I sit on a bench next to someone in the park, I find their view of events interesting. One of my friends once said, "Tony always wants to know why."'

Everything is personal for Tony, who combines English irony and North European rationalism with a heartfelt, almost reckless capacity for admiration that can be traced to her half-Italian heritage. Even her reason for selecting the Savoy Hotel as the setting for the Women of the Year Lunch was a personal one, she says.

'The manager of the Savoy back in 1955 was a man called Paolo Contarini, who had a small villa in San Remo, Italy, where my father, who had very bad bronchitis, used to go for the winter to get out of the London fog. So there I was, this fat little girl from his past, who turned up on Paolo's doorstep in London and said, "Can you help?" He liked the idea of women who contributed to the community meeting and helping to raise money for charity at the same time.' Floella Benjamin also praises the contribution in more recent years of the Savoy's head chef Anton Edelmann, who created a Caribbean menu for the five hundred Lunch guests at her request in 1996, the first year of her chairmanship.The experiment was so successful that Edelmann now lectures on Caribbean cooking. 'Men in particular have always liked the idea of the Women of the Year Lunch; maybe they had a slight conscience about their prestigious meetings that the papers always took notice of,' says Tony Lothian.

But the Women of the Year Lunch has consistently made the news. There have been many controversial moments, yet only once has it been disrupted by a protest. This came from the veteran peace campaigner Pat Arrowsmith, who stood up when everyone else was seated, whipped out a rubber bullet, yanked open her cardigan to reveal a Troops Out T-shirt and then bawled: 'I'm not here for Women's Lib. Get English troops out of Ireland!' The vice-president and co-founder Lady Georgina Coleridge, who had made her name as a magazine editor, was presiding over that particular Lunch. Stately as a galleon, she sailed across the room 'with every sign of composure', according to former chairman Anne Dickinson (now Phillips), 'and told Pat that she must not say any more. She didn't ask her to leave, but she asked her to finish her lunch. There was a gasp of shock – and then everyone carried on enjoying themselves.'

Then there was the occasion when the committee debated an invitation to the newly divorced Princess Diana to be royal guest of honour at the Lunch; some feared that it could be interpreted as taking sides in a royal divorce that had divided public opinion. And there have been several other tricky moments over the years. Princess Anne and Glenda Jackson sat side by side at one Lunch but, to the chagrin of Tony Lothian, didn't appear to communicate. And Sabrina, the stupendously endowed model, had belatedly asked to speak at the Lunch in a bid to change her dumb-blonde image. Unfortunately the list of speakers that year had already been fixed, so Sabrina walked out.

Encouraged by Tony, the comedienne Pamela Stephenson told colostomy gags and upset many older guests, while even the veteran Dora Bryan shocked some people at the Lunch with her blue jokes. 'We suffer from a small group of Pharisees,' says Tony.

The magician Fay Presto had been nominated by the Chief Commissioner of the Girl Guides, who did not realise that technically Fay was not qualified to attend because she had been born a man. 'We decided that if she wanted to come and she believed she was a woman, we should ask her as a woman,' recalls Tony. And was the

Chief Commissioner embarrassed by her inability to recognise a transsexual when she saw one? 'Not at all,' Tony says drily. 'You don't become head of the Girl Guides without having a sense of humour.'

Then there was the year when the first Lady Cobham was happily taking the seat of the second Lady Cobham before being persuaded by a committee member to sit elsewhere.

Yet the successes have always vastly outnumbered the sticky moments. There is the importance of the Lunch as a charity fund-raiser alone – for the Greater London Fund for the Blind until 1997, followed by NCH Action for Children for three years. The Frink Award, inaugurated in 1987 for women achievers who have overcome disability, was followed by the symbolic Empty Chair Award in 1996 for women who – because of imprisonment or even death – could not be there. Tony Lothian likes to quote the response of the late Mother Teresa when the Albanian-born nun, founder of the Missionaries of Charity, was nominated for the Lunch: 'She said she might come if she could bring a bag to put her food in and take it back to the London homeless.'

The singularity of the event, together with the high celebrity turnout, caught the attention of the press from the outset. 'It is a field day for rubber-necks who, with all the excitement of small boys train-spotting, collect real-life close-ups of celebrities,' wrote Audrey Slaughter in the London *Evening Standard* on the occasion of the Lunch's 25th anniversary back in 1980. 'Intrepid passers-by along the Thames Embankment are likely to be engulfed by a tidal wave of women all trying to get into the Savoy Hotel by the inadequate doors, totally ignoring the bemused attempts of the top-hatted doormen to impose some control. For some reason it attracts attempts at ridicule by men (though they now copy it with their Men of Distinction Luncheon) with outdated remarks about female hats from male reporters (at least three-quarters of the turnout tomorrow will be hatless) and frosty disbelief at being rejected by companies hiring PRs to get their women execs in on the act.'

The Scottish journalist Liz Taylor painted a similar picture in the *Scotsman* eleven years later: 'Edwina Currie beaming in emerald green and a sun-tanned Kate Adie in black... This must be the most truly egalitarian and meritocratic gathering in Europe, if not the world... Guests are selected regardless of age, class, discipline, race or colour...'

Daily Mail columnist Lynda Lee-Potter got the point of the Lunch immediately when she was nominated (several times) as a guest. 'The five hundred guests were there because our expectations of ourselves were that "anything is possible",' she subsequently wrote in her column. 'There were surgeons, pilots, police superintendents, editors, politicians and, as always, it was inspiring and fun. If anybody had told us that we live in a man's world and that there was much more pressure on men than women to be successful, we'd have laughed like drains. In many ways, the pressures on women today are enormous because we know that the chances are there, if we've got the guts and brains to take them. Many career women do decide later to stay at home when they have children, but it's rubbish to say their professional training has then been a waste. Achievement and knowledge gained in the past is never negated and children do grow up.'

As the Women of the Year Lunch grew in stature, however, so the critics started carping. This was almost axiomatic, since the press – as Tony Lothian knows full well from her media background – must always find a new angle. Jane Gordon, writing in *Today* newspaper in 1989, commented: 'Hardly a week passes by these days without some kind of wimmin's award. It is almost as if no one has told the women's magazines who sponsor these events that, at 46.2 per cent of the workforce, we are less of a minority and well on our way to being a majority.' But that is exactly what is being celebrated by the Women of the Year Lunch.

To do Gordon justice, she reserved greater criticism for the Women of the World lunch. 'Although Women of the World boasted Princess Diana as guest of honour, their collection of wittering, award-winning women was lacklustre compared to Women of the Year where Princess Margaret held court,' she wrote. So successful did Gordon feel the Women of the Year Lunch to be that 'if anyone needed a pioneer now, it was probably the working man'.

Not all the critics were female, of course. Like Jane Gordon, Peter McKay in the London *Evening Standard* also picked up on the fact that two women's luncheons were being held on the same day. 'Women of the Year suggests to me doughty do-gooders who have fought against male arrogance to establish dominion of the female gender, while Women of the World conjures up thoughts of slit skirts, hotel bars and no questions asked. The kind of women who organise these ridiculous functions are – like men who like to closet themselves continually with other men – as pompous and sexless as Freemasons and Rotarians. Individually I am certain that each and every one of them is charming. But en masse, I would sooner sup with a convention of sausage salesmen in Skegness,' wrote McKay.

David Thomas, who has made a reputation for himself as a satirical writer on the so-called sex war, considered the Women of the Year Lunch to be 'no less degrading than the Miss World contest. Both make the sexist assumption that women are a special case, which does women no favours. It assumes they can't make it as people,' he claimed.

'Of all the invitations I haven't received this month, the

event I will be least sorry to miss is the 41st Women of the Year Lunch,' wrote columnist Charlotte Raven in the *Guardian*. Only because, apparently, she 'already knew that girls were just much better in all respects than boys'. So why not simply celebrate it? Indeed, the critics of the Women of the Year Lunch seemed to be fascinated, if not obsessed by it: Barbara Amiel in the *Daily Telegraph* devoted a column item to the Lunch for two years running. Although she had turned down an invitation to it the first time, she wrote that she was pleased to see that 'the sporting Lady Lothian turned her atheist cheek and invited me back'. In fact Tony is a Roman Catholic.

The point about the Women of the Year Lunch is that none of its guests needs to feel ashamed of discussing the apparently trivial alongside the world-shaking subjects. 'One woman said to me, "It's the only event where you can talk about children and pantihose and world events,"' says Floella Benjamin.

Significantly, many of the criticisms of the Women of the Year Lunch were vague in the extreme. Columnists strained every sinew to try to find something negative to say. In 1991 Rhoda Koenig wrote in the London *Evening Standard*: 'There is something dated about titles like Woman of the Year... when prizes are given out for the best female this or the best woman that, a faint children's party air hangs over them...' She was wrong: the Women of the Year have always avoided prizes.

'The fact is that any restriction on applicants for excellence condescends to them...' Koenig maintained. 'Abolishing the sex distinction would also make awards much more competitive by removing the protection of being judged only against others with the same problems in getting to the top. And those problems are formidable indeed. Women get less education and job training than men, and have to face more discouragement and contempt.' This sounds like a very good argument, in fact, for women banding together and going to the Women of the Year Lunch in order to swap notes, give mutual advice and generally compare war wounds in an upbeat atmosphere.

Floella Benjamin is a woman who has more reason than many to celebrate her own success against all the odds. 'I hope I have brought to the Lunch a feeling that anything is possible,' says Benjamin, who made her name as a children's television presenter. A remarkably focused and positive woman, she is not the kind of person you would ever associate with hurt feelings. And yet she suddenly becomes hesitant as she makes an unexpected admission. 'Sometimes you get the feeling that people are surprised a black woman is chairman. And when you work with children, you are not taken as seriously.'

A particular affinity has developed between Floella and Tony, whom Benjamin described as a 'mentor' during a profile of Floella on BBC1's *This Is Your Life*. Both are people of vision. Floella's chairmanship ends in 2000 – as it must, according to the rules of the company set up to preserve the name of the Women of the Year.

Both she and Tony are determined that the event will never lapse into a charitable gathering of Ladies Who Lunch, hence the institution of the Assembly in 1997 in order to give the occasion added gravitas for those guests keen to engage in debate over controversial issues. 'There has always been a conflict between those who saw the Lunch as an easy money-maker for charity and those who saw it as an event to honour and recognise the work of women across the board,' says Tony. 'Year after year, we have jealously guarded the integrity of every nomination so that it enhances the integrity of those who receive it.' Tony claims to have been inspired in her aims by Lady Stansgate, the mother of politician Tony Benn. 'She appealed to me to fight for the women's movement; she said, "Don't let Women of the Year become a social occasion."' In fact it fulfils both functions, a balancing act that Tony would like to maintain for as long as possible.

Tony describes Floella as the spirit of the Women of the Year, exemplifying the new woman who sees beyond divisions, with an outlook that is both classless and colourless. Benjamin emigrated to England from Trinidad when she was ten, an experience evoked in poignant detail in *Coming to England*. 'I soon began to notice people staring at us,' she wrote. 'I thought it was because we were wearing brightly coloured clothes, our very best clothes. They all had on such dull, drab colours: black, navy and grey, as if they were going to a funeral. What I didn't realise was that staring was something I was going to have to get used to...

'When I arrived at the school, many of the children rushed over and touched me then ran away giggling. I thought they were being nice to me. At that time, I didn't realise it was because I was different, a novelty, something to be made a fool of and laughed at...The work the teacher gave us was so easy and simple compared to the work I was used to. Yet the teacher treated me like an idiot because she couldn't understand my Trinidadian accent even though I could understand her...Some boys came up and spat strange words at me, words that I had never heard before but from their faces I knew they were not nice. They were words which told me that I was different from them and that they felt my kind shouldn't be in their country. I looked at them, confused and baffled like a trapped, helpless creature. What was "my kind" and why shouldn't I be in the country I was brought up to love? The land of hope and glory, mother of the free...That was the day I realised that in the eyes of some people in this world, I was not a person but a colour...

'In Trinidad there were people of different races, from

all over the world, and they lived together in harmony... So why all the fuss in England?... Even going shopping was an ordeal. [My sister] Sandra and I would stand at the counter waiting to be served but would be ignored, treated as though we were invisible, and that hurt. Other West Indian children in my school had experienced the same hostility. We were treated without any respect and we were bundled together as coming from the same place.

'Our individual identity was never acknowledged. We had come from different islands... and spoke with different accents. We were brought up with different cultures and music. Each island in the Caribbean was as different as France is from Finland and as Spain is from Sweden – even we had to learn to understand each other.

'I couldn't understand why English people knew nothing about our different countries while we knew so much about theirs... I, too, was coming into contact with Jews, Italians, Africans and West Indians from other islands, but I didn't treat them as if they were worthless beings with no feelings. So many British people thought we had come from a land of coconuts and palm trees, huts and beaches, not realising that our buildings, history and food had strong European influences. In fact, we probably knew more about British history and culture than most of them.

'My uncle, like so many other West Indians, had fought and died for Britain in the Second World War. Hundreds of West Indians had joined the Army and the Air Force, and had fought to protect Britain, to make her a safe place to live. Little did that generation of West Indians know that their gallant action was to go unrecognised and forgotten and that many of their descendants would have to go through a gruelling survival course on arrival in Britain, and be made to feel unwelcome and unwanted in the celebrated motherland.

I came to England feeling special, like a princess, but was made to feel like a scavenger, begging for a piece of what I thought was mine. I had been told that I was part of the British Empire. Was that a lie? My dreams and visions had been shattered but I was in England now and there was no turning back. I had to learn to survive.'

And survive she most certainly did. 'If you belong to a large family, you learn from a very early age to be extremely competitive...Being so competitive made me a high achiever at school, both academically and as an athlete...Motivating others was easy for me because at home it was a way of life.' And it was at school that she discovered her gift for performing. As she sang and danced in a solo spot at the Christmas concert, 'something took over my body...

'I had no idea why it had taken a song-and-dance routine to change their perception of me, all I knew was that...they saw me differently...I had overwhelmed them with my energy until their prejudices were swept away. At that moment, I knew that in order to make a success of my life...I would have to work twice as hard as anyone else and be twice as good. I had to develop the ability to make people see me as a person, someone with feelings, pride, dignity and intellect.'

Although Benjamin is referring to colour prejudice, the same words could be applied to the kind of opposition that many of the guests at the Women of the Year Lunch have encountered in a man's world of work. In the Afterword to her book she explains that she wrote it 'to give young people, both black and white, an insight into the circumstances that brought a whole generation of West Indians to Britain'. Benjamin regards the hundreds of West Indians who came to England, Scotland and Wales in the late fifties and early sixties as 'pioneers'. The same can be said for so many of the Women of the Year.

'To feel you belong is a most important necessity in

life,' she concluded. 'This feeling was denied thousands of West Indian children who came to Britain, but at least they had their memories of the homes they had left. The next generation, however, were born into a turmoil of not knowing enough about their roots and how they came to be born in Britain. I hope this book will go some way in helping people to find their identity, to discover where they came from and to feel proud of themselves.'

So positive is her personality, however, and so vivid are the evocations of her Trinidadian heritage, that the overall impression left by Floella's book *Coming to England* is a joyous one. One of the first black performers on British television, Benjamin first made her name in the musical *Hair* before becoming the face of *Play School* for a record six years, from 1976 to 1982. Many acting and writing projects later, she now runs her own production company making children's programmes. A natural teacher who believes in the power of drama to educate, her work with the Campaign for Racial Equality (CRE) and Lord Murray's NCH Action for Children charity has also made her a useful go-between and adviser for government ministers who want to connect with community leaders. She is right, however, when she says that work with children is shamefully undervalued in comparison with work with adults; children's TV presenters, it seems, are rarely taken as seriously as those who front prime-time shows. Yet Floella was first nominated by Tony for the Women of the Year Lunch in 1990 precisely because she had made an impact on Tony's own family.

'I think it came about that I was chosen because Tony's grandchildren knew of me. Tony has a great network of young people; in fact, she would ask all sorts of people, like the person serving fish and chips, who they thought should be invited to the Lunch. After doing *Play School*, I was well established. It was then that I was approached by Tony, who saw that we were like-minded in many ways.

'When I got this letter from someone called Tony, I remember thinking, "Is this a man or a woman?" It was a very friendly letter, almost too friendly, very familiar. I thought, "Who is this man writing to me in this very familiar fashion?" But Tony has this genius for instant intimacy, for sounding as if she has known you for a long time. I was still expecting to meet a man, and I was taken aback by this woman with a black eyepatch, strong, funny, gentle, caring, a woman who can make you feel as if you can fly... She makes you feel as if you are the most important person in her life. She cracks jokes immediately and makes fun of herself to put others at their ease.

'And she seldom takes "no" for an answer. We were standing in the receiving line five years ago when I first became chairman. Tony was supposed to greet Princess Michael of Kent, who was our royal guest that year, but her legs were very tired and she asked me to do it instead. So I had to go to the River Entrance to greet the Princess and think very fast. Your brain is working treble time, because you're remembering everyone's name and giving the royal guest all the information on each person. At the end I was exhausted.

'But that's the sort of thing Tony would land you in: she trusts you. She made me cope. She makes you realise what your capabilities are. I'm truly grateful to Tony for supporting me as the first black chairman. You are not often given the opportunity to be in that position.

'I felt this kind of understanding, this bond with Tony. We can talk about world issues together, we can laugh; the day Nelson Mandela was freed we both danced and laughed and cried. Like Tony, I want to try and counteract the evil that's going on in the world. Tony is a good woman and everything she does is for the well-being of others. She does it because she wants to make a difference.'

For Benjamin, the Women of the Year Lunch was already something of a legend by the time she joined it. 'The BBC used to televise it every year, but they stopped doing outside-broadcast events because they hadn't got the money. Yet they still show it on the news now. Growing up, I used to look forward to seeing the event on TV and wish I could be there. When I got the invitation, I was flattered and at the same time I was wondering, "Why me? Why was I chosen?" I was totally bowled over and overwhelmed by being there: I was gobsmacked to see all the great women there. Two years later I was asked to join the committee and then I was asked to be chairman of speakers and speeches before being asked to be chairman of the whole event.'

So close did they become that Tony and Floella travelled to Moscow where 'Floella danced and sang for the cosmonauts in Star City', while Tony made a recording of her book *Valentina: First Woman In Space*. A strong-minded, highly motivated person, Benjamin believes that she manages to 'hold things together' because she has 'the respect and understanding of many people outside the organisation. I hope I have made the life of chairman look easy, but it's hard, hard work. It's like being a producer: you have to take on board everybody's problems.

'A speaker might not know they have to speak at a given time, for instance; in 1999, Helen Bamber had thought it was an evening event, not a lunch, though luckily she found out in time. You would be surprised how nervous some well-known people are before speaking in front of five hundred women, so that sometimes I have to talk them into it. I think it's because they feel they are letting the side down in front of their own sex if they don't do well.

'Then there are times when women say, "You have never invited me." Usually it's purely an oversight: you might overlook what they have done, unless you know them personally. Some people perceive it as an elitist event, but we go out of our way to get unsung heroes. We always ask women from the regions to tell their newspapers they have been nominated as one of the Women of the Year, so that the message gets around the country. No matter what job you have, you are perceived to be the greatest in that area if you are invited to the Lunch. It's as simple as that.'

At five-foot-five, Floella is no taller than Tony but just as dynamic in her direct way. 'People think I'm taller, but it's how I carry myself,' she shrugs, patting the top-knot that has become her trademark. 'That's the confidence you have to bring to your role.

'Some people ask why they're not sitting at the front at the top table, and we say, well, every table is a top table. Very rarely do people get upset. We really do try to make everyone feel important. Now we have come up with the idea of putting the guest-of-honour table down the middle with every other table surrounding them, so it will be like theatre-in-the-round: everyone will be able to see the top-table guests who represent the different professions.'

To mark the millennium, the committee has nominated Nelson Mandela as the Greatest Man of the Century and Valentina Tereshkova as the Greatest Woman of the Century to attend the Lunch in the year 2000. And for the first time ever, men have been invited to a tea-and-champagne party after the Lunch in tacit recognition of their behind-the-scenes support over the years. It's an experiment that is likely to continue, for the Women of the Year Lunch and Assembly has always been keen to distance itself from an anti-man agenda. This is a day that seeks to unite rather than divide.

A big influence in Floella's life is her mother Veronica Benjamin, a teacher of Caribbean cookery who, along with Prue Leith, has been nominated as a guest of the Women of the Year Lunch to represent the culinary arts. Reared on matriarchal West Indian discipline, Floella has her own view on the eternal question of how to balance the two worlds of home and work without excluding men from the equation.

'I'm into cross-gender, making sure that you are treated the same whether you're a man or a woman. In fact,' she adds, 'I see we women bringing gender problems upon ourselves. Don't feel as if you are competing against men – and don't make men feel inadequate: they have to play their part for the well-being of society.

'I think women have an empathy; that's a quality they must not lose. I also think women can compromise: they don't feel their ego is dented if they have to reach a compromise, they don't feel as if they have lost face. If a man has to back down, he feels he is not a man, whereas women just want to get to the next stage. Very rarely will you find a woman saying, "Let's go to war." In this spirit women don't want their sons or daughters to die in a war, so we have to look at women as leaders in a different way to men.

'All the qualities you need to run a good home are skills to be brought into the workplace, so just give us a chance. We can prove we can do it. I think perhaps that women are forgetting what's happening in the home and are giving up these responsibilities to work in the outside world. That's why we are coming unstuck with stress problems and with drinking too much.

'I want women and men to go back to the drawing-board: men and women need to move forward in a unified way in solidarity. Women are the ones who nurture sons, and they need to re-train their boy-children into thinking differently. If they pamper their boy-children and pander to them, cleaning their rooms and doing their washing, they are training their boys to expect another woman to do this when they get married.

'I phone up my son Aston if I'm going to be late and I ask him to vacuum the stairs and so on. He's a very good cook and his friends say to him that they wish they could cook like him. But that's because I've taught him to do it.'

It is precisely Floella's kind of logical forward thinking that characterises the women at the Lunch. The Women of the Year's light shines on many pioneers, and a glance through some of the 'firsts' who have attended the Lunch over the years cannot help but make inspiring reading: Diane Abbott, the first black woman MP; Gee Armytage, the first woman Champion National Hunt jockey; Tracy Axten, the first police officer instructor for riots and domestic violence; Heather Baillie, the first woman Formula One racing driver/instructor; Eva-Maria Beck-Coulter, the first woman chairman of the Reform Club; Rosie Boycott, the first woman editor of a national broadsheet newspaper; members of the first all-women expedition to the North Pole; Samantha Brewster, the first woman to sail single-handed round the world, East to West; Ffyona Campbell, the first woman long-distance walker; Patricia Chapman, the first woman editor of the *News of the World*; Pauline Clare, the first woman Chief Constable; the Hon. Lady Cosgrove, Scotland's first woman Supreme Court judge; Flight Lieut. Sally Cox, the first woman RAF fighter pilot; Agnes Curran, the first woman governor in charge of an all-male prison; Lynne D'Arcy, the first woman to run a brewery; Penny Davies, the first woman on the Board of Directors, Coca-Cola/Schweppes Ltd; Trudi de Haney, the first black woman trade-union official; Baroness Dean of Thornton-Le-Fylde, the first woman to lead a major industrial trade union, SOGAT; Ruth

Deech, the first woman principal of a mixed Oxford college; Elizabeth Earnshaw, the first British woman referee at the Open Golf Tournament; Tracy Edwards, the first woman to captain an all-female crew around the world; Sue Ellen, the first woman managing director of United Racecourses; Pennie Evans, the first woman station manager for British Rail; Sue Farr, the first director of marketing for both TV and Radio at the BBC; Rev. Christine Farrington, the first woman Cathedral Deacon; Allison Fisher, the first woman to join the men's professional snooker circuit; Baroness Flather, the first Asian woman mayor in the UK; Emma Ford, the first woman falconer; Clara Freeman, the first woman on the Board of Directors of Marks & Spencer; Captain Lisa Giles, the first woman captain of White Helmet Motorcycle Display Team; Kate Glover, the first woman member of the National Society of Master Thatchers; Dr Jane Glover, the first woman conductor; Buzz Goodbody, first woman director of the RSC; Alex Greaves, the first woman jockey to win a major handicap; Professor Susan Greenfield, the first woman director of the Royal Institution and presenter of its Christmas lectures; Dr Elaine Griffiths, the first woman in Britain to perform adult cardiac surgery; Barbara Harmer, the first and only woman Concorde pilot; Linda Haye, the first black woman to serve on the Police Complaints Authority; Frances Heaton, the first woman director of the Bank of England; Councillor Rosemarie Higham, the first woman coal merchant; Professor Judith Howard, the first woman Professor of Chemistry in the UK; Professor Sue Iverson, the first woman Professor of Psychology at Oxford University; Professor Carole Jordan, the first woman President of the Royal Astronomical Society; Captain Yvonne Kershaw, the first woman to captain a Boeing 747; Pam Liversidge, the first woman President of the Institution of Mechanical Engineers; Maureen MacGlashan, the first woman Ambassador to the Holy See; Lucy MacSwiney, Britain's first female paragliding champion; Ann Mallalieu, the first woman president of the Cambridge Union; Genista McIntosh, the first woman director of the Royal Opera House; Dame Barbara Mills, the first woman Director of Public Prosecutions and Head of the Crown Prosecution Service; Nicolette Milnes-Walker, the first lone woman to sail the Atlantic; Jenny Pitman, the first woman racehorse trainer to win the Grand National; Rev. Dr Kathleen Richardson, the first woman president of the Methodist Church; the Venerable Judith Rose, first woman Archdeacon in the Church of England; Baroness Scotland, the first black woman QC; Kathryn Shannon, the first female hotel doorman; Linda Sharp, the first woman head keeper at the London Zoo; Susan Shaw, the first woman member admitted to the floor of the London Stock Exchange; Liz Skinner, the first woman allowed to compete in the Isle of Man/TT races; Dr Jane Somerville, the first woman cardiologist in charge of the first heart transplant; Nicola Swan, the first woman to walk from the Arctic to the North Pole; Jane Tabor, the first international woman tennis umpire; Veronica Uchendu, the first black woman master baker in Britain; Marion Woodard, the first British International Judo Referee; and Louise Woolcock, the first co-head of Rugby School.

Beat that if you can. Yet who would have thought that the inspiration behind such an Establishment list was an Edwardian stone-thrower who changed the destiny of women?

Chapter Two
Pankhurst the Equaliser and a Woman Called Tony

Of all the events that liberated women in the twentieth century, the greatest was enfranchisement. Winning the vote gave women a voice and an official stake in the community. Emmeline Pankhurst is therefore indisputably the woman of the century for her services to female humanity. Women across the spectrum, from business leaders to astronauts to tree-dwelling eco-warrior queens, owe the opportunity for self-determination that we now take for granted to the deceptively fragile figure of Mrs Pankhurst. Interestingly, the female vote, considered to be a crucial election decider, is now courted by politicians as never before.

The Women of the Year Lunch and Assembly has always honoured pioneers, and Tony Lothian cites Mrs Pankhurst and Hildegard of Bingen as her two major inspirations. In many ways, Pankhurst embodies the spirit of the Lunch, acknowledged by the depiction of the Equal Rights Millennium Stamp in executive chairman Floella Benjamin's souvenir programme of the 1999 Lunch. The Pankhurst battle-cry 'Deeds Not Words' was emblazoned upon artist Natasha Kerr's striking textile image of a suffragette woman behind bars, created from a newspaper archive photograph found in London's Fawcett Library. 'I was trying to encapsulate as many aspects of the suffragette story as possible...that they went to prison, that they were women, that they were trapped or felt trapped, the window-smashing campaign. The woman looks timeless, so she could stand for any woman from any place or any era who feels trapped,' explained Kerr.

Along with Marie Curie and Florence Nightingale, Pankhurst featured prominently among the seven women whom Tony chose to profile in a seven-part series she made for Thames TV in 1981. Tony describes Emmeline as 'that fearless fighter for women's rights, whose statue on the Embankment rightly reminds us that torture, brutal antagonism and prison sentences had to be endured to win votes for women'.

Before the nineteenth and twentieth centuries, there existed precious few women in public life who provided any kind of inspiration for their sex. The Abbess Hildegard of Bingen, the twelfth-century poet, composer, herbalist, theologian and leading political figure who corresponded as an equal with popes and emperors, is seen as a pathfinder by Tony Lothian: 'She described the making of men and women into one flesh brutally and beautifully.' But Emmeline Pankhurst, at a much later time, embodied the spirit of friendship and unity between women that is so well mirrored by the Women of the Year Lunch. As Tony wrote: 'I believe the firmest friends can be made working for a shared ideal and one example is the life of Emmeline Pankhurst.'

That same 1999 programme of the Women of the Year Lunch and Assembly contains a tribute to the Pankhurst women by Helen Pankhurst, granddaughter of Emmeline and daughter of Sylvia. 'What singled out the suffragette movement from previous calls for women's suffrage in the UK seems to have been the recognition that they had to come together to build a movement for social trans-formation,' Tony continued. 'Asking men politely to share their public power would not be enough. In the process of asking women to demand change, loudly and consistently despite the numerous setbacks, women themselves gained confidence and abilities...using pomp and pageantry to make their point...The Pankhursts stood for justice, principles and bravery. At a time when women were second-class citizens, their activism helped millions of women to gain more fulfilling lives.'

Helen Pankhurst is the Head of International Programmes and the Africa Programme Officer at Womankind Worldwide, the only UK charity that campaigns globally for women's economic, social and political equality. There is another link via Women of the Year Lunch and Assembly director Lady Morris of Kenwood, a former director and trustee of Womankind Worldwide who still keeps in touch with the organisation. Helen points out how Emmeline and her daughters Christabel, Sylvia and Adela also operated from a global perspective, something that is central to the international outlook of the Women of the Year Lunch. Parochial it most certainly is not.

Emmeline's granddaughter has passed the surname of Pankhurst on to her daughter Laura, with her son Alexander taking his father's name. It seems crucial to preserve the name of Pankhurst for future generations to remind people just how forward-looking the family was. Pankhurst argued that her sex actually gave her an advantage over men. And yet she was simply reflecting her education at a girls' boarding school, which had always stressed the moral superiority of women. Once upon a time that concept had been used to put women on a pedestal, far above the hurly-burly of daily life; but Pankhurst, full of indignation against injustice, turned it into a weapon of empowerment which would allow women to take an active part in the battle against poverty, misery and ignorance. In her 1978 introduction to a paperback edition of Emmeline's autobiography,

My Own Story, Jill Craigie wrote of 'the passion for the oppressed which burned in her [Emmeline] as a form of genius'.

'Women care more,' Emmeline wrote. 'They have more practical ideas about relief and prevention of poverty than men...My daughters and I sought a way to bring about that union of young and old which would find new ways and blaze new trails.' Yet like the great eighteenth-century thinker Mary Wollstonecraft, whose *Vindication of the Rights of Women* fired the first feminist broadside, she always sought to build alliances with men. And men have certainly never been seen as the enemy by the organisers or guests of the Women of the Year Lunch. In 1955 Charles Scott-Paton had helped to organise it.

Men certainly played their part in the early struggle for the enfranchisement of women, yet the suffragette movement of the late nineteenth and early twentieth centuries remains the largest campaign ever mounted by women in history. Even today, its sheer longevity and scale staggers the imagination: no Women's Liberation march of the seventies or single-issue campaign of the nineties could possibly compare with this historic female resistance to the Government. The first Women's Suffrage Societies in Britain were formed in 1867 in Edinburgh, Manchester and London, with two more founded in Bristol and Birmingham a year later. Mrs Millicent Garrett Fawcett (who always referred to herself in the traditional patriarchal way as Mrs Henry Fawcett) founded the National Union of Women's Suffrage Societies in 1898, yet by the beginning of the twentieth century her supporters were no nearer winning the vote. A radical solution was needed.

The response of Emmeline's army was a strategy of attention-seeking tactics that ranged from heckling to shattering shop windows, slashing paintings and chaining themselves to railings. The brutal reaction of the police, however, was out of all proportion to the deeds of the demonstrators. Pankhurst's campaign lasted from 1903 to 1914, during which time thousands of suffragettes were imprisoned, forcibly fed during hunger strikes with long tubes inserted up the nose and down the throat. One woman, Emily Davison, became a martyr in June 1913 when she died under the hooves of a horse in front of the King and Queen at the Derby. In that same year, Mrs Pankhurst, then aged fifty-five, was imprisoned six times under the notorious Cat and Mouse Act (devised to free weakened women protesters until they were strong enough to be incarcerated again), though she was too high-profile to be force-fed.

Pankhurst's campaign for women's suffrage was a testament to the power of female networking, a relatively informal arrangement by the standards of the male-run Establishment. Certain similarities can be seen with many subsequent women's campaigns, such as that waged at Greenham Common against Cruise missiles and the peace initiatives by Ulster women across the religious divide; representatives of both groups have attended the Women of the Year Lunch.

Although the suffrage movement was led in the main by middle-class women, the suffragettes had to organise their protests from home in the first instance. Their gender barred them from the great clubs, most notably the Palace of Westminster, where the high-level deals were struck. Yet the Pankhurst suffragettes soon learned to be streetwise. In the autumn of 1906 they set up their headquarters in an office at Clement's Inn, adjacent to Fleet Street, to maximise the opportunities for publicity. 'Never lose your temper with the press or the public is a major rule of public life,' wrote Christabel Pankhurst, who had taken a first-class degree in law that summer and was, in the opinion of her mother, a born politician. 'We never made that mistake. We liked the public, we even liked the press...the journalists who interviewed us seemed to be quite sympathetic and we suspected that their copy was touched up in newspaper offices by those who had no first-hand knowledge of the movement, and that they themselves were perhaps under instruction "not to encourage it". Yet even exaggerated and distorted reports, which made us seem more terrible than we really were, told the world this much – that we wanted the vote and were resolved to get it.' This media-savvy attitude found echoes seventy years later in the Greenham Common women, whose anti-nuclear protest made headlines round the world even while they were being demonised as hairy-legged lesbians by the tabloids.

Luck, however, always plays its part in destiny; as the actress and author Maureen Lipman once remarked with her supportive husband, the playwright Jack Rosenthal, in mind: 'Behind every successful woman is an awfully kind man.' That's certainly true of Tony Lothian's husband Peter, a man never too self-important to send a fax on her behalf, and of Keith Taylor, Floella Benjamin's husband and business partner. Quick to acknowledge men's contribution to women's progress, they all remember that Mrs Pankhurst began the crusade for female suffrage with her husband in the late nineteenth century.

Although Emmeline Goulden was raised to her full potential by a father who seemed remarkably enlightened by the standards of his day, he was enough of a man of his time to comment on one occasion, 'What a pity she wasn't born a lad.' It was Emmeline's great good fortune to marry a Victorian New Man: Dr Richard Pankhurst, one of the earliest campaigners for votes for women. He drafted the first enfranchisement, the Women's Disabilities Removal Bill which was introduced into the House of Commons in 1870.

It was Richard Pankhurst who also drew up a crucial

piece of legislation that gave women control of their own money for the first time: the Married Women's Property Act of 1882, a watershed in the history of women's emancipation. Prompted though it may have been by many wealthy men's fear of handing over their property to a son-in-law who might gamble away an heiress's fortune or even murder her for her estate, at last it gave women rights over the assets they brought to the marriage.

That a married woman could be such a hostage to fortune seems medieval to the modern mind. Marriage, however, was historically regarded as a transfer of property from one man to another, a view that survives in some cultures in the dowry system. Only when the vast numbers of newly rich Victorian industrialists began to discover that their daughters were targets for unscrupulous fortune-hunters did anyone begin to acknowledge that the age-old system was wide open to abuse.

Emmeline married Richard in 1879, a union that lasted, in her words, 'for nineteen happy years' until his sudden death in 1898. In 1894, when her children were old enough to be left in the care of nursemaids, she had begun working as the only female on Manchester's Board of Poor-Law Guardians. In that capacity, she made many imaginative as well as basic changes to the grim lives of bread-fed paupers in the Manchester workhouse. After the death of her husband, Emmeline took paid employment as a Registrar of Births and Deaths. It was the pitiful plight of the young unmarried mothers she encountered in her new job that showed her at first hand how women always seemed to bear the brunt of poverty and exploitation.

'I was shocked to be reminded over and over again of the little respect there was in the world for women and children,' she wrote later. 'I have had little girls of thirteen come to my office to register the births of their babies...I found that the child's own father or some near male relative was responsible for her state. There was nothing that could be done in most cases...If civilisation is to advance at all in the future, it must be through the help of women, women freed of their political shackles, women with full power to work their will in society.

'It was rapidly becoming clear to my mind that men regarded women as a servant class in the community, and that women were going to remain in the servant class until they lifted themselves out of it.'

On 10 October 1903, Mrs Pankhurst invited a number of women to her house in Nelson Street, Manchester, in order to form a new, women-only society called the Women's Social and Political Union (WSPU). Although the motto they adopted was 'Deeds Not Words', at first they hoped to bring about female suffrage via a private member's bill rather than resorting to direct action. Yet when the first suffrage bill in eight years was brought before the House of Commons, it was cynically 'talked out' by a preceding bill about the need for lights on the back as well as the front of carts travelling at night on public roads. The Roadway Lighting Bill's promoters' sabotage of the suffrage bill with their long-winded jokes and anecdotes was a delaying tactic that enraged Emmeline. It was a defining moment: she realised then that the suffragettes would never be taken seriously unless they took destiny by the scruff of the neck.

'I felt', she recorded grimly in her diary, 'that the moment had come for a demonstration such as no old-fashioned suffragist had ever attempted.' And, as she also wrote in her autobiography, the time had come for a calculated risk. 'We had to do as much...guerilla warfare as the people of England would tolerate.' Emmeline called upon the waiting women assembled in the Strangers' Lobby to demonstrate outside the House of Commons there and then. The police moved them on twice, pushing and shoving the demonstrators, before reluctantly agreeing to let them hold a meeting in Broad Sanctuary near Westminster Abbey. Here they made speeches and passed a resolution condemning the Government's action in 'allowing a small minority to talk out our Bill. This was the first militant act of the WSPU.' Things were never to be the same again.

Only the outbreak of the First World War brought a halt to Emmeline and Christabel's 'women's war', as the fight for female suffrage came to be called. As Emmeline put it, 'For the present at least our arms are grounded, for directly the threat of foreign war descended on our nation we declared a complete truce from militancy which was answered half-heartedly by the announcement that the Government would release all suffrage prisoners who would give an undertaking "not to commit further crimes or outrages".' One argument advanced by the opponents of female suffrage was that women did not play a part in the armed defence of their country. No one could accuse the suffragettes of being unpatriotic, however: even *The Suffragette* newspaper was renamed *Britannia*. Yet they felt they co-operated with the Government from a position of strength: that of moral superiority. 'There can be no real peace in the world until woman, the mother half of the human race, is given liberty in the councils of the world,' concluded Mrs Pankhurst.

'She was really a great equaliser,' says Tony Lothian, 'just as our Assembly proves that men and women are equal in ability if not in opportunities. The war helped the suffragettes because women were needed. Emmeline was brought up in a chemistry of reform, and she didn't care about being politically correct. She encouraged people to throw stones.'

Although Emmeline is commemorated by a statue and Christabel by a plaque on the Embankment outside the

House of Lords, there is no memorial or plaque to the radical Sylvia. A more committed pacifist than her mother and sister, she refused to play politics and abandon the suffrage campaign in order to support the war effort. As a result, she was expelled from the WSPU. Yet, just as Emmeline is Tony Lothian's particular heroine, so the socialist Sylvia also has her champion on the committee of the Women of the Year Lunch and Assembly. The retired engineer and trade-union official Barbara Switzer, one of the directors of the Women of the Year who was first nominated for the Lunch by the late Mikki Doyle, set up the Sylvia Pankhurst Memorial Committee in 1999 in order to raise funds for a statue to Sylvia by sculptor Ian Walters, to be placed on College Green outside the House of Commons within two years. In this way the Memorial Committee hopes to ensure that Sylvia's achievements are not overshadowed by those of her charismatic elder sister and mother.

The work of women at home and at the Front as nurses and ambulance-drivers did indeed prove invaluable to the war effort, so much so that in 1918 the Representation of the People Act finally gave women the right to vote – so long as they were over thirty and fulfilled certain property criteria. Not until 1928 was full female suffrage granted to 21-year-olds, giving women electoral parity with men at long last.

Women had finally won the propaganda battle for equality; and in 1917 the Pandora's box of contraception was opened when Marie Stopes published her book *Married Love*. The contraceptive pill, developed half a century later, would come to be seen by some as the ultimate liberator of women, though evidence of associated health risks eventually made it a controversial option. 'It certainly liberated men,' comments Tony Lothian. By the end of 1918, women were finally allowed to stand for Parliament. The Sinn Feiner

Countess Markievicz, the first woman MP to be elected to the House of Commons, was in Holloway Prison at the time and so did not take her seat. The Tory Nancy Astor was the first woman MP to do so in 1919. There were other heartening signs of progress, with a handful of women entering the professions of medicine and university teaching at this time.

The Second World War liberated women still further when they took over the jobs of conscripted men; yet many firms, together with the teaching profession and the Civil Service, still operated a marriage bar after the war. Women had to hide their wedding rings for fear of being asked to leave work when they got married in order not to take a job away from a man. When the men returned from the war, the women were expected to go meekly back into the kitchen in order to allow their menfolk to resume their rightful place at the helm of society. The triumphs of the equalisers seemed to be dead in the water.

From the vantage point of the twenty-first century, 1955 now seems like a vanished world. Although the entertainment industry fielded plenty of female stars, prominent figures in science, business or public corporations were rarely female. One notable exception was Dorothy Hodgkin, the scientist who was made a Fellow of the Royal Society in 1946 and was to win the Nobel Prize for Chemistry in 1964. Needless to say, Hodgkin was a great supporter and a distinguished speaker at the Women of the Year Lunch.

When the Campaign for Nuclear Disarmament was formed in 1957, two-thirds of its support came from women. Indeed, its first secretary was a woman: Peggy Duff. With the sixties there came a major breakthrough: 1963 saw the first flight by a woman in space. As a result of her historic journey, the Russian Valentina Tereshkova, who always insisted on describing herself merely as a 'straightforward aviation engineer', was honoured as an Astronaut of the USSR and a Hero of the Soviet Union. Her codename was the Chekhovian 'Seagull'; after successfully orbiting the earth forty-eight times, taking an hour and a half for each orbit, Tereshkova landed safely on 19 June after three days.

To this day, Valentina remains the only woman ever to have accomplished a solo flight in space. Her vision of a Planet Earth that was 'so small, so fragile and in danger' led to a unique understanding with peace campaigner Tony Lothian, to whom she gave her only press interviews. 'For me, I felt like a worm looking at an eagle,' Tony now recalls of their encounters, recorded in *Valentina, First Woman in Space*. Valentina had proved that women and men could be equal in the new dimension for living.

Tony writes: 'I believe that the Lothian/Tereshkova understanding proved that women from East and West could have a connection with each other: we need not be divided into tribes. And that was particularly evident when I first met Valentina: we found that we were two women very worried by the annihilation of the globe through atomic warfare. We were worried about the same thing and we found it easy to talk about it and find ways to advance peace.'

As an international guest of honour in 1984, Tereshkova went on to give one of the most memorable addresses in the history of the Women of the Year Lunch and Assembly by focusing on the 'nuclear menace' and calling upon the 'women of our two countries' to work together for world peace. 'The women I met in Russia cried for peace, convinced that the great patriotic war had wiped out Russia,' writes Tony. 'But we have to demonise someone, so we demonised the Russians – and there was quite a lot of resentment at asking Valentina to the Lunch during the Cold War.' Nevertheless what had been a considerable gamble in those pre-Gorbachev days paid off triumphantly at a Lunch with the theme 'How to be First'. Alongside Tereshkova were speakers such as Brenda Dean, the first woman in the UK to lead a major industrial trade union. 'We gave the first woman in space a standing ovation,' remembers Tony. 'Valentina is proof that Pankhurst was right. Emmeline believed that women could equal men in the value and quality of their work. Valentina proved that men and women can be equal in space. And after that she had a daughter – who is now an orthopaedic surgeon.

'The suffragettes were equalisers not only for women, but for humanity: there was this huge gap in the power of humanity because women weren't allowed to take part,' Tony continues. 'But men are not always antagonistic towards women, and that's what Emmeline made use of. Valentina also likes and respects men: she worked with them on space and now she works with them in Russia's Star City on her engineering research.'

Tereshkova's achievement in space preceded an age of radical sexual and social change. David Steel's bill to legalise abortion became law in 1967, applauded by all those women who had campaigned for that sixties article of faith: a woman's right to choose. Simone de Beauvoir's *The Second Sex*, Betty Friedan's *The Feminine Mystique* and Germaine Greer's *The Female Eunuch* became key texts in the fight for liberation as the mass of women began to wake up to a brave new world of multiple choices for females. '*The Female Eunuch* changed me completely, turned me inside out,' says Tony, who dreams of balance, not gridlock, on controversial subjects such as abortion. The suffering of the pre-born is an issue where she has found herself out of step with her radical contemporaries, but where she is now more in tune, she believes, with younger women.

During the fifties and sixties, Tony Lothian was well

placed to meet a wide cross-section of people across the globe. After earning her journalistic spurs on a mothers' magazine, she had been offered a current-affairs column on the Glasgow-based *Scottish Daily Express* as a result of an introduction to its then editor, the legendary Ian McColl, by her friend and fellow journalist Lorna Blackie – an equally legendary Scottish writer. To try her out, McColl had asked Tony to send him a 400-word think-piece on the Prime Minister Harold Wilson's statement on trade sanctions against the then Rhodesia, which achieved independence from Britain and renamed itself Zimbabwe in 1980. Her article made the centre-spread the following day. Hearing about the circulation boost she had achieved for *The Catholic Mother*, McColl said, 'If you can get me 20,000 more readers, you're hired.'

Initially there was opposition from some quarters – and there exists no harder hack than a Scottish journalist of either sex – to the hiring of a titled lady. Yet Tony toughed it out, proved her worth and was to hold down the job of columnist for ten years during the social upheavals of the sixties and early seventies. For obvious reasons, hers was a dream job – writing on such subjects as working wives, crime, drugs and youth, abortion, divorce on demand, test-tube babies, sex education, Flower Power, a woman Prime Minister and women at the top.

As Tony puts it, 'The sixties were turning traditional morals inside out; I aimed to be balanced, but that was not politically correct at the time. This gave me profound respect for the media men and women who told the truth.' And this led to a joint venture with her friends and fellow Women of the Year colleagues Mikki Doyle and Renée Goddard. What she would most like to be remembered for, she now says, was the annual Valiant for Truth award, co-founded in 1974 with Mikki and Renée.

The Women of the Year team were again praising men. Among the winners for their services to truth have been such prominent media movers and shakers as Kate Adie, Robert Fisk, Conor Cruise O'Brien, Jon Snow and Pat Seed, the Lancashire journalist who raised a million pounds for a cancer scanner after contracting the disease and who wrote the cancer-confronting book *One Day at a Time*. On the wooden shield they won was the John Bunyan inscription: 'I do not repent me of all the trouble I have been at to arrive where I am.' The majority of winners were men, who still vastly outnumber women in the ranks of the foreign correspondents. Nevertheless Kate Adie and Ann Leslie, two distinguished female practitioners of that dangerous trade, have both been guests at the Women of the Year Lunch.

As well as column-writing, Tony also branched out into freelance interviewing. Like all born interviewers, she has a strong sense of balance and humour together with an intense curiosity about people and their lives. Her spirit, she says, was 'fed by interviews: Margaret Herbison, Odette, Coretta King, Jehan el-Sadat, Petra Kelly'. All of these became associated with the Lunch.

Besides her press contacts, she met medical workers through her work for the Royal Colleges of Gynaecologists and of Nursing. When Peter Lothian was sent as a UN delegate to New York, to the Geneva Disarmament Conference, the European Parliament in Strasbourg and to Africa for the Foreign Office, she found herself meeting high-level politicians. And when, as a member of Women in Media and patron of the National Council of Women, she became an active campaigner for equal opportunities, Tony also met many influential women leaders. 'These varied contacts proved to me that when disparate people know more about each other, they become tolerant in practice, even if they do not agree in principle,' she wrote in her book on Valentina Tereshkova.

In 1970 Sally Alexander, a former actress and trade-union student at Ruskin College, Oxford, helped to organise the first Women's Liberation Conference in the UK, to discuss plans for a Sex Discrimination Act and to campaign for contraception and abortion on demand; six hundred women attended, and the crèche was run by men. That same year saw a protest by a hundred feminists at the Miss World competition at London's Royal Albert Hall, hurling leaflets, smoke and stink bombs, bags of flour and plastic mice in all directions. The first Women's Liberation march took place in 1971, demanding equal pay, equal education and job opportunities as well as free contraception, abortion on demand and free 24-hour nurseries.

True, it was the middle classes at the forefront of such rallies, with the vast majority of women too preoccupied with family and work to join demonstrations. Nevertheless there was an inevitable trickle-down effect as the message of what the detractors pejoratively referred to as 'Women's Lib' began to spread through society. Meanwhile, in Ulster, the first moves towards cross-party unity were being made by women's groups who had become disenchanted with the tribal bitterness of the Troubles; representatives of Ulster's middle-ground politics regularly attended the Women of the Year Lunch.

In mainland Britain, two landmark pieces of legislation – The Sex Discrimination Act and the Equal Pay Act – came into force in 1976, although they were to prove notoriously difficult to implement in many instances where wily employers exploited loopholes. By the late seventies and early eighties, media women were becoming a formidable force. In 1980, Kate Adie covered the Iranian Embassy siege. The radical organisation Women in Media was later succeeded by Women in Film and Television and Women in Journalism.

Over the last century the historical contribution made by black women such as Mary Seacole has often been overlooked. The Women of the Year has ended this tragic exclusion by celebrating all women's achievements, no matter what colour they are. Black women such as Merle Amory and Diane Abbott were by now entering politics in the eighties. Yet the business world remained very much a man's domain. As late as 1988, statistics showed that women formed only six per cent of the total of UK directors and ten per cent of senior managers.

The nineties brought further high-profile progress when Stella Rimington was appointed the first-ever female head of MI5 and when the first C of E women priests were ordained – much to the well-documented disgust of many of their male counterparts. It says a lot for the rapid progress of women in general that the notion of a woman minister – which had been introduced into the Church of Scotland well before the Church of England – seems completely normal and natural from the perspective of the twenty-first century.

The nineties also saw further developments in the kind of spontaneous grass-roots protests so often associated with women. Young women figured prominently among the armies of tree-dwelling or tunnelling eco-warriors who began campaigns in the nineties against road-building schemes that threaten the environment. From 1995, demonstrations against the conditions surrounding live animal exports to the Continent were led by middle-aged or elderly women, among them the writer Carla Lane, the animal campaigner and former fashion model Celia Hammond, the actress Dora Bryan and the world-famous nutritionist Audrey Eyton, a regular Women of the Year Lunch and Assembly attender.

Women are also making their mark on the emergent new technology of the twenty-first century. Writing about Martha Lane Fox and other female dot.com entrepreneurs behind many on-line e-commerce companies, commentators began to refer to the phenomenon as 'she-commerce'. So often, however, it seems a case of one step forward and two steps back for women. Unwanted pregnancy fears were followed by sterility fears. Postponing childbirth until their late thirties or even early forties, some found they had missed biology's window of opportunity during the fertile younger years. Increasingly, solutions were sought through in-vitro fertilisation; could women win?

In the first issue of the women's magazine *Aura*, launched in March 2000 by Women of the Year speaker Eve Pollard's publishing company Parkhill, Germaine Greer wrote: 'When wanting a child became irrational, I stopped doing it. I still have pregnancy dreams...[but] my life is full of baby surrogates, animals and birds that need nursing, that run to meet me when I open the door...' Yet she remained philosophical about the realities of motherhood: 'Even by proxy, it's mostly a case of letting go...Though I have no child of my own, I spend days with young adults who have less difficulty letting me into their lives than my own children would have had. I never suffered as mothers do when their children are rejecting, are ill or in trouble.'

Meanwhile, back at the career coalface, research had shown that while girls were doing consistently better than boys at school, their skills were less likely to be rewarded at work. The popular press then indulged in one of its regular fits of the vapours over why the schoolboys were performing less well, without bothering to ask what would become of the over-achieving but under-rewarded schoolgirls. However, the guest-lists for the Women of the Year Lunch and Assembly continue to provide a vast range of high-achieving role models to inspire future generations of women. And the can-do message certainly seems to have spread. In a London *Evening Standard* interview published in 2000, the 27-year-old American film star Cameron Diaz declared: 'In my generation, women have always been able to do anything.'

No matter how exhilarating such an atmosphere of achievement can be, it seems there is still no room for complacency among women who want to make their mark in society while also reserving the right to raise a family. The author Shirley Conran is founder and chairman of Mothers in Management, an organisation that campaigns to ease the stress-burden shouldered by working mothers. At a conference it held in March 2000, there were calls for 'smart hours' to replace the long-hours culture that threatened family life. At the beginning of the twenty-first century, the cards were still stacked heavily against many women ... so much so that the Prime Minister's wife publicly acknowledged it in a key speech at London's King's College that same month.

Here a lead had been given by the solicitor Joanne Gubbay, since June 1999 company secretary of the Women of the Year and a partner with the firm Berwin Leighton. Gubbay's involvement with work-life balance issues began after she became pregnant with her first child in 1993. Since then she has proved herself a successful part-time pioneer in general commercial litigation, working four days a week.

'Very often part-time jobs can be a demotion, because there is still a great culture of presenteeism in this country, of having to be seen at your desk. I was the first part-timer in my firm, but now there are several,' says Gubbay, an acknowledged 'wave-maker' who in 1997 launched a businesswomen's network called the Adelaide Group on behalf of her firm.

'I agree very much with the points that Cherie Booth made about working mothers in her King's College lecture, although I thought her speech was quite optimistic,' she says. 'I know her professionally, having worked with her on some public-law issues. When I first instructed her, Tony Blair was shadow Home Secretary and her clerk was much more interested in the fact that she was the actor Tony Booth's daughter. She's lovely, a real down-to-earth Scouser. Because I knew her professionally, I asked her to be the first speaker and honorary president of the Adelaide Group.' As a result, Gubbay became involved in the Woman Lawyer Forum, 'which brought me into the work-life debate'.

Highlighting the continuing scandal of the pay differential between men and women twenty-four years after the Equal Pay Act and the dilemma for working mothers who lose their footing on the career ladder by choosing to work shorter hours, Booth had in her lecture coined the evocative expressions 'the female forfeit' and 'the mother gap'. Projecting a hope that the pay gap would be closed by the year 2005, she added: 'If employers want to succeed in the twenty-first century, they need to think seriously about the quality of life of their employees. The number of women in the workforce is set to overtake the number of men and employers will have to recruit and retain the best available people.'

The need, therefore, for a leading women's Assembly to publicise, celebrate and shore up women's achievements against all these considerable odds seems greater than ever. The value of women's work to the community offers an incentive for women to throw new stones to obtain equality. But what does Pankhurst Power mean now? Perhaps it means reinventing the wheel of working life and campaigning for more flexi-time to enable employees – men as well as women – to spend more time raising the next generation. With gridlock on the roads, and a home-working revolution on the horizon, why should commuters continue to descend upon the same congested cities and stuffy offices like so many thousands of worker ants? By the beginning of the twenty-first century, two million people in the UK were working from home and the Labour Government had floated the idea of paternity leave – to be met with a predictable outcry from small businesses. Once again, women are expected to patch up the wounds inflicted on family life by an increasingly workaholic culture that takes its lead from America, not Europe. In Germany, you are considered inefficient if you are still at your desk beyond 6 pm.

With working mothers forever being cast as the scapegoats when family life goes wrong, the quest for the Holy Grail of a work–family balance goes on. Back in the pioneering days of 1955, when the Women of the Year first attempted the dream of an all-female forum that exemplified the work on which communities depend, who would have thought that the continuing controversy about the rival claims of work and family would still force so many women to play the game of Snakes and Ladders at the beginning of the following century?

Chapter Three
The Best of Women:
Odette Hallowes and Others

'We have always avoided personality cults,' remarks Tony Lothian. 'I think readers will resent a recurring commentary by me. How do we explain or excuse it? I see my main contribution to have been as supervisor of the guest list. From the beginning I have been the gatekeeper, sorting out which women were authentic achievers.

'The journalist Susan Raven, a distinguished former editor of the *Sunday Times* magazine and the creator of its "A Day in the Life" column, wrote that I was a professional impresario. I can relate to that. Certainly my head is like a computer, holding information on a wide stretch of women's work. But the final achievement in bringing an unprecedented variety of valuable work together was not by one person. It was the result of women working together with no barriers of colour or creed. I believe I am useful now as a sort of Greek Chorus, to remind those who never knew or have forgotten about how a small idea has become a great force.'

Yet in her millennium message for the Lunch in the year 2000, the Russian cosmonaut Valentina Tereshkova, the first woman in space, singled out Tony Lothian's work for special praise. 'The dialogue between women of different countries has become a mark of our times. How can we not praise the enormous contribution of my dear friend Lady Antonella Lothian to international co-operation and understanding of the women of our planet? The voice of the Women of the Year Assembly is heard in Australia, America, Africa, Asia and in Europe.

'This is a result of your efforts, my dear Tony, of your energy, an achievement of your life. I am grateful to my destiny that made it possible for us to meet each other and allowed us to contribute our efforts to the cause of uniting peoples of different countries and beliefs in the interests of strong peace on our Earth and in the Universe,' wrote Tereshkova, now the president of the Russian Centre for International Scientific and Cultural Co-operation.

In a world where women are achieving more than Pankhurst ever dreamed possible, what are the criteria for selecting Women of the Year? 'I think that authentic achievers are those whose legacy lives on,' is the view of anaesthetist Dr Beverly-Jane Collett, one of the directors of the Lunch. 'This perpetuity can be in an ideal, a change in the *modus operandi*, in a way of thinking. But I think it must change the way people think and act – not only for now but for future generations ... to the greater good.'

'Don't get too hung up on the iconography,' Tony warned me at an early stage of this book. 'We have fun at our Lunches as well, you know.' But with such icons as Tereshkova, not to mention Odette Hallowes on board from the very beginning, it's rather difficult not to get hung up on the iconography of the Women of the Year Lunch. One day Tony, not usually preoccupied by traditional girlie talk about handbags and lipstick, began reminiscing to me about how carefully kept Odette's nails always were. There was a purpose behind this frivolous observation, as there is always a serious purpose behind her apparently chance remarks. 'She was very French,' was Tony's way of explaining the courage of her late friend, one of the co-founders of the Women of the Year Lunch.

Odette had become an international heroine for her services to Britain and France during the Second World War. Awarded the George Cross for gallantry, this French-born British spy for the Special Operations Executive (SOE) had been subjected to torture by the Gestapo after she was captured on a mission. Her toenails had been torn out during interrogation at the notorious Fresnes prison in Paris.

Betrayed by a weak link in the chain, Odette did not betray her fellow agents. She was sent to Ravensbruck concentration camp for more than a year, where she was put on starvation rations in solitary confinement for trying to organise an escape. After her homecoming in 1945, it took three operations on her injured toes before Odette was able to wear shoes again. Until then, she had been able to walk only on her heels. Of such details is the story of real courage made – a theme which she was to address later at the Lunch.

The policies of Germany's Third Reich under its Chancellor Adolf Hitler had a lasting effect upon the personal lives of three women at the heart of the Women of the Year Lunch. And thus, in a curious way, its history has become a microcosm of the history of the fight against injustice and oppression. Odette, who died in 1995 at the age of eighty-two, was the most famous of the three. Given that the war had been over for only ten years, it was inevitable that some of the women attending the first Lunch back in 1955 would have seen active service of some kind. However, the legendary Odette, as her obituary in *The Times* pointed out, was at the very centre of resistance to Nazism. She was indeed the best of women, the supreme anti-dictatorship role model for an event that has brought together women of all races and backgrounds. Asked whom she would nominate as the very best of women, Tony Lothian immediately names Odette.

'Odette thought that my idea of a Women of the Year Lunch and Assembly was a wonderful one, and that absolutely put the seal on it,' she recalls. 'The fact that Odette was vice-president impressed many people. Odette was everybody's hero; I had met her through mutual friends, and she taught me about how much torture the human body can take; she was always very physically frail as a result. But she had this shining, strong spirit. She was always well dressed – very simple, just right. There was always a sort of edge to the way she looked.

'She was lovely-looking. I have often wondered how much the element of beauty – and I know this is not a feminist thing to say – has to play in women's influence on people; beautiful women do seem to have a special influence.' Pausing to reflect, Tony adds rather sadly, 'But beauty is also the undoing of some women, like Marilyn Monroe.

'I often asked Odette what enabled courage. With her, it was a mixture. She said to me that as she was spiritual in belief she derived a great deal of courage from prayer in her cell. When she was really desperate, she remembered having kissed the feet of Christ for reassurance. And she wasn't being histrionic; she really meant it.

'Her great love of Peter Churchill, the organiser of the SOE, gave her courage. She said she just could not betray him, reveal his name and what part he played in the Resistance. That's another very female thing. They broke her physically – there were certain things she couldn't overcome – but only temporarily.'

Although she married three times – Roy Sansom in 1931, Captain Peter Churchill after the war in 1947 and Geoffrey Hallowes, who also served with the SOE, in 1956 – this self-effacing woman, who modestly styled herself 'housewife' in *Who's Who*, became universally known simply as Odette. Anna Neagle played the title role in the 1950 film *Odette*, based on the book by Jerrard Tickell that paid tribute to Odette's unswerving dedication. Odette herself returned to Ravensbruck in 1994, the year before her death, to unveil a plaque commemorating the SOE women who had died there. Awarded an MBE in 1945 and the George Cross in 1946, she was made an officer of the Légion d'Honneur in 1950.

It was no coincidence that this supreme exponent of female courage should become a co-founder of an organisation to celebrate women's achievements and raise money for the blind; for after the war, Odette had immersed herself in charity work to help the vulnerable and underprivileged. As *The Times* obituarist put it: 'Her wartime experiences had taught her two great truths: that suffering is an ineluctable part of the human lot, and that the battle against evil is never over.'

Tony Lothian was also to be profoundly affected by Nazism, but as a horrified spectator rather than a victim. When Tony was sixteen, she was sent to school in pre-war Germany where the experience of National Socialism proved to be a defining one: 'After basically amiable Italian fascism, the horrendous master-race eugenics in Germany turned me upside down,' as she puts it. 'From then on, I was driven by an obsession to protect the voiceless weak.'

An army doctor's daughter, Tony describes her peripatetic youth thus: 'My mother was twenty when she married my father, who was fifty-five. They separated when I was four years old and she married again. I was very much an only child until my half-sister was born; it was a life of no fixed abode, as happens if your father is a serviceman. My heart's home was with a foster mother in a smallholding in the Tuscan hills or with my grandmother in a flat for retired civil servants in Rome. The rest of the time I lived in England.

'I don't remember my childhood in Egypt except that my Italian mother admired the ancient culture while my Yorkshire father benevolently said he wouldn't be surprised if God was an Englishman. Mixed races seemed inevitable to me and that helped when later I met so many from all over the world. Travelling did not encourage robust health, and I was always ill. When, in my forties, I lost an eye through cancer, it was just one more physical problem to be dealt with like the rest.

'Childhood loneliness was lifted by day-dreaming, nearly always of myself leading a campaign against injustice. Apart from dreams, I was shy, insecure and frightened. An experience of spirituality came later. After that, strength was provided by praying and becoming a Christian. Someone said "You are devout"; I answered, "Not devout – I am desperate!" I always remember Gandhi's remark: "I love Christ but not Christians. They are so unlike him."'

Her glimpses of the collective madness that engulfed Nazi Germany in the thirties make chilling reading in her book *Valentina: First Woman in Space*. 'The thirties in Italy were ruled by Mussolini. But Italian-style fascism often included disregarding regulations, so for me dictatorship meant only that: provided no one asked disturbing questions, those who wished to live in peace could do so. I remember that one of my two uncles, an uncompromising soldier, was never promoted because he opposed fascist corruption in the armed services, but the only time I can remember being frightened by fascism was when Mussolini, copying Hitler, issued decrees which discriminated against the Jews.

'The persecution of the Jews was relentless and to witness how they were categorised as sub-human by the description 'Semite' and denied dignity as individuals transformed my thinking. I became a very un-comfortable member of the school, particularly when I followed up carefully concealed rumours of atrocities against the Jews told to me by a house-cleaner. I challenged the upright Christian citizens who befriended me to share my repulsion, but they did not want to know. The principal of the school asked my mother to get me back to England.'

In her autobiography, Tony recalls how the Odette story became a legend for those who had survived the war. 'Even before I met Odette Hallowes, she exemplified for me, as for many others, the proof that even in the deepest pain of war the human heart and mind can be brave enough not to be broken.'

In 1981 Tony recorded an interview – which, as with her taped encounters with Valentina Tereshkova, she prefers to call 'a conversation' – with Odette. 'She typically played down her own courage,' Tony writes in her forthcoming autobiography. 'If anyone could torture Odette later, it would be by singling her out for praise.'

Asked to define fear, Odette had replied, 'Fear is the unknown. Not knowing the answer. If you fear an operation, it is because you don't know if it will be successful or not. After it, you fear less even if the worst happens. Before torture, I knew what I maybe had to put up with. When I was captured and they started torture, I wasn't sure how much I could take. I said to myself, "If I survived the last minute, I can take the next minute."' And when Tony asked 'Do you break after a time?', Odette replied simply, 'I didn't expect to, as I preferred to die.'

Describing herself as the 'perfect prisoner – not bitter', she said without irony that she had found plenty of free time to think about things in prison. And she defined courage as 'not giving up. To keep hoping. Self-respect is what Rochefoucauld said: "To do without witnesses what one would do in front of the world." But courage is not giving up what you believe you should be doing.'

Odette believed that courage is helped by 'looking

one's best. Every evening when I was condemned to death, I thought I must go to my death looking respectable. Looking my best! When my stockings wore out, I made what was left of the stockings into small hair rollers. Every day I turned my skirt an inch so that it would not be worn more on one side than another.

'When I went to be interviewed, because of my torn feet I couldn't wear my shoes. But I wasn't going to be seen shoeless by the man I was interviewed by – the Commandant of Ravensbruck.' Indeed, she thought that he 'was certainly interested' in her. 'That was one way of keeping up courage. I was not going to the firing squad not looking my best.'

Odette told Tony that the time when she felt most fear was when she 'had to make a decision which would influence the life of her children, because it meant parting from them without knowing when she would see them again. Her saddest day was the day on which she had to leave her children, though self-sacrifice was the characteristic she admired most in a human being. But her happiest moment was at the end of the war, when she felt she had done her best in difficult circumstances and had the great joy of returning home to her daughters.'

Odette's outstanding record makes her one of the most remarkable people ever to be associated with the Women of the Year. According to Tony's autobiography, 'Odette's most hated human characteristic was weakness of heart and soul, and she despised those who would not accept their responsibilities to other human beings. She abhorred sectarianism, tribalism, colour prejudice and, indeed, narrow-mindedness with all its dangers. Her beliefs might be seen as a blueprint for the Lunch.'

One senses that Tony Lothian is a more fallible and therefore more approachable human being. And yet Odette was far more vulnerable than one might guess from the look of that beautifully lacquered carapace: 'She was always dying a little, like me, and would always say to me that she couldn't possibly last another day,' recalls Tony, who has fought a number of serious illnesses.

'Odette was blind in one eye,' says her widower Geoffrey Hallowes, musing over the strange coincidence that left all three of the original founders of the Women of the Year Lunch afflicted by eye problems. 'My late wife's eye was damaged from birth with three or four scars on the iris. So she was blind in one eye when she went to France on her missions. She was able to read; she had some vision in it, but it was very poor vision.'

Emphasising how important the Women of the Year Lunch was to Odette, he recalls how he used to 'drop her off at the Savoy every year. She always went to the Lunch whenever she could. Odette would always tell me about the people who were at the Lunch; she was always amazed at the sheer numbers of women who had achieved something remarkable in their lives. She would take her granddaughter Sophie along to the Lunch sometimes,' adds Geoffrey. 'Female friendship was important to her; she enjoyed the company of other women, even though towards the end of her life she wasn't able to attend the Lunch.'

It was a good marriage, and Geoffrey remembers his late wife with enormous tenderness. They had no children together, but he talks fondly of her six little great-grandchildren – only one of whom she ever knew. Two of them, however, are named Odette after her.

When Tony married Peter at that temple of Roman Catholic Baroque, Brompton Oratory, she married into the hereditary aristocracy that she has often found comical. 'For a professional journalist, it was a problem when I became Lady Lothian. Being a doctor's daughter and the granddaughter of a doctor, I was accepted for what I did and who I was; but on marrying Peter, I suddenly assumed an identity that had nothing to do with me. It is sensible that hereditary titles are now out of the House of Lords; although Peter is an hereditary peer, I think titles give people the wrong shape. They open the wrong doors and shut all the good ones.' Or as she once put it in an interview with the *Daily Express*, 'It's stupid for people to live in their own little history boxes.'

A woman-friendly woman – it would be rather difficult to be president of the Women of the Year Lunch otherwise – Tony revelled in the contacts she made while working on the Mother's Union magazine, *The Catholic Mother*. Her assistant editors were Grace Hough, wife of a Derby bank clerk, Mary Stott (not the future *Guardian* women's editor of media legend but a sharp-witted Crown Derby employee) and Derby councillor Mary Harper, later mayor of Derby. 'They were the three musketeers,' says Tony. 'We worked brilliantly together.' The magazine's readers were, in Tony's words, 'the most lovable and instructive influence of my life...miners' wives, dockworkers' wives, farmers' wives and fishing communities in Hull...the mothers were certainly the best human beings it could be anyone's privilege to know. They will always remain as my ideal of the best of women.'

With the help and hindrance of what she calls 'an eccentric Irish nanny straight out of Nancy Mitford', Tony also managed to raise a family. 'But I mostly looked after the children myself. My one outstanding bonus is this enormous energy, which is not based on healthiness because I've always been ill. As a child, my asthma was dreadful; and I've also had four miscarriages. 'I would,' she admits, 'have loved ten children.'

Instead she has six. 'My eldest, Mary, is a Montessori teacher. Michael is very much a Conservative idealist, involved in charities such as Shelter; he was very effective in initiating the peace process in Northern Ireland. My second eldest daughter Cecil is vice-chairman of Save the Children, Clare works for mental health, Elizabeth is a trustee of the British Library and my youngest, Ralph, is a music man like his father. He worked at Sothebys and now he's an estate manager in Derbyshire.'

It was on the country-house circuit that she became friends with Lady Georgina Coleridge, a character of renowned wit and style who has always been known as Lady G. The daughter of a Scottish marquess, the former Lady Georgina Hay was one of the first great role models for British women journalists...not to mention women racehorse owners.

A legendary editor (and later publisher) of *Homes & Gardens* from 1949 to 1963, Lady G is one of the only two surviving original founders of the Lunch – Tony Lothian being the other. Sadly, Georgina has become profoundly deaf. 'One of the best aspects of the Lunch is the good time that everybody has,' says Anne Dickinson, a long-standing friend of Lady G's who was first invited to attend the Lunch because of her distinguished career in public relations. 'The buzz in the room is terrific, and when Georgina's hearing started to fail, she found the noise levels in the room impossible to deal with.'

Yet she remains as sharp as ever, barks out good-humoured answers to probing questions and snorts with laughter as a paradox or a joky thought occurs. Despite the fact that she never smoked or drank, Lady G, the author of a racy book on racing, would qualify as the most clubbable of media people. She too lost an eye to illness but, like Tony Lothian, did not let the lack of full eyesight cramp her style.

Still lending her name to the Lunch and Assembly but no longer actively involved with it, Lady G leads a life of quiet retirement near Ashford in Kent and devours Edgar Wallace thrillers supplied by her devoted daughter, Frances Smith. Like a character from Evelyn Waugh,

Georgina lists her recreations in Debrett's as 'racing, writing, cooking, nothing highbrow'. It was Lady G, Frances points out, who had the idea of asking matrons and other women administrators in hospitals along to the Lunch. 'It laid the foundation of the list.'

Most emphatically not a political animal of any persuasion, she immediately saw the fund-raising potential of a charity Lunch when Tony first mooted the idea. 'Georgina, Violet [Attlee] and Odette were amused at the ideals I kept waving at them like angry flags,' admits Tony. 'They were all friends of mine, and I said to them one by one, "Would you support me?"'

'Georgina was well placed, right at the heart of journalism as one of the first really successful women editors, and her husband Arthur Coleridge was an executive on *Reader's Digest*. It was a great media marriage. They both believed in the Assembly.'

Originally a writer for such society glossies as *Harper's Bazaar*, Georgina climbed the executive ladder with the help of Alice T Head, her first woman boss and editor (later to be managing director) of *Good Housekeeping* when it was launched in 1924.

'There were very few women in women's magazines before the war; *Woman's Own*, for example, was edited by a man. In a way I felt like a pioneer,' Lady G recalls. 'But I succeeded Miss Head, as we called her. She was completely disregarded by women, who thought she was an old fogey, but she had been absolutely beautiful as a girl. She was the most highly paid woman in England and she terrified men.' Another heroine was Odette: 'I thought she was wonderful; I had met her through Tony. I admired her for her acceptance of what she had been through and her absolute dignity; I would have been a coward.'

In her trademark tortoiseshell glasses and Simone Mirman hats, Lady G cut a wonderfully chic and imposing figure at the Lunch – where she was affectionately known as Brown Owl. 'It reflects her kindness, strength, total integrity and judgement. She has a gift for getting to the point and seeing what needs to be done,' says Diana Makgill, who has been associated with the Lunch – first as a guest and then as the diplomatic protocol officer – since the late sixties.

Georgina cheerfully admits to having found some of the more earnest speakers at the Lunch 'rather heavy', a criticism that Tony readily acknowledges. 'Women speakers don't want to be trivial, they want to talk about serious matters,' she explains. Lady G was just retiring as chairman of the Ladies Committee of the Greater London Fund for the Blind when she first met Tony, and they both knew the president well: an outstanding man called Paul Hyde-Thomson, who was himself blind.

'He suggested that I should succeed Georgina as chairman of the Fund and I accepted with the proviso that I could only become involved in projects for improving the welfare of the blind,' says Tony. 'I refused to become involved with the usual glitzy fund-raising round of balls, fashion shows, film premières – and more balls.'

Instead Tony suggested bringing leading women professionals together for lectures and conferences to meet each other and at the same time raise funds for the charity. The logo of the Women of the Year Association was eventually to become 'Women who distinguish themselves through their work and are united to promote a charitable cause'. A flutter of ladylike doubts was immediately expressed within the Fund's Ladies Committee; and in those pre-feminist days, people feared it might be hard to find enough distinguished working women. Yet Hyde-Thomson and Georgina were both enthusiastic from the beginning.

'During my time with the Mother's Union journal, I found that wherever I went there was always one remarkable woman without whom the village, town or whatever would have collapsed. I met women of outstanding talent in schools, hospitals, local radio stations and voluntary services without whose efforts and expertise national life might be halted,' Tony writes.

'But this was 1955 ... a time when women's work was just not recognised. I wanted to change this. I wanted to bring together a cross-section of working women who had distinguished themselves in their careers to enable them to meet each other and hear the views of world-famous women on important issues.

'I had heard of a lunch club which always had a waiting list "because anyone who attended was bound to be sitting next to someone interesting". I asked, "Can I join?" The answer was "No – it's only for men." So it struck me, why shouldn't women have the same opportunity? I looked for supporters for my plan and as I was seeing Odette Hallowes regularly, I asked her,' says Tony. 'Then I said, "We must have a socialist flag flying. We must have Violet Attlee." So it was with Georgina, Odette and a little later, Violet, that the new venture began.'

During the Second World War, Tony had worked as a nursing auxiliary and lived through the deaths of friends 'who had not wanted to go to war'. As she wrote in her book *Valentina*, 'First World War patriotism was out of fashion in the Second World War. My contemporaries faced being killed, resigned to obey orders – while dulled and dogged civilians in the Blitz waited for a world fit for heroes. I voted for Attlee and socialism [after the war].

'Seeing the Jews suffering in Nazi Germany had sown in me a seed of motivation to try and protect the helpless. I believed wholeheartedly in the ideal of reverence for life taught by Albert Schweitzer. I came to feel this particularly about racist attitudes to my black friends, as my work enabled me to meet many from the

Caribbean...it seemed to me that, having defeated the Nazis, the democracies of the rich North now adopted similar master-race attitudes in their dealings with the poor South.'

The way Tony Lothian's mind works explains the way in which the Women of the Year Lunch broke down race as well as class barriers by inviting black women of merit across the board. As Tony puts it, 'We changed history quietly, in a background way.' Here, she says, Violet Attlee's influence was low-key but pervasive.

Elected leader of the Labour Party in 1935 after pursuing a career as a barrister, social worker and lecturer before entering politics, Clement Attlee had become Prime Minister when Labour won a landslide victory in the general election of 1945 on a Keynesian programme of social reform. Attlee presided over the creation of the Welfare State as we know it, setting up a National Health Service, nationalising the railways and power industries and passing a National Insurance Act to provide a medical service through taxation and thus protect the population, as the saying went, from the cradle to the grave.

In 1951, the Conservatives were returned to government. Attlee remained Leader of the Opposition, however, until 1955 when Hugh Gaitskell succeeded him; that year Attlee went to the House of Lords and Violet, a devoted wife who had served her husband so loyally, immersed herself in the new cause of celebrating women's work. The timing for Violet's involvement was perfect.

'Violet was a very typical socialist; we always looked for authentic people of real merit and integrity for the Lunch,' explains Tony. 'Like Mary Wilson, who succeeded her, she was a free spirit: an intelligent, good woman. She and Clement used to ask Peter and me to lunch at the Athenaeum Club, and I always remember Clem saying to us, "The intelligentsia hate the British people, but not half as much as the British people hate the intelligentsia."

'They were real people; they never played to the gallery. Violet always thought her role was at home, making Clem's life possible' – a view that was to be reflected in Countess Attlee's speech at the Women of the Year Lunch in 1958.

Tony remembers that at first Violet Attlee was sceptical about whether the 'real people' would bother to make the great trek to the Savoy. 'Violet said to me, "You won't get the matron of Derby hospital to come to the Savoy." She was seldom wrong, but I thought she was wrong about that – and I was right. The matron enjoyed having a day out in London. She liked the experience of listening to important women speaking about important issues and she went on to the theatre in the evening, so it all came together – and still does.'

Peter's work at the Foreign Office had brought Tony into contact with many worldwide women achievers at official social functions, some of which she helped Elizabeth Douglas-Home to organise when Elizabeth's husband Sir Alec was Prime Minister. She remembers Lady Home as 'the most brilliantly clever woman I have ever met. We always asked her but she never came to the Women of the Year Lunch. She was nervous that we might be anti-men. In the year she could have come, sadly it was too late; she was no longer in this world.'

Yet even with Tony as the chief jockey, the Lunch very nearly fell at the first hurdle, as it were. In its second year, the Savoy found itself catering to only 381 women instead of the planned five hundred.

'People were still very puzzled by the idea at that stage,' Tony admits. 'The numbers went down because the professional women we invited were all of a particular merit and not socially inclined. They didn't want to come along to what they thought was simply a

Ladies Who Lunch event; they were nonplussed and suspicious that it was just a charity bash. But when word got around, when they came to understand that the Lunch was all about women of merit nominating other women of merit, they became interested. We have been over-subscribed ever since 1959.'

The Women's Liberation movement of the late sixties and early seventies was to make women's issues fashionable. But back in 1955, women could not have launched the Lunch completely by themselves; men were needed. Few people now remember the part played by Charles Scott-Paton; a professional fund-raiser for the Greater London Fund for the Blind who afterwards founded the Men of the Year Lunch.

Equally essential were the waiters and the toast-master: the legendary, beetle-browed Ivor Spencer, who started up a school of toast-masters and whose solid presence as a stalwart of the Lunch helped from the beginning. 'He upheld the Lunch for nearly thirty years,' says Tony Lothian.

At first the four founders planned to launch the Lunch on a date convenient for working women – 19 May, 1955 – but a general election was called shortly after that date. As a gushing *Leicester Mercury* put it, 'The Marchioness of Lothian, whose home at Melbourne Hall on the fringe of our county continues to give delight to Leicestershire visitors, is chairman of an interesting event planned . . . for May 19 . . . When the date of the [General Election] became known, it was obvious that many guests would be engaged in preparation for that day. So the Lunch, to which leading women in science, the arts and professions are being invited, has been postponed until September 29.'

Tony's most vivid memory of 1955 was of 'sitting on the floor in Charles Scott-Paton's house, surrounded by reference books, from which he and I made the first lists of important women to be invited. The reference books provided not too few, but too many! Mayors, actresses, doctors, authors, dentists, scientists, engineers, lawyers, explorers, educationalists...It was not so much a question of providing recognition for hundreds as for thousands, and the space at the Savoy was limited.

'So our lists were built on the most balanced selection we could identify. The absolute requirement was that all those asked must have distinguished themselves by courage, artistic or academic achievement, business or professional talent – in short, excellence in a chosen career.' To achieve balance and variety was the most difficult part.

Yet it became more complex than that. As she put it to me: 'What became increasingly clear was the challenge to separate the celebrities built up by spin doctors who would live for a day and die in a day from the often unknown and unsung women without whose work the lives of everyone else would come to a grinding halt.'

A committee was formed from the outset, meeting twice a year to finalise the guest list drawn up from nominations by each committee member in her particular field of expertise. From the beginning, the names on the committee's list represented forty categories of work and influence. Tony Lothian became the first president of the Women of the Year, with her co-founders Georgina Coleridge, Odette Hallowes and Violet Attlee as the vice-presidents. They were to be followed later by Mary Wilson, the tennis player Virginia Wade, Edna Healey, Glenys Kinnock, Diana Makgill, Ruth Morris – and Renée Goddard.

The third woman with a direct experience of the peculiar horrors of Nazism, Renée Goddard is yet another example – the Lunch can boast so many – of a remarkable achiever whose career deserves a book in itself. Associated with the Women of the Year Lunch since 1972, she was head of scripts at the late Lew Grade's former independent television company ATV and, as such, one of the first women executives and programme-makers of British broadcasting. A half-Jewish refugee from Nazi Germany who had tried to hide her race by becoming a member of Hitler Youth, Renée came to England after her father, an outspoken Marxist critic of the National Socialist government, was imprisoned and eventually shot in a concentration camp.

'My father was in the Reichstag, the German Parliament, as the leader of the Communist Party. He was Jewish but had married outside his religion; he was neither a Stalinist nor a Trotskyist, just a Marxist. He was accused of helping to burn down the Reichstag and was imprisoned for two years before being put in Dachau and several other camps. He was executed by firing squad in 1940. My mother was working for the Communist Party too and she was imprisoned the same day as my father. My mother escaped from jail after being let out on bail and went illegally to Czechoslovakia and eventually to England, where she sent for me and my sister and my grandmother,' recalls Renée.

In England, Renée, then called Renate, grew up with the human-rights lawyer Ben Birnberg after his mother Naomi, who served on various refugee committees, had taken a fancy to the girl when presenting her with a school prize and invited her into her home. 'My mother was pleased because she didn't know what to do with me,' recalls Renée.

'So I grew up with Naomi until Churchill said "Collar the lot" and then I was interned as an enemy alien. I was put in Holloway Prison and then in jail on the Isle of Man for a while. But I feel that most people are displaced now,' Renée adds perceptively. 'We don't live where we were born; and we marry people from totally different backgrounds.'

When she met Tony Lothian, it was Renée who suggested that she copy the example of the Israeli general Moshe Dayan by wearing a piratical black eyepatch – which has since become one of Tony's most distinctive trademarks. Renée also has vivid memories of an early meeting: 'I went to her cottage in Chelsea. On the floor there was a cold Batchelor's soup and bread; that was my lunch. I was absolutely amazed,' says Renée, who had by now come to the conclusion that Tony was a kindred spirit. In other words, both of them were creative eccentrics, or perhaps eccentric creatives?

'In 1970 Tony had a marvellous idea for a TV programme that looked at what women's priorities would be if they were government ministers,' Renée continues. 'So I said, "Let's create a programme about a women's parliament." We eventually made some of those programmes and did well with them on ITV. Tony played the Speaker of the House, a Betty Boothroyd prototype.' The protective Renée calls Tony 'the motor' of the Women of the Year Lunch: 'She works at it every day. Tony *is* the Lunch, everybody knows that." It was, Renée feels, 'the first outfit that really fought for the professional woman's status. When I was at ATV, its own club wouldn't let me in because I was a woman. Lew had said that middle management should take clients there, but I wasn't allowed in. I couldn't wear trousers in the studio, either.'

And just as she feels protective of Tony, so Renée feels proprietorial about the spirit of the Women of the Year Lunch. 'It took twenty or thirty years to get so popular and so well-known; it's absolutely unique. People want it, and it has taken all this time. So many gatherings don't last, but even my daughter Leonie and many other people's daughters are now members of the Lunch.'

Renée has always supported the changes introduced over the years to adapt to the changes in society, such as a greater sartorial informality. She was in favour, however, of retaining certain formal aspects – much appreciated by the guests – which in her view represented a cornerstone of the Lunch. Thus she favoured an established venue and opposed dropping the Loyal Toast, read with the message to all from the charity's royal patron Queen Elizabeth the Queen Mother, and the saying of grace, traditionally read by leaders of different denominations, most recently the Salvation Army, Rabbi Julia Neuberger and Methodist lay preacher Sybil Phoenix. Such traditions epitomise the ethical aspirations of the Lunch.

Renée and Tony were later to team up with Shirley Conran and Audrey Eyton, author of *The Complete F-Plan Diet*, to put on the pioneering Health Festival in 1985 which effectively launched the health-food movement in Britain.

They remain almost as close to each other as a fondly grumbling old married couple, yet not even Renée could replace Mikki Doyle, a lifelong fighter against fascism, in Tony's heart. Here was another great element in the Women of the Year chemistry.

Born Miriam Levental to East European Jewish parents in New York, Mikki Doyle was to become one of the best-known (and best-loved) characters on the tiny stage of British communism when she joined the *Morning Star* as women's editor. Even diehard capitalists liked Mikki, a warm and funny human being with a genius for friendship and a talent for eloquent communication. For Tony, her friendship with Mikki was to symbolise the way in which the Women of the Year Lunch brought so many different tribes together. As Tony put it, such a bond between a Christian and a Communist proved that 'when women meet, there is always more to unite than to divide'.

Mikki's first husband had been an English communist. That, together with the experience of bringing up two children during the Depression, shaped her left-wing politics. By a strangely sad coincidence, she, like Tony, Georgina and Odette, had suffered eye problems. In her case, she had been nearly blinded in a racist attack by hooligans at the 1949 Peekskill concert given by the iconic black singer Paul Robeson. That same year she married her third husband, the Glasgow-born Charlie Doyle, a leading member of the American Communist Party and one of the first targets of the McCarthyite witch-hunts. She came with him to London in 1953 when he was deported from the United States.

After a couple of years of factory work in England, Mikki went into advertising – which she described in her usual direct way as easy 'because of years of writing political pamphlets – and just being American'. She joined the *Morning Star* in 1967 and became a key figure in the emergent feminist movement. Cancer was first diagnosed in 1979; it was later followed by a coronary, which she fought with the same zeal that she applied to everything in life. In her speech at the 1982 Women of the Year Lunch, she talked of how, three years and eleven operations after she had been told she had cancer, she was still fighting for a better world where all could live in peace and dignity.

She and Tony had first met each other in Women in Media, the feminist campaigning organisation Mikki had co-founded, during the seventies. 'We all called each other Sister, but it really became true of Mikki and me,' Tony was later to write. 'She and her husband Charlie, and Peter and I, genuinely loved each other, so much so that when asked who he would want to be with on a desert island, Peter replied without hesitation, "Mikki and Charlie Doyle." The outside world saw our polarised philosophies, Christian and Communist, as not to be reconciled, but in actuality Mikki and I sometimes feel like one person and we even look and dress alike.'

Retired trade-union leader Barbara Switzer, one-time

deputy general secretary of the manufacturing union TASS, recalls Mikki, whom she succeeded on the Women of the Year committee, as 'more than a friend but also a teacher'. Switzer is the current president of the National Assembly of Women, an organisation aiming to bring women together to campaign for equality, peace and the elimination of poverty. It was founded in 1952 at the height of the Cold War, with Mikki one of its earliest members. Barbara now pays tribute to her 'encouragement, much-needed advice, common sense and tolerance', typical Mikki qualities.

Having found a like mind in Mikki from the beginning, Tony Lothian asked Doyle to join the Lunch committee. 'Mikki became a real pillar of strength,' she recalls, adding, 'She and Valentina have been closer to me than sisters.'

Floella Benjamin believes that friendship and understanding beyond the frontiers of class, colour and creed, as exemplified for nearly half a century by the Women of the Year, is the key to its apparently timeless appeal.

Chapter Four
Pageant of Personalities

Hearing about the lives of Tony, Renée, Mikki and the many other vivid personalities associated with the Women of the Year Lunch is like reading a book about the history of the times. And it says much for its all-embracing spirit that two of those now accepted as women of influence are the capitalist Margaret Thatcher and the communist Mikki Doyle, who have both been distinguished speakers at the Lunch. As the first female British Prime Minister and the leader of a party not known for promoting its women members, the pioneering Thatcher was to fulfil many of the criteria that led to a nomination for the Women of the Year Lunch.

But the history of the Lunch includes some setbacks along the way. Tony Lothian suffered serious health problems in 1970. She took a short sabbatical from her Women of the Year work, asking Lady Georgina Coleridge to preside over the Lunch in her place. The arrangement worked so well that the two women rotated the chairing of the Lunch between them for a number of years. They understood each other, one picking up where the other left off. 'Lady G had real presence,' remembers Diana Makgill, 'and Tony is a one-off. She's a unique personality. It's rare to find someone as professional as she is and such a good homemaker, a good wife and mother, at the same time.'

Tony was soon back in business, both in London and Australia. Although the Women of the Year Lunch remains a unique event, one of its most exciting spin-offs was the formation of the Australian Women of the Year Lunch in 1975 when 250 women attended a sister event in Brisbane. The concept of a Down Under edition, as it were, had been brought to Australia by Elizabeth ('Libby') Escolme Schmidt who had helped to organise the Lunch in London. A teacher and trainer who began her career in Papua New Guinea, she has been nominated for many businesswoman awards throughout Australia and specialises in training and mentoring programmes – in particular for women.

In the mid-seventies, the macho culture of 'mateship' still held sway throughout Australia; the average Australian man would have fainted clean away at the thought of talking to and interacting with a group of women when he had his mates to bond with instead. When Libby was first invited to the Lunch in London, she had been working for British Airways as the first Australian to be involved with the airline's public image and middle-management training. Then she had married and moved to the Outback. Because she was so keen to get involved, she became a committee member in absentia; and then she had her Big Idea.

'I asked the committee in London if I might emulate the Lunch in Australia and they said yes. But in 1975 it was quite a risk, as there was nothing like this for women in this macho country. I was told I would be ridiculed and that women would be too modest to turn up!' Libby now recalls. No faint-hearted feminist, Libby persevered. The first affirmative reply to an invitation came from the then Labour Prime Minister Gough Whitlam's wife Margaret. 'She has been a great supporter – and others followed,' says Libby. Now, not only has the Lunch raised money for the National Heart Foundation, the Neurological Foundation and the Royal Flying Doctor Service in Australia but, as Libby points out, it has been the first truly serious networking organisation for Australian women. It also invited leading Aborigine women to attend.

Because of the vast distances that must be travelled in Australia, the Lunch is held in a different city each year. Close contact with the London committee of the Women of the Year Lunch has been maintained in order to ensure that the Australian sister event followed the format and remained true to the traditions of the London Lunch.

Valentina Tereshkova had seen Australia from space during her solo flight. And through what has become her special bond with Tony Lothian, Valentina agreed to speak at the Australian Women of the Year Lunch ten years after her historic address to the London Lunch in 1984.

Another valuable spin-off developed when the Women of the Year Association was set up in 1980 in order to protect the name. Betty McLeish, an Elder of the Church of Scotland, became its administrator. Dr Erna Low, the travel pioneer, was joint chairman with Pat Gregory, chairman of women's football, and Tony Lothian was appointed founder president. In 1996 the Association nominated Tony for an honour, which she received. She was awarded an OBE for her services to women and to the disabled. The association holds informal meetings with guest speakers – Coretta King, Social Democratic Party co-founder Shirley Williams, broadcaster Esther Rantzen and novelist P D James have been among them – four times a year in London, with membership drawn from working women representing many different fields.

The voice of the Women of the Year was becoming ever more widely heard. Tony was invited to Russia in 1987 to attend the World Congress of Women as a representative of the Women of the Year Association. She rang Mikki Doyle up in a panic to enlist her company on the trip because she spoke no Russian. Mikki had many contacts there, and their joint attendance at the Congress went so well that the following year Tony found herself on her way back to Moscow as an international delegate to the Orthodox Church's Millennium celebrations. This time the atheist Mikki Doyle did not go with her. In her book *Valentina: First Woman In Space*, Tony records that she arrived at the same time as the Archbishop of Canterbury, Billy Graham, Archbishop Tutu and four Vatican cardinals – and received exactly the same hospitality because Valentina had asked that she should be well looked after.

During that week, Tony found herself being asked to convey what was to be an historic message to the then Prime Minister Margaret Thatcher. Metropolitan Juvenaly of Moscow, who had been to school with Valentina in their native Yaroslavl, wanted Mrs Thatcher, whom he had met on her visit to Russia the previous year, to know that the Russian Orthodox Church 'was now free because she had enabled America to look at Russia and Russia to look at America and this had made *perestroika* possible'.

Also charged with taking a record of Russian church music and the seal of St Vladimir to Mrs Thatcher, Tony wrote to the Prime Minister's secretary to ask permission to leave these gifts in a plastic bag with the name of St Vladimir printed on it at Ten Downing Street without giving the police a fright.

The secretary wrote back suggesting a meeting with Mrs Thatcher so that the gifts might be handed over in person. As a slightly mystified Tony put it in her book, 'I was not a Conservative. I consistently criticised the Thatcher cutbacks in the social services. I had never joined the prevalent chorus of admiration for the Prime Minister, but now I was to give her a message from

Moscow which indicated that she had saved humanity from atomic war.'

When Tony met Maggie it was the day of the Piper Alpha oil-rig disaster and Tony wondered whether the Prime Minister might cancel their meeting as a result. However, she was summoned to the House of Commons instead of Number Ten. Tony recalls, 'The last time I had spoken to Margaret Thatcher was thirty years earlier to discuss her speech at the Women of the Year Lunch. The theme was "If Not You, Who?" and she had chosen Anna, teacher of Victorian values to the King of Siam. Then she had been a little-known Conservative politician, only recently appointed to the Board of Trade. Now she was one of the most famous women in the world – not least in Russia.

'Mrs Thatcher, hand outstretched, gave me a kind, unpretentious welcome. She looked red-eyed and tired but was the sort of sympathetic listener one could talk to. I read her the message from the Moscow Metropolitan. She listened carefully. I gave her the plastic bag and we took out the presents as if it was Christmas. I had to kneel on the floor to get the record out; she knelt to help me.'

Unbending though the Iron Lady usually was on matters of state, she did like to keep in touch with her inner housewife, as it were. It was one of those informal moments that are quite common among women of all ranks – but rare among men. The Princess of Wales was also to kneel impulsively at a Lunch on a later occasion in order to whisper in the deaf ear of an elderly Salvation Army general.

No mention was made of the Women of the Year but after Thatcher had praised Valentina as 'a very fine person', Tony ventured to suggest that although in the future the Prime Minister's current triumphs would probably be forgotten, Mrs Thatcher's grandchildren would remember the part she had played in solving the crisis of misunderstanding between the USA and the USSR and thus averting a potential atomic war. 'Yes, but we must not let down our guard,' replied Thatcher. Despite that typically vigilant remark, Tony Lothian nevertheless credits her with 'an outstanding contribution to peace' by encouraging the Russians and Americans to meet. This, Tony believed, had been 'the turning of the tide in East–West relations'. Rarely is this aspect of Margaret Thatcher's premiership mentioned these days. 'Throughout,' added Tony, 'she had been sincere, humble and wise. I wished Valentina had been there too.' Humility is not a quality normally associated with the Iron Lady.

'I owed the meeting to Valentina,' says Tony Lothian of Tereshkova, who in 1995 became the first woman to hold the rank of general in the Russian Air Force. 'She is always a disciplined soldier but like many Russians, if she loves you it is genuine and generous. I was frightened of letting her down. I told her that Catherine the Great gave banquets to bring rival factions together. She was like a Russian empress, but with no pretensions.'

Born in 1937 in the village of Maslennikovo near Yaroslavl on the Volga river, Valentina left school at sixteen and began working at a tyre factory and then a textile factory. She went to night school in the evenings to study to become a technician and learned to parachute at a local air club. After Gagarin became the first man in space in 1961, Valentina applied to join the Soviet Space Research Programme and was among the first group of women to be trained for space flights. From 1968 to 1987 she was chairwoman of the Soviet Women's Committee and thus well placed to forge links with other women's groups worldwide as the Cold War became 'less frozen', to quote Professor Margaret Gowing.

The committee had nominated Valentina as the international guest of honour at the Women of the Year

Lunch in 1984, for two reasons. Not only had she earned her place in history, but it was hoped that Valentina's presence at an occasion to raise funds for Britain's disabled would establish the important principle of friendship across frontiers. At the time, relations between the two countries were anything but friendly and British athletes had been told to boycott the 1980 Moscow Olympic Games after the Russian invasion of Afghanistan. Tony Lothian recalls a prophetic speech by Margaret Gowing, Oxford Professor of the History of Science, at the Lunch of that year when she warned of the devastation of Planet Earth by a possible future atomic holocaust. The previous year the economist and environmentalist Barbara Ward had also issued the plea to save Spaceship Earth with the words: 'We either love or die.'

Who better to address the Women of the Year Lunch four years later than this remarkable female cosmonaut? When Tony first met her at the press conference to publicise the Lunch, where Tereshkova was immediately asked about the Russian invasion of Afghanistan by an American woman reporter, her first impression of Valentina was of a woman of dignity and self-containment. Tony stood up and pointed out that, as chairman, she would have to give 'Madame Tereshkova' the opportunity for a counter-question about US involvement in Vietnam. That silenced the American, who later said to Tony: 'I never knew you were so pro-Russian.'

As Tony wrote in her own defence, 'I *had* thought I was on the side of justice. Valentina, who had seemed distant, even suspicious, at first meeting me, had given me a long look from the platform. As we went outside for photographs, she took my arm. Sisterhood among women had not happened with my American friend, but it had happened between Valentina, Elizabeth Zolina [her interpreter] and me.' Later Valentina came up to

Tony and told her, 'You were very fair this morning. I was grateful to you.' And thus began an inspirational friendship across the world. So thoroughly committed was Tereshkova to the concept of a unique forum for women that she coined the evocative phrase: 'the Voice of the Women of the Year'.

But how to get permission from the Russians in the first place for Valentina to speak at the 1984 Lunch? Once it had been decided that she should be approached, the Women of the Year Lunch Committee unleashed their secret weapon – Diana Makgill. A ceremonial officer in the protocol department of the Foreign Office who looked after the wives of the various heads of states on official visits, Diana was at the time in charge of looking after the royal and international guests of honour and overseeing the programme on the day of the Lunch. That included arriving at the Savoy long before the sniffer dogs did – an essential security procedure for any event attended by a member of the royal family.

The Russian ambassador to Britain at that time was a Mr Popov: 'a rather jolly man,' as Makgill recalls. 'I had contacted Mr Popov to ask permission for Valentina to address our Lunch; the Russian Embassy also had a very good cultural attaché called Yuri Mazur who was a huge help. Valentina was coming to London to address the Royal Aeronautical Society, and Mr Mazur worked very hard on our behalf to get her to our Lunch as well.

'Getting Valentina was a highlight for me; it took nearly a year to arrange. I would see Mr Popov at parties or at Westminster and I would say to him, "Have you heard?" I'm sure he would often want to duck when he saw me across a room.'

The warmth and understanding that was to develop between Tereshkova and Tony reassured the Lunch's founder president, already a lifelong peace campaigner, that 'the more we find out about the lives of those in other communities, the less likely it is that there will be conflicts resulting in the unnecessary suffering of war. As friends, Valentina and I had crossed the barrier between West and East, capitalism and Communism, democracy and dictatorship; and we had proved that genuine co-operation is possible even in supposedly impossible circumstances. We had tried and we had succeeded in building a bridge between like minds...' The international dimension which was now part of this unique women's forum was to give the Women of the Year Lunch a world-famous reputation.

Valentina Tereshkova will always be one of the icons of the Women of the Year. Yet the event creates a plurality of attitudes; and those outsiders who ask 'Who is the Woman Of The Year?' miss the point. To single any one person out above all others would be a betrayal of the democratic spirit of the Lunch. Inevitably, however, among the pageant of personalities that have passed through the doors of the Savoy, there have been some unforgettable world and community leaders and inspirers.

The late Princess Diana; Martin Luther King's widow Coretta King; Queen Mata'aho of Tonga; Jung Chang, the author of *Wild Swans*; Uta Bellion of Friends of the Earth; the late Petra Kelly of Germany's Green Party ('like Joan of Arc', according to Tony Lothian); Josephine Henderson of Battersea Dogs' Home; Simone Veil ('the French face of feminism'); Pearly Queen Grace Smith; Sylvia Dunn, President of the National Association of Gypsy Women; Rita Restorick, Ulster mother of a murdered son; women from the small Scottish town of Dunblane where sixteen primary schoolchildren and a teacher were murdered in 1996 by the gunman Thomas Hamilton; the actress Joanna Lumley; the tennis broadcaster and former Wimbledon star, Virginia Wade; Margaret Thatcher; Germaine Greer; writer and actress

Jennifer Saunders, creator of the decade- (and generation-) defining TV satire *Absolutely Fabulous*; and fifteen-year-old Annabel Schild, held captive by Sardinian bandits for seven months, to name just a few.

Certainly the history of the second half of the century is mirrored in the Assembly. As Maureen Castens, director of the newly established National Library of Women, wrote: 'We are looking to expand the remit of the archives collection to include women of achievement in the latter part of the twentieth century and beyond. The archives of the Women of the Year organisation will in themselves provide a rich source of material for future historians – representing, as they do, an unparalleled insight into how women have identified and honoured women of achievement over a period of great change in society.'

Royal attendance reflects this change. The Lunch's longest-serving committee member and vice-president, Lady Airlie, has been a lady-in-waiting to the Queen since 1973, the year that the Lunch began inviting royal guests. 'It sounds a bit conceited, but for years we didn't think we needed a royal,' says Tony Lothian. 'Then the Duchess of Kent did something that we really respected, so we invited her along as our royal guest of honour.'

Among the royals, the late Princess Diana was, for Tony Lothian, 'magical. In fact, she was mesmeric – absolutely mesmeric.' The committee had not asked Diana to speak at the Lunch; the legend of Shy Di had become so fixed in the public mind that everyone assumed she would not want to make a speech as royal guest of honour. So it was in a non-speaking role that she attended on two occasions.

'One of my greatest regrets is that we didn't ask Diana to speak; it was assumed that she didn't like public speaking. But she seemed to love the occasion. I don't know if it was heartfelt or not, but she seemed to be totally interested in the other person,' Tony recalls. 'I thought it was genuine, myself. She was also very quick-witted, so much so that she could hold her own in any argument. She was anything but stupid but she had been brought up in a climate where it was important to be self-deprecatory. You didn't show off, you ran yourself down; she was essentially very, very English. I have seen so many air stewardesses who look and behave and speak like Diana – that blonde Englishness . . . Diana told me at the Lunch that she thought love was stronger than anything. I said cynically that I thought money was stronger than love; but she said, "No, Tony, love is."

'I think both Marilyn Monroe and Diana were rather childlike in their vulnerability,' she adds. 'Although, if anything, Marilyn may have been more like Fergie. At the time she came to the Lunch in 1991, Fergie was very beautiful, I thought: those green eyes and red hair. But she didn't establish a good connection with the audience, when she spoke: I rather think they were not expecting humour from her. She spoke without her notes, which she had torn up. And she was funny, but perhaps too superficially.'

Key achievers nominated for the Lunch value the democratic eclecticism that makes it unique and differentiates it from other fund-raising events. In 1990, when the shepherdess Katy Cropper caused a stir by bringing along her collie Trim, the Savoy tried to bar the dog, which was wearing its best green bow, from the Lunch. Katy stood her ground and said, 'If she doesn't go in, neither do I – I am only here because of her.' Katy and Trim made a good double act when they finally gained entrance, as the actress Diana Rigg recalls. 'The thing about the Lunch is the wonderful mix of people,' says Dame Diana.

Widely acknowledged as one of Britain's leading actresses for her performances in such roles as Medea, Diana Rigg first attended the Lunch in the seventies. She had already become a massively influential role model for women as the karate-kicking Emma Peel in the sixties in the escapist TV series *The Avengers*. For many, Mrs Peel was a superwoman and an early embodiment of female empowerment. 'Then there was quite a long gap until I came again. I remember sitting next to the shepherdess of the year, who had taken on this male bastion and beaten all these men. She brought her collie dog along, which behaved immaculately. She was the prettiest thing you ever saw; the dog was, too. It got some titbits from both of us; a certain amount of Hoovering went on under the table.

'It's a huge privilege to meet all these extraordinary people,' adds Rigg. 'It's not remotely solemn, not pompous. You go out on a high; it's a brilliant idea to celebrate women's achievements without being aggressive. You come out of the Lunch thinking, "How I like my sex, I really, really like them." I like them for their honesty for the most part. It's a tough audience: strike a phoney note and everyone would recognise it. I do rate women very highly, and you just don't meet the simpering women at this Lunch. I think of simpering women as having two faces: the hard, driven one and the one that simpers. The façade is only there for men, and that's pretty pathetic. But at the Lunch, you meet women who are honest and strong and funny.

'I'm not usually a great luncher, because when I'm working, the idea of getting all tarted up to go to a lunch makes the heart sink. But I love this occasion. Kate Adie I met at the Lunch, and nobody could deny that she's the best in her profession of journalism. I think she's tops.'

As for her own profession, Dame Diana believes that women in the theatre have made great progress in recent years. 'I'm in a career where you can't be supplanted by men, though some complain that men are paid more. But I feel very strongly that we are a potent force. At one stage, women as a subject for drama were not considered interesting. But from the mid-eighties onwards, lots of new plays about or around the subject of women proved to be immensely successful with the public. They were ciphers before then, pouring tea or gently flirting; you never got the blood and guts. Now a play about women can be a great pull. Now male playwrights write about women – because they find them interesting.

'There's nowhere to go but up for women. I think they should feel that they can have it all, the young should have this wonderful sense of having it all. After all, what is all? All to one person is not very much to another. You lead your life,' concludes Dame Diana.

Another hugely influential artist associated with the Women of the Year Lunch is the internationally renowned singer/ songwriter Joan Armatrading, who works with the management committee. A computer buff, she designed the Women of the Year website. In 1998, Armatrading wrote a warm personal tribute: 'I don't recall the exact year that I first attended a Women of the Year Lunch; I believe it was around 1982. But I do recall the excitement I felt when Lady Lothian wrote to me with an invitation. I had heard of the Lunch and was fascinated to see the one woman who would be singled out as the female achiever for that particular year,' she wrote, referring to a common misconception. 'To my delight, when I attended the Lunch I discovered that it was in fact all the women assembled who were named "Women of the Year".

'What a fantastic idea. And what an eye-opener. I had no real notion of the extent of women's achievements. And I could hear snatches of conversation from people all around as each person in turn marvelled as they came to the same realisation as me. Which was the under-played magnificent achievements of women.

'There were women from all walks of life. There were mayoresses, bankers, union leaders, Members of Parliament, stockbrokers, peace-makers, scientists, surgeons, artists, singer/songwriters, the list was endless. I had never been in a room filled with so many women and the place was buzzing. I don't have a funny or sad anecdotal story connected to the "Women of the Year". What I do have is a very happy feeling that the "Women of the Year" exists. It's wonderful that Lady Lothian was inspired to bring together so many women in order for us to see what we can and have achieved. And the Lunch itself is an inspiration for women to continue to aspire to greatness.

'As one leaves the Savoy Hotel where the Lunch is held, one is automatically looking forward to the year ahead and anticipating the next "Women of the Year". It's wonderful that the Lunch has celebrated women for over forty years. Long may it continue.'

Gail Rebuck is widely acknowledged as one of the most dynamic women in publishing. Chairman and chief executive of Random House, she remembers 'sitting on the top table next to Joan Armatrading; we have sort of kept in touch ever since. That kind of thing is what gives the Lunch its unique flavour. Any gathering of women who have achieved so much in very diverse occupations is very exciting and energising. Not only is the multiplicity of talent at the Lunch breathtaking, but there's also a warm welcome – which is an unusual combination. It builds confidence and is quite unique. It's eclectic and fascinating: you could be sitting next to an important scientist or someone in the legal profession.

'Each table seems to be an extraordinary mixture: I have always come away from it, thinking, "I have met some extraordinary people." The sheer diversity is what's awe-inspiring. There's a unique atmosphere and a great deal of excitement, and to make these kinds of contacts is incredibly helpful.'

The punk pioneer Poly Styrene – in real life Marian J Elliott – achieved fame in the seventies when her band X Ray Spex was riding high in the charts with some extraordinarily far-sighted songs. She recalls the key year of 1976: 'I remember writing [the song] "Genetic Engineering", which now seems quite prophetic. It's sad in a way, but I do hope scientists will be responsible with gene therapy and remember while playing with the materials here on earth, they are not the original creator, or the Godhead, of these things that existed long before them and will continue to do so with or without them. Frankenstein and Bionic Man have been there for the playwrights. But Dolly the Sheep [the first sheep cloned by scientists] became a reality. I hope humanity stays in tune with nature that has been created by the Supreme Artist.' Tony Lothian respects in-depth thinking, and Poly Styrene is the kind of visionary who has always been associated with the Lunch.

But no matter how famous the names, all are keen to acknowledge and encourage the contribution of those who are not well known. The novelist Doris Lessing, whose best-known novel *The Golden Notebook* is a landmark text in contemporary women's writing, recalls how she 'very much enjoyed being one of the guests at the Lunch I attended. To see so many remarkable women together, while knowing what it must have cost at least some of them to achieve such excellence, was an experience I shall not forget. It is an admirable thing, this Lunch, and does nothing but good.'

International guest of honour in 1997 was Queen Noor of Jordan, the widow of King Hussein, who contributed a letter to this book that speaks for the achievements of her countrywomen. 'I was particularly honoured to participate in the Women of the Year Lunch and Assembly as it provided a unique opportunity to share with the extraordinary achievers in the audience some factual anecdotes about women in Jordan, and our region, who make a difference daily. While they have not achieved milestones for women on a global scale, they, too, are pioneers, entrepreneurs, artisans and active citizens. Their work has enabled them to find a worth they never knew they had, to break down social and economic barriers and given them the strength to persevere in the face of prejudice and criticism. I consider them the unsung grass-roots heroines of the region.

'My beloved husband, King Hussein, strove from the early days of his reign to promote the role of women. I well remember his pride when, just over two years ago, the Women of the Year gave me such a wonderful opportunity to focus the limelight on the marvellous women who bravely overcame all odds to become an inspiration to their sisters, their menfolk and their families, and whose achievements ultimately touch their neighbourhood and their nations.'

Again, it is the international dimension which has fascinated people and helped to make the Lunch so memorable. The Belfast-based trade unionist and peace campaigner Baroness Blood says that the first Lunch she attended 'blew my mind. It was 1998, the year that a lot of things were happening with the peace process in Northern Ireland. It was decided that myself and my colleague Anne Carr should go over to the Lunch and represent Mo Mowlam, who was Secretary of State for Northern Ireland at the time.

'I found myself sitting beside a woman from Jerusalem who was doing the most fantastic work in bringing people together; hearing her story made ours seem insignificant because her son had been killed just before she came to the Lunch. We also heard the story of a young woman suffering appalling racial abuse.'

Lady Blood is a founder member of the Women's Coalition, one of the newest parties in Northern Ireland which has brought together Republicans and Unionists, nationalists and loyalists, rural and urban women. 'So far it has been highly successful. The Coalition was formed in 1996 to get women to the peace talks; prior to that, there had been no women at all at the table.' Her involvement with the Lunch came about, she believes, through Tony Lothian's eldest son Michael Ancram, who has been a Tory government minister in Northern Ireland. 'An event like the Lunch gives us an outlook on the rest of the world,' she points out. 'In Northern Ireland, we are inclined to be inward-looking.

'Women have a special knack of cutting through bureaucracy, and women have borne the brunt of the Troubles in Ulster. At the Lunch, we heard stories of women doing that all over the world.'

Another important figure at the Lunch has been the leading neuroscientist Susan Greenfield, the Oxford University pharmacology professor and first woman director of the Royal Institution. Greenfield, who has presented a science series on BBC2 and was the first woman presenter of the Royal Institution Christmas Lectures, was voted fourteenth most inspirational woman in the UK by *Harpers* magazine. Such an accolade is as much to do with her glamorous dynamism, one suspects, as with what an admiring Tony Lothian calls Greenfield's 'awesome' brain.

'Things are changing for women in science but there are still relatively few women professors. Women can be there at the junior level, but running laboratories is another matter. It's impossible to be really dedicated to science and to have a family; I chose not to have children because of that. But I think the world can survive without my genes being passed on. If you don't publish as a scientist, you are dead in the water,' Greenfield warns. 'And it's harder to run a lab when you have been out of it for a while because of family reasons. This is one of the real problems facing women in science. You either put off having children until you have tenure in your late thirties, which isn't necessarily the best time to conceive, or you don't have them at all. Young women science students these days believe they can have it all. Their generation is much more confident and chummy, and they've grown up in an atmosphere of girl power, but they're in for a shock when it comes to combining work and family.'

Yet Greenfield remains an optimist and finds inspiration in the Women of the Year Lunch. 'It's a very exciting event: I like the occasion because it's so upbeat. Often one finds a gloom where people whinge, but the Lunch is very positive and makes for a very different atmosphere. You are not sitting there as a member of an oppressed minority.'

So repeatedly there is the same impression, the same question. Where else but at the Assembly could scientists rub shoulders with actresses, rock singers, monarchs, peace campaigners and human-rights activists? The all-embracing nature of the Lunch means a great deal to Doreen Lawrence, who has fought an unremitting campaign in the glare of the media to bring the killers of her son Stephen to justice. Doreen, a guest in 1998, believes that the Lunch 'symbolises where women are at the turn of the century; it stands as a beacon for the world to see. I am proud to be associated with the Lunch and Assembly because it brings together all sections of the community, which makes all women feel special. What I most like about the Lunch is that women are recognised for their achievement no matter what their ethnicity.'

There were two Lawrences present at the Lunch the year Doreen was honoured as a 'woman of courage'. She was joined by fellow guest of honour Frances Lawrence, whose husband Philip, a North London headmaster, had been stabbed to death in 1995 while trying to protect a pupil who had been attacked by a gang at the school gates. 'This is a great opportunity for us to support each other,' Doreen told the waiting reporters outside the Savoy. That year teacher Alison Moore, who had returned to her school after being assaulted in order to teach the children about the effects of bullying, was also numbered among the Lunch guests.

A wide ethnic representation had been one of the features of the Lunch from the very beginning. Leading human-rights activist Indira Patel of the UK Asian Women's Conference is an international speaker on such crimes against women as bride-burning, forced marriages, trafficking in women and so-called honour killings. She recalls how 'thrilled and honoured' she was to be invited to the event that recognised the achievements of women 'from different religious, cultural and social backgrounds, based on merit and not on social status, class or politics, sitting together on one of the longest main tables I have ever seen'.

The event nevertheless brought home to her the fact that although 52 per cent of the world's population are women, 'even today women are paid only 80 per cent of men's wages for the same work, are first to be fired in a recession, are routinely subjected to economic discrimination, assault, rape, sexual exploitation and even murder, only because they are women. The old saying that a long journey begins with single steps applies to the efforts of women like Lady Lothian in seeking a just and fair world for all. I would like to light a candle and pray that all the dreams of the organisers of the Women of the Year Lunch and Assembly come true.'

Journalist and *Official Sloane Ranger's Handbook* co-author Ann Barr, now serving on one of the Women of the Year sub-committees, praises the sheer diversity of a Lunch at which she found herself sitting with a shepherdess and a woman falconer. Valentina Tereshkova's speech she remembers as a particular highlight: 'Everyone perhaps expected a speech that wouldn't challenge prejudices, but Valentina was very radical. She was incredible: she stood up and gave this heartfelt speech that suggested women could get together to end the Cold War. It was a most moving occasion, but at first the audience were silent from sheer shock: they were astonished at this major initiative. It was a real breaking down of barriers.'

Lady Morris of Kenwood, a director of the Women of the Year Lunch and Assembly, values the Lunch for the way in which 'it brings together women of like mind; it's a form of networking and it focuses women's minds on important issues'. She comes from a family 'that is expected to give service to the community'; her brother is the QC Greville Janner. And the biggest female influence upon Lady Morris is 'Barbara Castle: I admire her for saying, "Don't ever talk of retiring, just talk of a change of direction."'

The work of many Women of the Year is known all over the world. Lunch and Assembly director Eleanor Angel is sales administrative director of Angels, the largest and most famous theatrical costumiers in the world. A family-run concern that started up in 1840, it numbers many women among its 140 employees. After being asked to join the Lunch and Assembly committee, Eleanor then organised the Frink Award. Like every other woman associated with the event, she finds that it gives her a unique and valuable perspective on other women's lives. 'The interest and joy of the Lunch is that it brings together so many varied people who all want to know each other's story,' she says. 'It really recognises people's achievements; every person there is special. There are various groups who object to the event being all women together, but as far as I'm concerned, women will let their hair down and relax more than if there were men around. This is something that men don't always understand. There's intimacy and informality at an all-women event; people will talk to each other.'

Among the many subjects who have sat for the distinguished portrait painter June Mendoza are the Queen, Prince Charles and Princess Diana, the Queen Mother, Princess Anne, Margaret Thatcher and her successor as British premier, John Major, Yehudi Menuhin, Georg Solti, Joan Sutherland and Paul Tortelier. One could hardly be nearer the heart of the Establishment than that, yet Mendoza sent the least pompous of letters about her involvement with the Women of the Year. 'Being included in that gathering of those hundreds of vibrant vitality girls is my annual fix. A day in the presence of the collective force of all that intelligence and activity at work in this world is not only rewarding stimulation but, to one whose work is necessarily solo, my comfort blanket. I treasure belonging to such a sorority. I raise a very large glass of excellent red to all of them.'

So many different voices. For example, one active committee member is the Cambridge University academic and lecturer Sylvana St Andrews – wife of the Duke of Kent's elder son, the Earl of St Andrews. She has been associated with the Lunch since 1990. A Fellow of Hughes Hall and a lecturer at St John's College, she specialises (as Sylvana Tomaselli) in the history of political theory in general and eighteenth-century writers such as Edmund Burke and the proto-feminist Mary Wollstonecraft in particular. She brings an historical perspective to bear, therefore, upon the progress of women; and in her own field of academia she points out that most Cambridge colleges are nearly 40 per cent female. 'There are many more women teaching at university level now and many seminars on gender and women's issues; and that was not the case ten years ago.'

Yet Sylvana is no ivory-tower academic. She enjoys the Lunch's broad mix: for her it is an opportunity to meet 'women I would otherwise never come across. I remember meeting the first woman master-thatcher and the first policewoman to ride in a motorcade escort, lawyers, writers, engineers, trade-union women. One meets women from a large variety of professions because of the unique feature of the Lunch in covering a really wide area of achievement.

'There's a very good atmosphere: everyone is pleased to have been asked and to meet so many other women across the spectrum. It brings together very different women, including those who are not particularly concerned with women's issues; it cannot help but have an influence, given the fact that it attracts women of influence.'

In March 1973, Susan Shaw had become the first woman member on the floor of the London Stock Exchange, reversing the single-sex policy of 200 years. 'The men started clapping, and someone kissed me on the cheek,' she remembers. 'There was no hostility – although there had been hostility at first when I and several other women applied for membership. But the London Stock Exchange had merged with the provincial Stock Exchange and they already had a woman in Manchester, so there was no way they could stop me. A few years later, when I was pregnant with my second child, I remember one of the jobbers looking at my stomach and saying to me, "How come the two of you came in on the same badge?" Once women members were in place, I never felt conscious of machismo in the City; instead I found nothing but the hugest courtesy. And my clients were very pleased when I was nominated for the Women of the Year Lunch: to them, it was the cherry on the cake.'

In 1985, Shaw was invited onto the Women of the Year committee as a representative of the City and finance, serving as chairman for a year from 1986. 'I have made the most wonderful lifelong friends through the Lunch,' says Shaw, one of whose most abiding memories was the 'wonderful' speech that the opera singer Jessye Norman made as Coretta King's representative one year.

The campaigning barrister Helena Kennedy QC found herself being nominated for the Women of the Year Lunch as a result, she believes, of 'being at the forefront of campaigns to change the law on recognising rape in marriage as a crime. I became seen as an advocate of the reform of the legal profession, particularly as it affected women. In law schools, 50 per cent of the students are now women. Women are changing the profession; we have also seen an increase in the number of women judges. There have been very significant changes in my professional life.'

Baroness Kennedy first attended in 1987 when the actress Emma Thompson and Dr Pauline Cutting were on the panel of speakers; two years later she herself addressed the Lunch. 'I remember that wonderful human-rights combination of Emma, who's very much involved with human rights, and Pauline, who was working in Palestine with refugees. One of the great things about the Lunch is the diversity. I remember sitting next to a woman cheese-maker, a woman coal-merchant and a very eminent eye-surgeon. It's not just people we know in the public eye: the Lunch also includes women whose success stories are not spoken of enough. Tony Lothian makes no distinctions as to people's backgrounds. She's a galvaniser, a pretty special dame.'

For Women of the Year treasurer Trish Morris-Thompson, the highlight of the Lunch was 'meeting Queen Noor, sitting next to the great nun-reformer Sister Lavinia Byrne – who is identifying reforms to the function of nuns in the church – and Maureen Lipman, a heroine of mine. You sit next to famous people and you realise they are human; the Lunch is a great common denominator. To me, the Women of the Year Lunch and Assembly has three valuable functions: to bring together a world tribe of women who have all made a contribution to improving life, to give an opportunity to my colleagues in nursing to rub shoulders with scientists and authors in recognition of their equal status and to raise funds for a legitimate cause.'

Morris-Thompson was originally asked to join the committee as a representative of the nursing profession, one of the biggest employers of women and also at the forefront of campaigns on work-life issues. 'We raised it first,' she points out. 'Now it has been identified throughout the health industry.' As ever, Women of the Year have found themselves at the heart of research into improving women's lives.

Sally Becker, dubbed the Angel of Mostar in newspaperspeak, was invited to the Lunch in 1993 on the strength of her charity work in Bosnia when she drove an ambulance into the besieged city of Mostar to rescue injured women and children. That same year Susan McHugh, the Dublin woman who founded the Peace '93 movement because of her outrage at the IRA bomb which killed two children in Warrington, was one of the speakers, and she asked for a one-minute silence to remember the victims.

Recognising as it does the achievements of women for nearly half a century, not only is the Women of the Year Lunch a broad church, but also a broad-minded one. Dropped by one charity when it was revealed that she was acting as a parent to three children after her female partner had been artificially inseminated, the comedienne Sandi Toksvig was welcomed by the Women of the Year Lunch as a guest of honour in 1994. The previous year Julie Hasler, who arrived with a tattooed upper torso and a nose-to-ear chain, had been invited on the strength of her twenty-two books on the art of needlepoint.

Retired trade-union official Barbara Switzer recalls how she and former Tory minister Edwina Currie, now a novelist and broadcaster, found themselves at the same table. 'I know of no other event that involves such a wide cross-section of people. When Edwina realised who I was, she verbally attacked me over a statement made by a male colleague at a recent trade-union conference. We were unlikely table companions in the normal run of things,' says Switzer, 'but after I had dealt with the attack we settled down and enjoyed ourselves. Such is the nature of the Women of the Year Lunch...'

Tony Lothian's late friend Mikki Doyle, the link with unions for the Women of the Year Lunch, had invited key women officials to join the committee in order to ensure that females in very traditional male-dominated industries were adequately represented.

'I had first got involved in union matters during the seventies when I found myself speaking on platforms. I was invited to the Women of the Year Lunch in 1983 after becoming the first woman general president elected to a major manufacturing union: SOGAT, the Society of Graphical and Allied Trades. It was such a shock to some officials when I got elected; shivers went through them when they realised they were going to have to start accounting to a woman,' remembers Baroness Dean. 'Subsequently I was the first woman to be elected as general secretary of SOGAT. Two-thirds of the membership were men. But I'm in no doubt that I wouldn't have stood a dog's chance if it had been an appointment instead of an election. There were moves afterwards to make election candidates put only their initials down; if I had put down B. Dean, people wouldn't have connected it with Brenda Dean. That was the kind of pettiness I encountered.

'I always refused to pick women's issues in an overtly

feminist campaign; I got the men to vote for me because I didn't want to be marginalised. But despite the 1976 Equal Pay Act, women's earnings were still way behind those of the men. I negotiated time off for women workers to have cervical smear tests; I also opposed the idea that women were working only for pin-money, which had meant that they were the first to be made redundant.

'As President, I still encountered attitude problems,' adds Baroness Dean. 'One of the Fleet Street managers had placed a bet that I wouldn't get the job; and my two deputies had been invited to a Christmas party held by the national newspapers in Manchester, whereas I wasn't. I remembered how the whole room stopped talking when I appeared; I thought that was a typical attitude. They were embarrassed, they didn't know what to do. It was little things like that. But I started to change the culture of the boys' club – because drinking with them and going to the races wasn't my scene.'

Being a pioneer can be lonely. For Baroness Dean, the Women of the Year Lunch and Assembly is a chance to 'recharge the batteries of inspiration. It made me realise that someone as impressive as Valentina Tereshkova is a woman like the rest of us. That brought home to me the inspirational nature of the Lunch; you sometimes think you are out there on your own, but when you get to the Lunch, you realise you aren't.'

Association with the Lunch gave Dr Vivette Glover, a leading researcher at Queen Charlotte's and Chelsea Hospital's Royal Post-Graduate Medical School, a chance to 'move a little out of the closed scientific community. The Lunch allows one to meet interesting women from very diverse spheres.'

Tony Lothian, in particular, cited by Glover as a major influence: 'Tony looks for the good and the interesting in people, quite irrespective of background.' And former chairman Val Arnison, a leading public-relations consultant who was first asked to join the committee in 1975, has long admired the presiding spirits of the Lunch, Tony Lothian and Georgina Coleridge. 'Tony has been totally committed to encouraging women over the years and recognising where women have taken themselves. She's incredibly enthusiastic and won't give up; she's a very warm person. Georgina, of course, was one of the first women to reach the heights in the magazine world; she's a lovely person, great fun with an enormous sense of humour. Although they are different, they are both great enthusers and would go all out to get where they wanted to get.'

For Arnison, as for every attendee its sheer diversity is what makes the Lunch so special. 'There were so many women one was privileged to meet, such as the *Wild Swans* author Jung Chang and the surgeon Pauline Cutting.' Her successor as chairman was the dress designer Paddy Campbell, a former actress who launched her first collection back in the seventies and is now well established as a leading fashion designer. One of her regular clients is Cherie Blair.

Paddy Campbell's talents were tested during her chairmanship when Jeanne Moreau, confirmed as the international guest of honour in 1993, cancelled her appearance at the eleventh hour. 'My horror story is that two days before the Lunch, Jeanne Moreau's assistant said she couldn't come after all because of a strike at Charles de Gaulle Airport. I had a nervous breakdown for five minutes and then I asked my friend, the national-newspaper editor Eve Pollard, to speak instead. She gave a wonderfully witty speech.

'Princess Margaret was my royal guest of honour that year and I was quite nervous of that, but she couldn't have been nicer. The following year, in 1994, I was lucky enough to get Helen Suzman as international guest of honour; the wine was supplied by a South African wine producer, and I discovered that her daughter was one of my best customers. In 1995 we got Simone Veil to be our international guest of honour. She was the most famous woman in France and that year had been chosen to meet the Queen for the 50th anniversary celebrations of the end of World War Two on the beaches where the Normandy landings were made.

'At the age of sixteen Simone Veil had been picked off the streets of Paris and sent to Auschwitz with her sister. She was seated next to me at the Lunch, and when she realised that I speak reasonable French, she talked to me about her family and her sons. Hearing Simone Veil's story was my most treasured moment from the Lunches. I'll never forget her scraping her plate clean; it brought home to me what she had been through,' adds Paddy. 'Sadly, her sister had survived all the Auschwitz horror, only to be killed in a road accident when she was still young.

'There were a lot of wonderful moments at Lunches over the years: I remember Valentina Tereshkova bringing me apples from her garden. And for the 40th anniversary I got the Savoy to give us the wine free as a tribute to Tony.'

Just about every innovative woman of our times has represented one of the 40 categories of work at the Lunch, among them Deborah Oliver and Jennie Page of the Millennium Dome, Dorothy Kuya, Janet Boateng and Gayle Morrison, chairman elect of the Lunch and the executive producer behind many Granada TV programmes. The increasingly high profile of women in sport has also been reflected in the choice of guests, with the late Marea Hartman – backbone of the British women's Olympic team – heading the list of sports stars closely associated with the Women of the Year. Tessa Sanderson, the only woman to have competed in five consecutive Olympic Games, brought her gold medal along to the Lunch on her first visit, while other guests of honour have included Sally Gunnell, Denise Lewis and Dame Mary Peters, Ulster's finest athlete. The Scottish-born Liz McColgan offered her world record-breaking shirt up as a raffle prize at the Lunch, while the broadcaster and former Wimbledon champion Virginia Wade, one of the organisation's first vice-presidents, has never missed a Women of the Year occasion and works tirelessly for the cause of women in tennis. 'After the Lunch,' she once said, 'you leave the Savoy feeling as if anything is achievable.' It's a reaction shared by all the guests at such a unique occasion.

Never let it be said that this event is afraid of diversity or challenges. For neither death nor imprisonment, as it turned out, were to prevent a woman from taking her rightful place at the Women of the Year Lunch.

Chapter Five
Themes of the Lunches

From the beginning, the Women of the Year Lunch was all about serious fun. The sheer novelty of such an event in the second half of the fifties meant that themes aimed to be innovative and were sometimes deliberately whimsical in order to encourage original reactions from the celebrity speech-makers. More recently, the Lunch has become an important forum for world issues on which world-famous women have spoken. Yet the occasion has never lost that sense of serious fun.

Its instant fame rather took the Women of the Year Lunch by surprise back in the early days; and it was not until the director of the newly established Women's Library contacted the committee for extensive information that the organisers realised the immense value of the Lunch as a record of social history. That is why the earliest speeches survive only in newspaper reports in the London *Evening Standard* on the day and in *The Times* the following day. 'We've got the most abysmal archives of any organisation I know; for a few years we never kept anything,' says Tony, cursing cheerfully. Anne Dickinson, chairman for three years, recalls how every speaker was nervous. 'No matter how seasoned they were at the art of public speaking, each one felt that the Women of the Year Lunch was the ultimate platform – since they would be judged by their female peers. 'That sea of female faces is quite tough and daunting. Although the atmosphere is always very positive, you always feel that your own sex is looking at you quite critically.'

Baroness Sharp of Hornsey, head of the Civil Service, joined the actress Hermione Gingold and Viljaya Lakshmi Pandit, the Indian stateswoman who became the first woman president of the United Nations Assembly from 1953 to 1954, on the very first panel of speakers in 1955. Lord Normanbrook, Secretary to the Cabinet, had suggested that Madam Pandit, who was Nehru's sister, should be the international guest of honour. 'I don't think Tony ever noticed people's colour,' says Shirley Conran. 'This was very unusual back in 1955, because a lot of people in those days *did* notice the colour of someone's skin.' 'Even in a world leader,' Tony adds. So from the very beginning, the Women of the Year Lunch had set out its stall on the world stage and emphasised discernment by inviting an illustrious Asian stateswoman to be one of the three speakers.

This discernment has continued in the selection of Lunch guests and in the organisation's international awareness ever since. Sharista Ikramullah, leader of the Pakistani delegation to the United Nations, spoke alongside Dame Edith Evans and the author Rosamund Lehmann the following year. 'Sharista had a little bare midriff showing through her sari,' recalls Tony, 'and it was sticking out a bit. I remember her saying, "I'm getting fat. I *must* get thin there." Ikramullah's great passion was the position of women: her speech said the West undervalued the importance that countries like Pakistan gave to women.'

The following year the theme was 'The Verities', with Odette Hallowes speaking about courage alongside a woman police chief. 'I've always been obsessed with the verities – death, injustice,' admits Tony. 'The great

Russian writers remind us of them; they are the great issues, even if they don't make you happy. I think I'm rather a sad person anyway: I live with a lot of melancholy. Like Pagliacci – the clown that must not cry. On with the motley, on with the Lunch and on with the job. And I think some of the guests feel like me.'

In 1958 the Ministry of Health's chief medical officer had warned of an increasingly dangerous addiction to sedatives, stimulants and tranquillisers, heavily marketed to housewives. The Lunch theme that year was 'What Makes A Woman Happy?' to which the actress and comedienne Joyce Grenfell drily replied in her speech: 'Taking my roll-on off.' Violet Attlee, by then Countess Attlee, joined her on the panel of speakers to tell an audience of five hundred women that putting Lord Attlee's slippers by the fire gave her more happiness than anything else. Relief found in sedatives was not mentioned.

In 1959 Countess Mountbatten, wife of the last Viceroy of India, proved a particularly impressive speaker as she talked about her work as a crusader for people in need all over the world. That idiosyncratic actress Margaret Rutherford provided the humour, speaking alongside headmistress Diana Reader Harris and the leading fashion model of her day, Bronwen Pugh.

The following year's theme, 'If Not You, Who?', invited speakers to say who they would most like to be. The last in order of speaking was a newly-elected Tory MP named Margaret Thatcher. She told Tony Lothian: 'I don't mind when I speak.' And her message that day was quintessential Thatcher.

Tony remembers: 'Ailsa Garland, the women's editor of the *Mirror* and then editor of *Vogue*, said she wanted to be Eve in the Garden of Eden, and Elizabeth Longford – Lady Pakenham – wanted to be Queen Victoria, but I was struck by the fact that when it came to Mrs Thatcher's turn, she said she wanted to be the governess

Anna Leonowens from the musical *The King and I* – which had premièred in the West End that year – in order to teach the Siamese children British values.

'I saw no signs of future genius in her that day, I must say. But although it seems politically incorrect to say so now, I believe she did go on to turn the tide of history by saying that the Russian President Gorbachev was a man she could do business with.'

The brilliant pageant of stars continued in 1961 with Dame Ninette de Valois, the governor of the Royal Ballet and the founder of the Royal Ballet School, Angele Delanghe, the only woman member of the Incorporated Society of London Fashion Designers, Mary Grieve, editor of *Woman* magazine, Patricia Hornsby-Smith MP, Janey Ironside, Professor of Fashion at the Royal College of Art, and the actresses Anna Neagle and Molly Weir. They spoke on the theme of 'Success'. This, after all, was the exhilarating year in which two British women had reached the Wimbledon tennis final: Christine Truman and Angela Mortimer, who took the title.

Unfortunately only the final speech survives in the archives, but it is a disarming one that demonstrates above all the pomposity-free spirit of the Lunch. The popular Scottish actress Molly Weir gave a lively address on the subject of success and was not intimidated by the Great and the Good gathered before her. Far from trying to stun them into submission with showbusiness anecdotes, her homely stories carried the universal message that women do not have to be Zelda Fitzgerald's 'beautiful idiots'.

In 1961, the privations of the home front in the Second World War were still relatively fresh in the collective consciousness. Weir, one of Scotland's best-loved comediennes, pressed the right buttons by remarking, 'As I knew full well I couldn't possibly compete on the same level as the previous speakers, much less with an audience like yourselves, I've decided to concentrate on the small domestic successes which have amazed me and saved me many a hard-won penny.' And what could be guaranteed to appeal more to an audience of women than the story of how Weir managed to usurp the male prerogative of knowing one end of a screwdriver from the other and mending her own wireless in a national emergency? Not to mention her memory of six children sleeping in their grandmother's bed; a sure sign of her times.

On 12 April 1961, the Soviet test pilot and cosmonaut Yuri Gagarin became the first man in space. Not one to miss an opportunity, the following year the Women of the Year Lunch addressed the theme 'What Is Woman's Place in Space?' 'We have always been very responsive to the news,' explains Tony Lothian. 'From the outset, the Lunch was all about how women were aware of what was happening and what they were doing about it.'

Among the speakers in 1962, the year of Marilyn Monroe's death from an overdose, were the legendary *Daily Mirror* journalist Marje Proops, the Reverend Mother Clare, an Anglican Deaconess, consultant obstetrician and gynaecologist Josephine Barnes, glider pilot Ann Welch, comedienne Tessie O'Shea and a Mrs H G Hazelden – billed as the *wife* of a test pilot in the year of Concorde's maiden flight. Today no mere consort would be invited to the Lunch, of course, unless she had done something important in her own right.

Other achievers present were flying instructor Elizabeth Overbury, the scientist Lady Fleming, Winifred T Barker, Chief Superintendent of the Metropolitan Women Police, the poet Kathleen Raine, the Maharani of Jaipur, the actresses Dame Edith Evans and Irene Handl, and the prima ballerina Beryl Grey.

In 1963 Prime Minister Harold Wilson's wife Mary, a vice-president of the Lunch and a poet, was among the guests of honour; she was, says Tony Lothian, loved and respected by all who worked with her. One of the speakers was the dress designer Mary Quant, ultimate symbol of the Swinging Sixties. After addressing the theme 'Is Happiness a Lost Art?', she was later to write in her autobiography that the Women of the Year Lunch had been a most frightening day in her life.

No transcripts survive, alas, although Quant is remembered for a great speech that included some mild jokes before sitting down again. Perhaps she was in awe of Colonel E I W Hobkirk, prison and Borstal governor, Colonel Mary Booth of the Salvation Army or Dame Marie Rambert, founder and 'directress' of the Ballet Rambert. Quant was well known for being modest about herself but she was confident enough in her own field to launch a stinging attack on Paris fashion the following year, describing it as out of date. Her designs, she said, were aimed at girls who were 'tired of wearing essentially the same as their mothers'.

Attending as a guest of honour in 1964, the actress Tsai Chin said that the 'no men' rule of the Lunch 'shouldn't be encouraged'. One wonders what she found to talk about with prison governor Miss M E G Stocker, Brigadier J E Henderson or Air Commandant Dame Jean Conan Doyle. Or, indeed, what they thought of the theme, 'My Favourite Man', wittily and candidly explored by author Edna O'Brien, jazz singer Annie Ross, marriage-bureau director Heather Jenner and Felicity Green, assistant editor of the *Daily Mirror*.

Felicity attended the year afterwards, as did another influential journalist, the *Observer*'s Katharine Whitehorn, pioneer of the irreverent confessional column and a witty commentator on dodging domestic drudgery. The theme in 1965 was 'The Chance of a Lifetime': an appropriate subject for the Labour MP Jennie Lee, who went on to become Education Minister and founder of the Open University.

The onward march of media women continued in 1966. One of the Lunch speakers was the editor of *Honey* magazine, Audrey Slaughter, talking on the subject of 'The Bee in My Bonnet'. That was the year in which Britain's capital was christened Swinging London and British youth officially recognised as world style leaders.

The theme of 1967 was a provocative one: 'Have We Gone Too Far?' Among the guests of honour were television presenter Joan Bakewell and the broadcaster Jean Metcalfe.

The speakers interpreted the theme widely. The Russian ballerina Svetlana Beriosova regretted hideous sixties architecture that had gone too far in dehumanising housing. She had been to Glasgow and seen no extra room for the baboushka in the tenement flats.

With the sixties in full swing, speeches at the Lunch reflected the mood, particularly with such speakers as Ann Mallalieu, first woman president of the Cambridge Union, and Shirley Williams, then Minister of State for Education and Science.

Female singers were making their mark on the sixties pop scene and the Lunch was not slow to recognise this, with Lulu a guest of honour in 1967 and Julie Driscoll a speaker twelve months later. The subject then was 'Whatever Next?', a theme inadvertently put forward by Edna Healey, who was thinking of something else when, as a vice-president of the Lunch, she was asked to suggest a subject. That same year, 1968, Mrs Mary Whitehouse was a guest of honour – though not a speaker. She had founded her National Viewers and Listeners' Association three years before in order to 'clean up' television.

The following year was the first Lunch attended by the former actress Renée Goddard, head of the script department at ATV. The theme was 'Shadow Cabinet', an idea that Renée and Tony later turned into a television series: how would an all-women Cabinet run the country?

'We chose that theme because I was getting very edgy about women not being put into top government jobs,' recalls Tony. 'I thought hospital matrons would be able positively to reform the National Health Service because they knew what was needed.' It was a timely year in which to envisage British women in top political jobs, since seventy-year-old grandmother Golda Meir had been elected Prime Minister of Israel that March.

Sheila Scott, the round-the-world solo aviator, played the role of Minister of Transport for a day, columnist Harriet Crawley was Minister for Youth, financial columnist Marie Jennings was Chancellor of (the Exchequer) Waste, *Nursing Times* editor Peggy Nuttall was Minister of Health and Social Security, Joanna Spicer 'swapped' her job as the BBC's Assistant Controller of Television Developments to 'become' Minister of Communications and the actress Irene Worth 'became' Home Secretary. The actress Sheila Hancock, the final speaker, was the Minister for Women. No doubt Sheila Thomas, invited along as a guest of honour by virtue of being the mother of sextuplets, listened keenly to how women would run the country and make life easier for those working at home.

With Myrella Cohen QC, later to be a judge and a patron of the Suzy Lamplugh Trust, among the speakers in 1970, the theme that year reflected the tough world outside: 'Aspects of Violence'. That was the year in which, besides the escalating violence in Ulster over the controversial 'shoot to kill' policy alleged against the Royal Ulster Constabulary, the American President Richard Nixon sent US troops to attack communist bases in Cambodia. Four students protesting against the American war in Vietnam were shot dead by National Guard soldiers at Kent State University in Ohio, leading to the cruel jibe by pro-war factions: 'The Kent State Four / Should Have Studied More.'

The Lunch was also highlighting the community

contribution made by women's organisations, with Delia Dalton, president of the National Federation of Business and Professional Women's Clubs, a guest of honour. Caroline Coon, co-founder of the civil-liberties organisation Release that had been set up to help those arrested on drugs charges, was one of the speakers. The theme in 1971 was 'Quality in Life', and the journalist Jilly Cooper, later to become more famous as a best-selling author, was among the guests of honour.

In fact, although the committee has always been careful to make sure that all professions are represented, the media count was becoming heavier. Betty Kenward, editor of the famous Jennifer's Diary in *Harpers & Queen*, Margaret Alexander, social editor of *The Times*, Joan Bakewell, Winefred Jackson, Woman's Page editor of the *Sunday Telegraph*, TV reporter Angela Huth, the BBC's Woman's Hour editor Wyn Knowles, *Woman's Own* editor Jane Reed and *Nursing Mirror* editor Yvonne Cross were all guests of honour that year.

The theme of 'Freedom' in 1972 led to Glenda Jackson and the late *Guardian* columnist Jill Tweedie tackling a subject that could have been made for such well-known (if, in Jill's case, self-styled faint-hearted) feminists.

The following year saw the first royal speaker, the Duchess of Kent, giving a speech on the subject of achievement. It has aways been emphasised that royal guests must justify their presence with a noteworthy achievement in the year they attend, and of all the royals, the Duchess is the one who has been most often associated with the Lunch over the years. Her daughter Lady Helen Taylor became the royal guest of honour in 1999. The achievements of Women's Liberation, a term that seems dated at the beginning of the twenty-first century, were highlighted with Mary Hobbs, spokesman (so the programme termed her) for the Nightcleaners' Association and Women's Liberation Movement, among the guests of honour. In the kind of juxtapositions which characterise the Lunch, she and Betty Kenward of Jennifer's Diary sat together while Betty Parsons, teacher of relaxation, was seated alongside Marie Patterson, National Woman Officer of the Transport and General Workers Union.

With so many different perspectives present at every Lunch, it remained important to unite people – and not divide them. Although the message of Women's Liberation had been well and truly absorbed by a committee that was always forward-thinking, it was never intended to alienate the middle of the road. The theme chosen for 1974, 'The Importance of Being a Woman', covered the waterfront.

Thus Dr Una Kroll, parliamentary candidate advocating the rights of women priests, sat in the company of the cookery writer Marguerite Patten, the actresses Diana Rigg and Gayle Hunnicutt, the fashion designer Laura Ashley, yachtswoman Eve Bonham, film producer Betty Box, Methodist minister Kathleen Burgess and stunt artist Roberta Gibbs.

The image of women as sex objects was at the heart of feminist concern, reflected in the 1975 theme 'Image or Reality?' The author and broadcaster Germaine Greer, speaking for the first time at the Lunch, analysed it, according to Tony, with her customary wisdom. Betty Lockwood, chairman designate of the Equal Opportunities Commission, was also on the panel of speakers. Writer Anna Raeburn and Erin Pizzey were among the guests of honour so feminism was well represented.

The choice of guests of honour that year also underlined how the Lunch always responds to the developing news agenda over the previous twelve months. Two airline stewardesses who had been held hostage at Heathrow and policewoman Margaret Liles, heroine of the Tube train crash at Moorgate, were among them.

Also present was the sculptor Elisabeth Frink, whose gift of a trophy in her name eventually inspired a special award for disabled women achievers.

The theme in 1976 was 'Yesterday, Today and Tomorrow'. Anna Raeburn gave what Tony Lothian calls 'an extraordinarily human and inspiring speech'. But it was also a year in which to highlight the women's peace movement in Ulster, representatives of which attended the Lunch. Royal guest and fellow speaker was the Duchess of Gloucester, presiding over a top table which included the farmer Hannah Hauxwell whose tough working life had been immortalised in a television documentary. Also present were the yachtswoman Clare Francis, later a best-selling novelist, and Heather Brigstocke, headmistress of St Paul's School for Girls.

The following year Erin Pizzey addressed the theme of 'Loyalty' alongside the actress Penelope Keith. The founder of Chiswick Women's Aid, Erin had become embroiled in controversy. As she spoke, protesters staged a noisy demonstration outside the Savoy in response to her controversial suggestion that some women might be drawn towards violent men. For her part, Erin protested at what she saw as the politicisation of the women's refuge movement, which, she felt, was becoming a platform for various groups with axes to grind. The then chairman Anne Dickinson remembers Pizzey's speech as 'very moving and powerful – she spoke in a very gentle way'. Among the guests of honour were Betty Williams, representing the Northern Ireland Peace People, broadcasters Esther Rantzen and Angela Rippon, and the acclaimed cellist and rising star Jacqueline Du Pré.

'The Art of Survival' was the theme in 1978, with round-the-world yachtswoman Naomi James speaking on a panel which included the *Woman's Own* editor Jane Reed.

Of all the amusing guests over the years, the *Hello Dolly!* musical star Carol Channing was probably the most flamboyant. She illustrated the 1979 theme of 'Gifts' by bringing along a paste diamond – 'I thought it was real,' said Tony enviously – to show exactly what she considered to be a girl's best friend. That year was particularly strong on showbusiness with the author Jackie Collins, the entertainer Marti Caine, actresses Francesca Annis and Jane Lapotaire and the singer and actress Elaine Paige among the guests of honour. The inclusion of Maureen Flowers, the professional darts-player, helped to redress the balance.

By 1980, the Lunch had become so well established in the national calendar that it was decided to start keeping records of speeches on a regular basis. That year the theme was '25 Years Back – 25 Years On'. Only Professor Margaret Gowing's speech on 'Science, Space and Survival' has safely survived, but it remains one of the most influential and far-sighted ever made.

Addressing a gathering that included the actress and comedy writer Victoria Wood, the singer Kate Bush, the dog trainer Barbara Woodhouse and Rabbi Julia Neuberger among its guests of honour, Gowing – first woman professor of science at a UK university – proposed restraint rather than unthinking advancement in science. She issued a prophetic warning.

'Science in the last twenty-five years – I suppose most non-scientists ask: what difference has it made in our everyday lives? Surprisingly, not all that much. We have had a wide diffusion of inventions made earlier and small cumulative advances but few completely new revolutionary science-based inventions. The Pill, yes, and the laser. But what else? 1980 is very like 1955 although – to go back in twenty-five-year leaps – 1955 was vastly different from 1930 and 1930 even more different from 1905. However, microchips, biotechnology, etc. now herald a new era of dramatic change.

'But let us lift our eyes from everyday life to the heavens

– as men and women have done ever since they walked on two legs instead of four. The stars and heavens have been their source of wonder, their fount of religious, philosophic, scientific and mathematical speculation and also their means of navigation by land and sea. In the last twenty-five years, the heavens have been the most exciting realm of science. Scientific theory and experiment, aided by extraordinary science-based technology, have found a distant universe inconceivably vaster than we supposed and have told us how and when it probably began and what it is made of.

'Nearer home in the solar system, man has acquired a new dimension – space, has travelled in it and made direct contact not only with the moon but with some of the planets – something unimaginable twenty-five years ago except in science fiction. This, too, heralds revolutionary change and, as astronomers observe light that began its journey towards us millions of years ago, the very concepts of time – carving it up into the past, the present and the future – seem meaningless.

'And so back to earth. Television pictures of astronauts circling the globe succeeded – where generations of cosmologists had failed – in convincing the layman that the earth is but a small planet, finite and vulnerable. But space exploration has also shown the earth to be infinitely precious and unique in the solar system, teeming with life among the wastelands of its neighbours. The supreme challenge for the next twenty-five years and beyond is to keep the earth uniquely living, to preserve it from a holocaust which would leave much? most? all? of it – who knows? – as desolate as it was thousands or millions of years ago. The threat is the arms race and it is science-based.

'Nuclear physics – one of the finest fruits of the human intellect – had led to the atomic bombs which ended the Second World War. For a brief decade, these primitive bombs, carried in aeroplanes, did preserve a balance of terror. But then came terrifying escalation: hydrogen bombs with no theoretical limits to their size: missiles, chemical and biological weapons. The sublime atomic irony of which Churchill spoke, with survival as the twin brother of annihilation, was true no longer. Ever since, any brief balance or equilibrium of arms has been swiftly upset by the inventiveness of scientists and technologists, futile though it is when existing weapons could destroy every man, woman and child on earth several times over.

'Yet defence claims a large proportion of research and development in many countries, and in this inventive fever the multilateral arms control, let alone disarmament, that we need so desperately can scarcely begin. The scientists have a leading role in arms control alongside the politicians, the military and, increasingly we hope, public opinion. They have been pioneers...But can they go further?

'Scientists in every country have their powerful established institutions, close to governments and in communication with each other. Proud of their internationalism, can they take a major rather than a minor lead in urging mutual restraint on ever more scientific development of weaponry? This restraint of science is more important than any conceivable advance of science in the next twenty-five years. Science could take the lead in mankind's race to survive.'

In 1981, the theme 'Who Cares?' looked at that most unsung area of women's work: caring for the disabled. As the Lunch's first international guest of honour, Zimbabwean President Robert Mugabe's first wife Sally gave a very constructive speech on work for the disabled. 'It is our grand ambition to give every disabled person the independence that is his right,' she declared, outlining how the African – formerly Dutch – Reformed Church had begun the process of help outside the immediate family for the blind, deaf and dumb at the beginning of the twentieth century. The war of liberation, she said, had, 'like all wars', brought an even greater need for help, with 10,500 people disabled in various ways; a grim reminder of the price to pay.

Then the writer Christopher Nolan's mother Bernadette spoke for disablement research. 'Being the mother of a speechless, severely physically disabled son, I recognise the hurdles ahead. We have as yet taken but the first step towards making people aware that normal intelligence can lie behind the hopeless image of the physically disabled who lack speech as a mode of expression. I would dearly hope that through his own writings, my son Christopher may, as it were, open a door through which the able-bodied may glimpse a world which was heretofore a total mystery to them.'

Eight years later Jim Sheridan's Academy Award-winning film *My Left Foot* earned Daniel Day-Lewis an Oscar for his portrayal of Christy, who was born with cerebral palsy and typed with his toes. Bernadette concluded, 'I will read a poem written by Christopher, a poem in which he appeals to the caring heart of women to join with him in defence of the defenceless.'

The international guest of honour the following year was Jehan El-Sadat, the widow of Egypt's assassinated President Sadat. She also stirred hearts as she spoke brilliantly on the subject of 'Life Begins at...' 'Perhaps your task, as women of goodwill and compassion in Britain, is more difficult than our own. We still have some of the old rural traditions of family solidarity, which make people take pride in caring for the handicapped and underprivileged. But in advanced industrial societies, people tend to rely on social security and national health schemes to relieve them of responsibility for their fellow mortals. Indifference is bound to set in, and your task is to fan the flames of the old virtues of helpfulness, love and caring, in an increasingly bureaucratic society.' This was indeed a challenge.

Mrs El-Sadat also spoke from the heart when she said that 'the vocation of peace is particularly suited to our role as women. But I am also certain that it is an ideal shared by millions of people of both sexes everywhere. When my husband was cruelly killed, I received countless messages from all over the world stressing his heroic contribution to the cause of peace.'

Mikki Doyle's speech was similarly inspiring. 'If they thought I could talk on how life begins (or ends) when you have cancer, I must admit it's an honour I could have done without!' she began. Describing how she had been a fighter all her life, this one-time 'angry young woman' had fought against world starvation, senseless wars and discrimination against race, sex and creed. 'Today, I'm an angry old woman, still fighting and enjoying the fight. And while my sight is somewhat impaired as a result of Peekskill, my vision of a better world has not changed.' She had graphically described how a rock had hurtled through the windscreen of a coach in which she and many children were travelling en route to the concert 'to defend the right of the great Paul Robeson to sing'.

Then came comedienne Pamela Stephenson's controversial contribution. Addressing an audience that included the widow of the Falklands hero Colonel 'H' Jones VC and the eleven-year-old mathematics genius Ruth Lawrence, and wearing a hat with an enormous pair of donkey ears, Stephenson argued for a woman comedian's right to raise laughs by behaving as badly as a man. And she had the jokes to prove her point. One gag in particular – about a fashion-conscious woman who refused to have a colostomy operation because she couldn't find shoes to match her bag – had the tabloids in an uproar, although an admiring Tony Lothian was quoted in the *Daily Star* afterwards as saying, 'We ask women to say what they think. I thought it was real wit. If anybody was upset, they needn't come next year.'

It was the only honest response to make. Particularly as Tony had asked Pamela to speak on anything except politics or religion. As Pamela put it, sex was the only thing left... Anne Dickinson, chairman that year, vividly recalls the impact of her speech. 'It went down like a lead balloon with some of our guests, but I got the impression that Pamela was being deliberately provocative. She knew what she was doing and she knew it would make the headlines. I did quite enjoy it myself,' adds Anne, 'although there were some nose-wrinkling moments. But the problem was that I was sitting next to a nun and I didn't dare look at her throughout Pamela's speech.'

The committee hoped they had played it slightly safer the following year with the theme 'A Woman's Best Friend'. Shirley Conran summed up the spirit of the Lunch by identifying female friendship. The Lunch had always led the way for female solidarity, but Conran articulated the case for it. 'The most valuable thing in my life is... my address book... It is the basis of my system for living and working and having fun. And the most important things in it are the telephone numbers of my close friends... When I need emotional support of any kind, I head straight for my wonderful female friends.

'I feel that today we are in a pioneer period just as much as those women who crossed America in covered wagons... We are pioneers of the emotions – both in the personal world and in the business world... In a world where, during the last twenty years, so many forms of relationship have been inspected and found phoney – and where the divorce rate is now one divorce in three marriages... there seems to be one growth area of stable relationships... that of women to women...

'This camaraderie has always existed among men but is only just starting to develop among women, partly because in a society where a woman's identity no longer rests on her exterior appearance and her husband, there is less and less cause for petty jealousy.' Conran was right, for although Women's Liberation had officially begun in the late sixties and early seventies, it was not until the eighties that career women began to make significant progress in the professions and in the business world.

'To illustrate what I mean,' continued Conran, 'in my mother's day if you had a wonderful recipe you kept it to yourself and if you passed it on to your best friend you carefully left out the most important ingredient...There is much talk at the moment of networking among women in the business world. But let's remember that all the women here today are here because they are a success in their own right and they are therefore in the position to be a mentor to younger women in their field of business. Would it be too much to hope that any woman here today who is not already helping a younger woman up the ladder would walk out of this luncheon and find one to guide? Networks should be forming downwards as well as upward...It seems very obvious to me that, in a world where other relationships are not necessarily stable or permanent...a woman's best friends are...her best women friends.'

An alternative option was provided by Nobel Prize winner Professor Dorothy Hodgkin, a woman of international stature who was confident enough in her achievements as a scientist to assert that an understanding husband could be a woman's best friend.

'When I first told my colleagues in Oxford that I was going to marry Thomas Hodgkin, one of them said, "Well, you are marrying one of the most interesting men I know, but you won't have a quiet life." I think in many ways this was true; we had a very eventful life, but his mother also remarked in her old age, "It seems to me you have a very quiet relationship, both of you dependent on the other and yet sure of one another"...

'He had a tremendous natural sympathy with people who would tell him almost straight away their troubles, their problems; and everyone he would invite home so that our house was always full. He loved company, he loved conversation, food and drink, and other people loved him accordingly...He wrote a long poem about his life...the early parts...have a good deal about marriage in them. "So you see how I think of friendship" [he wrote]. "Someone who will last one's life, / With whom to share all one's thoughts and problems, / All one's joys and sorrows, / Someone whom to see, to be with and to remember, / Is a very great delight."'

The racehorse trainer Jenny Pitman and the actress Jane Lapotaire completed the circle by nominating members of their family as best friends. For divorced single parent Lapotaire, her ten-year-old son had become her 'really best friend'. Like Shirley Conran, she had experienced 'a change in women's attitudes to each other, and this is reflected in this Lunch-gathering today.' She added: 'There was a time when the good jobs would be likely to go to the blonde girls with good figures and the rest of us saw them as a threat to us and to our opportunity to work. Thanks to the women's movement, this has changed...

'Women now tend to be much more helpful to each other – encouraging, supporting, giving advice. When I was doing Piaf at the Other Place in Stratford, sharing a single dressing-room with four other women who had smaller parts than I did, those cramped, scantily subsidised conditions gave perhaps one of the most joyful experiences of my life because all four helped me to put Edith Piaf together with a generosity and love and attention to detail – not always helpful and not always sensitive – but it was there, and fifteen years ago when I first came into the business, it would not have been there.'

As for Pitman, she considered her farmer father to be her best friend 'of all time'. She went on, 'It was undoubtedly due to my father that long before I became a trainer, I knew my way around what one could describe as a "man's world"'. 'He's the greatest judge of horseflesh that I know, as well as the best friend I've ever had. Dad bought me a pony when I was fourteen months old...I was always Dad's girl. My life consisted of helping him around the farm from the moment I could walk...I wonder, sometimes, if my family ever noticed that I was a girl!

'I hated dolls, which Dad quite understood, though it hurt my mother that I refused to have anything to do with a Christmas present which had real blonde hair, arms and legs that moved, and which cried "Mama" in a horrible reedy voice when I turned it upside down. Dad understood that I'd much rather have had a new pair of wellies so that I could tramp round the farm by his side...I've always gone to Dad with the bigger problems in my life.

'Today, when buying a racehorse...I always take Dad with me. I value his opinion of a horse more than any other...He misses nothing...He's not a very emotional man, and he's always showed us how much he cared for us in the way he brought us up...But for all his reticence, we know he cares. I shall never forget the day that Corbiere won the Grand National, just seven months ago, not purely because an ambition had been achieved, or because I was the first woman trainer, but because, for the first time in my life, I saw my father moved to tears. I actually saw tears running down his cheek. I had never seen him cry before. He is my best friend.'

The Woman of the Year Lunch has never been afraid of emotion. The final speaker, Dorienne Wilson-Smillie of the Programme for Woman and Development, Commonwealth Secretariat, won admiration when she nominated her foremothers as her best friends. By that, she meant 'my myth of myself...centred around my foremothers, not my forefathers (I know little about the males of the line). It was the women, transported to an alien and brutalising environment, who reared the children...In Jamaica women were the ones who impelled and led slave rebellions. On many occasions refusing to work unless they were given time to tend their children and their gardens, they managed to force an amelioration in slave conditions. Through them, I saw that change is possible and that like them, in however small a way, I could contribute to changing the world and, in particular, the world as far as women are concerned...

'Perhaps', she concluded, 'it's difficult for you to think of a concept as a best friend. Shirley Conran's best friends are other women. Perhaps I go back one stage further. It is difficult to be a loving, caring, giving friend unless you first have a strong sense of yourself. So, I say, a sense of self-respect of your own worth, and confidence in that worth – that is a woman's best friend.'

In 1984 the Lunch invited Valentina Tereshkova, first woman in space, to be the international guest of honour. The theme that year was (what else?) 'How To Be First.' 'Even though she had to communicate through an interpreter, it was a very moving and wonderful speech,' recalls Anne Dickinson. For the majority who heard it, a summit had been reached.

Addressing an audience that included the singer/songwriter Joan Armatrading, the actress Julie Walters, the TV presenter Anne Diamond and the restaurateur Prue Leith, Valentina explained: 'It is both hard and easy to answer your question on how I was to become the first woman cosmonaut...What is important is that many women in my country might have been in my place. Why is that so important? Because my space flight was a logical step along the road that Soviet women had covered from illiteracy and lack of rights to genuine equality in all areas of life. Today more than 90 per cent of Soviet women work or study. They make up more than half of the country's experts with a higher or specialised secondary education and about half of all Soviet scientists and industrial engineers. They represent half of all elected deputies in local governments and more than a third of national MPs.'

She then described how she had been born again in space: 'It is hard to put into words the feeling you have when sophisticated technology obeys a woman's hand. When I piloted the ship, I felt proud for women of the world and I thought that women could and should be ever active in managing a planet which is just another huge spaceship...Old as the world itself is the striving of women of all times and people to bring up their children to enjoy a peaceful and happy life. It is a woman's heart that can measure all the depth of suffering that war inflicts on mothers, widows, orphans. Unless it is prevented, the merciless fire of nuclear war would not spare a single nation or a single continent. Our planet is big enough for us to live in peace on it, but it is far too small to be exposed to nuclear menace.

'In working against this menace today, we women and mothers are protecting not only each her own home but our common home – Planet Earth. More than forty years ago, when the war flared up, the British women, the British mothers were among the first who responded to the appeal by the Soviet women to unite for protecting life,' she added, evoking the old alliance that Churchill had considered to be – under Stalin – necessary. 'And today, recognising the responsibility for fortunes of the present and future generations, we are called to do whatever possible for preserving peace and life on our beautiful planet. So may our meeting today help towards better understanding and greater friendly ties between women of our two countries for the sake of peace,' concluded Tereshkova. It was an historic speech.

This was a voice from the new dimension of space, the dimension for life in the future. It was followed in 1985 by the theme 'Hope' appropriately enough. Two royal guests gave speeches: Princess Anne and Queen Mata'aho of Tonga. The latter was there to talk about the hope given by the care of the disabled and handicapped of her Pacific island, a coral atoll whose flatness had led, she said, to the saying that 'the Tongan's mountain is his heart'. The Queen ended by asking to 'borrow an attempt from the immortal words of one of England's greatest sons: "The quality of service is not strained. It droppeth as the gentle rain from heaven, it is twice blessed, it blesseth him who gives and him who receives."' In paraphrasing Portia in *The Merchant of Venice*, the Queen's message was that women were the messengers of hope.

Anne Dickinson, who was sitting next to her, remembers the Queen's 'emotional' speech with affection. 'She was a deeply religious woman and she moved herself to tears which came plopping down on the table. To console herself, she then consumed After Eight mints.'

With characteristic realism, Princess Anne set about her own definition of hope. 'For instance, every time I climb on a horse, I hope that I'm not going to fall off. I also hope that, if I do come off, I will be fit enough to drive the horsebox home, due to the fact that nobody else can. The aggro of finding somebody else who will do it involves more time than it's worth.' She added: 'In my experience with the Save the Children Fund fieldworkers, they have wanted to do something and sometimes giving hope is the best they have been able to achieve. That of course is talking about their work at its worst, famine relief at its worst. It is perhaps the most obvious vision of hope; those children, we hope we are saving them. We may well ask for what... Mothers – perhaps they hope for live babies, but they probably also hope not to be pregnant again. They have hope in these situations because their backs are to the wall and the only way is up. Life can only improve or end altogether.

'I suppose I'm a pessimist at heart,' she admitted, 'but you know even pessimists have hopes. No hope paralyses emotions and confidence, without hope no one would help themselves, never mind anybody else. When I meet groups of young people, schoolchildren of all ages and groups of handicapped children... they've looked and listened and understood that there are many much worse off than they are. And they are happy to help. They are learning. And we must always be ready to learn, then there is always hope and there can be happiness.'

She concluded, 'If there is one common hope in this room just now, I can fulfil it. I'm going to sit down.'

In 1986 the international guest of honour, Coretta King, widow of Martin Luther King, was prevented from coming by illness. Instead she delivered her speech on the theme of 'Vision' by satellite.

The TV reporter Kate Adie gave the first speech, drawing upon her wide-ranging experience of other worlds as a foreign correspondent and illustrating her anecdotes in her famously crisp style. In that, she was very reminiscent of Princess Anne. And like the princess, Adie has a dry sense of humour. She sent herself up with a story about how she first entered journalism as a local radio reporter. 'My first, and last, assignment on Radio Durham as a football reporter: big match, said the sports editor, take the radio car, report every fifteen minutes, please... Piece of cake, I thought... as I delivered a breathless report. Bit foggy here at Evenwood, I added. Fifteen minutes later, the other half of the pitch was completely obscured... So, being as honest as possible, with limited vision of the game, I delivered a score probably unique in BBC sport: "As you join us after thirty minutes, it's Crook Town nil, Evenwood Town at least one, possibly three." '

Then she became more serious and talked about the reason why she had been invited to the Lunch. 'Let me tell you that a month ago I stuck my nose out during a small disturbance in Northern Ireland to see what I could see. A shower of missiles was raining down. I got hit hard. Let me assure you that this was no moment of glory or heroism. There is nothing heroic about being hit on the nose by a potato. So I hope I'll just go on, looking, and trying to say honestly what I've seen, as long as my vision isn't impaired by bricks, bullets and medium-sized King Edward potatoes.'

Coretta King's vision of 'the human spirit' followed. It is, she said, 'available to all people of good will ... If we resolve to pursue a vision of justice, compassion and peace, we can create a new world where all people have enough to eat, where no one lives in fear or poverty, and where the blessings of freedom are firmly established all over the planet. In this faith and in this spirit, together we shall overcome.' Reflecting the call to be compassionate, singer Toyah Wilcox talked of a blind girl at one of her concerts whose poems 'were an inspiration in my life' and of two deaf boy fans who heard music through their hands and feet. 'To me, these three people recognised reality with clarity.'

The Lunch can be an occasion in which speakers respond to the themes with unusually personal revelations. The theme of 1987 was 'Survival'. Dr Pauline Cutting, a surgeon in the Palestinian refugee camps in Lebanon and a heroine of the six-week siege, movingly described her work at Bourj el-Barajneh camp.

But it was the actress Emma Thompson's revelation that proved to be the unexpected one. She talked with candour about her grandmother, who had been in service from the age of fourteen and had been impregnated by her employer with his wife's complicity, in 'an early attempt at enforced surrogate motherhood'. All this was astonishing to those who had assumed that the Cambridge-educated Thompson, whose late father Eric had created the best-selling children's TV programme *The Magic Roundabout*, came from a privileged background.

Thompson went on to relate how both husband and wife had tried to persuade her grandmother to let them have the child, since she had no means to support it. 'Gran refused...and left their service with dignity, a swollen belly and no references...a story that would never have seen the light of day if it had not been wrung out of my grandmother amidst protests that it "wasn't important" and "didn't matter now". But it is precisely these stories that "don't matter now" that make up the bulk of women's undocumented, untaught, unsung experience...

'I always felt excluded by history lessons at school. None of it seemed to apply to me. I remember thinking, is that what it's all about then, life? Producing males who go forth and do things?...Women have not thought of their story as important. That's the main reason why so little of it has survived. Gran's story gave me a personal connection with the past...It is up to all of us now to bring the history of women to the surface, to tell our stories and to honour, as this Lunch does, our achievements. Here's to their survival.'

The theme of 1988 was 'Give Me Time'. The Duchess of Kent, the royal guest of honour, talked of how reassuring she found it when 'so many young people...use the time of their strength to help the weak'.

Baroness Tessa Blackstone, who was to become a key player in the New Labour think-tanks of the nineties, stressed the subject of women's continuing exploitation, arguing that a woman should not have to make the cruel choice between building 'a family which is the source of her emotional strength' and building 'a career which is the source of her economic independence and her self-esteem'.

Another future Baroness, the barrister Helena Kennedy, spoke the following year on the theme of 'Help'. 'I have just had framed for my chambers a poster which shows the Statue of Justice just as it appears on top of the Old Bailey. The caption reads: "The symbol of Justice is a woman". She must have had the time, the money, the legal know-how... and someone to look after her kids,' she began.

The future QC, readily acknowledging the help behind the scenes that all career mothers need, pointed out, 'It is an important reminder that in order to function, many of us are the receivers of help, and that help in turn enables us to be givers of help. And of course it is usually other women who are the source of that help... whether they be members of our family... mothers or sisters, people who work for us or with us, or just friends... the mutual support of women as colleagues and friends has been a particular help to me...

'It is particularly unfashionable now in the eighties to talk of helping people,' she added, 'and some of the most important helpers in our society, such as social workers, nurses, psychiatrists and now even doctors, are scorned for giving this priority... But one of the exciting developments is that many more young women are coming into the law, bright, committed women, who so long as they are given the right encouragement will have an enormous impact on the law and the legal system... If one thing has become clear from the utterances of some judges, it is that they have little understanding of the experience of women, of the changed status of women.'

One of the best pieces of advice she had ever been given, she said, was by a female QC, who told her to conquer her nerves in front of judges at the Court of Appeal by imagining them all sitting naked in the bath. And Kennedy admitted that there were advantages to being a woman: 'Having had three babies in six years, there are many of my clients walking the streets free men who attribute their acquittal to my pregnant state while defending them. It definitely helped...'

Considering, in the same context, the conduct of rape trials in which women in the witness box felt violated twice over by having their personal histories scrutinised, Kennedy also called for some representation for women rape-victims in the courtroom – an argument that has become widespread in the legal profession at the beginning of the twenty-first century. It was first expressed as an appeal to the Women of the Year, so often the mirror of important events.

A non-speaking Princess of Wales was the royal guest of honour for the 1990 Lunch, the highlight of which was the passionate speech by Germany's Green Party MP, Petra Kelly. As international guest of honour, she appealed to women to save the planet. The theme was 'Challenge of the Nineties', and Kelly had no hesitation in making her challenge: 'I have only four to five minutes in which to tell you that we, the women of the world, must reweave this world! Reweave this Planet Earth which has no emergency exit!' she declared before backing up her rhetoric with sobering statistics: 'Women represent half the global population and over one-third of the labour force and yet we women receive only one-tenth of the world's income and own less than one per cent of world prosperity. And yet we are responsible for two-thirds of all working hours. Not only are the women of the world most of the poor, most of the starving and illiterate, but women and children constitute more than 90 per cent of all refugee populations.

'The overlooked factor in the power of women as a

world political force is the magnitude of suffering combined with the magnitude of women: women constitute not an oppressed minority but a majority – of almost all national populations and of the entire human species.' Women, she continued, should 'feminise' power. The dangers, as Kelly outlined, were ominous ones directly affecting women as the carriers of future generations.

'The fate of women is a critical determinant of the fate of whole societies. Toxic pesticides, herbicides, chemical pollution, leakage from nuclear wastes and plants like Sellafield and acid rain usually take their first toll as a rise in cancers of the female reproductive system and in miscarriages, stillbirths and congenital deformities.'

Her own sister Grace, she said, had died of cancer at the age of ten, a victim of the 'poisoned world we live in ... It is women's work which must compensate for the destruction of the ecological balance. Just one example: deforestation results in a lowering of the water-table which in turn causes parched grasslands and erosion of the topsoil; women, as the world's principal water-haulers and fuel-gatherers, must walk further to find water, to find food for animals and to find further cooking fuel.' Women can, she said, 'make our opposition known as consumers, as mothers of children, as women who can influence their partners and as women who support other women in solidarity.'

The sailor Tracy Edwards MBE followed Petra with a speech that echoed many of Kelly's concerns. 'When taking on the *Maiden* challenge, I was very sure of myself, who I was and where I was going. Little did I know just how much it would affect how I think...' she admitted. 'I had never been outspoken about the rights of women, preferring to worry only about myself. But after the prejudice we encountered whilst putting the *Maiden* project together and the sheer force with which people opposed us, I was devastated.

'Today, more than ever, women have got to make the difference. In America they are calling the nineties the 'decade of the woman'. I think they're right... During the race, we were the only team, bar one, out of twenty-three yachts that didn't have any crew changes; whilst the other crews competed and argued among themselves, the women on *Maiden* were sensitive towards each other and directed their competitiveness towards the other boats. Our feminine failings worked for us, not against us. The time has come to change our ways of thinking and our attitudes towards each other... Where do women belong in the nineties? Well, a woman's place is in the office, a woman's place is in politics, a woman's place is in the home; but now, as always, a woman's place is clearing up the mess!'

Edwards was followed by Professor Margaret Turner-Warwick, outlining her vision of medicine in the nineties. 'I am an unrepentant positive thinker,' she admitted as she called for more preventative measures against disease, not least in healthier lifestyles.

In 1991 the theme of 'Harmony' set a challenge for the Duchess of York, the royal guest of honour. She had arrived with an official speech but, in the event, extemporised. 'I am a Libran,' confided Fergie, 'and (so my Sun Sign Book says): "People born under the sign of Libra dislike seeing others suffer and do what they can to help those in dire straits. Another characteristic of a Libran is their love of harmony and beauty." Harmony for me', she added, 'can also mean a reasonable chance at the beginning of each day of getting Beatrice and Eugenie off to a peaceful start with the minimum of hassle and the maximum amount of breakfast inside them... It's at these sometimes fractious moments that I have my harmonious thoughts...'

Sunnie Mann, whose former wartime fighter pilot husband Jackie had been kidnapped on the streets of

Beirut, had demonstrated fortitude under great stress ...but confessed that 'I don't believe in harmony any more. I have lived with anything but harmony over the past three years since my husband Jackie was kidnapped,' she said, 'and I discovered what it was like to have to live alone in a war-torn country without electricity, water or friends. But I still believe harmony can exist and I found some peace of mind with my dogs and horses. Animals give you all their love and devotion without asking anything in return except to be wanted by you.

'But years ago I did believe in harmony when the nurses took the bandages off Jackie's eyes after being blind for a week – the result of his last horrendous crash flying Spitfires during the Battle of Britain. I ran down the ward, crying, "He can see, he can see." Then I felt that miracles could happen and there was love and harmony in the world at that time...I would like to send a message to all blind people. Take courage from Jackie's story. Keep your faith in God and keep holding on as I had to do during my darkest days in Beirut with only a little white poodle dog to keep me sane.'

Jane Glover, the conductor, used music as a metaphor. 'There's a process in music known as the enharmonic change. This is what happens when a particular chord in one key becomes the pivot for sending the music in another direction. And there are times in our lives when we must identify these, literally, turning-points, and work through discord to regain our concord. This afternoon we have all been inspired to survive our enharmonic changes by our fellow guest Sunnie Mann. Two years ago her life in Beirut became a veritable cacophony of fear, devastated hope and despair. But she fought through those dissonant years until her harmony was restored by Jackie's release just a few weeks ago.

'I watched in tears as they both came down the steps of the aircraft at RAF Lyneham and a musical image, from Haydn's *Creation*, burst into my mind. It was the jubilant moment which comes after the Representation of Chaos. With the words "and there was light", the music explodes into a massive, triumphant C major chord. That, I believe, is harmony."

Ann Leslie of the *Daily Mail* pointed out that it was not necessarily in her interests, as a foreign correspondent, to wish for universal harmony. 'If harmony reigned, frankly, I'd be out of a job – and I rather like my job.' She made the equally valid point that 'a woman who strives too much for harmony ends up becoming a doormat for the world's bullies to wipe their boots on'. Yet she believed that 'you must cling to the belief that harmony is possible. When, as a result of drought and civil war, you watch an Ethiopian child – the same age as your own – dying in the dust, it's your job as a foreign correspondent to remind the world, "It doesn't have to be like this."'

Instead she hoped for more moments, such as the night the Berlin Wall came down and the day when Nelson Mandela 'took his first steps to freedom after twenty-seven years', when 'it can be like this instead'. Wisely, she concluded with the thought that 'it's only by continually refusing to accept that fact [disharmony as the world's natural condition] that we can ever hope to achieve some degree of harmony in the future.'

Fellow speaker Floella Benjamin exemplified the promise which later led to her being described as 'the Spirit of the Women of the Year'. She rose above and beyond divisions, bringing the laughter and life of the Caribbean to shine on a speech about 'learning to live in harmony with myself'. Benjamin argued for a new moral code: 'Today the word "morals" conjures up a prim Victorian attitude. But...in a world where everyone seems corruptible by money, power, drugs, greed and fame...morals are what we must teach our children, not when they are thirteen and fourteen, but from an early age, and by our example.'

The positive attitude continued in 1992 with the theme 'Community'. Although royals are supposed to avoid politics, the Duchess of Kent edged very close to them when she voiced her indignation at the stockpiled food mountains which mocked world famine. 'I am sure I cannot be the only person who feels baffled and indeed affronted to read of unimaginable amounts of food which cannot be sold, or which are even destroyed, and so many millions starving,' said the Duchess, who also talked of 'the consequences of famine, corruption, endless warfare, racial tensions. We see the dead and the wounded, the refugees, the homeless and the helpless and children crucified by the "opposition of events".' She went on to list 'the great names of service to the community: Leonard Cheshire, Sue Ryder, Father Kirkpatrick, the Samaritans, Dr Alec Dickson, Mother Teresa . . .' And guests of the Women of the Year Lunch are, she added, 'pioneers in many of the forms of sharing and service which I have been describing'.

After surviving so many privations herself, Dr Jung Chang had immortalised them in her best-selling book *Wild Swans*: the true story of three generations of Chinese women during the transition from feudalism to communism in three different communities. 'For ten years, from the age of fourteen to twenty-four, I lived through Mao Tse Tung's violent Cultural Revolution, which was something like George Orwell's 1984 in real life,' her speech began. 'I have told the stories of my family in my book *Wild Swans*. I am here today because of its success. But for many years, this was the book I found too painful to write. It was my mother who urged me on, and my husband who helped me . . . I want to say that love in our family and community is something that we cannot live without.'

Comedienne Helen Lederer gave a speech about the insecurity of the comic community, often due, she said, to 'unhappiness'. And Janet Street-Porter, then the Head of Youth and Entertainment Features at the BBC, talked of the dreams in the community of youth: 'In the middle of this tidal wave of consumerism and growing racial tension in Europe, there is the voice of young idealists calling for community...Television has a responsibility to allow air time for the views of the young dreamers...For a way forward, we must not merely listen to the young, we must learn from their dreams too.'

'Bringing Down Barriers' was the perfect theme for the black QC Patricia Scotland and the Fleet Street editor Eve Pollard in 1993. Among the guests were the super-model Kate Moss, Lady Longford, international aid worker Sally Becker and Barbara Mills, Director of Public Prosecutions. 'I remember watching the 1987 election campaign on television with my son, who was seven at the time,' said Pollard, then editor of the *Sunday Express* and later to be the chairman of her own magazine empire. 'After seeing a shot of Neil Kinnock, he turned to me and said, "But Neil Kinnock can't be Prime Minister, he isn't a girl!" Perhaps there's hope if you get them young.'

Patricia Scotland, later Baroness Scotland, talked inspiringly of the greatest barrier being 'the self: every person is the architect of their own good fortune'. And Susan McHugh, founder of the Ulster peace campaign Peace '93, talked movingly of the Northern Ireland barrier called 'history'. Perhaps, she suggested, 'a new barrier should be the creation of a chasm between that past and today's urgent need for mutual accommodation and the tentative hand of friendship'. Barriers, she said, were easily erected. She refused to accept that the violence was entrenched. 'Non-violence is a powerful and just weapon...it is a sword that heals.' Again, an historic challenge had been made.

In 1994, the QC Presiley Baxendale, the astronaut Helen Sharman, the pop singer Yazz and the author Joanna Trollope were among the guests of honour listening to a panel of speakers, headed by the veteran anti-apartheid campaigner Helen Suzman as international guest of honour, on the theme of 'What Matters Most'. The Duchess of Gloucester, the royal guest of honour, talked of the contrast between her native Denmark, where the state takes all responsibility for people from the cradle to the grave, to Britain, where 'the freedom to help other people...is least discussed, because it is totally unnoticed and taken for granted'.

Writer, comedienne and fellow Dane Sandi Toksvig paid tribute to 'one of my great heroines, Helen Suzman, a tireless campaigner for equality in South Africa. It always worries me that when the Day of Judgement comes, God will turn to me and She'll say, "What did you do with your life?" To which I'll have to reply, "Showing off and getting a laugh."...What matters most is getting a laugh...' But on what mattered most at this Lunch, she scored a serious point: 'The question I get asked most is why there are so few women comics and I think it's because we don't necessarily want to play humour as an aggressive squash game.'

With a 40th anniversary to celebrate in 1995, the Women of the Year Lunch posed the question: '40 Years On – Have We Come a Long Way, Baby?' In her opening speech the founder president looked back to Pankhurst. 'The Pankhurst monument reminded us how torture, brutal antagonism and prison sentences were endured to win votes for women. How many who pass it on the Embankment recall that she began her crusade with her husband? And that their shared ideal was to liberate half the world so that through enfranchised women the whole world would secure better laws?

'Emmeline believed, "Women care more. They have more practical ideas about the relief of poverty than men." Has that proved to be true?' asked Tony. 'Has half a century of voting influence by women reduced the world's poverty significantly? From the Conference in China, the strongest message has been that the rich minority in the world is getting richer, while the huge majority of poor is getting poorer to the point of destitution. And we see a reflection of this in our own surroundings where six hundred homeless are estimated to die on the streets of Britain every year.

'I do not mean', she added, 'to cast a shadow on our comfort here in the Savoy. I feel confident, and I need to so as to keep my job, that achievers have earned the right to relaxation, not least when they combine it with raising funds for the disabled! But even so, perhaps we can admit the irony of the Western system which seeks to provide the Pankhursts' "practical ideas" to relieve poverty and yet places international delegates looking for solutions about famine in luxurious official settings.

'When I researched the suffragettes' resolve to obtain gender equality, it was for a television series and it struck me that the description "feminist" could sometimes be misleading about them. Emmeline Pankhurst was a radical equaliser. She wanted to free women, convinced that with this freedom women could and would help all humanity.

'But did women's involvement, which she and her colleagues were prepared to die for, develop into the influential collective force they hoped for? Have women with the vote ensured significantly that there is less discrimination in the world...? And even more essentially, why have women together not yet insisted on starting to put an end to wars while the face of war grief is still usually everywhere – the face of women?' After citing Coretta King's belief in 'non-violent social change', Petra Kelly's ideal of sustainable development to prevent ecological catastrophe, Nobel Peace Prize winner Betty Williams' Walk for Peace 'to explode the cement ceiling of tribal prejudice in Northern Ireland', Valentina Tereshkova's appeal for 'One World – One Family' and Mikki Doyle's shared dream with Tony herself of 'reverence for all Creation', the founder president posed the question: 'Do these ideals hand on a torch for the future to carry on further? Or are they like shooting stars lighting up the darkness only for a brief spell? Can we sit back and say we have come a long way, baby? Or, if world humanity is to be helped, is there still a long way to go?'

International guest of honour that year was Simone Veil, former President of the European Parliament. She acknowledged that equality – not to mention the vote – came later to the women of her native France than to the women of Britain and other northern European countries. 'France would wait until 1944. In this way, General de Gaulle recognised the role of women in the French Resistance, but today there are still less than six per cent of women in the National Assembly and the Senate...A mother's parental authority equal to the father's, participation in managing the couple's common possessions, and even the abolition of the obedience owed to a husband, came about in France and in other European countries only in the sixties,' she said.

Calling for a quota system to enable women to enter politics in greater numbers, Veil pointed out that the key to progress lay in new technology and in better working conditions and hours. 'It may seem that women have come a long way, since, on the legal level, they have in principle acquired equality. Reality, however, is very different,' she admitted. 'It is easier to change laws than mentalities and practice...Consequently, a greater participation by women in political power would enable a better response to people's aspirations and needs.'

By 1995 the Labour Party had introduced a controversial quota system for getting more women into Parliament. The *Daily Mail* headlined a picture of the victorious women MPs of the 1997 General Election as 'Blair's Babes'.

Equal Opportunities Commission chairwoman Kamlesh Bahl warned against complacency in her speech. Having unsuccessfully applied for 250 jobs 'at a time when there was a great shortage of newly qualified graduates applying for articles', she reluctantly realised that 'either gender or race discrimination' was against her. 'Discrimination is insidious. It saps your confidence and your self-esteem. It bars you from tried and tested career paths,' she said. Sensing a 'bit of a backlash at the moment' against women's advancement, she talked of 'the life cycle of inequality' that still faced so many women a quarter of a century after the Equal Pay Act was put on the statute book. There had been significant achievements over two decades, she said: girls in co-educational schools were now taught the same subjects as boys, women could apply for credit without a male guarantor, jobs, with a few exceptions, were advertised as being open to both men and women, dismissal from employment on the grounds of pregnancy was now unlawful and married women were now taxed separately. Again there was a history lesson to be learnt from the opinions of the Women of the Year.

The 40th anniversary of the Lunch, Bahl believed, should be symbolised by a ruby, the jewel that is traditionally used to celebrate 40th wedding anniversaries. 'According to Ben Jonson in *The Alchemist*, "the perfect ruby...can confer honour, love, respect, long life. Give safety, valour, yea and victory..." Ruby Wax spoke next with a combination of irony and honesty that made hers one of the most memorable speeches ever given at the Women of the Year Lunch. Her success, she believed, was all due to her father's constant criticism of her when she was a girl: that, together with the example of her mother's life, was a warning not to become a domestic drudge.

'Have we come far in these last 39-and-a-half years? Well, for one thing, 39-and-a-half years ago we'd all be in our pillbox hats exchanging recipes... squealing with delight at each other's engagement rings... so we've moved on a bit,' she said. 'And certainly in my profession things have changed. When I started I don't remember too many women comedians. The woman was the brunt of the joke, not the voice. She was considered "funny" back then because she was a bad driver... which they all were, or a mother-in-law. So I'd say we've come far.

'I know from watching my own mother, who had a brilliant mind and was well educated, that she spent a life of frustration and [was] finally in a continual state of rage. She was far smarter than my father, but backed his needs...' But were women, Ruby demanded, any more liberated in the sixties? Far from saving themselves sexually for Mr Right, they found that 'it was compulsory to sleep with anyone in your eye-range...'

'The seventies gave us the image of Power Woman... Mother Earth replaced by Ms Clark Kent... And just as fast as Ms High Power got up that corporate ladder, she got broody to breed and morphed into the "Woman who has it all". Time never moved that fast. We were dizzy with the speed of it all. And so we got it all, including the stress and probably the early heart attacks that were once a man's domain... Though how you juggle them... maybe the next generation can figure it out. Good luck.

'I just know I'm so glad I got to be in the first generation of women that have been allowed to be men... How I got where I got? God knows... I feel like I jumped without a parachute and landed on target without a map.' And the spur was the way her father constantly belittled her. 'I can honestly say I got successful just to spite him...Thank God we've finally arrived at a time where women can have what men always did...the freedom to pursue your passion. And once you've tasted it, it's like seeing the sun for the first time.'

As a video of that Lunch records, there was a slightly stunned silence for a few seconds after her broadside... but Tony Lothian likened Wax's understanding of the human condition to that of William Shakespeare. Wit and wisdom never failed to be a favourite combination for the Women of the Year.

Tackling the theme of 'Balance' the following year, Victoria Wood spoke with ad-libbing brilliance on the subject of balancing the demands of motherhood and profession. International guest of honour was Vigdis Finnbogadottir, the then president of Iceland, and royal guest of honour Princess Michael of Kent. The latter talked about balancing privilege with obligation to others, while the Icelandic President focused on the balance of nature, a vital issue in Iceland where, she explained, soil erosion from too much tree-felling and over-grazing had become a serious problem.

Such views were important for the Women of the Year because maintaining balance has always been the most difficult challenge. Heather Rabbatts, then the chief executive of the London Borough of Lambeth, gave her view on balance in crisis management. Until she was head-hunted to turn it around, Lambeth Council had been saddled with one of the most shambolic reputations in the capital. 'I got to this meeting where I had a sea of people waiting to see me and my mobile rang and it was my...thirteen-year-old son, who said to me, "I can't find my sports shorts." Now I've got people about saying, "We owe millions to here and we have a crisis and every newspaper in the world is on the phone to me" and I have got all these people waiting in my office, so I was saying to my son (you know sons of thirteen, they never look for anything), I was saying, "Have you looked in the top drawer, the second drawer?" However, what it meant was that all these people had been in crisis, sweat pouring down their brows which men in grey suits often seem to experience. Yet I felt totally calm because, believe you me, if we hadn't found the shorts, that would have been disaster!'

Floella Benjamin argued at the same Lunch for 'an equal and balanced partnership with men, free from discrimination and chauvinism' as she talked about the different balances – between Caribbean and English, career woman and mother – in her life. Replying to a criticism of the Lunch in the *Guardian*, she added: 'I hope the person who wrote it will come and see me and ... I will take her to some schools where I do assemblies in the morning with girls who think they can never make it and that's why we have to come here and have an occasion like this ... to prove women do succeed.'

Consort to the most Westernised of Arab leaders, King Hussein's wife Queen Noor was the international guest of honour at the 1997 Lunch. In a new development, the event honoured three champions of courage, who exemplified 'the best of women'. As Tony Lothian put it in her introductory address: 'We highlight three women we particularly respect and acclaim because they have shown us how the valour to overcome evil is stronger than tragedy. Doreen Lawrence's innocent eighteen-year-old son Stephen was murdered for racist reasons by killers who still go unpunished. It is a sad victory, but a notable one that Stephen's death annulled colour differences because now he is a son, a brother, a grandson for us all to love and mourn as our own. His murder unmasked the Pigment Barrier as the evil blasphemy which it is and thus defeated racism.

'Lisa Potts had told us that one moment she was an ordinary nursery nurse and the next she was confronting a madman killing her child charges. Her response ... and the wounds she suffered because of her courage are now history and she is back running a church crèche on Sundays.

'Rita Restorick's 24-year-old son Stephen was murdered by an IRA bullet while serving as a soldier in Ulster... now she has become an active peace campaigner. We have seen her photograph standing outside Stormont, holding high a notice-board appealing for support for the peace talks. Three champions of courage, exemplifying the vote reformers' vision of what "Woman Power" can do for humanity.'

The theme that year was 'Making a Difference' and dress designer Vivienne Westwood, the great revolutionary of British fashion, was joined on the panel of speakers by the Labour MP Harriet Harman, the then Minister for Women, followed by CND crusader Joan Ruddock. Harman spoke about how Labour's New Deal for Lone Parents to get them back to work did not represent criticism of single mothers.

'For too long, the democratic processes of this country have been dominated by men – men on public bodies; men in Parliament; men in Government. Men have been responsible for making decisions that have a profound effect on the lives of women. And yet we all know – and I expect most of us have had personal experience – of how incapable some men are of understanding women, their issues and their place in society,' Harman stated. 'Is it any wonder that women have felt disconnected from democracy; disheartened by their lack of representation; and dismayed that issues which should have been at the top of the agenda have been at the bottom of the agenda of those in power?' She ended with a quote – 'I do not wish women to have power over men, but over themselves' –

from Mary Wollstonecraft, whose most famous works, *Vindication of the Rights of Men* and *Vindication of the Rights of Women*, have been edited by the Cambridge academic Sylvana St Andrews, present at that Lunch.

As the new century approached, the themes became more serious and focused. In 1998, the Duchess of Kent, Anna Scher, whose London theatre school for talented youngsters has helped to develop many future stars, and the actress and writer Meera Syal talked of, what Tony Lothian called 'Tomorrow's Children', with Meera giving an acutely apposite Asian point of view.

In keeping with the Lunch's new tradition of honouring special heroes, the programme contained addresses by three nominated Women of Peace – Mo Mowlam, then the Secretary of State for Northern Ireland, Alison Moore, the junior-school music teacher attacked by racists, and Esther Wachsman, whose son had been murdered by Arab terrorists in the Middle East. The Duchess of Kent talked about the work of the Women of the Year's new charity, NCH Action for Children, while Maureen Lipman spoke movingly of the late Linda McCartney, a posthumous recipient of the Empty Chair Award.

As principal of a pioneering theatre school, Anna Scher had worked all her life with children of all backgrounds and races. 'Speaking as an Irish Jewish integrationist who once held the somewhat dubious distinction of being the only Jewish girl in the convent, my...world view [is that] tomorrow's children of all ages need a sense of belonging in a community.' True to the spirit of the Women of the Year, Scher encouraged 'children of all ages to speak out against racism, ageism and sexism...Mahatma Gandhi said, "We must start with the children," and I have followed that to the letter these past thirty years.'

Three ten-year-old children – Alvina Benjamin-Taylor,

Tinu Adeniadele and Maya Cheetham – spoke that year, telling the guests what in their view was important to tomorrow's children: peace and having their mothers there to give them a hug when they needed it. At the end of her speech Alvina brought the house down with her impression of Tony Blair's 'Education, education, education' speech.

The Lunch and Assembly again showed the courage of its convictions in 1999 by choosing the theme 'Human Rights'. International guest speaker was the actress and producer Linda Gray, whose eighties image as an emoting soap-opera actress in the long-running American TV series *Dallas* had been been replaced in the late nineties by her United Nations appointment as an Ambassador of Goodwill. She took the challenge of the theme seriously, speaking of her own learning experiences when she tried to teach in the Third World while novelist Kathy Lette gave a witty extemporised speech about the experience of being married to a human-rights lawyer.

Helen Bamber and Sheila Cassidy, who had been elected Resistance Women to carry the baton handed on by Odette Hallowes, gave moving personal testimonies. When she was twenty, Bamber left Britain for Germany as one of the first psychosocial workers to enter Belsen concentration camp after the war. As a result of those experiences, she founded the first medical group with Amnesty International and in 1986 became the director and founder of the Medical Foundation for the Care of Victims of Torture. In her speech she tackled the subject of rape as a war crime, once again making the Women of the Year a platform for the most important issues of the day. Pointing out how the International Criminal Tribunal in Arusha, Tanzania, had determined that rape is an act of genocide when women are assaulted because they are members of an ethnic group, she talked of how, on visits to Uganda, Palestine and Northern Ireland, she had watched female survivors of torture and organised violence play a prominent part in trying to resuscitate their communities. For Bamber, the strength of women being treated at her medical foundation for the victims of torture proved extraordinarily heartening.

Dr Cassidy had been imprisoned and tortured by General Pinochet's military regime in Chile in 1975. Even as she spoke, Pinochet had taken refuge on a wealthy estate in Surrey and resisted extradition to Spain on human-rights charges. As she put it, 'There's a limit to how often one can talk about one's own torture, but I have done what I could over these past few months with the Pinochet affair so much in the public eye.'

Cassidy, who now works with cancer patients in the Plymouth Oncology Centre, conveyed sad memories without bitterness. 'I had never heard of human rights until I was suddenly deprived of my own in Chile in 1975 ... I found myself right in the middle of one of the bloodiest military coups of modern time ... My crime was to agree to treat a revolutionary with a bullet in his leg,' she continued, after analysing the causes of revolution by describing what the Brazilian bishop Helder Camara calls the spiral of violence. 'A week later, I was arrested in the house of friends. They shot the maid dead and carried me off blindfolded to a torture centre on the outskirts of town where they stripped me naked and interrogated me with electric shocks.

'I spent the next three weeks in solitary confinement and then five weeks with a hundred or so other young women, all of whom had been tortured as I was – many of them more violently. I became close to those women – heard their stories and admired their courage until we were sisters under the skin. How then could I not work for their release when I was sent back to the United Kingdom? That's how I became a human-rights activist: someone who spends time and energy trying to make things even marginally better for those who are poor or in any way oppressed.'

Among the guests of honour that year were the eleven middle-aged Yorkshirewomen who had posed nude for the Alternative WI calendar to mark the new millennium. They were nominated by Maureen Lipman, firstly because of the thousands of pounds they had raised for leukaemia and lymphoma research after the tragic early death of WI member Angela Baker's husband John, and secondly because of the way these free spirits had changed the image of the Women's Institute for ever. Serious fun, indeed. Since then, their story has been taken up by Hollywood and a film is under way.

Presiding over the 1999 event as royal guest of honour was Lady Helen Taylor, invited because of her work in the contemporary art world. She also represented a younger generation at the Lunch, which is always looking for new talent in every profession. As Anne Dickinson, who resigned from the committee when she retired from professional work, so frankly puts it: 'We have always sought fresh blood; we always fought against the idea of being a collection of mouldy old ladies.'

Yet it was to be invisible guests who had the most extraordinary impact of all upon the Women of the Year.

Chapter Six
The Empty Chair

In 1989 the Burmese people elected a woman Prime Minister, Aung San Suu Kyi. However, she could not take up her post because the military government that rules Burma placed her under house arrest. Two years later she was awarded the Nobel Peace Prize. And she did attend the Women of the Year Lunch in spirit if not in body, thanks to the idea of leaving a chair symbolically empty for her. Thus began the Empty Chair reserved for women who – due to circumstances beyond their control – could not be there.

This was the brainchild of the author and actress Maureen Lipman who was first introduced to the Lunch by her friend, the television producer Linda Agran. 'Linda got me onto the committee in 1995. I found it completely fascinating,' admits Maureen, who was given responsibility for organising speakers and speeches. 'I hadn't been on a committee since my youth-club days. People like Diana Makgill are marvellous characters; once you break through the formal crust, they're as straight as a die. The Lunch has been very much an influence for good, and I've really enjoyed the whole thing; I've gained a lot from it. Especially ending up at the Savoy bar after the Lunch with a group of hilarious women: the Victoria Woods, the Kathy Lettes and the

Ruby Waxes. Yet even they, she says, become anxious about whether they should tone down their acts in front of such a disparate audience of all ages. 'I had to reassure Kathy that this was an adult group of women. Her speech was about human rights in the home, as the wife of a human-rights lawyer, and she was great.'

Lipman herself has marched and campaigned in support of human rights. In the spring of 2000, she joined a demonstration to protest at the predicament of the 'chained' women whose Orthodox Jewish husbands refuse to grant them a divorce. 'We were marching in Golders Green on a Sunday morning, and the police wouldn't let us march more than three abreast because they said it would hold up the traffic. I'm not Orthodox myself, but this whole situation of chained women is chauvinistic: it leaves women very vulnerable. It's a human-rights issue; and another way', she observes, 'of binding women's feet.'

One of her fondest memories of five years on the committee was the experience of going round the lobby of the Savoy Hotel with fellow Women of the Year director Sylvana St Andrews to drum up interest in the blind children's painting competition that had been organised for the Frink Award.

The Frink disability trophy was introduced to honour the achievements of women who had overcome physical disabilities and excelled in a wide variety of fields, which included computer programming, engineering, sculpting and gymnastics. In 1986 Britain's leading sculptor, Dame Elisabeth Frink, sculpted a bronzed winged eagle that represented the 'transcendent progress of women' and offered it to the Women of the Year.

Frink, who died in 1993, had always shared the passionate commitment to peace that has been such a consistent feature of the Women of the Year Lunch. During the Second World War, the airstrips where she lived as a teenager were targeted by the enemy. Even when she was evacuated to school in Exmouth, that area of the West Country experienced a series of bombing raids. The horror of war was a theme that ran throughout her work, and she attended the Women of the Year Lunch as an artist with a worldwide influence. She admired and supported the achievements of her own sex, once saying, 'I am inspired by women flying high and flying free.'

Frink would have approved of a typical piece of lateral thinking by Maureen Lipman. The plight of Aung San Suu Kyi had been on Lipman's mind for some time. 'We talk so much about juggling work and family, but hers is the most dramatic situation with her family back in Oxford. She's a shining light of democracy and womankind. That's what it [the Burmese government] is afraid of.'

Burma had been granted independence from Britain in 1948, but the army abolished the country's first and only civilian government in 1962 and installed a military junta instead. Aung San Suu Kyi is the daughter of the opposition leader, General Aung San, who was dubbed Burma's George Washington for his role in helping to end British colonial rule. He was assassinated in 1947 by a political rival with a machine-gun and the country was taken over by a military dictatorship. Aung San Suu Kyi had left Burma in 1960 at the age of fifteen when her mother was appointed ambassador to India. She studied abroad and eventually settled in the UK, marrying a British academic. But when she came back to Burma in 1988 to visit her then-ailing mother, she found herself at the epicentre of the political upheaval.

The ruling junta had agreed to Burma's first free elections in thirty years, although it expected to control the ballot box by a mixture of tactics. The outspoken Aung San Suu Kyi was placed in solitary detention in her home and barred from running for government because of her public utterances, such as 'The people of Burma really want freedom, but first they want freedom from fear.' Her party, the National League For Democracy, went on to win 81 per cent of the vote. This was not what the junta had planned at all, and they threw most of her supporters into jail. Aung San Suu Kyi was placed under house arrest and has since gone on hunger strike, found herself vilified in government smear campaigns, and even denied a visa to visit her husband in Britain before he died of cancer in 1999. Yet even as a prisoner, she remains the focal point in Burma for opposition to the rule of the generals. Rather than go into exile and desert her people, she endures imprisonment in her own home.

When Lipman first proposed the idea of the Empty Chair being reserved for Suu Kyi she had decided to step down from the committee because of other commitments. 'As a sort of exit visa, I suggested inviting a guest who couldn't come but whom we would invite none the less. So why not have an empty chair for that guest?

'I then got a letter back from Tony, proclaiming me as the new Messiah, so all thoughts of leaving were dismissed. The idea split the committee in half, however: half thought it was not a good idea and half thought it was great.' Eventually it was adopted and Lipman stayed on to help launch the new project.

To put the idea into its historical context, however, Tony Lothian recalls how this mark of respect was first suggested in the sixties by a group of Jewish guests who wanted to emphasise that Jewish women of distinction were excluded from national activities in the Soviet Union. 'They proposed paying for a ticket and keeping the place empty for a nominated Jewish woman achiever from Russia who was not allowed to travel. The request was not acceded to because it was considered impossible to monitor with absolute fairness whether the nomination fulfilled the necessary criteria. But the possibility of an Empty Chair remained on the back burner and some years later it was given new inspiration by Maureen.

'Nevertheless, honouring great work of women living outside the UK and prevented from attending remains a problem. Nobel Prize procedures provide an indication of how recognition can be given without involving political or religious prejudice. But it is not easy to separate the recognition of these women heroes from politics or sectarian issues. Obviously it was admirable and important to support democracy in Burma but preventing the death of innocent victims in Ulster is closer to home and relatively easier to monitor. Still, it was worth the effort of trying to be just; and in the end a still-divided committee had to agree that had been proved possible. As much as Maureen, the leading influence in favour of the Empty Chair was Floella Benjamin.'

One committee member feared such a citation might become 'theatrical'. To which Lipman replied: 'The word "theatre" comes from the Greek word "to see". We need theatre to make us see things afresh...I think it is important to distinguish what is political from what is humane.' The treasurer, Trish Morris-Thompson, submitted a formal nomination of Suu Kyi as 'hero of the year', pointing out that the proposal would 'reflect and embrace the objective of the Women of the Year Lunch. This, as I see it, is not only to celebrate women's individual achievements but their heroic contributions to each nation's culture and society.'

Then came the dangerous delivery of the Women of the Year citation to Aung San Suu Kyi in person. Glenys Kinnock, a Member of the European Parliament and a vice-president of the Women of the Year Lunch, was the messenger. She carried the citation with her when she posed as a tourist and took a day trip to Burma from Bangkok airport. The main purpose of her mission was to record a secret interview with Aung San Suu Kyi in which the imprisoned leader urged the international community to boycott Burmese tourism, investment and trade to undermine the junta. Linking up with a Dutch journalist and another woman in the ladies' lavatory of a Rangoon hotel, Glenys used the roar of the hand-driers to muffle her voice as she discussed the arrangements for getting to Aung San Suu Kyi's house and walking past the armed guards outside.

Glenys brought back a letter for Maureen from Aung San Suu Kyi in which, referring to one of Lipman's jokey column items in *Good Housekeeping* about how her mother had found the fat glossy a bit heavy to lift, she wrote, 'I would just like you to tell your mother that *Good Housekeeping* isn't at all heavy.' 'It was', says Lipman, 'amazingly moving to think of her reading my mother's jokes while she was imprisoned.'

Maureen's address to the Lunch in 1996 upheld the spirit of the Women of the Year. 'We are, and always have been, Ladies Who Lunch in every sense but the Stephen Sondheim one. We do not lunch to pass time away. We come together in pleasant surroundings to raise money for the blind, to reinforce our faith in women's achievements and to have fun. The Women of the Year Lunch is, for me, affirmation of the late, great, Hugo Gryn's life motto: "To practise tolerance, cherish harmony and to celebrate our differences."

'Tony Lothian and Odette Hallowes, the women who began Women of the Year forty years ago, were pioneers for change, and though a successful career is now easier to achieve for women, life is more complex, the stakes are higher and the struggle for equality continues.

'In the spirit of this belief...we would like to direct our attention to those women who, for reasons domestic, political, economic or physical, do not have our precious freedom...to fulfil their potential. Today we wish to inaugurate, in their honour, those absent women who struggle against oppression and with whom we share responsibility in the fight for change. So this is, to misquote Hemingway, a grace for those under pressure.

'On behalf of the Women of the Year, we would like to nominate the leader of the elected NLD party in Burma, Nobel Laureate Aung San Suu Kyi, as the first recipient of this citation. We are a non-political organisation but we cannot and do not separate politics from humanity. Suu Kyi symbolises all the most admirable qualities in woman and mankind. Many of her colleagues are imprisoned. She is free to leave her country but as the military will not let her return, she chooses to remain there, in increasing danger and under close surveillance, without personal security and separated from her Oxford lecturer husband Michael Aris – unable to watch the day-by-day growth of her children.

'Journalists refer to her frail beauty – Bernard Levin got it right when he called her the "iron feather". She has chosen the difficult road of principle. She has shown real courage ... with patience. The military junta have now prevented the crowds of supporters from converging at her house each week to hear her quiet words of resistance ... She does not see herself as a heroine or a saint. "Saints are only sinners who go on trying," she says. Suu Kyi is a woman trying to do her job. The job she was elected to do ...

'We believe that, like Mandela and Luther King, Suu Kyi will achieve her aims through the principles of non-violent protest and through the Empty Chair we send her our respect, our admiration and our solidarity ... Meanwhile, our prayer today is for her safety and for a few seconds, I would like us to just visualise sharing her life as today we share each other's ... And perhaps today, although she can't be with us, we can be with her.'

Lipman's words made world news, as the Women of the Year Lunch has done again and again. 'Two years later we gave the award posthumously to the late Linda McCartney, and some people didn't agree with the idea of a vegetarian meal in honour of Linda's beliefs,' recalls Maureen. 'But Paul McCartney gave everyone there a posy, so it turned out well.'

In 1997 Linda McCartney had been invited to the Lunch, but by then the vegetarian campaigner, who died of cancer in April of the following year, was too ill to attend. Like the Princess of Wales, who perished that year in the fatal Paris car crash, Lady McCartney had never hesitated to act on behalf of favourite causes. She wrote angry letters on behalf of stranded whales in 1992 and sent a veggie Christmas hamper to the women protesters against the Greenham Common cruise missiles in 1993. Always her own woman, she earned her place among the Women of the Year.

In September 1998 Maureen wrote to Sir Paul: 'I will be saying a few words at the Women of the Year Lunch to honour the memory of your beloved wife. I will talk for a minute about the Empty Chair, about Aung San Suu Kyi, the first recipient, and about why we chose this year to have a vegetarian lunch in memory of Linda. It will be a form of grace, of which she had such an abundance...

'I hope in some way that we manage to remind mothers, lovers, working women and members of the human race of her unique and continuing contribution to our lives. Should you wish to join us on the day,' she added, 'we would, of course, welcome you with open arms...if that's not too daunting a prospect.'

Sir Paul confessed himself 'chuffed' and added, 'It's a pity us blokes can't go.' Some members of the committee suspect to this day that he may have been too shy to be a token bloke. But Lipman perseveres. 'I have been fighting for men to come to the Lunch ever since I joined,' she adds. 'Paul McCartney said he didn't feel brave enough to come. I think he may have meant that it would have been a very emotional event for him. But I would like to invite along men who have enabled women, who have improved the lot of women.'

Maureen continues to support the Women of the Year. 'It's not a religion, it's a Lunch. It doesn't change the world, one mustn't get pretentious. But if we do good with our Lunch, it's even better.

'It's a Lunch for busy women, and on the other side you have Tony's ideals about changing society. You couldn't have an event like this without Tony and Odette, and in a sense there's a permanent Empty Chair there for Odette. She should be up there always in the Legions of Honour. The Women of the Year Lunch was created when it was desperately needed – and we have all benefited from those pioneers.'

Chapter Seven
Could Women Change the World?

The only thing that really matters, Barbara Castle once observed, is altering attitudes – an observation often quoted when the Women of the Year has challenged entrenched attitudes.

With guests from all walks of life, of all colours, creeds and nationalities, the event has consistently encouraged necessary change. 'We have taken our own line on racism, on Ulster and on leading women who are under-valued at the time. Understanding has developed from us remaining true to our principles,' says the founder president. 'When women meet, totally free of conventional constraints, they often find unity. There's an empathy about protection. Perhaps we are all mothers, not necessarily physical ones, but we protect the weak. This is something women have in common. There's a shared informality when women meet, but it's deeper than that. Emmeline Pankhurst said that we *care* more.'

Tony Lothian is something of a visionary, as has been shown in her innovations for health and media awards. Certainly it was her original vision which became the driving force for the Women of the Year. 'In my old head,' she remarks, 'I have this great landscape of women.' And by 1997, the Women of the Year Lunch had become a world-famous institution. But maintaining a high standard was not easy. In the early nineties, Lady Georgina Coleridge's hearing problems had become so severe that she stood down from direct involvement with the Lunch. No longer able to rotate the responsibility with Georgina of presiding over the Lunch under the old amicable arrangement, the founder president carried on in her nose-to-the-grindstone way.

'My father's family is from Yorkshire and they thought there was no alternative to work and getting on with it. I think I have been a workaholic,' she admits. But in 1997 Tony Lothian's seemingly indestructible endurance was severely tested. 'I had a stroke, a small one; but it put my legs out of action. I find walking difficult; the nerves go, it's like polio.' Yet she was up and – well, not quite running, but certainly back in harness. That indefatigable spirit of hers seems to rally when physical problems present themselves; and Tony has been sailing on a powerful second wind ever since. And forcing herself back into the fray.

In 1998 a major organisational restructuring took place when the Women of the Year Lunch was established as independent from charity control. It became a not-for-profit company limited by guarantee which raises money for charity. The former members of the main committee became directors and Tony Lothian continued as founder president with Floella Benjamin as non-executive chairman until the year 2001. Until 1997, the Greater London Fund for the Blind was the sole charity that benefited from the Lunch, with a million pounds raised over the forty-two years since the Lunch began. From 1997 the charity chosen to receive the results of fund-raising on a three-year arrangement was NCH Action for Children.

The Lunch and Assembly had become such an important forum, with a growing database of nominated guests who were experts in forty categories of working life, that the establishment of an independent annual debate on important issues was a logical next step. It was held at the Savoy on the morning of the Lunch, and an annual survey with questions for each of the nominated guests was commissioned beforehand, to find out what women wanted.

'Before becoming a company,' Tony writes, 'a poll had been taken asking members of the committee whether they wished to make fund-raising the priority or whether advancing progress for women's issues was the main aim. The majority replied that they wished to work for women first and foremost while combining this, as always, with raising funds for the disabled. So it was agreed to work on for women. But the debate between money and ideals was never far away, and ideals brought their own problems. To steer an objective passage in the stormy sea of bitter sectarian, racist and ideological prejudices, in the second half of the twentieth century, was a major challenge for the survey questions. It was something to be proud of that so many prejudices were successfully thought out and a valid example of impartiality arrived at.

'Impartiality was a useful contribution for human progress at a time when increasingly unprecedented dangers needed Pankhurst-type wisdom and co-operation to establish safeguards.' This still worries Tony. 'I believe that watchdogs are needed to control the conflicting commercial interests of money-making giants. I hope women will use their influence through customer power. Otherwise I fear that the new forces of mental manipulation will prove too powerful for human fragility to oppose them.

'So many interests stand to gain. The armaments industry, the pharmaceutical industry, the fertility industry, the food industry and also, above all, wars and rumours of wars. I had always believed passionately that the women reformers had been right to believe that women could together find ways to end war. The women of Sparta did not do too badly – by going on sex strike – but we need to find other solutions; and progress is made when women meet.

'For the peace process, Valentina has brought in an extra-terrestrial element as a pioneer woman who had seen from space the interrelationship of the human species living on a fragile globe at the constant mercy of destruction. She is a New Woman who has proved that women are as able to live and work in the new dimension of space as men. She has become a leader for peace, advocating global morality as a simple and strong belief that could prevent global annihilation.' The Lothian/ Tereshkova sisterhood has proved that it was worthwhile for humans to try to meet and learn about each other, rather than destroy each other. 'Living together, even enemies find understanding. This happens to hostages imprisoned with their abductors. It happens even more conclusively meeting and talking in a climate of mutual respect which leads to enjoying each other's company, regardless of conventional barriers.

'In the twenty-first century, could New Woman change history and even save the world?' Tony wonders. 'The reformers' hunger strikes were instrumental in obtaining voting power for women and now customer power is a new weapon which women can use to control commercial irresponsibility.'

She adds: 'It is difficult for women to oppose and expose the financial giants determined to exploit them, but the consumer movement has valiantly reacted. Women customers now make use of their power to complain by refusing to buy. Unfortunately, manipulated by commercial hidden persuaders, some minority groups have claimed they speak for the majority and they even deny a voice to other women who think differently. This causes rigid gridlocks when what we need is calm, objective studies of issues, such as armaments sales, food modification and pro-life and pro-choice measures to deal with unwanted pregnancies. Our Assembly discussions aim to provide accurate information. Agreeing to differ is essential; but to find out what women really want needs a high standard of information if women are to make a properly informed choice.

'The Women of the Year now contributes two new ways to establish authentic answers to the question "What do women want?" One is through the Assembly Forum co-ordinated by a leading scientist, Professor Nancy Lane, aiming to voice both sides of each controversy, through the views of indubitable experts on, for example, the Millennium Dome and genetically modified foods. The audience agreed to differ but they were satisfied that they had been given the opportunity to base their choice on balanced expert information.'

In 1997 Dr Lane had succeeded the astronomer Heather Coupar on the committee of the Women of the Year Lunch to represent women's scientific achievements. A lecturer and researcher into cell biology at Cambridge University and a Fellow of Girton College, the Canadian-born Lane recalls how she had been asked to create a provocative discussion on a subject of substance. Women for the most part had not been trained in science, so were perhaps unaware of many scientific issues. 'I was asked to put the idea of the Assembly in place. It was conceived to maintain a diversity of opinion by airing important issues with speakers for and against. We discuss the ethical views on an issue rather than the precise scientific validity, because women respond to debating ethics.' Indeed, she hopes that the Assembly will also debate the issue of cloning in future because 'women are very interested in the surrogacy issue that comes with that. Women are the vehicles for carrying children, but very often they haven't had a voice on these issues – sadly, in my view.'

'What started as an experiment is now a fixture,' writes Tony Lothian. 'The same result was provided the following year by a questionnaire for guests which asked for answers to important questions, mainly serious but some more frivolous. In this anonymous but genuine exercise, some surprising conclusions were revealed. It was to be expected that Nelson Mandela and Richard Branson were favourite men, but a few found it irritating that Margaret Thatcher was a favourite woman. But here again it was valuable as a reminder that women as a family need to agree to differ.'

Genetically modified crops was the first topic covered in the survey, and nine out of ten reported eating organic foods. At the other end of the spectrum, one-third of them also ate GM foods. All of them said that they wanted more information about the extent of the use of GM foods and called for greater transparency on the part of biotech companies, retailers and wholesalers in this market. Since women the world over are the main buyers of food for the home, their views influence hitherto hidden persuaders.

As for social, health and sex-education issues, the vast majority (93 per cent) agreed that the National Health Service should continue to be responsible for basic services, and more Women of the Year were critical of police attitudes than supportive of them.

A healthy 84 per cent believed in teaching children the value of cultural diversity in Britain, reflecting the multi-cultural backgrounds of many guests at the Lunch. More than three-quarters are educated to degree or HND level or above, and nearly three-quarters are working full-time.

From answers given, a picture emerges of the usual juggling of priorities, with many women regretting 'cramming things in', arriving 'late all the time' and 'putting things off'. They identified the inability to say no and the habit of working long hours as their biggest professional weaknesses.

Other answers are equally interesting. Asked to nominate their first, second and third choice of British Woman of the Century, they ranked Emmeline Pankhurst first ('the catalyst establishing women's position in modern society' and 'first steps to equality' were some of the comments), Margaret Thatcher second ('challenged men on ability, not gender') and Marie Stopes third ('enabled women to manage their fertility and so responsible for the greatest change in women's lives: freeing them from their biology').

As for the Woman of the Millennium, Queen Elizabeth I came first ('her utter steadfastness to her call to be queen, her calm devotion to duty, her intelligence'), Marie Curie second ('she used her intellect for the good of mankind, with continuing results') and Mother Teresa third ('for her great humanity and giving throughout her life').

When asked who she would nominate, the actress Dame Diana Rigg says: 'I would go for Elizabeth I. She was so completely her own woman and she stood alone. She was in a position of immense power and she led an extraordinary life that was very dangerous, but she took England into a glorious age. I would love to have been her; she was an intellectually acute lady until she died. Here was a woman who set a standard. I would love to play her,' she adds, 'but I'm a bit old now – except to play her in later life.'

So, Thatcher apart, which women leaders of the past inspire women leaders now? Public-relations consultant Val Arnison, who was asked by Lady Georgina Coleridge to bring sponsorship to the Lunch for the first time, cites the late Gina Franklin – a PR giant who was one of the first to set up her own agency – as a major inspiration. 'Women have done well in this field because they are good communicators and organisers with an eye for detail and an enormous determination to get on with it. Women start much earlier in the business now; you see a lot of young women PRs. Public relations is now accepted at management level, but whether you call it corporate relations or public affairs, it's all about advising or counselling.'

One of the legal profession's wiser counsels, Helena Kennedy QC, nominates her own 'doughty' mother as her Woman of the Millennium, with Mary Robinson – head of the UN Human Rights Commission and former President of Ireland – running her a close second. For both Glenys Kinnock and Barbara Switzer, Emmeline Pankhurst's daughter Sylvia would be the Woman of the Millennium. Describing Sylvia as the kind of 'socialist feminist' she admires, Glenys also adds Mary Wollstonecraft and Barbara Castle to her list.

'My choices are political feminists,' she says bluntly. 'The face of poverty is female and one urgent issue to tackle is that of the 125 million children not in primary school, two-thirds of whom are girls.' Castle is also the choice of Brenda (now Baroness) Dean, like Barbara Switzer a woman trade-union leader honoured at the Lunch for her achievements in a male-dominated world. Baroness Dean points out how, at nearly ninety, 'Barbara Castle is still an active speaker. She's a trailblazer for women, like Golda Meir – who I also admired for being there at the birth of a nation.'

For Dr Vivette Glover, an internationally known medical researcher, Dorothy Hodgkin 'showed me that it was possible to be a first-rate scientist and a woman'. The neuroscientist Susan Greenfield is a great admirer of the achievements of Hodgkin, too, as well as of Marie Curie. 'But my hero would be Rita Levi-Montalcini, who was a neuroscientist in Mussolini's Italy, set up her own laboratory and won the Nobel Prize in 1986. She was Jewish; I'm half-Jewish myself so I can appreciate how she fought against a great deal of adversity.'

Dr Nancy Lane also nominates Dorothy Hodgkin:

'She won the Nobel Prize for her input into crystallo-graphy, but she was a mother as well – and she encouraged a lot of women in her laboratory who are now her scientific children, dotted around the country. She encouraged the female scientific community and she was extremely kind to me.' As for Women of the Year treasurer Trish Morris-Thompson, a nurse who has risen to become chief executive of the Birmingham Women's Health Trust, her Women of the Millennium would be Florence Nightingale, Princess Diana, Mother Teresa and Mo Mowlam.

Doreen Lawrence's all-time heroines are 'the writer Maya Angelou in the arts and Princess Diana for supporting people in adversity'. And stockbroker Susan Shaw nominates Edith Cavell, the British nurse shot by the Germans for aiding the escape of Allied soldiers from Belgium during the First World War, as her Woman of the Millennium: 'a lady who stood for all that I value most in humankind: loyalty, bravery and humanity.'

The fashion designer and Francophile Paddy Campbell nominates Eleanor of Aquitaine, who ruled over twelfth-century France and England, as her Woman Leader of the Millennium. 'As for the position of women in my own industry, they have always been leaders – we haven't got much of a war to fight. The supreme difficulty is carrying on with a full-time job after you have children; in France, they make childcare tax-deductible.' Yet women associated with the Lunch remain optimistic. 'In journalism there has been a huge leap forward for women,' says Shirley Conran, pointing out how 'women generally have just got more businesslike and confident'.

The year 2000 had been declared the Year of the Culture of Peace by the United Nations. The Women of the Year, records Tony Lothian, 'looked for the figure-head which shed the strongest light on peace. Replying to the questionnaire, there was an unexpected development.

The chosen leader was not a woman, but a man: Nelson Mandela. The citation in voting for him as the Leader of the Century by the Women of the Year was spoken by Valentina Tereshkova: 'By his own example he has taught humanity that hatred and revenge can be transformed into forgiveness, acceptance and positive action to heal separated communities. It is not an easy road but it is the only road to peace away from war.' With Mandela and Tereshkova as shining lights to guide them, could women change the world?

In her letter of acceptance to the Year 2000 Assembly, Tereshkova hailed Mandela as 'a symbol of solidarity of peoples of different race, creed and nationality'. The Women of the Year Lunch had become a microcosm of that solidarity: 'The dialogue between women of different countries has become a mark of our times,' continued Valentina in her letter.

With hindsight, we can see that the twentieth century perfected the dark art of war with the development of weapons of mass destruction by the armaments industry; and at the beginning of the twenty-first century, tribal-hatreds between peoples seem as threatening as ever. Peace is not easy to find.

The heartening news, however, is that women have increasingly played a vital part in resistance and peace movements during the century just passed: with the highly dangerous missions of Odette and others in occupied Europe, with the struggle against apartheid and other cruel regimes of all political persuasions, with the alliances between women of all creeds to try to end the Troubles in Ulster, with the Greenham Common women's peace camps that campaigned against cruise missiles.

The Greenham Common campaigners have been represented at the Lunch by Wendy Roseneil, a psychologist who has been associated with the Women of the Year since the sixties when she was a journalist. A former editor of *Parents* magazine, Roseneil has been following the peace-campaign trail laid by her late mother Pat O'Connell – a CND activist and member of the Committee of 100 who was jailed alongside Bertrand Russell for civil disobedience at an anti-nuclear rally in Trafalgar Square in 1962.

Wendy, Pat, and Wendy's sociologist daughter Sasha Roseneil – who, in the spring of 2000, published a history of the Greenham Common women's campaign in the eighties – represented three generations of protesters at the cruise missile base in Berkshire and helped to 'rock down' the perimeter fence surrounding the base. Women, Wendy feels, are natural peace campaigners, which is why they have so often been at the forefront of protest against war: 'We create life in our bodies and we find it incomprehensible that people should want to kill others. Planned genocide is incredibly primitive.'

So who are the true heirs to the Pankhurst breakthrough? Some would feel that Wendy Roseneil is one. Tony Lothian is in no doubt that Princess Anne is another. 'She has made the most of every talent and refuses to be either a feminist or exclusively feminine: just herself. When she made up her mind to become an Olympic showjumper, she did – and all her colleagues respected her. She's a very remarkable woman. She runs everybody off their feet on these African visits for her Save the Children charity, leaves them gasping. She is a complete professional in her work as well as a mother. In a sense, she also throws stones: she can't endure inefficiency. We were less than efficient at a Lunch one year and got the names of the people she was being introduced to wrong; she pointed out the names on their lapel badges. We had absolutely no excuse for inefficiency.

'She has the same sort of charisma as her father; they are two royals whom I admire for their work. And I admire the whole Kent family. They provide the perfect balance of kindness with professionalism. The Duchess is a real Yorkshire countrywoman. She told Floella, 'Call me DOK' – short for Duchess of Kent.

'It's been hard work to keep up the standard of not letting down women,' reflects and sums up the founder president. 'Authentic has been the word throughout – and authentic is what we believe in as well as achieving work done well. The vote reformers believed, "You have to hit where it hurts if you are going to alter attitudes." They chose property as the area that hurt commercial interests - and consequently earned respect and attention. What we have done, instead of throwing stones, is to show the immense value of women's work. We believe that if we can confirm the contribution made by women to the community, most of it unpaid, the views of women will be taken seriously. If women gave up their jobs, the community structures would collapse. A reminder is also needed that women still face many difficulties in their working lives.'

Lawyer and Women of the Year director Anne-Marie Piper, who failed her eleven-plus but nevertheless managed to get to university from a secondary modern school, believes that 'it's still necessary to highlight the achievements of women; they don't have the same career pattern as men'. Now she specialises in the law relating to charities and is a partner in her London solicitors' firm, Paisners, which has done much pro bono work for the Women of the Year Lunch and Assembly.

Stockbroker and former Lunch chairman Susan Shaw thinks that it's easier for women to go into the City now than at the start of her career in the sixties. However, she emphasises that 'there's still this glass ceiling, very much so'.

Yet Tony Lothian, a watchful gatekeeper who never seems to sleep, continues to worry away like a terrier at the question: 'What is the voice of the Women of the Year?'

She says, 'In the new millennium it will still be in recognising the value of women's work. Why do women come away from the Lunch on such a high? They say that it's because they have suddenly realised how much women can do. This, then, is the voice of the movement. We celebrate the value of varied women's work as a reminder that no matter where in the world, this vast human asset should not be taken for granted. What women want deserves to be respected and listened to and provided for. But, of course, adequate, accurate information must be given to women and not hidden from them, so that they can make informed choices.'

As the QC Helena Kennedy says of the Lunch: 'It always makes you feel good about women.' And most of all it has helped, in its microcosmic way, to change attitudes, to bring different peoples together and to enhance world understanding. There could be no better feel-good factor than to make a significant difference to society. Recalling once again Lady Stansgate's exhortation to make the Women of the Year far more than a social occasion, Tony Lothian says: 'I think we have kept the faith.'

And so say all of us.

Epilogue
by Floella Benjamin

Women have come a long way; perhaps not as far as we would like but we are making our mark in places our mothers would never have imagined. I have been the chairman of the Women of the Year Lunch and Assembly for the last five years and every time I stand up to address the five hundred women at our Assembly I think of my mother. I see her face smiling in resignation at the limitations that were placed upon her as she fought to make a difference for her daughters. She, like thousands of other women, paved the way for the success and progress of our generation.

We have battled against everything our mothers had to tolerate and tried to make progress in every way possible. However, I sometimes feel we have lost our way and are steering towards a conflict with ourselves as we try to battle forward into the unknown. My association with young people gives me the opportunity to hear their views and what I hear leads me to believe that a gender crisis is imminent. If we don't defuse this situation soon we will be set on a collision course that will put paid to all that our mothers and grandmothers struggled and worked for over the last century.

Men are finding it hard to cope with the new-found 'girl power'. Women are prepared to have babies without them, be their own bosses, work to support themselves and only be dependent on men on their own terms. All this is having a huge impact on young men and they are becoming vulnerable, or feeling left behind or inadequate and resentful. Many of them are adopting a 'laddish culture' to counterbalance the new woman's attitude, which is having disastrous consequences on families. Suicides among young men are higher than ever. These issues, coupled with men's failures to cope with women's success in the workplace and worries about not measuring up as men in the way their fathers and grandfathers did, are matters women have to be concerned about.

Women of the Year have always led the way in highlighting the moral, environmental, health, social and economic dilemmas which society has had to face in the name of progress. Our surveys have always focused on issues long before they become topical. So in this new, fast-changing world, women have to be sure that they are on the right course and do not forfeit all that they have worked for.

Our children's well-being must also be in the forefront of our minds when we think of the future. They are tomorrow's workforce. The quality of care, attention and leadership we show them now must be of the highest, especially in the first three years of their lives, as this will affect their ability to form responsible relationships and lead the way. If we do not address these responsibilities, our mistakes will come back to haunt us. Paid childcare should not be the only option for women who want to go back to work; nor must the nurturing work of mothers who stay at home be devalued. Men should be enabled and encouraged to play a major part in the early formative years of their children, by giving women the option to be the breadwinners. Perhaps this is where full-time financial allowances for both housewives and househusbands should be introduced.

Whether it is men or women who stay at home to look after the children, one of the main messages we must teach them is that gender is not the yardstick by which we measure people. Women and men must come to an understanding and agree to compromise and the youth of today must play a major role in doing this. Many young people, both women and men, already having difficulty in finding suitable partners to spend the rest of their lives with, which could have a dramatic effect on family life. A way to unify and build bridges between genders needs to be found if we are to avoid putting more and more pressure on society and the congruent backlash on our children.

Women of the Year holds the key to better understanding and, as I have said, it is a leading light for the way women run their lives. Personally, I see the future of the Lunch in the hands of the under-thirties. In fact, the Lunch was started by a group of under-thirties. So, in 1999, a Young Consultative Group was formed, who have been quite inspirational. They represent a new generation which accepts and takes full advantage of the advances women have made. But it is important that they know of the past and the long and winding road which has brought us to this point. That is why the writing of a book, which tells us how we have come as far as we have, is important for the future. We are the flagship for women's achievement.

It is essential to carry this legacy forward into the new century. Young women need our wealth of experience to help them build their working, home, love and social lives. They need look no further than Cherie Booth for a brave example of balancing high professional standards with high standards of parenthood. Can today's young women have everything? Do we have the answers yet? Can we make more changes for them or do they take it from here? These are the questions and answers we have tried to encompass here, while also remembering the funny side of life. For we must not forget that laughter is the best therapy for stress, frustration and illness.

My own inspiration has come from Tony Lothian. Her ideals and dreams for nearly fifty years have been to highlight women's work in the interests of society. I have tried to continue her dream in a humble way by striving to make a difference with my leadership style, which is one of empathy and consideration for all. I have tried to give the Lunch a distinctive corporate identity with our brooch, our logo and our brochure. It has been a huge responsibility representing so many women, and I could not have done what I have without the support of a wonderful committee around me. My chairmanship is also, for me, a gift to my mother for all the adversities she had to face and to prove to women, especially those from less privileged backgrounds, that if you work hard, persevere and believe in yourself, then anything is possible. When I stand before the guests at our Assembly and see a woven cultural patchwork of achievement which has helped to make Britain great in the workplace, I realise that we must do whatever it takes to keep Tony's dream alive and to pass the baton on to our future leaders. Her vision has been an historical achievement, for she has continued where Emmeline Pankhurst left off and for that we must all thank her. She is a true inspiration and I am honoured to have been part of her vision.

The story of the Women of the Year has now been told. It takes us to the end of the last century. But after the Millenium Celebration of the Value of Women's Work the banner will be further unfurled.

Speakers and Guests of Honour 1959–1999

As they appeared in the Women of the Year guest lists

Tuesday 29th September 1959
(5th Annual Lunch)
NO THEME

Speakers:
The Countess Mountbatten of Burma, CI
  GBE DCVO
Mrs Alison Munro
Mrs Rosemary Mudie
Miss Diana Reader Harris
Miss Margaret Rutherford
Miss Bronwen Pugh

Guests of Honour:
Dame Peggy Ashcroft DBE
Air Commandant Dame Henrietta Barnett
  DBE ADC
Lady Violet Bonham Carter DBE
Colonel Mary Booth CBE
Professor EM Butler DLit
Miss Leslie Caron
Miss Enid Chanelle
Miss Harriet Cohen CBE
Lady Cynthia Colville DCVO DBE JP
Brigadier Dame Mary Colvin DBE TD
  ADC
Baroness Elliot of Harwood
Professor Margaret Fairlie Hon LLD
Miss Ailsa Garland
Miss Barbara Goalen
Miss Beryl Grey
Miss Hilda N Harding
Miss Olive M Hirst
Miss Lena Horne
Commandant Elizabeth Hoyer-Millar
  OBE Hon ADC
Miss Eileen Joyce
The Viscountess Kilmuir DBE
Dame Laura Knight DBE
Miss D Knight Dix QC
Lady Littlewood BSc JP

Miss Virginia McKenna
Miss Marjorie Marriott OBE
Madame Prunier, Chevalier de la Légion
  d'Honneur
Dame Sybil Thorndike Casson DBE
Madame Vernier

Thursday 6th October 1960
THEME: IF NOT YOU, WHO?

Speakers:
Miss Ailsa Garland
Commandant Dame Elizabeth Hoyer-
  Millar DBE Hon ADC
Miss Evelyn Laye
The Lady Packenham
The Dowager Marchioness of Reading
  GBE CStJ
Mrs Margaret H Thatcher MP

Guests of Honour:
The Lady Mayoress of London (The Hon
  Lady Stockdale)
Miss EC Bather OBE
Colonel Mary Booth CBE
Miss AF Bull
Miss Enid Chanelle
Brigadier Dame Mary Colvin DBE TD
  ADC
Dame May Curwen DBE
Professor Margaret Fairlie Hon LLD
Miss Christina Foyle
Miss Judy Grinham
Colonel EIW Hobkirk CBE TD
Dame Katherine H Jones DBE RRC
Dame Laura Knight DBE RA
Mrs Elizabeth Lane QC
Miss Marjorie Marriott OBE
Miss Nancy Martin
Miss Anna Massey

Mrs M ildred Pace MIPA
Dame Felicity Peake DBE
Mrs Lorna Pegram
Madame Prunier, Chevalier de la Légion
d'Honneur
Miss Bronwen Pugh
Miss Janet Quigley MBE
Baroness Ravensdale of Kedleston
Miss Audrey Russell FRSA
Miss Joanna Scott-Moncrieff
Miss Hannah Stanton
Air Commandant Anne Stephens MBE
Sister Dorothy Thomas GC
Miss Christine Tidmarsh
Miss Tsai Chin
Madame Vernier
Miss Nan Winton
Miss GV Woodman
Mrs Grace Wyndham Goldie

Thursday 6th October 1961
THEME: SUCCESS

Speakers:
Dame Ninette De Valois DBE, Governor
of Royal Ballet and Founder of Royal
Ballet School
Miss Angele Delanghe, only woman
member of the Incorporated Society of
London Fashion Designers
Miss Mary Grieve, Editor of *Woman*
The Rt Hon Patricia Hornsby-Smith DBE,
MP
Mrs Jane Ironside, Professor of Fashion,
Royal College of Art
Miss Anna Neagle CBE

Guests of Honour:
The Lady Mayoress of London (The Hon
Lady Waley-Cohen)
Lady Dorothy MacMillan
Viscountess Astor, former leading fashion
model
Miss Winifred Barker, Chief
Superintendent, Metropolitan (Women)
Police
Lady Violet Bonham Carter DBE, MP
Colonel Mary Booth CBE, Salvation
Army
Mrs Kay Brebner, Director, The National
Magazine Co Ltd
Dame Barbara Brooke DBE, Vice-
Chairman, Conservative Party
Organisation

Miss Marian Care, first Head Gardener of
Westminster Abbey
Miss Enid Chanelle, Director of Fashion
House
Miss Sybil Connolly, Dress Designer
The Hon Beryl Cozens-Hardy JP, Chief
Commissioner for England, Girl
Guides Ass.
Commandant Jean Davies OBE Hon
ADC, Director, WRNS
Professor Margaret Fairlie LLD FRCOG
FRCS
Miss Iris Franklin, President, Women's
Advertising Club of London and
Company Director
Miss Ailsa Garland, Editor of *Vogue*
Miss Beryl Grey, Prima Ballerina
Dame Florence Hancock DBE, Ex-Chief
Woman Officer, Transport and General
Workers' Union; Director of
REMPLOY
Miss Kathleen Harrison, Actress
Colonel EIW Hobkirk CBE TD, Prison
and Borstal Governor, Greenock
Mrs Jenifer Howland, Photographic
Model
Miss Evelyn Laye, Actress
Air Commandant Dame Alice Lowrey
DBE RRC QHNS, Matron-in-Chief,
PMRAFNS
Madame Simone Mirman, Milliner
Miss Dorothy Neville-Rolfe MA,
Principal, House of Citizenship
Miss Mervyn Pike, Asst Postmaster
General
Madame Prunier, Chevalier de la Légion
d'Honneur
Miss Janet Quigley, Asst Head of Talks,
BBC (Sound)
Brig JE Rovett-Drake MBE ADC,
Director, WRAC
Miss Audrey Russell FRSA, Broadcaster
and Scriptwriter
Miss Joanna Scott-Moncrieff, Editor,
Woman's Hour, BBC
Miss Margaret J Smyth CBE, President,
Royal College of Nursing
Air Comm Dame Anne Stephens DBE
ADC, Director, WRAF
Miss Doreen Stephens, Editor, Women's
Programmes, BBC Television
Sister L Thomas GC, Nursing Sister
Miss Christine Tidmarsh, Fashion Model
Mrs Mirabel D Topham, Director of
Grand National Racecourse

Tony Lothian

Odette Hallowes

Lady Georgina Coleridge

Floella Benjamin   Mikki Doyle

Renée Goddard

Valentina Tereshkova

Aung San Suu Kyi

Coretta King

Emmeline Pankhurst

Violet Attlee

A panorama of guests who have attended Lunches over the years

1966

1966

1974

1975

1975

1975

1976

1977

1979

1981

1986

1987

1987

1989

1989

1990

1994

1995

1995

1996

1996

1996

1996

1996

1996

1996

1996

1996

1997

1996

1997

1997

1997

1997

1997

1997

1998

1997

1998

1998

1997

1998

1998

1998

1998

1998

1998

1998

1998

1998

Madame Vernier, Milliner
Miss Mollie Weir, Actress
Mrs Ann Welch, Vice-Chairman, British
  Gliding Association
Dame Rebecca West DBE, Writer
Miss Nan Winton, Broadcasting
  Personality
Miss GV Woodman, Master Bookbinder
The Lord Mayor of York, (Alderman Mrs
  Ivy G Wightman JP BA)
Miss Anna Zinkeisen ROI RDI, Artist

Thursday 4th October 1962
THEME: WHAT IS WOMAN'S PLACE IN SPACE?

Speakers:
The Reverend Mother Clare, Deaconess,
  Community of St Andrew (Anglican)
Miss Josephine Barnes MA DM MRCP
  FRCS FRCOG, Consultant
  Obstetrician and Gynaecologist
Mrs Marjorie Proops, of the *Daily Mirror*
Mrs Ann Welch MBE, Glider Pilot; Vice-
  Chairman, British Gliding Association
Mrs HG Hazelden, Wife of a famous Test
  Pilot
Miss Tessie O'Shea, Artiste

Guests of Honour:
The Lady Mayoress of London (Lady
  Hoare)
Miss Shirley Abicair, Zither Player
Mrs Bridget Auty, Wife of Test Pilot
Miss Winifred T Barker, Chief
  Superintendent, Metropolitan (Women)
  Police
Colonel Mary B Booth CBE, Salvation
  Army (retd)
Mrs Nancy Bryce, Wife of Test Pilot
Mrs Anne Burns BA, Scientific Civil
  Servant
Miss Enid Chanelle, director of Fashion
  House
Professor Kathleen Coburn MA BLitt
  IODE, Editor of *Collected Coleridge*
Miss Elizabeth Cowley, BBC *Tonight*
  Programme
Commandant Jean Davies OBE Hon
  ADC, Director, WRNS
Miss Angele Delanghe, Director of
  Fashion House
Mrs Eileen Dickson, Editor, *Harper's
  Bazaar*
Dame Edith Evans DBE

Lady Fleming MD, Scientist
Lady Frankau MD, Physician
Lady Gamman, MP
Miss Ailsa Garland, Editor, *Vogue*
Miss Beryl Grey, Prima Ballerina
Miss Irene Handl, Actress
Miss Hilda M Harding, Bank Manager
Miss MA Harwood, Bank Manager
Mrs Sybil M Hathaway OBE, La Dame
  de Serk
Begum Ikramullah
Miss Winefride Jackson, Woman's Page
  Editor, *Sunday Telegraph*
H.H. The Maharani of Jaipur
Mrs JE Kelley MA, Governor, HM Prison,
  Holloway
Miss Rosamond Lehmann, Author
Miss WM Lodge, Social Editor, *The
  Times*
Miss Dawn Mackay, Headmistress,
  Heathfield School
Mrs M Marriott OBE, Matron,
  Middlesex Hospital
Madame Simone Mirman, Milliner
Miss Anna Neagle CBE, Actress
Mrs Elizabeth Overbury, Flying Instructor
Miss RN Pearse OBE BA, President,
  Association of Headmistresses
Madame Prunier, Chevalier de la Légion
  d'Honneur
Miss Joan Quennell MBE JP, MP
Miss Janet Quigley MBE, Assistant Head
  of Talks, BBC (Sound)
Miss Kathleen Raine, Poet
Brigadier JE Rivett-Drake MBE ADC,
  Director, WRAC
Miss Anna Russell, International Concert
  Comedienne
Miss Audrey Russell FRSA, BBC
  Broadcaster, Scriptwriter
Miss Joanna Scott-Moncrieff, Editor,
  Woman's Hour, BBC
Miss Antoinette Sibley, Prima Ballerina
Sir Commandant Dame Anne Stephens
  DBL MBE Hon ADC, Director, WRAF
Miss Doreen Stephens, Editor, *Woman's
  Hour*, BBC
Miss Noel Streatfeild, Novelist
Mrs Margaret Thatcher MP JTPS,
  Ministry of Pensions and National
  Insurance
Sister Dorothy L Thomas GC, Nursing
  Sister
Miss Mirabel D Topham, Owner, Grand
  National Racecourse

Madame Vernier, Milliner
Dame Irene Ward DBE MP JP

Thursday 10th October 1963
THEME: IS HAPPINESS A LOST ART?

Speakers:
Miss Doreen Stephens, Editor, Women's
  Programmes, BBC Television and
  President, Women's Press Club of London
The Hon Charlotte Bingham, Author
Miss Hy Hazell, Actress
Miss Mary Quant, Dress Designer

Guests of Honour:
Miss Josephine Barnes MA DM MRCP
  FRCS FRCOG, Consultant
  Gynaecologist
The Rev Mary Biddle BA, Congregational
  Minister
Dame Joyce Bishop DBE MA,
  Headmistress (retd)
Miss Enid Chanelle, Managing Director,
  Fashion House Group
HE Mme del C Chittenden, Costa Rican
  Ambassador
The Rev Mother Clare, Deaconess,
  Community of St Andrew (Anglican)
Air Commandant Dame Jean Conan
  Doyle DBE Hon ADC, Director,
  WRAF
Miss Annelli Drummond-Hay, Show
  Jumper
Miss Christina Foyle, Director
Miss Ailsa Garland, Editor
Mrs Myrtle Reeves Gorgla, Liberian
  Consul General
Miss Beryl Grey, Prima Ballerina
Colonel EIW Hobkirk CBE TD, Prison
  and Borstal Governor
Mrs Jennifer Howland, Photographic
  Model
Miss Ida Kar, Photographer
Miss D Knight Dix QC, Queen's Counsel
Miss Mabel G Lawson OBE MB CHB
  SRN, Pres. Royal College of Nursing;
  Ntl Council of Nurses of UK
Miss Moura Lympany FRAM,
  International Concert Pianist
Miss Millicent Martin, Actress
Mme Simone Mirman, Designer/Milliner
Miss Veronica Papworth, Editor
Mrs Phyliss Perkins, Teacher/Runner:
  WAAA 880 champ. Ex world record
  holder, 3x880 Relay and 1500m Relay

Miss Janet Quigley, Pres. International
  Assoc. of Women in Radio & TV
Dame Marie Rambert DBE, Légion
  d'Honneur, Founder and Directress,
  Ballet Rambert
Dame Barbara Salt DBE, Diplomat
Sister Dorothy Thomas GC, Nursing
  Sister
Mme Vernier, Designer and Milliner
Mrs Harold Wilson

Monday 12th October 1964
THEME: MY FAVOURITE MAN

Speakers:
Miss Felicity Green, Assistant Editor,
  Daily Mirror
Miss Heather Jenner, Founder and
  Director, The Marriage Bureau, W.1
Miss Edna O'Brien, Author and
  Playwright: *The Country Girl; The Girl
  with Green Eyes* etc.
Mrs Gabrielle Pike JP, Chairman,
  National Federation of Women's
  Institutes
Miss Annie Ross, Jazz Singer

Guests of Honour:
Miss Winifred Barker, Chief
  Superintendent, Metropolitan (Women)
  Police
Miss Molly Bishop (Lady George Scott),
  Artist
Colonel Mary Booth, Salvation Army
Mrs Ernestine Carter OBE, Women's Page
  Editor, *Sunday Times*
Miss Enid Chanelle, Managing Director,
  Fashion House Group
Miss Tsai Chin, Actress
HE Mme del C Chittenden, Ambassador
  for Costa Rica
Woman Police Constable Margaret
  Cleland GC
Miss Harriet Cohen CBE, International
  Concert Pianist
Air Commandant Dame Jean Conan
  Doyle, Director, WRAF
Mlle Angele Delanghe, Haute Couture
Miss Nora Downey, Woman's Page
  Editor, *News of the World*
Commandant Margaret Drummond OBE,
  Director, WRNS
Mrs Vivienne Entwistle, Portrait
  Photographer

Miss IPM Freeston MA, Principal, Westminster Tutors
Miss Ailsa Garland, Editor, *Woman's Journal*
Miss Beryl Grey, Prima Ballerina
Miss Hilda Harding, Bank Manager
The Countess of Harewood
Mrs Denis Healey, Social Services, wife of MP
Brigadier JE Henderson Hon ADC, Director, WRAC
Professor Mrs Janey Ironside Hon DES RCA, Professor of Fashion, Royal College of Art
Miss Alison James, Advertisement Manager, *Harper's Bazaar*
Miss Moura Lympany, International Concert Pianist
Miss Beatrix Miller, Editor, *Vogue*
Mme Simone Mirman, Designer/Milliner
Dr Sylvia Munro JP, Pres. Nat. Fed. Business & Professional Women's Clubs, Gt Britain & NI
Miss Julia M Nash, Show Jumper
Miss Patricia Neal, Actress
Miss Mary Quant, Dress Designer
Dame Barbara Salt DBE, Diplomat
Miss Alice Saxby MVO, Hospital Matron
Dame Margaret Shepherd DBE, Chairman, National Union of Conservative & Unionist Assoc.
Miss MEG Stocker, Governor, HM Prison
Sister Dorothy L Thomas GC, Nursing Sister
Miss Ann Townsend, Show Jumper
Miss Florence Udell SRN SCM, President, National Council of Nurses
Miss Jane Wildman, First Woman Chairman, Oxford University Student Council

Monday 4th October 1965
THEME: THE CHANCE OF A LIFETIME

Speakers:
Miss Drusilla Beyfus, Features Editor, *Weekend Telegraph*
The Reverend Sister Jude MA EdB, Director, Child Welfare Clinic
Miss Jennie Lee MP, Joint Parliamentary Under-Secretary of State, Department of Education & Science
Miss Beryl Reid, Actress
Miss Monica Sims, Editor, *Woman's Hour*, BBC

Guests of Honour:
Mrs Alison Adburgham, Fashion Correspondent, *Guardian*
Miss Maxine Audley, Actress
Miss Honor Balfour, Political Journalist
Miss Winifred Barker, Chief Superintendent, Metropolitan (Women) Police
Miss Josephine Barnes MA DM MRCP FRCS, Gynaecologist
Colonel Mary Booth CBE, Salvation Army (Rtd)
Miss Mary Cartwright FRS MA DPhil DSc, Mistress of Girton College
Miss Enid Chanelle, Co. Director and Chairman
Lady Georgina Coleridge, Director, *Country Life* & George Newnes Ltd; President, Women's Press Club, London
Dame Jean Conan Doyle DBE ADC, Director, WRAF
Her Excellency The Costa Rican Ambassador
Mrs Fleur Cowles Meyer, Writer and Artist
Miss Constance Cummings, Actress
Commandant Margaret Drummond OBE MA Hon ADC WRNS, Director, WRNS
Mrs Dorothy Dunnett, Portrait Painter and Historical Novelist
Miss Eunice Gayson
Mrs G Wyndham Goldie OBE
Mrs Myrtle Reeves Gorgla, Liberian Consul General in London
Miss Felicity Green, Assistant Editor, *Daily Mirror*
Miss Beryl Grey, Prima Ballerina
Miss Catherine Hall, General Secretary, Royal College of Nursing
The Countess of Harewood
Dr KM Kenyon CBE MA DLitt LHD FBA FSA, Principal, St Hugh's College, Oxford
The Right Hon The Lady Mayoress of London (Lady Miller)
Miss Ruth Lynam, Editor, *Harpers Bazaar*
Miss Mary Marquis, BBC, Scottish Compère
Miss Millicent Martin, Actress
Mrs Reginald Maudling, Politics
Miss Beatrix Miller, Editor, *Vogue*
Madame Simone Mirman, Designer/Milliner

179

Dr Sylvia Munro JP, Pres. Nat. Fed. Business and Prof. Women's Clubs, Gt Britain & NI

Mrs Gabrielle Pike JP, Chairman, National Federation of Women's Institutes

Mrs Mary Rand MBE, Olympic Athlete

Dame Barbara Salt DBE, Diplomat

Miss Anne Scott-James, Columnist, *Daily Mail*

Miss Dorothy Tutin, Actress

Madame Vernier, Designer/Milliner

Miss Pauline Vogelpoel, Organising Secretary, The Contemporary Art Society

Miss Katherine Whitehorn, Columnist, *Observer*

October 1966
THEME: THE BEE IN MY BONNET

Speakers:

Miss Hermione Baddeley, Famous Comedienne

Mrs Shirley C Becke, Chief Superintendent, Metropolitan (Women's) Police

Miss Thora Hird, Stage and Television Star

Miss Audrey Slaughter, Editor, *Honey* and *Petticoat* Magazines

Miss Theodora Turner OBE ARRC SRN SCM DN, Jubilee President, National Council of Nurses of the UK

Guests of Honour:

Mrs Sylvia Anderson, Writer and TV Producer of *Thunderbirds*

Miss Maxine Audley, Actress

Miss Hermione Baddeley, Actress

Miss Belinda Bellville, Dress Designer

Miss Drusilla Beyfus, Features Editor, *Weekend Telegraph*

Colonel Mary B Booth CBE, Salvation Army (Retd)

Mrs ER Cassie, Social Editor, *Daily Telegraph*

Miss Enid Chanelle, Company Chairman and Director

Miss Wendy Cooper, Hannen Swaffer Award 'Woman Journalist of the Year 1966'

Miss Elizabeth Cowley, BBC TV Producer

Miss Marian W Curtin SRN SCM, First Woman Pres. of NALGO and Hospital Matron

Commandant Dame Margaret Drummond DBE MA Hon ADC, Director, WRNS

Mrs Dorothy Dunnett, Historical Novelist

Miss Irene PM Feeston MA, Tutorial Director

Mrs Vera Finlay, Chairman, Scottish Conservative Party

Miss Felicity Green, Assistant Editor, *Daily Mirror*

Miss Beryl Grey, Prima Ballerina

Miss Marea Hartman MBE, Team Manager, Gt Britain Women's Athletic Team

Brigadier Dame Joanna Henderson DBE ADC, Director, WRAC

Air Commandant Dame Felicity Hill DBE ADC, Director, WRAF

Professor Mrs Janey Ironside Hon DES RCA, Professor of Fashion, Royal College of Art

The Lady Mayoress of London (Lady Denny)

Miss Ruth Lyman, Editor, *Harper's Bazaar*

Miss Mary Messer, Director, Printing Company

Miss Beatrix Miller, Editor, *Vogue*

Madame Simone Mirman, Royal Milliner

Dr Sylvia D Munro JP, Pres. Natl Fed. Business and Prof. Women's Clubs of Gt Britain and Ireland

Mrs Florence Nagle, Racehorse Trainer and Breeder

Miss Julia Nash, Horse Jumper

Mrs Patricia Neal Dahl, Actress – Oscar Awards

Miss Marguerite D Peacock BA Oxon, Journalist; first Woman President Elect, Institute of Journalists and NUJ

Miss Nadine Peppard, Sec. Natl Committee for Commonwealth Immigrants

Professor Mary Pickford DSc FRS, Physiologist

Miss Jean Plaidy, Writer

Miss Suzanne Puddefoot, Women's Editor, *The Times*

Miss Mary Quant OBE, Dress Designer

Mrs Mary Rand MBE, Olympic Athlete

Dame Barbara Salt DBE, Diplomat

Miss Audrey Slaughter, Editor, *Honey* Magazine

Miss J Stovell, Federation President, Soropotimists 1966

Mrs Margaret Thatcher MA BSc, MP
Miss Theodora Turner OBE ARRC, Jubilee Pres. Nat. Council of Nurses of the UK
Miss Dorothy Tutin, Actress
Twiggy, Top London Fashion Model
Miss Nora Walley, Pres. Brit. Assoc. of Women Executives of Gt Britain; Chairman and Managing Director, The Walley Group
The Lady Mayoress of Westminster (Mrs AL Burton)
Miss Anna Zinkkeisen ROI RDI, Artist

Monday 9th October 1967
THEME: HAVE WE GONE TOO FAR?

Speakers:
Madame Svetlana Beriozova, Prima Ballerina
Lady Chichester, Deputy Managing Director, Francis Chichester Ltd; Editor, *London Woman*
The Lady Mayoress of London
Miss Ann Mallalieu, first Woman President of the Cambridge Union
Mrs Shirley Williams MA MP, Minister of State for Education & Science

Guests of Honour:
Miss Joan Bakewell, Television Personality
Miss Josephine Barnes DM FRCS FRCP FBCOG, Consultant Gynaecologist
Mrs Shirley Becke, Chief Superintendent, Metropolitan (Women) Police
Miss Prunella R Bodington MA, President of the Headmistress Association
Colonel Mary Booth CBE, Salvation Army
Miss Mary Cartwright FRS MA, Mistress of Girton College
Miss Enid Chanelle, Director, Fashion House Group
Mrs Yvonne Cross, Editor, *Nursing Mirror*
Dame Ninette de Valois DBE, Director, Royal School of Ballet
Miss Josephine Douglas, Television Producer
Mrs Dorothy Dunnett, Historical Novelist
Miss Ursula Eason, Acting Head, BBC Children's Programmes
Miss IPM Freeston MA, Principal, The Westminster Tutors

Mrs JM Goodman, President, Royal College of Midwives
Miss Nellie E Harris FIPA, first Woman President, Glasgow Publicity Club
Miss Wendy Hawes, Hairdresser
Woman Superintendent Elizabeth Kay, Women Police, Glasgow
Miss Joan Kemp-Welch, Television Producer
Dame Laura Knight DBE RWC, Artist
Miss Margaret Lane (The Countess of Huntingdon), Author
Miss Beatrix Lehmann, Actress
Lulu, Singer
Miss Jean Metcalfe, Broadcaster
Madame Simone Mirman, Royal Milliner
Miss Barbara Mullen, Actress
Mrs Douglas Murray, Jubilee President, Scottish Women's Rural Institutes
Mrs Patricia Neal Dahl, Actress
Miss Carola Oman (Lady Lenanton), Author
Miss Marguerite D Peacock BA, first President of Institute of Journalists
Baroness Philips, Politician
Miss Mervyn Pike BA, MP
Miss Nyree Dawn Porter, Actress
Miss Charlotte Rampling, Actress
Miss Beryl Reid, Actress
Dame Barbara Salt DBE, Foreign Office
Miss Monica Sims, Editor, BBC *Woman's Hour*
Miss Audrey Slaughter, Editor, *Honey* and *Petticoat* Magazines
Miss Sally-Anne Stapleford, British Figure Skating Champion
The Dowager Marchioness of Reading GBE, CStJ (The Baroness Swanborough)
Miss Doreen Taylor, Managing Editor, *Border Life*
Professor Rosalyn Tureck Hon MusD, Concert Artist
Miss Virginia Wade BSc, International Tennis Player
Miss Nora Walley, Pres. British Assoc. of Women Executives; Managing Director, The Walley Group
The Lady Mayoress of Westminster
Mrs Mary Whitehouse, General Secretary, National Viewers & Listeners' Association
Mrs DM Wing, Governor, HMP. Holloway
Miss Irene Worth, Actress

Speakers:
Miss Julie Driscoll, Singer
Miss Marion Murtagh ACCA ACIS, Computer expert, who controls Britain's Computer Services (Birmingham) Ltd
The Reverend Sister Mary Perpetua FC, Hospital Administrator
Miss Susanne Puddefoot, Editor, Woman's Page, *The Times*
Dr Jane Somerville MRCS LRCP, Cardiologist-Physician, Member of the Transplant Team

Guests of Honour:
Brigadier The Hon Mary M Anderson MBE Hon ADC, Director, WRAC
Mrs Sylvia Anderson, Film Director/Producer
Miss PP Arnold, Singer
Mrs Joan Bakewell, Broadcaster
Frau Edith Baumann, Single-Handed Trans-Atlantic Competitor 1968
Mrs Shirley Becke, Woman Chief Superintendent, Metropolitan Police
The Baroness Birke JP, Associate Editor of *Nova*
Miss Sheila Black, Woman's Editor, *Financial Times*
Miss Mary Blakeley SRN SCM OHNC, President, Royal College of Nursing
Colonel Mary Booth CBE, Salvation Army
Mrs PEM Braund, Past Pres., Holborn Business & Professional Women's Club; Editor, Group Magazine
Mrs Pauline Crabbe JP, Magistrate and Social Worker
Miss Isobel Curry SRN SCM, Nursing Sister, National Heart Hospital
Mrs Dorothy Dunnett, Historical Novelist
Miss Jan Gay, *Evening Standard* Girl of the Year
Mrs Carmen Gronau, Art Expert; Director, Sotheby's
Miss Gena Hawthorn, International skiing champion
Mrs HE Hickson, President, Association of Inner Wheel Clubs
Miss Angela Huth, Broadcaster, TV Reporter
Miss Winefride M Jackson, Editor, Woman's Page, *Sunday Telegraph*

Mrs Kathie Johnson, Sheriff of Southampton
Commandant M M Kettlewell CBE Hon ADC, Director, WRNS
Mrs Jill Knight MBE, MP
Miss Patricia Lamburn, Teenage Group Director, IPC Magazine Division
Mrs Mollie Lee, Editor, *Woman's Hour*, BBC
The Lady Mayoress of London
The Hon Mrs Maurice Macmillan, Chairman, Women's Conservative and Unionist Party
Mme Simone Mirman, Royal Milliner
Miss Anna Neagle, Actress
Mrs Betty Parsons, Teacher of relaxation for ante-natal preparation
Miss MD Peacocke BA (Oxon), Past President, Institute of Journalists
Miss Sïan Phillips, Actress
Miss Nyree Dawn Porter, Actress
Miss Stella Richman, Television Producer/Director
Lady (Alec) Rose
Miss Sheila Scott OBE, Round World Solo Aviator
Miss Anne Sharpley, Journalist
Miss Audrey Slaughter, Editor-in-Chief, *Honey* and *Petticoat* Magazines
Miss Sally-Anne Stapleford, British Figure Skating Champion 1963–1968
Miss Rita Tushingham, Actress
Mrs Helen Vlachos, Editor, *Hellenic Review*
Miss Nora Walley, President, British Assoc. Women Executives, Company Director
The Lady Mayoress of Westminster
Mrs Mary Whitehouse, General Secretary, National Viewers & Listeners' Association
Miss Katherine Whitehorn BA, Journalist
Mrs Harold Wilson

Speakers:
Miss Harriet Crawley, Minister for Youth; Columnist; Past Editor of *Senate* Magazine; Author of *A Degree of Defiance*
Miss Marie Jennings, Chancellor of (The Exchequer) Waste; Financial Columnist;

Woman's Journal Chairman; Publicity
Committee of Women's Advisory
Committee; BSI Editor of
Publications
Miss Peggy Nuttall, Minister of Health &
Social Security; Editor, *Nursing Times*
Miss Sheila Scott OBE, Minister of
Transport; Round the World Solo
Aviator
Mrs Joanna Spicer OBE, Minister of
Communications; Assistant Controller,
BBC Television Developments
Miss Irene Worth, Home Secretary;
Actress
Miss Sheila Hancock, Actress

Guests of Honour:
Mrs Joan Bakewell, BBC & TV
Personality
Miss Josephine Barnes MA DM FRCP
FRCS FRCOG, Obstetrician and
Gynaecologist
Mrs Shirley Becke, Commander,
Metropolitan (Women's) Police
Miss Linda Blandford, BBC Personality
Mrs Joyce Butler MP
Miss Winifred Carr, Editor, Women's
Page, *Daily Telegraph*
Miss Wendy Craig, Actress
Professor Monica M Cole BSc PhD,
Professor of Geography, University of
London
Mrs Norma Corney, ITV Director
Miss Kathleen L Cottrell JP MA,
Headmistress
Miss Jane Drew FRIBA FIarb FSLA,
Architect
Miss Julie Driscoll, Actress
Mrs Dorothy Dunnett, Historical Novelist
Miss Fenella Fielding, Actress
Miss Renée Goddard, Head of Script
Dept, ATV
Miss Ronald Hallifax JP, President of
Mothers' Union
Miss Sheila Hancock, Actress
Colonel Elspeth Hobkirk CBE TD,
Governor HM Prison, Greenock
Miss Imogen Holst, Musician
Miss Winefride Jackson, Woman's Editor,
Sunday Telegraph
Mrs Christine Janes (Truman),
International Tennis Player
Miss Geraldine Jones, Ex-President of
Oxford University
Mrs Joanna Kelley MA, Assistant

Director of HM Prisons
"Jennifer", Mrs Elizabeth Kenward,
Social Editor, *Queen* Magazine
Mrs Anne Kerr MP, Labour MP for
Rochester and Chatham since 1964
The Reverend Elizabeth Kinniburgh MA,
Lecturer in Religious Education (First
Woman Ordained as Minister in
Church of Scotland)
Mrs Jill Knight MBE, MP
Dr Elizabeth Laverick PhD BSc FIEE,
AinstPsmiee (Herts) Head of Research
& Advanced Projects, Elliott-
Automation Radar Systems Ltd
Mrs Mollie Lee, Editor, *Woman's Hour*,
BBC
Miss Vera Lynn OBE, Singer
Miss Helene Middleweek, 1968 President
of Cambridge Union
Madame Simone Mirman, Royal Milliner
Miss Margot Naylor, Financial
Columnist, 'Money Mail'
Miss Suzanne Neve, Actress
Miss Meg Peacocke BA, Journalist
Lady Petty, Journalist, Wife of Agent
General for State of Victoria in London
Miss Mervyn Pike BA, MP
Miss Jean Rooke, Woman's Editor, *Daily
Sketch*
Mrs Ginette Scott, Mutual help, Mother's
Emergency Service
Miss Antoinette Sibley, Ballerina
Miss Audrey Slaughter, Journalist,
Evening News
Mrs Joanna Spicer OBE, Asst Controller,
BBC Television Developments
Mrs Sheila Thomas, Mother of Sextuplets
Mrs Julia Turner, 1969 *Daily Mail* Trans-
Atlantic Air Race
Miss Nora Walley, President, British
Assoc. Women Executives, Company
Director
The Lady Mayoress of Westminster
Sister Wilson MA (Oxon), Education

Monday 5th October 1970
THEME: ASPECTS OF VIOLENCE

Speakers:
Baroness Masham of Ilton, Life Peeress
Miss Myrella Cohen QC
Miss Joan Hall, Conservative MP for
Keighley, Yorkshire
Miss Jacky Gillott BA, Novelist, Journalist

Miss Buzz Goodbody BA, first woman to direct plays of Royal Shakespeare Company

Guests of Honour:
Miss Moira Anderson RSAM, Singer
Miss Eileen Atkins, Actress
Mrs Joan Bakewell, TV Personality
Mrs Shirley Becke, Commander, Metropolitan (Women's) Police
The Rt Hon Baroness Birk JP BSc (Econ), Journalist; Chairman, Health Education Council
Miss Mary Blakeley SRN SCM OHNC, President, The Royal College of Nursing
Commandant DM Blundell Hon ADC, Director, Women's Royal Naval Service
Miss Jane Bullen, Olympic Athlete, Nurse, Secretary
Mrs Maurice Bulpitt, 1970 President, Assoc. of Inner Wheel Club
Mrs Thelma Cazalet-Keir CBE, Ex MP, Writer
Mrs JC Cockroft, President, Women's Advisory Council on Solid Fuel
Dame Margaret Cole DBE OBE, Author; Local Government Education Chairman
Miss Wendy Craig, Actress
Mrs Delia Dalton, Co. Man. Director; President Nat. Fed. of Business and Prof. Women's Clubs
Miss Jessie Evans, Actress
Miss Dulcie Gray, Actress, Writer
Lady Holland-Martin OBE, Chairman, NSPCC
The Rt Hon Dame Patricia Hornsby-Smith, DBE MP, Conservative Member for Chislehurst
Miss Hattie Jacques, Actress
Miss Marie Jennings, Financial Columnist
Miss Glynis Johns, Actress
Miss Jean S Law QPM, HM Assistant Inspector of Constabulary
Mrs Mollie Lee, Editor, *Woman's Hour*, BBC
Mrs Gina MacKinnon OBE, Chairman, Drambuie Liqueur Co.
Miss Beatrix Miller, Editor *Vogue*
Madame Simone Mirman, Royal Milliner
Miss Sheila L Morrison FCIS, President, The Chartered Institute of Secretaries Women's Society
Dame Anna Neagle DBE, Actress

Miss Peggy Nuttall SRN MCSP, Editor, *Nursing Times*
Mrs Derek Parker-Bowles, Chief Commissioner of the Girl Guides
Miss RC Perkes SRN SCM MTD, President, The Royal College of Midwives
Mrs Robin Pleydell-Bouverie, Interior Decorator
Miss Stella Richman, Managing Director; Controller of Programmes, London Weekend Television
Miss Antoinette Sibley, Ballerina
Mrs Ailsa Stanley JP, Journalist
Mrs C Mary Stott, Women's Page Editor, *Guardian*; 1970 President, Women's Press Club
Mrs John Tilney, President, National Council of Women
Miss Dorothy Tutin, Actress
The Dowager Marchioness of Tweeddale
Miss Margaret Tyzack OBE, Actress
Miss Virginia Wade BSc, Tennis Player
Mrs Bernice T Weston, Attorney, Director of 'Weight Watchers'
Miss Freda Young OBE, HM Consul-General, Rotterdam

Monday 4th October 1971
THEME: QUALITY IN LIFE

Speakers:
Miss Dora Bryan, Actress
Miss Caroline Coon, Co-Founder of Release
Professor Alice Garnett BA PhD
Miss Renée Goddard, Scripts Director, ATV
Miss Nicolette Milnes Walker, Lone Atlantic Sailor

Guests of Honour:
Miss Margaret Alexander, Social Editor, *The Times*
Miss Sue Aston, Leading Show Jumper
Viscountess Astor, Owner/Manager, Chain of Boutiques
Mrs Joan Bakewell, Broadcaster
The Mayor of Cambridge, Councillor Mrs JAC Barker
Miss Jill Bennett, Actress
Mrs Vera Biggs
Miss Lorna Blackie, Company Director
Miss Mary Blakeley OBE, President, Royal College of Nursing

Miss Betty E Box OBE, Film Producer
Lady Chichester, Map Publisher
Her Excellency Miss GKT Chiepe MBE,
High Commissioner of Botswana
Dr Janet Cockcroft, President, National
Council of Women of Great Britain
Miss Ita Connors, Matron, Osborne
House
Miss Jilly Cooper, Journalist
Miss Wendy Cooper, Journalist and
Broadcaster
Miss Cicely Courtneidge, Actress
Mrs Yvonne Cross, Editor, *Nursing
Mirror*
Miss Margret Dalglish, Matron, King
Edward VII's Hospital for Officers
Mrs DG Dalton, President, Nat. Fed. of
Business and Professional Women's
Clubs
Miss Jane B Drew FRIBA FIarb FSIA,
Architect
Miss Sylvia Dutton, Matron, The London
Clinic
Mrs Winifred Ewing MA LLB, Solicitor
and Notary Public
The Duchess of Gratton DCVO JP
Miss Felicity Green, Woman's Page Editor,
Daily Mirror
Mrs Rosemary Hawley Jarman,
Authoress
Miss Angela Huth, Writer/TV Reporter
Miss Winifrede Jackson, Woman's Page
Editor, *Sunday Telegraph*
Miss Barbara Kelly
Mrs Elizabeth Kenward, Social Editor,
Harpers & Queen
Mrs J Knight MBE, MP
Miss Wyn Knowles, Editor, *Woman's
Hour* BBC
Mrs Mollie Lee, Retired Editor, *Woman's
Hour*
Miss Janet Lyle, Dress Designer, 'Annacat'
Boutique
Miss Winifred Mathews, Winner of the
Birmingham Post Competition
Dame Margaret Miles DBE BA,
Headmistress, Mayfield School, Putney
Madame Simone Mirman, Royal Milliner
Miss Jean Morton, Producer, *Women
Today*, ATV
Miss Jean Muir, Dress Designer
Miss Carola Oman CBE FSA FRSL,
FRHistSoc, Authoress and Historian
Mrs Sally Oppenheim MP

Mrs Nalini Pant, Gynaecologist, Wife of
High Commissioner for India.
Mrs Betty Parsons, Teacher of Relaxation
Miss Jane Reed, Editor, *Woman's Own*
Lieutenant Colonel Janet Saunders,
Salvation Army Officer
Miss Grace F Schofield SRN SCM
DN(Lond), Matron, University College
Hospital
Miss Sheila Scott OBE
Mrs Vinaya Teelock, Barrister, Wife of
High Commissioner for Mauritius
Miss Joan Turner, Actress
Lady Mayoress of Westminster
Mrs Mary Whitehouse
Mrs Hugh Wontner

October 1972
THEME: FREEDOM

Speakers:
Miss Dora Bryan, Actress
Miss Caroline Coon, Co-Founder of
Release
Professor Alice Garnett BA PhD

Guests of Honour:
HRH Princess Anne
Miss Margaret Alexander, Social Editor,
The Times
The Countess of Arran, Champion Power
Boat Driver
Miss Nadine Beddington FRIBA FSIA,
Vice-President, RIBA
Miss Mary Blakeley OBE SRN, President,
Royal College of Nursing
Miss Betty E Box OBE, Film Producer
Miss Barbara Buss, Editor, *Woman*
Mrs Jo Camp, Vice-President, Women
Caring
Miss Julie Covington, Actress
Miss Mary Dawney, Lady in Waiting to
HRH Princess Anne
Miss Janet E Fookes BA, MP
Miss Dulcie Grey, Actress
Miss Felicity Green, Woman's Page Editor,
Daily Mirror
Miss Catherine Hall, only Woman
Member of the Commission on
Industrial Relations
Miss Margaret Hall DES RCA MSIA,
Exhibition Officer at the British
Museum
Miss Diana Hart, Actress

Miss Patricia Hayes, Actress
Mrs Caroline Heller, TV Commission
  Officer for the ACTT
Miss Margaret Holt BA, Stockbroker
Miss Joyce Hopkirk, Editor,
  Cosmopolitan
Miss Harriet Hopper, first Woman on
  Nat. Comm. Amalgamated Union of
  Engineering Workers
Mrs Estée Lauder, Cosmetician
Lulu, Singer
Miss Monica Mason, Ballet Dancer
Dame Margaret Miles, Headmistress,
  Mayfield School
Madame Simone Mirman, Royal Milliner
Miss Jean Morton, Producer, *Women Today*
Mrs Derek Parker-Bowles, Chief
  Commissioner, Girl Guides Association
Mrs Marie Patterson, National Woman
  Officer of the Transport & General
  Workers Union
Mrs Sally Ramsden, President, National
  Federation of Business and Professional
  Women's Clubs of GB & NI
Miss Jane Reed, Editor, *Womans Own*
Miss June Ritchie, Actress
Lieutenant Colonel Janet Saunders,
  Salvation Army Officer
Miss Sheila Scott OBE, Pilot
Mrs Mary Stott, Columnist, *Guardian*
Mrs Christine Truman-James, Tennis
  Player
Miss Meriel Tutnell, First Woman Jockey
Mrs Jean M Tyrell, Chairman, Sirdar Ltd
Miss Virginia Wade BSc, Tennis Player
The Lady Mayoress of Westminster
Dr Cynthia L White, Senior Lecturer in
  Sociology, City of London Polytechnic
Miss Katherine Whitehorn, Columnist,
  Observer
Mrs Mary Whitehouse, Hon Gen. Sec.
  National Viewers & Listeners' Association
Miss Angela Wyatt, Editor, *Woman and
  Home*

Monday 8th October 1973
THEME: ACHIEVEMENT

Speakers:
HRH The Dutchess of Kent
Mrs Mary Wilson, Poetess
The Rt Hon The Baroness Seear, Reader
  in Personnel Management at the
  London School of Economics

Miss Jean Muir, Dress Designer
Miss Caroline Green, Actress
Miss Angela Lansbury, Actress

Guests of Honour:
Mrs Laura Ashley
Mrs Maralyn Bailey, Sailor
Mrs Maureen Baker, Design Director
Miss Josephine Barnes DM FRCP FRCS
  FRCOG, Consultant Gynaecologist
Mrs Jenny Barraclough, Documentary
  Producer
Miss Barbara Buss, Journalist, Editor of
  Woman
Miss Suzanne Cadden, Golfer, Winner of
  World Junior Golf Tournament
Dame Mary Cartwright DBE FRS ScD,
  Mathematician
Miss Sinead Cusack, Actress
Lady Douglas-Home
The Rt Hon Mrs Peggy Fenner MP,
  Parliamentary Secretary, Ministry of
  Food and Agriculture
Mrs John Forbes Love, Chairman,
  Church of Scotland's Women's
  Committee
Miss Catherine Hall CBE SRN, General
  Secretary of the Royal College of
  Nursing
Miss Susan Hampshire, Actress
Miss Doris Hare MBE, Actress
Miss Diane Hart, Actress
Miss DM Hawkins OBE SRN SCM MTD
Professor Hilde Himmelweit MA PhD
Mrs Mary Hobbs, Spokesman for the
  Nightcleaners' Campaign and Women's
  Liberation Movement
Mrs B Kenward, Social Editor, *Harpers &
  Queen*
Mrs MH Lampard JP, President, National
  Council of Women
Miss Betty Lockwood, Chief Woman
  Officer of the Labour Party
Lady Medawar, Chairman, Margaret
  Pyke Centre
Dame Margaret Miles DBE BA DCL
Madame Simone Mirman, Royal Milliner
Mrs Frances Anne Morris, Chairman,
  National Association for Family Life
Miss Donna Maria Newman, Pop Singer
Miss Anne Nightingale, Broadcaster and
  Journalist
Mrs Derek Parker-Bowles, Chief
  Commissioner, Girl Guides Association
Mrs Betty Parsons, Teacher of Relaxation

186

Mrs Marie Patterson OBE BA, National Woman Officer of the Transport and General Workers Union

The Rt Hon The Baroness Phillips JP

Major Elsie Pull, Salvation Army Officer

Mrs Sally Ramsden, President, National Federation of Business and Professional Women's Clubs of Great Britain and Northern Ireland

Miss Esther Rantzen, Broadcaster

Miss Jean Rook, Journalist

Miss Sheila Scott, Pilot

The Rt Hon The Baroness Sharples

Mrs Grace Smith, Pearly Queen

The Rt Hon Margaret Thatcher MP, Secretary of State for Education and Science

Miss Pauline Vogelpoel, Organising Secretary, The Contemporary Arts Society

The Lady Mayoress of Westminster

Miss Katherine Whitehorn, Columnist

Miss Billie Whitelaw, Actress

Miss R Yaffe, General Secretary, Union of Women Teachers

The Rt Hon The Baroness Young

October 1974

THEME: THE IMPORTANCE OF BEING A WOMAN

Speakers:

Miss Margaret Drabble, Author

Miss Andrée Grenfell, Managing Director, Elizabeth Arden Limited

Miss Mary Peters, Athlete

Dr Faith Spicer, Medical Director of London Youth Advisory Centre, Chairman of Inner London Juvenile Court Panel

Guests of Honour:

Miss Margaret Alexander, Social Editor, *The Times*

Air Commodore MG Allott ADC, WRAF Officer

Mrs Laura Ashley, Designer

Dame Josephine Barnes DBE MA DM FRCP FRCS FRCOG, Consultant Gynaecologist

Miss Mary Blair-Black BSc (Econ), Economic Survey Officer, Southern Region, British Railways

Miss Eve Bonham, Yachtswoman

Miss Betty E Box OBE, Film Producer

Miss Rowena Brassey, Lady in Waiting to HRH Princess Anne

The Reverend Kathleen Burgess, Methodist Minister

Miss Barbara A Edwards, Weather Forecaster

Miss Christine Anne Evans, Blue Button in the Stock Exchange

Miss Clare Francis, Yachtswoman

Miss Cecilia Freeman, Director, The Thames Motor Boat Co Ltd

Mrs H Gestetner OBE, Director

Miss Roberta Gibbs, Stunt Artist

Miss Dulcie Gray, Actress/Writer

Miss Anouska Hempel, Actress

Mrs GA Howard CEng MIMechE AMBIM, President, Women's Engineering Society

Miss Gayle Hunnicutt, Actress

Miss Sandi Jones, Broadcaster

Miss Barbara Kelly, Actress

Mrs Betty Knightly, Barrister, Parliamentary Candidate

Miss Wyn Knowles, Editor of *Woman's Hour*

Dr Una Kroll, Parliamentary Candidate for Women's Rights

Miss Margaret Lovell MIRP, Public Relations

Miss Ann Macpherson, Police Constable

Mrs Doreen Miller, Managing Director, Universal Beauty Club

Miss Janet Milne, Movements Manager, Heathrow Airport

Madame Simone Mirman, Royal Milliner

Miss Diana Napier Tauber, Company Director

Mrs Sheila Y Parkinson FANY, Corps Commander, Woman's Transport Service

Mrs Marguerite Patten FCFA, Home Economist and Cookery Writer

Miss F Richmond, Actress

Miss Diana Rigg, Actress

Her Honour Judge Rowland

Mrs Lois Sieff, Chairman of the Council of the Royal Court Theatre

Miss Auriol Sinclair, Race Horse Trainer

Mrs Dorothy Octavia Smith, Vice-Counsel of Portugal

Miss Cleo Sylvestre, Actress

Miss Tamara Ustinov, Actress

Miss Katherine Whitehorn BA, Journalist

Mrs Katie M Wilde MHCIMA, Flight
Catering Manager, British Caledonian
Airways
Lady Wontner, The Lady Mayoress of
London

Monday 6th October 1975
THEME: IMAGE OR REALITY?

Speakers:
Dr Germaine Greer, Author, Broadcaster
Miss Billie Whitelaw, Actress
Miss Betty Lockwood, Chairman
designate of the Equal Opportunities
Commission
Miss Joanna Nash, Journalist

Guests of Honour: In the presence of
HRH The Princess Margaret, Countess
of Snowdon
Miss Heather Ablard, Airline Stewardess;
hostage at Heathrow
Mrs Ruth Addison BA, Chairperson,
Union of Liberal Students
Miss Moira Anderson OBE, Singer
Air Commodore MG Arlott CB ADC,
Director of Women's Royal Air Force
Dame Josephine Barnes DBE MD FRCS
FRCOG, Gynaecological Surgeon
The Lady Elwyn-Jones, (Miss Pearl
Binder), Artist and Writer
Miss Barbara Brindley, Airline
Stewardess; hostage at Heathrow
Mrs Sandra Brookes, Chairman, National
Housewives Association
Mrs Elsie Clayton ACP, President,
National Union of Teachers
Mrs Shirley Conran, Writer and Designer
Mrs Roger Dawe, The Lady Mayoress of
Westminster
Dame Evelyn Denington DBE Hon
FRIBA, Hon MRTPI, Chairman of the
Greater London Council
Lady Donaldson, Author
Major Ellen Duff, Salvation Army
(Speaker for Grace)
Mrs Dorothy Dunnett, Novelist and
Portrait Painter
Mrs Kathleen Fox, President of the
National Council of Women of Great
Britain
Miss Elizabeth Frink CBE, Sculptor
Mrs Pauline Goodwin, World Champion
Wild Water Racing, Canoeist

Miss Hannah Gordon, Actress
Miss Beryl Grey, Artistic Director,
London Festival Ballet
Miss Catherine Hall CBE Hon DLitt,
General Secretary, Royal College of
Nursing
The Rt Hon Baroness Hornsby-Smith
DBE, Consultant
Alderman Mrs Pat Jacob JP, Chairman,
National Federation of Women's
Institutes
Her Excellency The Lady Khama, Wife of
the President of Botswana
Baroness Robson of Kiddington
Miss Patricia Lamburn, Director, IPC
Magazines
Miss Margaret Leighton CBE, Actress
Policewoman Margaret Liles, Moorgate
heroine
Lady Medawar MA BSc, Chairman,
Margaret Pyke Centre
Mrs Jessie Moon, President, Association
of Inner Wheel Clubs in Great Britain
and Ireland
Mrs Marie Patterson, Trade Union
National Women Officer
The Baroness Pike, National Chairman,
Women's Royal Voluntary Service
Mrs Erin Pizzey, Chairwoman, Chiswick
Women's Aid
Miss Joan Plowright CBE, Actress
Miss Winifred Prentice OBE, Hospital
Matron, President of the Royal College
of Nursing
Miss Anna Raeburn, Writer
Mrs Bridget Raynes, Manager, Customer
Relations, British Caledonian Airways
Miss Jane Reed, Editor, *Woman's Own*
Her Honour Judge Rowland
Her Worship, Councillor Mrs B Sindius-
Smith, Mayor of Kensington and
Chelsea
Miss Kathleen Skillern, Commander,
Metropolitan Police
Rabbi Mrs Jacqueline Tabick BA DipEd
Mrs Susan Thomas BA, National
President, National Association, Ladies
Circles Great Britain and Ireland
Dr Grace Thornton CBE MVO, Secretary,
Women's National Commission
Mrs Mary Whitehouse, Hon. General
Secretary, National Viewers and
Listeners' Association
The Rt Hon Mrs Shirley Williams,
Secretary of State for Prices and

Consumer Protection, Member of
Parliament for Hertford and Stevenage

Miss Pennie Yaffe DipPEd, General
Secretary, Association of Career
Teachers

Monday 11th October 1976
THEME: YESTERDAY, TODAY AND TOMORROW

Speakers:
Her Royal Highness The Duchess of
Gloucester

Mrs Helene Hayman, MP

The Marchioness of Lothian, Journalist
and Broadcaster

Miss Margaret Maden, Headmistress of
Islington Green School

Anna Raeburn, Journalist

Guests of Honour: In the presence of
HRH The Duchess of Gloucester

Air Commander MG Allott CB ADC,
Director of Women's Royal Air Force

Miss Katie Boyle, TV/Radio Columnist

Mrs Heather Brigstocke MA (Cantab),
Headmistress of St. Paul's Girls School

Lady Megan Bull MSc MRCP DPM
DCH, Governor of Holloway Prison

Mrs Major Irene Durman, Salvation
Army Officer

Mrs K Fox, President of the National
Council of Women for Great Britain

Ms Clare Francis BSc, Yachtswoman

Miss Hannah Hauxwell, Farmer

Miss Rosaline Kelly, President of the
National Union of Journalists

Commandant SVA McBride Hon ADC
BA, Director of Women's Royal Naval
Service

Miss Geraldine McEwan, Actress

Miss Millicent Martin, Actress

Miss Monica Mason, Ballerina

Miss Jean Morton, Head of Audience
Relations for ATV

Brigadier Eileen J Nolan Hon ADC CB,
Director Women's Royal Army Corps

Mrs Mollie Porter, Leader, Cairngorm
Mountain Rescue Team

Mrs Joan Pyke JP, President of the
Association of Inner Wheel Clubs

Mrs Pauline Roberts, British Caledonian
Airways Cabin Services Manager

Her Honour Judge Rowland

Miss Kathleen Daphne Skillern,
Commander of Metropolitan Police

Councillor Mrs H Stroud, Mayor of the
London Borough of Greenwich

Miss Una Stubbs, Actress and Dancer

Lady Vinaya Teelock BA, Barrister

Miss Diana Thorne, Amateur Rider

Dr Olga Uvarov DSc FRCVS, President of
Royal College of Veterinary Surgeons

Monday 10th October 1977
THEME: LOYALTY

Speakers:
Mrs Sheila Hocken, Author

Miss Penelope Keith, Actress

Dr Althea Leconite, Biochemist, Brian
Research Group

Erin Pizzey, Chairman, Woman's Aid

Dr Margaret Reinhold, Consultant
Psychiatrist

Guests of Honour: In the presence of
HRH The Duchess of Kent

Miss Margaret Alexander, Social Editor,
The Times

Mrs Kay Bolton, Chairman, National
Committee of the Standing
Conferences of Women's
Organisations.

Miss Eleanor Bron, Actress

Mrs Joyce Butler, MP

Lady Collins, Publisher

Mrs Iris E Dartnell, President, National
Free Church Women's Council
1977/1978

Miss Jacqueline Du Prè OBE FGsM
FRCM Hon RAM, Musician

Miss Gina Fratini, Dress Designer

Mrs JA Frieda (Lulu), Singer

Mrs JM Gilbert BPharm FPS, President,
Pharm. Soc.

Lady Grade

Miss Patricia Gregory, Hon. Sec. Women's
Football Association

Miss Beryl Grey CBE, Artistic Director,
London Festival Ballet

Mrs Daphne Hamilton-Fairley

Miss Maureen Laker, Social Editor, *Daily
Telegraph*

Miss Patricia Lamburn, Director, IPC
Magazines

Sister Mary Perpetua, Hospital
Administrator

Mrs Rosemary McWhirter

189

Lady Medawar MA BSc, Director,
    Margaret Pyke Trust
Miss Simone Mirman, Royal Milliner
Miss Jane Pugh, Lady in Waiting to HRH
    The Duchess of Kent
Miss Esther Rantzen, Broadcaster
Miss Jane Reed, Editor, *Woman's Own*
Miss EM Rees, SRN SCM, President,
    Royal College of Nursing
Miss Zandra Rhodes DES RCA,
    Textile/Dress Designer
Miss Stella Richman, Television Executive
Miss Angela Rippon,
    Newsreader/Broadcaster
Her Honour Judge Rowland
Mrs ES Rule, National President, UK
    Federation of Business and Professional
    Women
Commander KD Skillern, Metropolitan
    Police
Viscountess Stansgate, President of
    International Congregational
    Fellowship 1977
Miss Janet Street Porter, Television
    Presenter/Journalist
HE Lady Vinaya Teelock, Barrister-at-Law
Mrs H Waldsax, President, National
    Council of Women
Mrs Sheila Walker, Chief Commissioner,
    Girl Guides Association
Mrs Linda Cubitt, The Mayoress of
    Westminster
Mrs Betty Williams, Northern Ireland
    Peace People
Miss Penny Yaffe Dip Ed, General
    Secretary, Association of Career
    Teachers

Monday 25th September 1978
THEME: THE ART OF SURVIVAL

Speakers:
Miss Mollie Sugden, Actress
Her Honour Judge Rowland
Dr Anne Birchall, Archaeologist
Mrs Naomi James, Round the World
    Yachtswoman
Miss Jane Reed, Editor, *Woman's Own*

Guests of Honour: In the presence of
    HRH The Duchess of Kent
Miss Margaret Alexander, Social Editor,
    The Times
Dame Josephine Barnes DBE FRCP
    FRCOG, Consultant Gynaecologist

Miss Katie Boyle, Columnist, TV and
    Radio
Lady Bull MSc MRCP DCH, Governor,
    Holloway Prison
Mrs EA Coram, Chairman of National
    Union of Townswomen's Guilds
Dr Josephina de Vasconcellos FRBS Hon
    D Litt, Sculptor
Miss Monica Dickens, Author
Mrs Dorothy Drake, Director,
    Confederation of British Industry
Dr ME Duncan MB ChB FRCS Ed
    MRCOG, Research Obstetrician
Dr Jacqueline du Prè OBE FGSM Hon
    RAM, Hon RCM, Musician
Lt Colonel Irene Durman, Salvation Army
    Officer
Miss Gina Fratini, Dress Designer
Miss Patricia Gould, Matron-in-chief,
    QARNNS
Mrs Sheila Hocken, Author
Miss Victoria Holt, Author
Mrs MK Horsley, Ironfounder
Mrs Denise St Aubyn Hubbard,
    Skipper/Navigator
Miss Gayle Hunnicutt, Actress
Mrs Muriel Johnston, Cattle Breeder and
    Judge of Cattle (Farmer)
Mrs Eileen Kearney, Lady Mayoress of
    Westminster
Miss Penelope Keith, Actress
Miss Wyn Knowles, Editor, *Woman's
    Hour*, BBC
Dr Una Kroll MB BChir MRCGP, Med.
    Practitioner/Deaconess
Miss Maureen Laker, Social Editor, *Daily
    Telegraph*
Miss Patricia Lamburn, Assistant
    Managing Director, IPC Magazines
Miss Sue Lawley BA,
    Journalist/Broadcaster
Miss Yvonne Littlewood, BBC Television
    Producer/Director
Commandant SVA McBride Hon ADC,
    Director, Women's Royal Naval Service
The Countess of Mar and Kellie, Justice
    of the Peace
Brig JOE Moriarty RRC QHNS, Matron-
    in-Chief of the Army
Mrs John Nathan, Company Director
Miss Nanette Newman, Actress/Author
Miss Bridget Paton, Trade Union Official
Mrs M Patterson, TUC Officer
Mrs Erin Pizzey, Founder, Chiswick
    Women's Aid

Mrs Louise Pleydell-Bouverie, Interior
Designer
Miss Angharad Rees, Actress
Dr Margaret Reinhold MRCP, Consultant
Psychiatrist
Miss Stella Richman, TV Producer and
Restaurant Owner
Mrs Patricia Seed MBE, Journalist
Commander KD Skillern, Metropolitan
Police Commander
Ms Una Stubbs, Dancer
Air Commodore PJ Tamblin MA FBIM,
Director, Women's Royal Air Force
Lady Teelock, Barrister-at-Law
Mrs H Waldsax, President, National
Council of Women
Mrs Owen Walker, Chief Comm., Girl
Guides Association
Lady Wontner

Monday October 1979
THEME: GIFTS

Speakers:
Miss Carol Channing, Actress/Entertainer
Mrs Agnes Curran RGN RMN, Nursing
Admin, Governor, HM Prison, Dungavel
Baroness Ryder of Warsaw, Founder of
Sue Ryder Foundation
Mrs Judith Stone, UK Director,
International Year of the Child
Ms Poly Styrene, Writer

Guests of Honour: In the presence of
HRH The Duchess of Kent
Baroness Airey of Abingdon
Miss Margaret Alexander, Social Editor,
The Times
Ms Francesca Annis, Award Winning
Actress
Miss Mary Barnes, Painter and Writer
Mrs Patricia Batty Shaw JP, National
Chairman, Nat. Fed. of Women's
Institutes
Mrs Sandra Brown, TV Production
Executive
Miss Isabel Buchanan, Opera Singer
Miss Marti Caine, Entertainer
Miss Winifred Carr, Women's Editor,
Daily Telegraph
Miss Jackie Collins, Author
Mrs Mary Craig MA Oxon, Author,
Broadcaster
Ms Mikki Doyle, Women's Page Editor,
Morning Star

Dr Jacqueline Du Prè OBE FGSM FRCM
Hon RAM
Mrs Maureen Flowers, Professional
Dartplayer
Dame Margot Fonteyn de Arias DBE,
Prima Ballerina, President, Royal
Academy of Dancing
Mrs RW Forrester, Lady Mayoress of
Westminster
Ms Catherine Freeman, Television
Producer
Miss Elisabeth Frink CBE, Sculptor
Miss Catherine Hall CBE Hon DLitt SRN
SCM FRCN, Gen. Sec. Royal College
of Nursing
Miss Anita Harris, Entertainer
Mrs Edna Healey, Author
Mrs Diana Henderson, Event Rider
The Lady Home
Ms Sally Ann Howes, Actress
Miss Maureen Laker, Social Editor, *Daily
Telegraph*
Miss Jane Lapotaire, Actress
Mrs Penelope Mortimer, Author
Miss Elaine Paige, Actress/Singer
Mrs Marie Patterson CBE BA DSc, Nat.
Officer, Transport & Gen. Workers
Service
Baroness Pike, BA Hons Economics &
Psychology, Chairman, WRVS
Mrs Erin Pizzey, Founder, Women's Aid
The Lady Plowden DBE, Chairman,
Independent Broadcasting Authority
Mrs D Reid JP, Magistrate, Pres.,
National Council of Women
Her Honour Judge Rowland
Baroness Ryder CMG OBE, Founder, Sue
Ryder Foundation
Mrs Josephine Sandilands, Editor, *Woman*
Mrs Emma Selby Walker, Costume
Designer, Supervisor, ROH
Mrs Judith Stone BA (Oxon), Director,
International Year of the Child
Ms Honor Thackrah, Orchestra Manager,
Royal Opera House
Mrs Sheila Walker JP, Chief
Commissioner, Girl Guides Association
Mrs Mary Whitehouse, Hon. General
Secretary, National Viewers &
Listeners' Association
Her Excellency, The High Commissioner
of Zambia

Monday 20th October 1980
THEME: 25 YEARS BACK – 25 YEARS ON

Speakers:
Professor Margaret Gowing MA DLitt
FBA, Professor of the History of
Science, Oxford University
Baroness Jackson of Lodsworth DBE,
President, Institute for Environment
and Development
Miss Mary O'Hara, Singer
Mrs Marie Patterson CBE BA DSc, Trade
Union Official
Miss Sian Philips, Actress

Guests of Honour: In the presence of
HRH The Duchess of Kent
Miss Margaret Alexander, *The Times*
Miss Francesca Annis, Actress
Dr Jean Balfour FRSE DSc FE FOR JP,
Farmer, Forester, Chairman,
Countryside Commission for Scotland
Mrs Kingman Brewster, Wife of US
Ambassador
Mrs Sandra Brown, Equal Opportunities
Commission, Thames Television
Ms Iris Burton, Editor, *Woman's Own*
Miss Kate Bush, Singer, Songwriter
HE The High Commissioner for Canada
Lady Collins, Religious Publisher
Mrs Agnes Curran RGN RMN,
Governor, HM Prison, Dungavel
Ms Mikki Doyle, Woman's Editor,
Morning Star
Mrs Donald Du Parc Braham, Lady
Mayoress of Westminster
Mrs Catherine Freeman, Television
Producer
Miss Phyllis George FRCS, Consultant
Surgeon, The Royal Free Hospital
Miss Beryl Grey CBE DLitt DMus, Prima
Ballerina
Miss Catherine M Hall CBE Hon DLitt
SRN SCM FRCN, Royal College of
Nursing
Miss Susan Hampshire, Actress
Dr Dorothy Hodgkin DSC FRS OM,
Scientist
Miss Maureen Laker, *Daily Telegraph*
Ms Verity Lambert, Chief Executive,
Euston Films
Mrs Terry Marsland, Tobacco Workers
Union Official
Mrs Simone Mirman, Royal Milliner
Ms Fran Morrison MA, Television

Journalist
Mrs Penelope Mortimer FRSI, Author
Rabbi Julia Neuberger MA, Minister,
South London Liberal Synagogue
Ms Saidie Patterson, Life Vice-President,
'Women Together', Northern Ireland
Mrs Erin Pizzey, Chiswick Women's Aid
Ms Esther Rantzen, Television Producer
Ms Fiona Richmond, Actress, Journalist,
Broadcaster, Authoress
Professor BE Ryman MA PhD FRIC
FRCPath, Mistress of Girton College
and Professor of Biochemistry at
Charing Cross Hospital
Dame Cicely Saunders DBE FRCP
HonDSc, Medical Practitioner
Miss Sheila Scott OBE, Writer, Speaker,
Pilot, Explorer
Mrs Patricia V Seed MBE, Author
Miss Audrey Slaughter, *Sunday Times*
Poly Styrene (Ms Marian Elliott), Singer,
Songwriter
Miss Virginia Wade MBE BSc, Tennis
Player
Mrs Owen Walker JP, Chief
Commissioner, Commonwealth Girl
Guides Association
Miss Penelope Wallace, Chairman, Press
Club, Author
Ms Victoria Wood BA, Entertainer
Mrs Barbara Woodhouse, Authoress, Dog
Trainer

Monday 26th October 1981
THEME: WHO CARES?

Speakers:
Frances Cairncross, Journalist
Bernadette Nolan, Disablement Research
Zandra Rhodes, Dress Designer

Guests of Honour: In the presence of
HRH The Princess Anne, Mrs Mark
Phillips, GCVO
Ms Kate Adie BA, TV Reporter
Miss Margaret Alexander, *The Times*
Ms Molly Bishop, Portrait Painter
Miss Fiona Brothers, The Fastest Woman
on Water
Miss Dora Bryan, Actress
Miss Kate Bush, Singer/Songwriter
Frances Cairncross MA, Journalist
Petula Clark, Singer/Actress
Judge Myrella Cohen, Circuit Judge

Miss Joan Collins, Actress
Lady Collins, Publisher
Miss Gemma Craven, Actress
Miss Diana Dors, Actress
Mrs Elizabeth Emanuel MA, Fashion
Designer
Baroness Ewart-Biggs
Ms Jean Farrall, Women's Official,
National Union of Teachers
Miss Christina Foyle, Publisher/Book
Seller
Ms Decima Francis, Actress
Miss Felicity Green, Associate Editor,
Daily Express
Miss Susan Hampshire, Actress
Mrs Susan Harley MA, The Lady
Mayoress of Westminster
Ms Patricia Hewitt MA, General
Secretary, NCCL
Lady Home
Miss Mary Kenny, Journalist
Sister Jude, Child Psychiatrist
Miss Maureen Laker, *Daily Telegraph*
Baroness Masham, Member of House of
Lords
Miss Leonie Mellinger, Actress
Mrs Sally Mugabe
Mrs Bernadette Nolan, Disablement
Research
Ms Mary Peters MBE, International
Athlete
Mrs Erin Pizzey, Founder, Chiswick
Battered Wives Home
Miss Angharad Rees, Actress
Zandra Rhodes, Dress Designer
Miss Sheila Scott, Writer/Pilot
Mrs Pat Seed MBE MA,
Author/Journalist
Miss Faith Seward MBE BA DipEd, Spina
Bifida Association, President and
Teacher
Miss Janet Silver MPhil FVCO MBIM,
Opthalmic Optician
Mrs David Steel
Ms Muriel Turner, Trade Unionist
Mrs Jean Casselman Wadds, HE The
High Commissioner for Canada
Mrs Mary Whitehouse CBE, Founder,
National Viewers and Listeners'
Association
Lady Wilson, Poet
Mrs Margaret Wingfield CBE JP,
President, National Council of Women
Lady Wontner
Barbara Woodhouse, Authoress

Baroness Young, Leader of the House of
Lords
Mrs Susan Zwinoira, Wife of the High
Commissioner of Zimbabwe

Monday 25th October 1982
THEME: LIFE BEGINS AT...

Speakers:
Lucinda Buxton, Wildlife Photographer
Mikki Doyle, Woman's Page Editor,
Morning Star
Madame Jehan el-Sadat
Pamela Stephenson, Actress/Comedienne

Guests of Honour: In the presence of
HRH The Princess Michael of Kent
Mrs Hassan Abou-Séeda, HE The
Ambassador for Egypt's Wife
Miss Margaret Alexander, Social Editor,
The Times
Miss Muriel Rose Allan, Prison Governor
Mrs Eileen Armstrong, Co. Director, Park
Lane Hotel
Sister Anna (Hoare) MA (Oxon),
Religious Sister working in the
community for reconciliation in Belfast
and Northern Ireland
Dame Janet Baker DBE Hon DMus
FRSA, Singer
Lieutenant Colonel Jean Blackwood TD
WRAC, Commanding Officer, 37
(Wessex and Welsh)
Mrs Sondra Bonadie-Arming BSc MA,
Garden Designer
Dr Sally Bucknall BSc MSc MIBiol PhD,
Biologist
Miss Cindy Buxton, Wildlife
Photographer
Miss Annabel Croft, Tennis Player
Mrs Susan Crosland BA, Writer
Mrs Agnes Curran RGM RMN FIBM,
Prison Governor
Ms Mikki Doyle, Woman's Page Editor,
Morning Star
Miss Jane Drew RIBA, Architect
Lady Fisher, Co-Chairman/Founder of
Women Caring Trust
Miss Claire Francis, Yachtswoman
Dame Elizabeth Frink DBE, Sculptress
Miss Patricia Hart BA, Solicitor
Miss Margaret Hicks, Sailor
Mrs 'H' Jones
Miss Linda Kitson DipMA RCA, Artist

Miss Maureen Laker, Social Editor, *Daily Telegraph*

Miss Ruth Lawrence, entrant into Oxford University

Miss Sophie Laws BLitt MA, University Lecturer

Ms Ann Leslie BA, Journalist/Broadcaster

Miss Elizbath Lutyens CBE, Composer

Mrs Naomi Mackintosh BA Hon Soc, Senior Commissioning Editor, Channel 4

Ms Anna Markland ARCM, BBC Young Musician of the Year

Mrs M Morgan, President, Royal College of Nursing

Mrs Norah Owen, President, Institute of Public Relations

Ms Daphne Park CMG OBE MA, Principal, Somerville College

Mrs Sybil Phoenix MBE

Ms Erin Pizzey, Founder, Chiswick Women's Aid

Professor Lesley Rees MD FRCP, Professor of Medicine

Ms Annie Ross, Actress, Singer

Miss Patricia Routledge BA Hons, Actress

Mrs Margaret Rule FSA, Archaeological Director of The Mary Rose Trust

Madame Sadat, International Guest of Honour

Ms Anna Scher, Principal, Children's Theatre

Ms Selina Scott, Newsreader

Mrs Patricia Seed MBE MA, Journalist/Author

Miss Pamela Stephenson, Actress

Dr M Stoppard MD MRCP, Medical Broadcaster/Journalist/Author

Miss Ella Stothart CQSW CTBDip, Social Worker for the Blind

Miss Barbara Switzer, Trade Union Official

Miss Marion D Tickner SRN SCM OND, Chief Nurse, Moorfields Eye Hospital

Mrs Muriel Turner, Assistant General Secretary of the Association of Scientific, Technical & Managerial Staffs

Ms Jill Tweedie, Journalist/Author

HE Mrs Jean Casselman Wadds, The High Commissioner for Canada

Chief Superintendent Ward, Police Officer

Ms Fay Weldon, Author

The Lady Mayoress of Westminster, Mrs T Whipham

Mrs Margaret Wingfield CBE, President, National Council of Women

The Baroness Young MA Oxon, Government Minister

Monday 17th October 1983
THEME: A WOMAN'S BEST FRIEND

Speakers:
Mrs Shirley Conran, Writer

Professor Dorothy Hodgkin OM FRS, Nobel Prize Winning Scientist

Mrs Jane Lapotaire, Actress

Mrs Jenny Pitman, Race Horse Trainer

Ms Dorienne Wilson-Smillie, Programme for Woman & Development, Commonwealth Secretariat

Guests of Honour:
The Right Worshipful The Lord Mayor of Westminster

Ms Margaret Alexander, Social Editor, *The Times*

Mrs Laura Ashley, Designer

Miss Jane Bown, Photographer

Miss Fiona Brothers, Power Boat Racer

Miss Sheila Cameron QC, Vicar General, Church of England

Miss Heather Coupe, Organiser, Farm Women's Club

Miss Sharron Davies, Swimmer

Miss Brenda Dean, Secretary, SOGAT

Mrs Audrey Eyton, Writer

Dame Elizabeth Frink DBE RA, Sculptor

HE Lady Garland, Musician

Dr Jane Glover MA DPhil, Conductor

Mrs Molly Hattersley, Headmistress

Miss Maureen Laker, Social Editor, *Daily Telegraph*

Ms Verity Lambert, Director of Production, Thorn EMI Films

Ms Annie Lennox, Lead Singer, Eurythmics

Ms Ann Leslie BA, Journalist

Mrs Charlotte Lessing, Editor, *Good Housekeeping*

Mrs Terry Marsland, Deputy General Secretary, Tobacco Workers Union

Madame Simone Mirman, Milliner

Mrs Diana Moran, Breakfast Television Presenter

Mrs Frances Morrell, Deputy Leader, ILEA

Miss Virginia Nightingale, Horticulturist

194

Mrs Brigid Norris BSc, Science Teacher, Linden Lodge School for the Blind

Baroness Pike of Melton, Chairman, Broadcasting Complaints Commission

Baroness Platt of Writtle CBE MA CEng MRAeS, Chairman, Equal Opportunities Commission

Miss Arabella Pollen, Fashion Designer

Poly Styrene, Musician

Miss Sheila Quinn CBE, President, Royal College of Nursing

Her Honour Judge Rowland

Mrs Joan Ruddock, Chairperson, CND

Ms Selina Scott, Breakfast Television Presenter

Ms Gaia Servadio, Journalist

Ms Janet Suzman, Actress

Dame Olga Uvaruv DBE DSc (hc) FRCVS, Veterinary Surgeon

Mrs Jean Viall, President, National Council of Women

Miss Dorothy Webster CBE, Chief Nursing Officer, Royal College of Nursing

The Mayor of the City of Derby, Mrs Margaret Wood

Monday 22nd October 1984
THEME: HOW TO BE FIRST

Speakers:

Madame Valentina Tereshkova, Chairman, USSR Women's Council

The Right Honourable The Lord Mayor of London, Dame Mary Donaldson DBE

Ms Brenda Dean, President/General Secretary-Elect, SOGAT

Lady Antonia Fraser FRS, Author

Guests of Honour: In the presence of HRH The Dutchess of Kent

Mrs Jennifer Adams FILAM DipPRA, Superintendent of Royal Parks

Ms Margaret Alexander, Social Editor, *The Times*

Ms Joan Armatrading, Singer, Songwriter

Mrs Anne Ballard MAm, National Federation of Women's Institutes

Dr Ann Barrett MD FRCR, Consultant Radiotherapist

Miss JA Beak, Royal College of Midwives

Dr Tessa Blackstone BSc PhD, Deputy Education Officer, ILEA Resources

Mrs Lynda Chalker, Minister of State for Transport

Ms Caroline Charles, Dress Designer

Miss Heather Couper BSc (Hons), President-Elect of British Astronomical Association

Dr Anita Davies MRCP FF Hom, Physician

Miss Anne Diamond, TV-AM Presenter

Dr Elizabeth Evans BSc PhD, Research Fellow in Nutrition

Mrs Anne Gibson Dip Arch RIBA, Architect

Professor Margaret Gowing CBE FBA DLitt, Professor of History of Science, Oxford University

Mrs Tricia Guild, Interior Designer

Miss Audrey Head, Chairman, Unit Trust Association

Miss Virginia Holgate, Horse-rider, Olympic Medallist

Mrs Jennifer Jenkins MA Hon FRIBA Hon RICS, Chairman, Historic Buildings Advisory Committee

Ms Marie Jennings, Director, Public Relations Consultants Association

Miss Joy Kinsley, Governor, Holloway Prison

Miss Maureen Laker, Social Editor, *Daily Telegraph*

Ms Prue Leith, Restaurateur, Journalist

Dr Oonagh McDonald MP PhD, Opposition Front Bench Spokesman on Treasury and Economic Affairs

Ms Beatrix Miller, Editor in Chief, *Vogue*

Ms Debbie Moore, Business Woman of the Year, 1984

Mrs Francis Morrell, Leader, ILEA

Ms Anne Mueller, Deputy Secretary, Department of Trade and Industry

Ms Molly Parkin, Writer, Performer

Her Excellency Madame Popova

Ms Laurie Purden MBE, Editor, *Woman's Journal*

Miss Bridget Riley DLit CBE, Artist

Ms Deborah Rix, Presenter, BBC TV

Ms Joan Ruddock BSc ARCS, Chairperson, CND

Miss Tessa Sanderson, Olympic Gold Medallist

Miss Monica Sims OBE MA LRAN, Director of Programmes, BBC Radio 4

Siouxsie, Singer

Mrs Barbara Switzer, Deputy General Secretary, AUEW-TASS

Mrs Jean Viall, President, National Council of Women

Ms Julie Walters, Actress

Colonel Violet Wonfor BA, Director of Programmes, Tyne Tees TV
Ms EC Zolina, Interpreter

Monday 28th October 1985
THEME: HOPE

Speakers:
HM Queen Mata'aho of Tonga
HRH The Princess Anne, Mrs Mark Phillips, GCVO
Miss Heather Couper BSc FRAS
Miss Maureen Lipman

Guests of Honour: In the presence of HRH The Princess Anne
Mrs Latu Taumoepeau-Tupou, Wife of His Excellency The High Commissioner for Tonga
Lady Elizabeth Anson LLB, Proprietor, Party Planners
Ms Joan Armatrading, Singer, Songwriter
Miss Ann Barr, Journalist, *Observer*
Mrs Helen Beard, Social Ed., *The Times*
Ms Meg Beresford BA General Secretary, CND
Cathryn Countess Cawdor, Lady Mayoress of Westminster
Miss Judith Chalmers BA, Broadcaster, TV and Radio
Ms Chris Clyne, Fashion Designer
Judge Myrella Cohen QC, Circuit Judge
Miss Heather Couper BSc MSc SRN FRCN, Life Peeress
Miss Annabel Croft, Tennis Professional
Mrs Jennifer d'Abo, Chairman, Rymans
Ms Brenda Dean, General Secretary, SOGAT
Ms Margaret Drabble CBE, Writer
Deaconess Vivienne Faull MA, Chaplain, Clare College, Cambridge
Ms Jo Foley, Managing Editor, *Daily Mirror*
Miss Josephine Fowler BEd, Prison Governor
Mrs Ann Gibson DIPArch(HonsDist) RIBA, Architect
Lady Glendyne, Farmer and Cattle Breeder
Dr Jane Glover MA DPhil, Conductor
Dr June Goodfield BSc PhD, Author, Scientific TV Documentaries
Dr Germaine Greer PhD, Writer
Ms Marie Jennings, Director, PRCA

Mrs Kaeswardani Kassim, Wife of Malaysian High Commissioner
Ms Betty Kenward, Editor, Jennifer's Diary
Sq Leader Jo Kingston MBBS CRCP MRCS DipAve Med, Squadron Leader RAF, GP
Ms Dorothy Kuya SEN DipEd, Director, Equal Opportunities Agency
Miss Jennifer Laing, Deputy Chairman, Saatchi & Saatchi
Miss Maureen Laker, Journalist
Miss Barbara M Lee MBE, Orthoptist
Miss Maureen Lipman, Actress/Writer
Miss Sandra Lousada, Photographer
Ms Sue MacGregor, Broadcaster
Mrs Bo Maggs, Aerobatic Display Pilot
Mrs Mary Mayne, President, National Council of Women
Miss June Mendoza RP ROI, Artist
Ms Frances Morrell, Leader, ILEA
Lady Porter, Leader, Westminster City Council
Miss Sheila Quinn CBE BSc FRCN, President, Royal College of Nursing
Miss Jane Reed, Journalist
Ms Anita Roddick, Director, Body Shop International
Mrs Angela Rumbold MP CBE, Parliamentary Under-Secretary of State for the Environment
Dr Miriam Stoppard MD MRCP, Writer/Broadcaster/Doctor
Mrs Barbara Switzer, Deputy General Secretary, AUEW
Baroness Turner, Assistant General Secretary, ASTMS
Ms Catherine Walker, Designer
Ms Caroline Walker BSc MSc, Nutritionist
Dame Anne Warburton DCVO CMG MA, President, Lucy Cavendish College
Ms Billie Whitelaw, Actress

Monday 27th October 1986
THEME: VISION

Speakers:
Miss Kate Adie
Mrs Coretta King
Ms Toyah Wilcox

Guests of Honour: In the presence of HRH The Princess of Wales
Miss Kate Adie, TV Journalist
Mrs Margaret Anstey LLB(Hons), Solicitor

Mrs Anne Barker Poole SRN SCM HV Cert, Chief Nursing Officer, DHSS

Ms Meg Beresford, General Secretary, CND

General Eva Burrows, Salvation Army

Miss Lindka Cierach, Designer

Dr Vicky Clement-Jones MA (Cantab) MBBChir FRCP, Doctor and Chairman of BACUP

Dr Janet Gale-Grant BA MSc PhD

Mrs Tricia Guild, Interior Designer and Chairwoman, Designer Guild

Mrs Philippa Harrison, Managing Director, Macmillan (London)

Mrs Cathy Herring, Restaurateur/Hotelier

Mrs Sarah Hogg, Business and Finance Editor, *Independent*

Ms Sandra Lousada, Photographer

Councillor Mrs Terence Mallingson JP, Lord Mayor of Westminster

Mrs Mary Mayne, President, National Council of Women

Dr June Paterson-Brown MB ChB, Chief Commissioner, Girl Guide Association

Baroness Platt of Writtle CBE MA CEng FRAes HonDUniv, Chairman, Equal Opportunities Commission

Mrs Lisa St Aubin De Teran, Writer

Miss Emma Sergeant BA, Painter

Mrs Elizabeth Shields, Liberal MP

Miss Julia Smith, BBC TV Producer

Miss Patricia Tindale AADip RIBA, Architect

Mrs Rosemary Verey, Horticulturist and Author

Detective Chief Superintendent Thelma Wagstaff, Police Officer

Professor Dorothy Wedderburn MA Hon DLitt FIC, Principal, Royal Holloway and Bedford College

Ms Toyah Wilcox, Actress/Singer

Ms Dorienne Wilson-Smillie, Director, Women and Development Programme

26th October 1987
THEME: SURVIVAL

Speakers:
Ms Marisa Bellisario
Dr Pauline Cutting MB ChB FRCS MD(Hon) OBE
Miss Emma Thompson

Guests of Honour:
Her Honour Judge Nina Lowry, Circuit Judge

Miss Victoria Holt, Author

Mrs Frances Heaton, Merchant Banker

Mrs Rosie Barnes, MP

Mrs Marion Roe, MP

Dame Peggy Fenner, MP

Ms Judy Leden, World Women's Hang Gliding Champion

Ms Caroline Charles, Dress Designer

Lady Charles Spencer-Churchill, Interior Designer

Baroness Trumpington, Peer of the Realm

Lady Hulton, Sculpture Studio for the Blind

Miss Jenny Arnold, Pretty Polly

Miss Emma Thompson, Comedienne and Actress

Ms Marisa Bellisario, Managing Director and Chief Executive, ITALTEL

Baroness Gardner, Lady Mayoress of Westminster

Miss Sue MacGregor, Broadcaster

Mrs Valerie Strachan, Deputy Chairman, Customs and Excise

Miss Sophie Mirman, Chairman, Sock Shops

Miss Annette Maddick, Woman Police Constable

Mrs Gillian du Charme, Headmistress, Benenden School

Miss Harriet Walter, Actress

Miss Prue Leith, Restaurateur/Writer

Miss Jenny Greene, Editor, *Country Life*

Miss Wendy Henry, Editor, *News of the World*

Mrs Mary Bartholomew, Chairman, Shandwick Public Relations

Dr Pauline Cutting, OBE

Mrs Elizabeth Esteve-Coll, Director, Victoria and Albert Museum

Mrs Harold Phillips, President, St John Ambulance Brigade

Ms Judy Piatkus, Publisher

Deaconess Sheila Brown

Miss Gee Armytage, Racehorse Jockey

Miss Julia Mackenzie, Actress

Miss Ruby Wax, Actress

Mrs Rosemary Day, Head of London Regional Transport

Mrs Pat Heron, National Chairman, Standing Conference of Women's Organisations

Ms Gillian Ayres, Artist

Sister Winifred Dolan

Speakers:
The Duchess of Kent
Baroness Blackstone
Patricia Routledge

Guests of Honour: In the presence of
HRH The Duchess of Kent
Princess Dina Abdel Hamid, Author of
Duet For Freedom
Ms Joan Armatrading, Singer/Songwriter
Ms Michelle Barber, Director of Unit
Trusts
Mrs Rosie Barnes, SDP Member of
Parliament
Ms Meg Beresford, General Secretary, CND
The Baroness Blackstone, Master of
Birkbeck College
Miss Helena Bonham-Carter, Film Actress
Ms Catherine Bradley, Telecom-
munications Development Engineer
General Eva Burrows, International
Leader, Salvation Army
Ms Tsai Chin, Actress/Author
Miss Lindka Cierach, Dress Designer
Miss Heather Couper, Astronomer
Ms Brenda Dean, General Secretary,
SOGAT
Mrs J Ellerton JP, Chairman, National
Union of Townwomen's Guilds
Dame Peggy Fenner DBE, MP
Mrs Elizabeth Flach, Lord Mayor of
Westminster
Rev Mother Mary Garson, Pioneer
Founder, Houses for the Old and Frail
Mrs Fiona Gilmore, Managing Director,
Design Consultancy
Dr Jane Glover, Conductor
Ms Joanna Goldsworthy, Director,
Gollancz
Miss Christine Hawley, Architect;
Professor at London Polytechnic
Baroness Hooper, Under-Secretary of
State for Education
Miss Glenda Jackson, Actress
Ms Sue Lawley, Television Presenter
Mrs Lynda Lee-Potter, Feature Writer and
Columnist, *Daily Mail*
Miss Doris Lessing, Author
The Rt Hon Eleanor McLaughlin, Lord
Provost of Edinburgh
Mrs Eve Martin, President, National
Council of Women

Miss June Mendoza, Portrait Painter
Miss Sophie Mirman, Owner, Sock Shop
International
Mrs Sally O'Sullivan, Editor, *Riva*
Magazine
The Rt Hon Sally Oppenheim-Barnes,
Director of Boots; Chairman of
Consumer Council
Miss Su Pollard, Comedienne
Dr Usha Prashar, Director, National
Council of Voluntary Organisations
Miss Angela Rippon, Presenter for the
BBC
Her Excellency Dr Patricia Rogers, High
Commissioner for the Bahamas
Miss Patricia Routledge, Actress
Mrs Agnes Salter, Chief Executive,
Women's Institute
Ms Marie Staunton, Director, Amnesty
International
Dr Anne Szarewski, Specialist in
Gynaecology
Miss Fatima Whitbread, Javelin Silver
Medallist, Olympic Games 1988

Speakers:
The Hon Dame Lydia Dunn DBE LLD JP
Jean Boht
Helena Kennedy

Guests of Honour: HRH The Princess
Margaret, Countess of Snowdon
Mrs Val Arnison, Chairman of Luncheon
Executive Committee
The Rt Hon Mrs Susan Baird, Lord
Provost of Glasgow
Mrs Jean Boht, Actress
Ms Samantha Bond, Film Actress
Ms Darcy Bussell, Dancer, Royal Ballet
Company
Ms Carmen Callil, Publisher
Mrs Pauline Collins, Actress
Ms Annie Cassett, General Manager,
Reading Football Club
The Baroness Cox, Actress
Ms Brenda Dean, General Secretary,
SOGAT
The Hon Dame Lydia Dunn DBE LLD JP,
Senior Member, OMELCO
Mrs Joanna Foster, Chairman, Equal
Opportunities Commission

Ms Jenny Francis, Director, Networking PR
Ms Patricia Gallimore, Actress
Ms Maggie Goodman, Editor, *Hello!* Magazine
Mrs Robert Gunn JP, Presenting Boots Award
Miss Bridgit Hayward, The Really Useful Group
Mrs Edna Healey, Author
Miss Grete Hobbs, Hotelier of the Year
Dame Gwynneth Jones, Soprano
Ms Linda Kelsey, Editor, *Cosmopolitan* Magazine
Ms Felicity Kendal, Actress
Mrs Helena Kennedy, Lawyer
Dr Susan Lightman, Consultant Ophthalmologist
Lady Lothian, Founder President, Women of the Year Luncheon
Sister Patrick McDonnell, Sister of Mercy
Rabbi Julia Neuberger
The Duchess of Norfolk, Co-ordinator, Hospice Movement
Ms Sara Parkin, International Secretary, Green Party
Ms Eve Pollard, Editor, *Sunday Mirror* and Magazine
Mrs Rosalind Preston, President, UK National Council of Women
Miss Esther Rantzen, Television Producer
Her Excellency Mrs Rasgotra, Wife of Indian High Commissioner, Dietician
Miss Jo Richardson, MP
The Rt Hon Mrs Angela Rumbold CBE, Minister of State for Education
Dr Wendy Savage, Gynaecologist
Ms Sally Soames, Photographer
Ms Marie Staunton, Director of Amnesty International
Miss Maude Store, President, Royal College of Nursing
Ms Elizabeth Svendson, Director, Donkey Sanctuary
Ms Elizabeth Symons, General Secretary, Civil Service Union
Mrs Sarah Tyacke, Director, Special Collections, British Library
Miss Virginia Wade OBE, Tennis Professional
Professor Dorothy Wedderburn, Principal, University of London
Lady Wilson, Poet
Ms Anna Worrall QC, Barrister-at-Law

Monday 15th October 1990
THEME: CHALLENGE OF THE 90s

Speakers:
Frau Petra Kelly BA MA MdB
Miss Tracy Edwards MBE
Professor Margaret Turner-Warwick MA DM DSc PhD FRCP FRACP FRCP(E) Hon FFOM

Guests of Honour: HRH The Princess of Wales
Mrs Val Arnison, Chairman of Luncheon Executive Committee
Edna Astley, The Lady Mayoress of Westminster
Dr Yvonne Barton, Senior Petroleum Engineer, British Gas
Lady Blyth, Horse-breeder
Dame Margaret Booth DBE, High Court Judge
Mrs Valerie Bragg, Principal of Britain's First City Technology College
Miss Marti Caine, Entertainer, Author
Miss Tracy Edwards MBE, Skipper of *Maiden*
Mrs Elizabeth Esteve-Coll, Director, Victoria & Albert Museum
Miss Eldred Evans OBE, Architect
The Rt Hon The Baroness Flather, First Asian Peeress
Mrs Odette Hallowes GC MBE, Légion d'Honneur, Founder Vice-President, Women of the Year Luncheon
Miss Maggie Hambling, Artist
Ms Clare Hambro, Merchant Banker/Takeovers Regulator
Miss Christine Hancock, Gen. Sec. Royal College of Nursing
Lady Howe JP, Chairman, BOC Foundation
The Lady Jacobovitz, Wife of The Chief Rabbi
Frau Petra Kelly MdB, Leader of the Green Party, Federal Republic of Germany
Ms Helen Lederer, Actress
Miss Prue Leith OBE, Managing Director, Prudence Leith Ltd
Ms Frances Line, Controller, BBC Radio 2
Ms Davina Lloyd, Editor, *Practical Parenting*
Lady Lothian, Founder President, Women of the Year Luncheon
Ms Diana Luke, Radio Presenter

Ms Sue MacGregor, Broadcaster
Ms Nicola McIrvine, Equestrienne
Miss Detta O'Cathain OBE, Managing Director, Barbican Centre
Mrs June O'Dell, Deputy Chairman, Equal Opportunities Commission
HRH Princess Pilolevu Tuita, Honorary Chairman of Tonga Red Cross
Mrs Rosalind Preston, President, National Council of Women of GB
Ms Jane Priestman, Director of Architecture and Design for British Rail
Mrs Marion Rawlings OBE, Pharmacist
Miss Patricia Rawlings MEP, Member of European Parliament
Ms Fiona Reynolds, Assistant Director, CPRE
Ms Jo Richardson MP, Women's Affairs Spokesperson
Dame Rosemary Rue DBE, President-elect, British Medical Association
The Rt Hon Mrs Angela Rumbold CBE, MP, Minister of State for Education
Lady Scott, Photographer
The Revd Io Smith, Minister of Religion
Miss Jan Smith, Network Marketing Director, TSB
Miss Rosemary Spencer, Assistant Under-Secretary of State for the Public Departments in the Foreign & Commonwealth Office
Ms Janet Suzman, Actress
Professor Margaret Turner-Warwick, President, Royal College of Physicians
Mrs Jean Varman JP, Hon Chairman, National Federation of Women's Institutes

Monday 28th October 1991
THEME: HARMONY

Speakers:
HRH The Duchess of York
Mrs Sunnie Mann
Dr Jane Glover MA DPhil, Conductor
Ms Ann Leslie, Journalist
Floella Benjamin

Guests of Honour:
HRH The Duchess of York
Ms Kate Adie, Television Correspondent
Ms Melinda Appleby BSc, NFU Policy Adviser
Miss Joan Armatrading, Singer/Songwriter
Miss Val Arnison, Executive Chairman,

Women of the Year Luncheon
The Rt Hon Susan Baird, The Lord Provost of Glasgow
Mrs Elizabeth Bavidge JP BA, President, National Council of Women
Ms Marilyn Baxter, Planning Director, Saatchi & Saatchi
Ms Carole Blake, President, Association of Authors' Agents
Mrs Valerie Bragg BSc(Hons), Principal, City Technology College, Birmingham
Ms Catherine Burns LLb RGN RHI, General Secretary, Health Visitors Association
General Eva Burrows AO BA Med, World Leader, Salvation Army
Ms Darcy Bussell, Ballet Dancer
Dr Miriam Chung PhD, University Lecturer
Shirley Conran, Author
Mrs Jane Corner
Mrs Joyce Deane MBE BArch FRIAS RIBA, President, Royal Incorporation of Architects in Scotland
The Baroness Denton of Wakefield CBE Bsc(Econ), Deputy Chairman, Black Country Development Commission
Ms Jane Drabble, Assistant Managing Director, BBC TV
Miss Viviana Durante, Principal Ballerina, Royal Ballet
Ms Eldred Evans OBE SADG RIBA AAdipl (Hons) dipITP, Architect
Ms Pam Ferris, Actress
Mrs Joanna Foster, Chairman, Equal Opportunities Commission
Dr Jane Glover MA DPhil, Conductor
Miss Alex Greaves HND, Jockey
The Baroness Hamwee MA(Cantab), Solicitor
Miss Christine Hancock BSc(Econ) RGN, General Secretary, Royal College of Nursing
Mrs Josephine Henderson, Manager, Battersea Dogs' Home
Ms Angela Heylin, Chairman and Chief Executive, Charles Barker Holding
Miss Victoria Holt, Author
Mrs Carolyn James, Watercolour Artist
Flt Lt Rachel Johnson PMRAFNS, Nursing Officer, Royal Air Force
Miss Myra Kinghorn BLib FCA, Chief Executive, Investors Compensation Scheme

Dame Jill Knight DBE MP
Miss Joanne Lawrence, Director
Corporate Communications,
SmithKline Beecham
Miss Josie Lawrence BA(Hons), Actress
Miss Prue Leith OBE, Restaurateur and
Caterer
Ms Ann Leslie, Journalist
The Marchioness of Lothian FJI, Founder
President, Women of the Year
Luncheon
Mrs Josephine Lundberg, Managing
Director, Royal Academy Enterprises
Julia McKenzie, Actress
The Rt Hon Eleanor McLaughlin, The
Lord Provost of Edinburgh
The Hon Diana Makgill CVO, Vice-
Chairman, Women of the Year Luncheon
Mrs Anne Moran, President, National
Union of Teachers
Miss Jean Muir CBE RDI FCSD, Designer
Miss Eve Pollard, Editor, *Sunday Express*
Councillor Dame Shirley Porter DBE DL,
The Right Worshipful the Lord Mayor
of Westminster
Ms Jo Richardson, MP
Ms Clare Short, MP
Ms Susan Stockley, Chairman, National
Federation of Women's Institutes
Miss Rimma Sushanskaya, Violinist
Mrs Veronica Sutherland CMG BA MA,
Assistant Under-Secretary of State,
Foreign and Commonwealth Office
Ms Gwen Taylor, Actress

Monday 26th October 1992
THEME: COMMUNITY

Speakers:
HRH The Duchess of Kent
Ms Jung Chang PhD, Writer
Ms Helen Lederer BA, Actress/Writer
Ms Janet Street-Porter, BBC Head of
Youth & Entertainment Features

Guests of Honour:
HRH The Duchess of Kent
Ms Diana Abbott, MP
Miss Val Arnison, Executive Chairman,
Women of the Year Luncheon
Ms Zeinab Badawi BA(Oxon) MA,
Journalist/Presenter, Independent
Television News
Mrs Elizabeth Bavidge JP BA(Hons),
President, National Council of Women

Mrs Margaret Beckett, MP, Deputy Leader
of the Labour Party
Ms Jung Chang PhD, Writer
Miss Patsy Chapman, Editor, *News of the
World*
Professor Dulcie Coleman MBBS MD
FRCPath, Consultant Cytopathologist
Flight Lieutenant Sally Cox BSc(Hons),
RAF Pilot
Ms Marcelle D'Argy-Smith, Editor,
Cosmopolitan
Ms Lyndsey De Paul,
Singer/Composer/Producer
Mrs Ruth Deech BA MA, Principal, St
Annes College, Oxford
Dame Peggy Fenner DBE DL, MP
Mrs Joanna Foster, Chairman, Equal
Opportunities Commission
Mrs Rosalind Gilmore MA(Cantab) FRSA,
Chairman, Building Societies
Commission
Rabbi Amanda Golby LLB DipLib,
Minister of Religion
Ms Pat Hawkes, President, National Union
of Teachers
Mrs Frances Heaton BA LLB, Director
General, Takeover Panel
Mrs Bridget Hone BSc(Hons), Young
Farmer of the Year
Ms Lis Howell BA(Hons), Director of
Programmes, Good Morning TV
Ms Eva Jiricna DipArch RIBA, Architect
Dr Pamela Kirby BSc PhD, Managing
Director, Astra Pharmaceuticals Ltd
Mrs Lynda La Plante, Author/Scriptwriter
Ms Jean Lambert BA, Principal Speaker,
Green Party
Ms Joanne Lawrence BA MA MBA, Vice
President and Director, SKB
Ms Helen Lederer BA, Actress/Writer
Mrs Doris Lessing, Writer
Miss Louise Lombard, Actress
The Marchioness of Lothian FJI, Founder
President, Women of the Year Luncheon
Mrs Eve Martin, Co-Chairman, Women's
National Commission
Miss June Mendoza AO RP ROI, Portrait
Painter
Mrs Suzy Menkes MA(Cantab), Fashion
Editor, *International Herald Tribune*
Mrs Barbara Mills QC MA(Oxon),
Director of Public Prosecutions
Miss Pauline Neville-Jones MA(Oxon),
Deputy Secretary, Cabinet Office

The Baroness Perry of Southwark Hon LLD MA(Cantab), Vice Chairman, South Bank University

Ms Jo Richardson, MP

Miss Rebecca Ridgway, Canoeist/Outdoor Pursuits Instructor

Miss Tessa Sanderson MBE, Olympic Javelin Thrower

Ms Janet Street-Porter, BBC Head of Youth & Entertainment

Ms Ruby Wax, Performer/Writer

Miss Victoria Wood, Entertainer

Ms Dagmar Woodward, Hotelier of the Year

Ms Annette Worsley-Taylor, Managing Director, London Designer Collections

Monday 25th October 1993
THEME: BRINGING DOWN BARRIERS

Speakers:
Ms Eve Pollard, Editor
Susan McHugh, Founder, Peace '93
Miss Patricia Scotland QC, Barrister

Guests of Honour:
HRH The Princess Margaret, Countess of Snowdon

Ms Jenny Abramsky BA(Hons), Editor, BBC News and Current Affairs

Ms Dawn Airey, Controller of Network Daytime and Children's Programmes, ITV

Ms Valerie Amos BA(Hons) MA, Chief Executive, Equal Opportunities Commission

Ms Tasmin Archer, Singer/Songwriter

Ms Joan Armatrading, Singer/Songwriter

Miss Jane Asher, Actress/Writer/Jane Asher Party Cakes

Ms Sally Becker, International Aid Worker

Ms Reena Bhavnani BSc MSc MEd, Senior Research Fellow, City University

Mrs Jenny Bianco, The Right Worshipful The Lord Mayor of Westminster

Dr Fiona Caldicott MA BM BCh FRCPsych, President, Royal College of Psychiatrists

Paddy Campbell, Executive Chairman, Women of the Year Lunch

Ms Lynne Franks, Chairman, Lynne Franks PR

Miss Barbara Hamer, Concorde Pilot, British Airways

Miss Ruthie Henshall, Actress

Miss Betty Jackson MBE RDI, Fashion Designer

The Baroness James of Holland Park OBE, Writer

Miss Sarah Jones BA, Silversmith

Ms Diana Kershaw, Director of Planning and Development, Bristol City Council

Major Vanessa Lloyd-Davies MBE MA MB BS, Doctor, HM Forces

The Countess of Longford CBE ME Hon DLitt, Writer

The Marchioness of Lothian FJI, Founder President, Women of the Year Lunch

Mrs Susan McHugh, Founder, Peace '93

Ms Judy McKnight BSocSc, General Secretary, National Association of Probation Officers

Barbara Mills QC MA, Director of Public Prosecutions

Mrs Yvonne Moores Hon DSc, Chief Nursing Officer and Director of Nursing for England

Mademoiselle Jeanne Moreau, Légion d'Honneur, Film Actress/Director

Ms Kate Moss, International Model

Mrs Patricia Partington BA FRSA, President, National Association of Head Teachers

Miss Sybil Phoenix MBE, Counsellor, Methodist Local Preacher

Miss Amanda Platell BA(Hons), Director, Mirror Group Newspapers

Ms Sally Potter, Film Director

Mrs Patience Purdy MA, President, The National Council of Women of Great Britain

Mrs Gail Rebuck BA, Chairman and Managing Director, Random House UK Ltd

Ms Janet Ritterman, Director, Royal College of Music

Miss Deborah Rowland MA, Management Development Director, Pepsi-Cola International

Miss Alexander Shulman, Editor, *Vogue*

Ms Sally Soames, Photographer

Miss Patricia Scotland QC, Barrister

Mrs Susan Stockley, Chairman, National Federation of Women's Institutes

Mrs Veronica Sutherland MA BA CMG, Under-Secretary, Personnel

Ms Barbara Switzer, Ass. General Secretary, Manufacturing Science and Finance Union

Miss Elizabeth Tyson, Director, Philanthropic Programmes, SmithKline Beecham
Ms Katherine Wade, President, Oxford Union
Mrs Ann Wheatley-Hubbard OBE FRAgS, Master of the Worshipful Company of Farmers

Monday 31st October 1994
THEME: WHAT MATTERS MOST

Speakers:
HRH The Duchess of Gloucester GCVO
Mrs Helen Suzman, International Guest of Honour
Sandi Toksvig MA(Hons), Comedian

Guests of Honour:
HRH The Duchess of Gloucester, GCVO
Ms Diane Abbott MA, Member of Parliament
Pam Ayres, Writer/Entertainer
Miss Glenda Bailey BA(Hons), Editor-in-Chief, *Marie Claire*
Ms Sue Barker, Sports Presenter, BBC TV
Miss Presiley Baxendale QC, Barrister
Dr Fiona Caldicott MA BM BCh FRCPsych FAMS PRCPsych, President, Royal College of Psychiatrists
Paddy Campbell, Executive Chairman, Women of the Year Lunch
Mrs Jean Clark, President, National Council of Women
Mrs Suzanne Durr, South African Embassy
Dr June Goodfield BSc PhD, President, International Health & Biomedicine
Ms Sophie Grigson BSc(Hons), Food Writer/Broadcaster
Mrs Odette Hallowes GC MBE Légion d'Honneur, Founder Vice-President, Women of the Year Lunch
Miss Angela Hooper CBE, The Right Worshipful The Lord Mayor of Westminster
Mrs Patricia Hopkins AADipl RIBA, Architect
Ms Mary Hufford BA MA, Deputy General Secretary, NUT
Dame Jill Knight DBE, Member of Parliament
Maggie Koumi, Editor, *Hello!*
Dr Penelope Leach PhD, Psychologist/Author

Ms Maureen Lipman Hon DLitt, Actress/Writer
Lady Lothian FJI, Founder President, Women of the Year Lunch
Ms Sue MacGregor OBE, Presenter, BBC Radio Four
Mrs Anne Maguire, Author
Mrs Penny Marshall BA, Television Correspondent
Ms Sheila Masters LLB FCA ATII, Director, Bank of England
Mrs Marguerite Mitchell, National Chairman, Townswomen's Guilds
Dr Yvonne Moores DSC, Chief Nursing Adviser, Department of Health
Rabbi Julia Neuberger MA, Chairman, Camden and Islington Community Services NHS Trust
Miss Jennifer Page, Chief Executive, English Heritage
Ms Sara Parkin RGN, Environmentalist/Green Party
Her Honour Judge Pearce, Circuit Judge
Diana Rigg, Actress
Ms Janine Roxborough-Bunce MIPR, President, Association of Women in PR
Miss Galina Samtsova, Artistic Director, The Scottish Ballet
Miss Helen Sharman, Astronaut
Miss Clare Short, Member of Parliament
Ms Hilary Strong, Director, Edinburgh Festival Fringe
Mrs Helen Suzman, International Guest of Honour
Miss Janet Suzman Hon DLitt, Actress
Ms Sandi Toksvig MA(Hons), Comedian
Miss Joanna Trollope MA(Hons), Writer
Ms Elizabeth Tyson, Director, Corporate Responsibility Programmes, SKB
Ms Marina Warner, 1994 Reith Lectures
Yazz, Pop Singer

Monday 30th October 1995
THEME: 40 YEARS ON – HAVE WE COME A LONG WAY, BABY?

Speakers:
HRH The Princess Alexandra
Madame Simone Veil, International Guest of Honour
Kamlesh Bahl LLB(Hons), Chairwoman, Equal Opportunities Commission
Ruby Wax, Performer and Writer

Guests of Honour:

HRH Princess Alexandra, Royal Guest of Honour

Professor Judith Adams MBBS FRCR FRCP, Clinical Radiologist

Ms Mary Allen MA, Secretary-General, The Arts Council of England

Miss Barbara Amiel BA, Journalist

Ms Kamlesh Bahl LLB(Hons), Chairwoman, Equal Opportunities Commission

Dame Josephine Barstow DBE BA(Hons), Opera Singer

Mrs Liz Bavidge JP BA(Hons), Co-Chair, Women's National Commission

Dr Sheila M Brock MA PhD, Campaign Director, Museum of Scotland

Paddy Campbell, Fashion Designer; Chairman, Women of the Year Lunch

Dr Jane Carmichael MBE PhD, Managing Director, Danisco Seed UK

Mrs Pauline Clare BA(Hons) MIMgt, Chief Constable of Lancashire

Mrs Jean Clark, President, National Council of Women

Ms Lisa Clayton, Round-the-World Yachtswoman

Baroness Dean of Thornton-le-Fylde BA(Hons), Chairman of ICSTIS

Professor Ann Dowling MA PhD CEng FIMechE, Professor of Mechanical Engineering

Ms Margaret Drabble CBE, Writer

Mrs Audrey Eyton, Animal Welfare Campaigner

Ms Nicole Fahri, Designer

Ms Victoria Glendinning MA Hon DLitt FRSL, Writer

Alison Gomme BA(Hons), Prison Governor

Mrs Tricia Guild, Chairwoman/Creative Director, Designers Guild

Ms Sally Gunnell MBE, Athlete

Ms Anna Harvey, Deputy Editor, *Vogue*

Mrs Khanam Hassan, President, Moslem Women's Association

Lady Howe JP BSc, Chairman, Broadcasting Standards Council

Mrs Jan Kern, Commercial Director, Littlewoods International

Dr Alam Khan JP MB BS FRCS FRCOG FRCA, Consultant Anaesthetist

Miss Jennifer Laing, Chairman, Saatchi & Saatchi Advertising

Dr Nancy Lane OBE BSc MSc DPhil PhD ScD, Scientist

Ms S Lloyd-Roberts BA(Hons), Television Reporter

Lady Lothian FJI, Founder President, Women of the Year Lunch

HE Miss Maureen Macglashan MA LLM, HM Ambassador to the Holy See

Mrs Wenche Marshall Foster, Chief Executive, Perrier (UK)

Ms Sheena McDonald MA, Journalist and Broadcaster

Ms Pauline Milne DIPAD MA, Screenwriter

Dr Yvonne Moores Hon DSc, Chief Nursing Officer, Department of Health

Ms Sara Nathan BA(Hons), Editor, Channel 4 News

Mica Paris, Singer and Actress

Ms Allison Pearson BA (Cantab), Journalist

Ms Dawn Primarolo BA(Hons), Member of Parliament

Mrs Margaret Prosser, National Organiser, TGWU

Mrs Paula Ridley JP DL MA, Chairman, Liverpool Housing Action Trust

Miss Amanda Roocroft RGRNCM RNCM, Opera Singer

Ms Mary Ann Sieghart MA(Hons), Journalist

Baroness Smith of Gilmorehill MA, House of Lords

Mother Mary Agnes Soli, Sister of Mercy

Mrs Elizabeth Southey, National Chairman, NFWI

Ms Janet Street-Porter, President, Ramblers Association

Madame Simone Veil, International Guest of Honour

Ms Beverly Warner BA MSW, Regional Director, NSPCC

Miss Ruby Wax, Performer and Writer

Mrs Zelda West-Meads, Counsellor, Journalist and Writer

Miss Margaret Willes BA Dip Hist Arch, Publisher

Lady Wilson, Poet

Monday 7th October 1996
THEME: BALANCE

Speakers:

HRH Princess Michael of Kent, Royal Guest of Honour

Madame Vigdis Finnbogadottir, Former President of Iceland and International Guest of Honour

Ms Heather Rabbatts BA MSc, Chief
Executive, London Borough of Lambeth
Ms Victoria Wood DLitt,
Comedienne/Playwright

Guests of Honour:
HRH Princess Michael of Kent, Royal
Guest of Honour
Mrs Louise Aitken-Walker MBE, Former
World Champion Rally Driver
Mrs Julie Allison MA, General Secretary,
Royal College of Midwives
Miss Barbara Amiel BA, Journalist
Ms Janet Anderson, Member of Parliament
The Hon Mrs Justice Arden DBE MA
LLM, High Court Judge
Miss Joan Armatrading, Singer/Songwriter
Miss Jane Asher, Actress/Writer/Business
Woman
Floella Benjamin,
Broadcaster/Writer/Producer and
Chairman of the Lunch
Dr Susan Bewley MD MRcog MA,
Obstetrician
Miss Samantha Bewster, First woman to
sail single-handed round the world, East
to West
Miss Rosemary Brook MA FIPR,
President, Institute of Public Relations
Miss Deborah Bull, Principal Dancer,
Royal Ballet
Dame Fiona Caldicott DBE MA BM BCh
FRCP, Principal, Somerville College,
Oxford
Ms Sue Cameron MA,
Broadcaster/Journalist
Ms Naomi Campbell, Model
Mrs Pat Campbell, Vice Life President,
Women Together for Peace in N Ireland
Miss Anne Diamond, TV Presenter/Cot
Death Campaigner
Ms Rosie Eagleson LLB, General Secretary,
The Association of Magisterial Officers
Madame Vigdis Finnbogadottir, Former
President of Iceland and International
Guest of Honour
Ms Victoria Glendinning MA DLitt,
Author
Mrs Pat Greenhill OBE, Trustee of
Dunblane Fund
Mrs Valerie Grove MA, Journalist
Mrs Lois Hainsworth FCIJ FRSA,
President, Institute of Journalists
Rev Moira Harkes BD, Minister of
Religion, Dunblane Cathedral

Miss Claire Holder MA, Chief Executive,
Notting Hill Carnival
Mrs Tessa Jowell, Member of Parliament
Ms Helena Kennedy LLD, QC
Ms Maureen Lipman DLitt MA,
Actress/Author
Lady Lothian FJI, Founder President,
Journalist/Author
The Lady MacDonald, Cookery
Writer/Catering Specialist
Mrs Monica McWilliams BSc Dip TP MSc,
Northern Ireland Women's Coalition
Dr Angela Milner BSc PhD, Scientist, Dept
of Palaeontology, Natural History
Museum
Dame Pauline Neville-Jones DCMG MA,
Managing Director, NatWest Markets
Mrs Jenny Pitman, Racehorse Trainer
Ms Heather Rabbatts BA MSc, Chief
Executive, London Borough of Lambeth
Ms Jessica Rutherford BA PGCE FSA,
Head of Museums & Director of Royal
Pavilion Brighton
Mrs Pearl Sagar, Northern Ireland
Women's Coalition
Ms Daphne Todd HDFA, President of the
Royal Society of Portrait Painters
Ms Anthea Turner, TV Personality
Mrs Beryl Vertue, Chairman of Hartswood
Films/Film Producer
Ms Deirdre Vine BA, Editor, *Woman's
Journal*
Ms Ruby Wax, Actress/Writer
Mrs Grace Wedekind, President, national
Council of Women of Great Britain
Ms Vivienne Westwood OBE, Designer
Ms Victoria Wood DLitt,
Comedienne/Playwright

Monday 6th October 1997
THEME: MAKING A DIFFERENCE

Speakers:
HRH Queen Noor of Jordan, Royal and
International Guest of Honour
Rt Hon Harriet Harman MP
Vivienne Westwood OBE, Fashion
Designer

Guests of Honour:
HRH Queen Noor of Jordan, Royal and
International Guest of Honour
Madame Marie Ayoub, Wife of Jordanian
Ambassador

Mrs Mary Barnard, Chairman, Council of National Childbirth Trust

Professor Jocelyn Bell Burnell Bsc PhD

Mrs Uta Bellion MSc Civil Eng, Policy Director, Friends of the Earth

Ms Floella Benjamin, Broadcaster/Writer/ Producer and Chairman of the Lunch

Dr Mary Berry MA PhD MUSB, Founder and Director, Schola Gregoriana of Cambridge

Ms Christine Blower, President, National Union of Teachers

Ms Rosie Boycott, Editor, *Sunday Independent*

Miss Darcy Bussell OBE, Principal Ballerina

Ms Kay Carberry BA, Head of Equal Rights Department, Trade Union Congress

Ms Rita Clifton, President, Women's Advertising Club of London

Mrs Shirley Conran, Novelist

The Countess of Dalkeith BSc, Chairman, Museum of Scotland

Professor Mari Fitzduff PhD, Director, INCORE (Initiative for N Ireland Conflict Resolution & Ethnicity)

Miss Ann Foster, Director, Scottish Consumer Council

Captain Lisa Giles, Captain, The Royal Signals Motorcycle Display Team – The White Helmets

Mrs Ann Gloag, Managing Director, Stage Coach Holdings

Mrs Renée Goddard, Media Consultant

Mrs Valerie Grove MA, Journalist

Mrs Lois Hainsworth, President, Chartered Institute of Journalists

Mrs Harfiyah Abdel Haleem, Islamic Writer/Reviewer and Adviser, IQRA Trust

Ms Susan Hardwick BA, President, Association of Women in PR

The Rt Hon Harriet Harman MP, Secretary of State for Social Security and Minister for Women

Dr Mary Harris BSc PhD, Director General, Year of Engineering Success

Mrs Mimi Johnson BCom FRSA, National Chairman, Standing Conference of Women's Organisations

Ms Tessa Jowell MP, Minister of State for Public Health

The Hon Mrs Tessa Keswick, Director, Centre for Policy Studies

Mrs Doreen Lawrence BA, Civil Rights Campaigner

Miss Victoria Legge-Bourke LVO CVO, Executive Director, Goldman Sachs Int Ltd

Ms Kathy Lette, Columnist/Author

The Baroness Linklater

Lady Lothian OBE FCJI, Founder President, Women of the Year Lunch; Journalist/Author

Ms Joanna Macgregor BA, Virtuoso Musician

Mrs Helen McGrath OBE, General President, KFAT (Nat Union of Knitwear, Footwear & Apparel Trades)

Ms Claire Makin MBA FRCS, Chief Executive, Royal Institution of Chartered Surveyors

Mrs Eileen Meadmore, National Chairman, National Federation of Women's Institutes

Ms Joanna Moorhead BA, Journalist

Mrs Lorna Muirhead, President, Royal College of Midwives

Miss Deborah Oliver TD MA, Director of Communications, The Post Office

Mrs Sarah Parkin RGN, Director, Forum for the Future

Mrs Liz Paver FCollP FRSA, National President, National Association of Headteachers

Miss Lisa Potts, George Medal, Nursery Nurse

Mrs Rita Restorick, Peace Campaigner

Dame Diana Rigg DBE, Actress

Mrs Perween Warsi, Managing Director, S & A Foods Ltd

Mrs Grace Wedekind, President, National Council of Women

Ms Vivienne Westwood OBE, Fashion Designer

Ms Anne Weyman BSc FCA, Chief Executive, Family Planning Association

The Rt Hon Ann Widdecombe MA, MP

Dr Sheila Willatts FRCA FRCP MD, Vice President, Royal College of Anaesthetists

Miss Barbara Woroncow MA FMA, President, Museums Association of Great Britain

Mrs Rosalind Wright, Director, Serious Fraud Squad

Mrs Betty Yao, Managing Director of first Chinese Satellite TV Channel in Europe

Miss Kirsty Young, TV Presenter, Channel 5 News

Mrs Pat Zadora, National President, United Kingdom Federation of Business & Professional Women

Speakers:
HRH Duchess of Kent GCVO, Royal Guest of Honour
Anna Scher, Principal, The Anna Scher Theatre
Meera Syal MBE, Actress/Writer

Guests of Honour:
HRH Duchess of Kent GCVO, Royal Guest of Honour
Baroness Valerie Amos MA, Director, Amos Fraser Bernard
Miss Joan Armatrading DLitt, Singer/Composer
Ms Floella Benjamin, Broadcaster/Writer/Producer; Chairman of the Lunch
Miss May Blood MBE DLitt, Ulster Peaceworker
Lady Cecil Cameron BA, Deputy Chairman, Save the Children
Mrs Anne Carr, Co-ordinator, Ulster Women Together for Peace
Ms Caroline Charles, Fashion Designer
Ms Rita Donaghy OBE BA, Trade Unionist UNISON
Ms Charlotte Eager BA MA, Journalist/Editor, *Mensa Quest*
Ms Helen Fielding, Author
Professor Maria Fitzgerald BA PhD, Research Neuroscientist
Mrs Renée Goddard, Media Consultant
Ms Tanni Grey MBE, Project Co-ordinator for the BT Athletics Development Programme
Mrs Marjory Hall, National Chairman, Townswomen's Guilds
Dr Mae-Wan Ho, Author/Biologist, Director, Bioelectrodynamics Laboratory, The Open University
Ms Kelly Holmes, Athlete/Gold Medallist
The Rt Hon Baroness Jay of Paddington, Minister for Women
Ms Sue Lawley BA, Broadcaster, *Desert Island Discs*
Ms Frances Lawrence MA FRSA, Teacher/The Philip Lawrence Awards

Miss Victoria Legge-Bourke CVO, Executive Director, Goldman Sachs/Lehman
Miss Maureen Lipman DLitt MA, Actress/Author
Lady Lothian OBE FCJI, Founder President, Women of the Year; Journalist/Author
The Hon Diana Makgill CVO, Diplomatic Protocol Consultant
Ms Sue McGregor OBE DLitt, Broadcaster, *Today*
Professor Dr Susan McKenna-Lawlor PhD, Space Scientist and Astrophysicist
Ms Alison Moore, Teacher, Victim of Racist Violence
Mrs Lorna Muirhead SRN SCM MTD, President, Royal College of Midwives
Ms Elizabeth Murdoch BA, General Manager, BSkyB
Ms Dee Nolan, Editor, *You Magazine*
Ms Jennifer Page CBE, Chief Executive, New Millennium Experience
Dame Merle Park DBE, Director, Royal Ballet School
Miss Rachel Price, Manager, John Frieda Hairdressing
Ms Gail Rebuck BA, Chief Executive, Random House UK
Ms Joan Ruddock, MP, Lewisham & Deptford
Miss Jennifer Saunders, Comedienne/Writer
Mrs Vivienne Scantlebury, Banker
Ms Anna Scher, Principal, The Anna Scher Theatre
The Baroness Scotland QC, Barrister/Deputy High Court Judge
Ms Helen Sharman, Astronaut
Mrs Yasmin Sheikh, Author, *Successful Asian Women*
Ms Jill Sinclair, Managing Director, SPZ Recording Company
Lt Fiona Stewart, First Female Officer, Sword of Honour Award
Dame Valerie Strachen DBE DCB, Chairman of Her Majesty's Custom & Excise
Ms Meera Syal MBE, Actress/Writer
Mrs Penny Vincenzi, Novelist/Journalist
Mrs Esther Wachsman MA, Teacher, Director of Nachshon Wachsman Centre for Tolerance and Understanding
Dr Helen Wallace BSc PhD, Senior Scientist, Greenpeace

Professor Helen Wallace MA PhD,
Director, Sussex European Institute
Mrs Grace Wedekind AIL FRSA,
President, National Council of Women
of Great Britain
Ms Lesley White, Journalist

Monday 11th October 1999
THEME: HUMAN RIGHTS

Speakers:
Linda Gray, International Guest Speaker,
UN Ambassador for Human Rights;
Actress, *Dallas*.
Kathy Lette, Author
Helen Bamber OBE, Human Rights
Campaigner. Director, Medical
Foundation for the Care of Tortured
Resistance Women
Dr Sheila Cassidy BMBCh MA DSc DLitt,
Victim of Torture. Hospice Nurse,
Plymouth Oncology Centre

Guests of Honour:
The Rt Hon Janet Anderson MP, Minister
for Tourism, Film & Broadcasting
Miss Kamlesh Bahl CBE, Deputy Vice
President, The Law Society
Helen Bamber OBE, Human Rights
Campaigner. Director, Medical
Foundation for the Care of Tortured
Resistance Women
Professor Janet Bainbridge PhD, Professor
and Expert on GMF Foods
Floella Benjamin,
Broadcaster/Writer/Producer;
Chairman of the Lunch and Assembly
Sister Lavinia Byrne DD, Religious Sister
and Broadcaster
Helen Carey, Chairwoman, National
Federation of Women's Institutes
Dr Sheila Cassidy BMBCh MA DSc DLitt,
Victim of Torture. Hospice Nurse,
Plymouth Oncology Centre
Ms Wendy Cope MA FRSL, Author.
Shortlisted for Poet Laureate
Maureen Davies, Lifetime Achievement -
Top of the Class Teachers Award
Winner
Desree, Singer, Songwriter. Award for Best
British Female Artist
Jennifer Duguid, Consultant
Haematologist
Sylvia Dunn, President, National

Association of Gypsy Women
Dr Winifred Ewing MA FRSA LLD MEP,
President, Scottish National Party
Dr Christine Gamble, First Woman to be
Director of Chatham House
Daphne Glick BA MA MPhil PhD,
President, National Council of Women
of Great Britain
Mrs Renée Goddard, Media Consultant
Linda Gray, UN Ambassador for Human
Rights; Actress, *Dallas*
Professor Susan Greenfield DPhil DSc,
Professor of Physiology. First Female
Director, Royal Institution
Professor Germaine Greer PhD,
Author/Philosopher/Lecturer
Ms Marjory Hall, National Chairman,
Townswomen's Guilds
Barbara Hay CMG MBE, Immediate past
British Ambassador to the Republics of
Uzbekistan & Tajikistan
Miss Leela Kapila OBE FRCS, President,
British Association of Surgeons
Mrs Lucy Keaveney BA HDip, Ulster
Child Abuse Campaigner. Primary
School Teacher
Sarah Kestleman, Actress. Award winning
play *Copenhagen*
Mrs Glenys Kinnock BA, Member of the
European Parliament, Labour, Wales
Mrs Lynda la Plante, Author/Script Writer
Pinky le Grelle, Shoots for England in
International Competitions, eg
Olympics
Ms Kathy Lette, Author
Gemma Levine FRSA, Photographer
Lady Lothian OBE FCIJ,
Author/Journalist
Ms Norma Machell, Primary Teacher of
the Year
Ms Sheila McKechnie, Managing
Director, Consumer Association
Julie Mellor BA MSc, Chair of the EO
Commission
Ms Gloria Mills MBE, Equal
Opportunities Commission, UNISON
Mrs Trish Morris-Thompson MBA RGN
RM, Hospital Management
Indira Patel OBE, Teacher, Commodity
Trader
Ms Libby Purves, Broadcaster
Miss Jane Reed, Director of Corporate
Affairs, News International
Miss Emma Sergeant BA, Portrait Painter
and Draughtsman

Samantha Shaw, Dress Designer
The Baroness Smith of Gilmorehill DL,
President, Edinburgh Fringe Festival
The Lady Helen Taylor, Art Gallery
Director. Fashion Representative.

Susan Watts BSc Physics, Science
Correspondent, BBC *Newsnight*
Fiona Weir, Director of Campaigns,
Amnesty International
Vanessa Whitburn, Editor, *The Archers*,
BBC Radio

Guest Lists and Themes 1964–1999

As they appeared in the Women of the Year guest lists

Monday 12th October 1964
THEME: MY FAVOURITE MAN

Mrs Ruby F Adams
Miss MKM Aiken BA LLB
Mrs M Allday
Miss Diana Allen
Miss Avril Angers
Miss Eileen Asquith MFH
Viscountess Astor
Miss WM Attwood
Mrs ILE Austin-Smith FRIBA AA Dipl
Mrs Charlotte Baden-Powell AA Dipl
  ARIBA
Lady Balcon MBE
Mrs Aileen Ballantyne ARIBA AA Dipl
Dona Marina Bandeira de Carvalho
Miss DF Banister
Mrs Elizabeth Barber MA
Miss Frances Barker MA
Dr Rosetta Barker MB BCH BAO DPH
Miss Monica E Barnes SRN DN STD
  ONC MMS
Mrs S Barrett SRN
Mrs Marie Battle BSc MSc PhD
Dame Doris Beale DBE RRC OStJ
Mrs Geraldine Beamish
Mrs Eva Beecroft
Mrs Ellen Belchem
Mrs Jane Bell MBE BA
Mrs Ruth W Bell
Miss PJ Bennett
Miss BK Billot
Miss Kitty Black
Miss Sheila P Black
Mrs Jean Blackden LRAM (ELOC)
Miss Lorna Blackie MA
Lady Blane OBE
Mrs Paul Boissevain AIRBA
Mrs Gertrude Book
Miss Joyce Booth MSIA AMIPA

Miss M Bosson SRN SCM
Miss Lally Bowers
Mrs Beryl L Bowker ARIBA
Mrs Paddy Bowling
Mrs E Bowyer SRN SCM
Miss Kay Branston
Mrs Kay Brebner
Lady Brocklehurst
Miss ME Brown
Mrs Kathleen Browne SWA ARDS ATD
Miss NS Brymer RMPA RMN SRN SCM
Dr Alice E Buck MD ChB
Miss Margaret P Bucknall-Smith SRN
  SCM RFN
Mrs JS Budge MB ChB
Mrs Maurice Bulpitt
Mrs E Burr SRN SCM
Miss Mary Burr MA MPS
Alderman Miss M M C Burrows BEM JP
  CC
Miss H Langsdale Bussell
Miss G Hagar Butler SRN SCM MTD
Dr Lily C Butler MRCS LRCP DPH
Miss Hilda Butterworth BA
Mrs Lois Bygrave
Miss Juliann M Calder BSc EdB FEIS
Miss Joan Cambridge MSc G
Lady Campbell (Lizbeth Webb)
Miss Eila M J Campbell MA FSA
Mrs Wishart Campbell MA OStJ
Miss CM Carlisle LRAM
Miss Ann Caroll LRAM
Miss Phyllis V Carr ISO
Miss NW Carter PHC MPS
Miss JJ Caulton MSCP
Miss Judith Chalmers
Lieut-Colonel J B Chambers ARRC SRN
  SCM
Mrs DM Charlton OBE BSc
Miss Gladys Charlton SRN SCM
The Lady Chesham

Miss Gladys V Chesterman
Mrs Mavis A Chipperfield
Councillor Mrs J E Chrismas JP CC
Lady Clark
Miss Elizabeth L Clarke ISO
Mrs Elsie Clarke
Mrs ML Clarke FRCVS
Miss Mary Clegg MSc PhD
Miss Julia Clements (Lady Seton) FRHS
Miss CP Clyne SCM
Miss Myrella Cohen LLB
Miss EL Coleman NDD CDD
Miss Patricia G Coles MA
Mrs Margaret F Collett BA
Miss Patience Collier
Mrs Phyllis G Collins
Miss RO Corke
Miss Freda M Cowell BSc
Miss Doris L Cox
Miss Sheila Mary Crane ARRC SRN
  SCM
Mrs Vera D Crane BA
Miss Ethel M Cruickshank BSc PhD
  MRSH
Miss Rosalie Crutchley
Mrs LM Cumbers
Mrs LN Darbyshire BA
Miss VA Davidge MBE
Miss SA Megan Davies
Mrs Dorothy Day BA
Miss Lydia De Burgh RUA
Miss Mary Delane
Dr Gertrude M Delaney MB BCH BAO
  NUI
Mrs MA Dennis BSc
The Hon Lady de Zulueta
Miss Margaret M Dibb
Miss Nancy P Dibley LRAM
Dr Ursula M Dick MB BS MRCS LRCP
  RCOG
Miss Catherine M Dickie SRN SCM
Miss Jennifer Dickson ARE
Mrs JL Christian Dilcock
Miss Margaret I Dingle
Miss Gertrude C Dixon CBE DSc
Mrs Honor Dobbs
Mrs BA P Dobson OBE
Dr Honor Doyle MD BCH BAO MRCP
  DCH
Miss KM Draycott
Mrs NH Drury
Dr Madelaine Duke BSc MB ChB
Miss Joseen Duncan
Miss Angela Dunne
Mrs Kay Durrant

Miss Dorothy M Eade SRN SCM RMN
  BTA
The Mayor of East Retford, Councillor
  Miss Barbara W L Keal
Miss EM Edmonds
Miss MRJ Edwards MBE BSc FLS FMA
The Mayor of Liskeard, Councillor Mrs
  Eve Ellam
Mrs SS Elliott MBE
Mrs Brenda Ellis LSIA
Miss Betty Entwhistle LLB
Mrs Frederick Erroll
Mrs Aleda J Erskine
Miss Eileen Evans MSIA
Miss Hazel M Evans
Miss M Evans PHC
Councillor Mrs W G Evans JP, Chairman,
  Scarborough RDC
Miss WK Farmer MWES
Mrs MA Farr JP
Miss ME Faulkner MBE
Councillor Mrs Peggy E Fenner JP
Mme Lena B Fentiman LRAM ATCL
  MRST
Councillor Mrs V Ferrari
Mrs Fierz BSc
Miss Stella P M Fisher
Miss KM Fitzsimmons
Mrs Percyval H Ford SSStJ
Dr Mary I Foreman MB BS MRCS LRCP
Mrs Annabelle Forrest
Mrs Sylvia F Forster
Mrs Malcolm Foster
Mrs Catherine Foxell SRN SCM
Miss Judith E Frankel BSc QS ARICS
  MCQS
Mrs Anna M Frankl LLB LLD
Mrs Fraser-Tytler CBE TD JP
Miss Dorothy Freeborn
Miss Cecilia Freeman
Mrs Kathleen Freeman OBE
Mrs Eunice French MA
Miss Hermene French
Mrs J M Frizell LDS
Miss Dorothy Furbank
Miss IA Gallagher SRN RFN SCM
Mrs F W Garnett
Mrs Patrick Garrett
Dr V Jean Gavin JP MRCS LRCP
Miss Eunice Gayson
Mrs CM Geary-Knox
Mrs Doris Gerrard RBA
Mrs Audrey L Gilby FCIB
Miss Sylvia Gilley
Dr Camilla H Gillies MA

Mrs Guy Gluckstein
Mrs Edna Glyn
Dr Etheldreda Godfrey BSc MB ChB LM
Lady Nicholas Gordon-Lennox
Mrs PE Gordon-Spencer
Surg Lt Cdr C C Green RN MB ChB
  DRCOG FRCS
Mrs Gabrielle M Green
Mrs Helen M Green
Miss Joyce V Green ARIBA DA
Mrs MA Greenhough
Miss Anna M Greig LDS
Miss MG Greysmith BSc
Miss Phyllis Groves
Mrs ML Guays MBE
Mrs GI Habershon CC
Dr Jean Haine MB ChB
Miss Lucy Halford MSIA
Miss Garda Hall ARAM LRAM
Mrs Doris J Halley MBE BSc
Dr Margaret Hammond MB ChB
Miss CH Hampton
Mrs V Drummond Harcus ARRC
Mrs Leslie Hardern MIPR
Miss Isabella A Harker
Mrs MLR Harkness BSc
Mrs Rita D Harland
Miss Mary Harlow-Robinson ARCM
  LTCL
Miss Josephine Harris
Councillor Mrs Ruth Harrowing JP
Dr Margaret Hauxwell MB ChB
Mrs Kay Hawes
Councillor Mrs C M G Haynes CC
Mrs Esma M Hazelden
The Mayor of Buxton, Councillor Miss EI
  Heathcote JP
Mrs Ethel Heathcote FCIS
Miss Bridget Heaton-Armstrong
Miss Ellen Annie Heckford BA FCIS FVI
Professor E J A Henderson
Miss Romy Henning
Miss Constance H Henry MBE
Miss Rene Hetherington ARCA RBA
  ATD
Alderman Mrs E M Hews CBE
Dr J Heylen MB BS LRCP MRCS
Miss Jessie M Higgins RRC SRN SVM
  OStJ
Miss Mavis I Hilton MCSP
Mrs Julia Ferguson Hinchliffe Dipl Arch
  ARIBA
Miss Phyllis Hindle NDD
Miss Verna Hitchcock
Mrs Aubrey Hitching

Lady Hoare
Miss Moira Hoddell ARCA
Mrs JP Holt
Miss Mary Holt MA LLB
Miss Flora V Honywood
Miss Denise Hope
Miss Isaline B Horner MA
Dr Sibyl Horner CBE MB BS DPH DIH
Mrs MK Horsley
Mrs Myfanwy Howell CBE JP MA
Mrs AM Howker
Mrs Dorothy Hubball
Mrs Gladys Humm
Mrs Elsie M Hunt
Miss MB Hyde MSc MIBiol
Mrs Hyde Hyde-Thompson
Mrs Paul Hyde-Thompson
Councillor Mrs Godfrey Iredell CC
Mrs Celia L Jones
Dr Esther Jones
Miss G Mary Jones
Miss Hilary J Jones LLB
Mrs Marjorie E Jones
Miss Leonie Jonleigh RBA
Miss JR Joyce
Dr Winifred Kane MB BS DPH DCH
Mrs Phyllis AN Keates SRN SCM
Mrs Brian Keeling
Miss HS Keer MB ChB DTM H
Mrs MD Kemp
Mrs Mary P Kendrick BA
Dr Agnes Kennedy FFA RCS
Mrs Monica Kennedy ARIBA
Miss NW Kennedy
Dr Esther S Kerr MA MB BCH RCOG
  DOB
Mrs C Kerridge
Miss EM Killby OBE
Miss Alison King
Miss Dorothy A Kingsley LRAM
Mrs Beryl Kitz MA
Mrs Betty Knightly
Miss Marjorie Knights OBE
Miss Jenny Laird BA
Miss Amy Landreth
Dr Gwen M Langham-Hobart MB BS
Dr Jean M Langham-Hobart MB ChB
Miss Jean Lanning
Mrs Gwen Lansdell BA
Miss Eve Larsen
The Hon Lady Lascelles
Miss GES Leaver MBE
The Duchess of Leeds
Miss Margaret Leischner DES RCA FSIA
Miss Iris ME Lemare ARCM

Miss EM Leverson MBE
Councillor Mrs DM Levey JP
Miss J Lewis SRN SCM RFN
Dona Maria Ieda Linhares
The Mayor of Liskeard, Councillor Mrs Eve Ellam
Mrs JE Lloyd ARIBA
Miss Sheila M Lloyd MA BSc
Miss JM Ludford
Miss Robina Lund
Mrs IJ Lyons
Dr Isobel O Macalister MBE MB ChB DPH JP
Dona Hilda Macedo
Mrs Gena Mackinnon OBE
Dr Annie D Maclaine MB ChB
Miss Elizabeth G M Macmillan BVM & S MRCVS
Mrs Janet W Macnaughton
Miss KD Maddever OBE NDD
Third Officer S M Malham WRNS
Miss J Mann SRN SCM
Mrs Jean Marshall
Miss DE Martin
Mrs Rachel McBryde
Miss MC McCormack BDS
Councillor Mrs CN McGeorge SRN CC
Miss EA McMichael MA
Mrs Hilda M Menzies
Councillor Mrs Joan Merry
Miss Rosemary Meynell
Miss Lois Mitchison BA
Councillor Miss Diana H Moody
Councillor Mrs William Morley CC
Mrs F Morris
Mrs I Morris
Miss Jill Morris DES RCA NDD FRSA
Mrs BC Morton Palmer JP
Dr Margit Muller MD MRCS LRCP
Miss Agnes Mulvey RGN BTA
Dr Evelyn Munro MB ChB DPH
Mrs DJW Murray
Miss Margaret M Murray MBE SRN RMN RMPA
Miss F Murtland
Mrs Lilian Musson
Miss ME Myers RRC
Mrs Constance Nathan
Mrs Harold Needler
Dr Dorothy Neilan JP MB ChB DPH
Miss Marjory Nelson
Miss Evelyn New MSIA
Mrs VAB Newcomb FIPA
Councillor Mrs A M Newland
Miss IC Nichols MPS

Miss DE Nicolas MBE
Mrs Kathleen D Nock SRN IMA
Miss Theresa M Norman BSc MS
The Lady Normanbrook
Miss Sheila Norris
Mrs Anne C Norton FCA
The Lady Helen Nutting
The Mayor of Oldbury, Alderman Mrs Eva Pine MBE JP
Dr June Olley PhD BSc
Miss Eve Orme
Councillor Mrs B M Osborn JP CC
Miss Jean D Oswald LDS
Mrs Elizabeth Overbury
Miss KN Owen FCIB
Miss Margaret E Owen SRN SCM
Mrs JRM Page
Mrs Juliet Pannett
Miss AM Parker OBE SRN SCM RST
Miss Constance-Anne Parker
Mrs Marjorie Parkin
Mrs Molly Noyle Parkin ATD NTD
Miss Lily Pavey
Miss D Josephine Peace
Mrs M Peacock
Mrs Maeve Peake
Miss Eileen Peaker MA FRCog
Mrs Alison Pearce
The Hon Mrs Derrick Pease
Miss EA Peat SRN RFN
Dr EL Peet MB BS MD LDS
Miss Muriel A Pemberton ARWS FSIA ARCA WIAC
Mrs Eric Penn
Dr Joan K Perkins BA MB BChir DA FFARCS
Mrs Margaret Peters
Mrs Doris M Phillips MBE
Mrs Richard Piggott
Mrs Marion Plant DA LSIA
Mrs Ingrid Plowright
Miss Gwen Pollock
Dr Betsy Porter MRCS LRCP
Miss MG Powell
Miss Muriel Powell CBE
Madame SB Prunier
Mrs MH Purkiss-Ginn JP
Alderman Miss Rabagliati MBE
Mrs Godfrey Ralli
Mrs Rowland Rank
Lady Rankin
Mrs AEJ Rawlingson
Mrs Brenda Rawnsley
Miss W Rayment SRN SCM
Miss ME Rea

Miss Doris B Read
Miss Sarah M Read
Mrs William Read
Dr Elizabeth Rees MD
Mrs DC Reid
Miss M Rice SRN SCM
Councillor Mrs A Riddick CC
Mrs George Ritchie
Mrs E Rivers-Bulkeley
Dr Rosa Sutton Rivlin MRCS LRCP CPH
Dr Margaret J Roberts MB ChB DPH
Mrs Mary M Roberts BA
Mrs Hilda Robinson
Mrs MS Robinson MBE
Miss Georgie Rodgers
Miss NK Rodwell OBE
Dr Catherine M Rolant-Thomas MRCS
    LRCP LDS RCS
The Mayor of Romsey, Councillor Mrs P
    A Wellington JP
Mrs BP Ross-Esson FInstD
The Mayor of Henley-on-Thames,
    Councillor Mrs Monica Rowe
The Mayor of Royal Tunbridge Wells,
    Councillor Miss Clarinda Cox SRN
    SCM
Miss A Royalton-Kisch ARICS Dip Agric
The Lady Runcorn
Miss Agnes Russell
Miss Audrey Russell FRSA
Alderman Mrs Theresa Science Russell JP
Mrs Margaret E Ryder RMS
Mrs Flora M Sadler MA
Mrs Denise Salem
Mrs Julia Samson AC Dip Arch
Mrs Gerald Sanger JP
Mrs Hilda M Sargant
Miss EM Scott
Mrs Kathleen Scott Thorburn
Miss Joy Scully
Miss Mabel AL Sculthorp BA FIL
Major GA Sergant WRAC AMI MechE
Miss Brenda M Seymour BA LSIA
Miss AF Sharp SRN SCM DN
Mrs Laurie Newton Sharp
Miss Anne G Shaw CBE MA MIPRODE
Mrs Florence E Shaw
Miss Nan Shepherd MA LLD
Miss VD Shirtliffe BSc
Mrs L Silverston BA OBE
The Mayor of Slough, Alderman Mrs
    WM Watson JP
Dr Jessie Smailes MB ChB DPH
Miss Barbara E Smith
Miss EM Smith DN

Mrs Florence Smith
Lt Col EM Somerville OStJ ARRC
Miss Irene Southall FIHSG MWI
Mrs M Spencer
Miss Marian Spencer
Mrs B Spencer-Phillips
Councillor Miss Ann Spokes MA
Mrs Sproat MA
Mrs M Spurgin
Councillor Mrs Olive Standring JP
The Mayor of Stafford, Alderman Miss
    Iris Helen Moseley
Miss Jean E Stark
Mrs Leonora Steele SRN
Mrs Jocelyn Stevens
Lady Stewart OBE JP
Mrs Eileen Mary Strain
Miss June A Stubbs MSIA
Miss E Amy Studley
Miss E Summers
Miss Ethel Swinbank SRN
Mrs R Swinburne-Johnson
Miss Ursula H Tayler MIPA
Mrs Irene Thomas
Miss MA Thomas SRN RSCN
Miss Patricie E Thomas
Councillor Mrs ME Thompson
Mrs EM Thornberry MSR
Mrs Kitty DV Thorp
Miss Helena Tibau MBE
Dr Doreen M Tillotson MB ChB
Brigadier Margaret A Todd SRN SCM
Miss MM Torbet
Dona Zilah Mattos Totta
Miss BM Towle MBE
Miss Rachel A H Tripp ARCA
Mrs AGB Turner
Mrs L Tyson
Mrs Alison Uttley BSc
Madame Vernier
Miss BME Visick
Miss Rena Waddell
Miss Iris Wade
Miss Kathleen M Wade ARRC SRM
    RSCN SCM
Alderman Mrs Grace F Waggott JP
Miss Ruth Walder OBE
Mrs Richard Walker
Dr Vera B Walker MSc PhD MRCS LRCP
Miss Margaret Wallace SRN RMN SCM
Miss Nora Walley
The Hon Pamela Walpole OBE JP
Mrs Jean Walsh FPS
Miss Shirley Ward
Mrs Nellie Watson

214

Dr Barbara MQ Weaver PhD MRCVS
Miss Dora Webb RMS
Mrs EC Webster
Mrs EMH Webster OBE DStJ
Dr Mary A Webster MB ChB MRCS
    LRCP DObst RCog
Miss Molly Weir
Mrs PA Wells ARIBA
Councillor Mrs Mary Whipple BSc
Dr HRB White PLD
Alderman Mrs IG Wightman BA
Dr Frances G Wilcocks MB ChB DPH
Miss M Macklaier Wilkins BA
Miss EE Wilkinson MBE
Miss GG Williams SRN SCM RFN
    RNMD RMN
Mrs Margaret Williams
Miss May Williams
Miss Maureen Williamson
Mrs L Wills
Miss Rose Winslade MSIT MASEE
    AMIBM
Miss Hilda MM Wisdom FACCA FRVA
    SSStJ
Mrs Ann M Wiseman SRN
Mrs Alan A Withers LLB
Miss MM Wittich
Lady Wolfenden
Mrs Wonnacott
Mrs Catherine W Wood MA
Miss Cynthia Wood AADip ARIBA
    AMTPI AIARB
Miss Irene Wood
Councillor Mrs Gladys E Woodley
Miss FM Woolfit SRN
Mrs Kathleen Woolford
Mrs Dora Woolley
Mrs Mary Wright MB ChB
Mrs Barbara P Wroughton Dip Arch
    ARIBA
Miss Jean Zehetmayr ARIBA

Monday 4th October 1965
THEME: THE CHANCE OF A LIFETIME

Miss Joan Adair BA
Mrs RF Adams
Miss Margaret K M Aiken BA LLB
The Mayor of Aldeburgh, Mrs W B Agate
Miss Paula Allardyce BA
Miss Diana K Allen
Miss Margaret Allen BSc (Econ)
Mrs Jean Ames
Mrs Charles Anderson OBE

Miss Avril Angers
Mrs Lucie Arnheim FSIA
Mrs Janet Ashdown ARIBA
Miss Eileen Asquith MFH
The Viscountess Astor
Mrs Mary Atlee
Miss WM Attwood
Mrs ILE Austin-Smith FRIBA AA Dipl
Mrs Daphne A Alywin ARIBA
Mrs Charlotte Baden-Powell ARIBA AA
    Dipl
Lady Balcon MBE
Mrs Aileen Ballantyne AA Dipl ARIBA
Miss P Barclay-Smith MBE
Dr Rosetta Barker MB BCH BAO DPH
Miss Elizabeth Barling MA FIPM
Miss Doreen Barratt
Mrs S Barrett SRN
Miss Julia Bastian
Miss SB Bates SRN
Mrs EJ Battey MA BSc JP
Mrs Georgina Battiscombe
Miss AM Bayne ARIBA MTPI FRIAS
Miss Pauline Baynes MSIA
Mrs Geraldine Beamish
Mrs Ellen Belchem
Dr Anne Beloff-Chain BSc DPhil
Mrs Zoia Ann Beresford Dipl Arch ARIBA
Miss BK Billot
Mrs Jean Blackden LRAM (ELOC)
Miss Lorna Blackie MA
Lady Blane OBE
Mrs Barbara Boissevain ARIBA
Miss H Boleyne-Smedley SRN SCM
Mrs Gertrude Book
Dr D H Boon MRCS LRCP
Miss Joyce Booth MSIA AMIPA
Miss E Bowen
Miss E Bowyer SRN SCM
Miss Anita Brackley
Miss P Bridger MBE
Lady Brocklehurst
Mrs T Broome MBE
Miss ME Brown
Miss Agnes Browne SRN SCM
Miss Kathleen Browne ATD SWA ARDS
Dr AE Buck MB ChB
Mrs JS Budge MB ChB
Mrs BJ Bugden
Mrs M Bulpitt
Mrs ME Burgess FCA
Mrs E Burr SRN SCM
Miss Barbara Buss
Miss GH Butler SRN SCM MTD
Miss Jill Butterfield

Mrs JR Callis
Miss Joan Cambridge MSc G
Miss Elizabeth Cameron LLB
Mrs Wishart Campbell MA OStJ
Miss Jennifer Capon Dipl Arch ARIBA
Miss Ann Caroll LRAM
Miss MF Carpenter SRN SCM
Miss Winifred Carr
Mrs J Allan Cash
Miss Lee Cecil
Miss Margaret I Chalmers BSc PhD
Miss Madeline Chase
Miss GV Chesterman
Mrs Francis Chichester
Miss Tsai Chin
Mrs Mavis A Chipperfield
Mrs JE Chrismas JP CC
The Mayor of Christchurch, Cllr Mrs IA
    Stevenson JP
Mrs ML Clarke FRCVS
Miss Julia Clements (Lady Seton)
Mrs Anne Clough-Norton FCA
Miss Elizabeth Clowes SRN SCM
Miss CP Clyne SCM
Mrs JC Cockroft
Mrs Erna Cohn FSIA
Prof Monica M Cole BSc PhD
Miss EL Coleman NDD CDD
Miss Patricia G Coles MA
Mrs AR Collett BA
Mrs Elizabeth Colwyne-Foulkes BArch
    ARIBA Dip CD (L'Pool)
Mrs Audrey Compton FRIBA AA Dipl
Miss R Jean Conran BSc NFF
Miss Freda M Cowell BSc
The Deputy Mayor of Royal Tunbridge
    Wells, Cllr Mrs Clarinda Cox SRN SCM
Miss Doris Linda Cox
Dame Barbara Cozens DBE RRC
Mrs Charles Cross
Dr EM Cruickshank BSc PhD MRSH
Miss Rosalie Crutchley
Miss D Culver
Mrs LM Cumbers
Mrs E Dakeyne-Cannon
Mrs LN Darbyshire BA
Miss VA Davidge MBE
Dame Jean Davies
Miss SA Megan Davies
Mrs Phyllis A Dawson SWA
Mrs Dorothy Day BA
Miss Beryl Dean ARCA
Miss Gertrude Dearnley MD FRCOG
Miss Rosalind A Dease
Miss Mary Delane

Dr GU Delaney MB BCH BAO NUI
Miss Elizabeth Denby FRSA ARIBA
Mrs Margaret Anne Dennis BSc
Miss Dorothy A Denny OBE
Mrs Barbara Dent
Miss Delia Derbyshire BA LRAM
Miss Astra Desmond CBE BA RAM
The Hon Lady de Zulueta
Miss Margaret Mary Dibb
Miss Nancy P Dibley LRAM
Dr Ursula M Dick MB BS MRCS LRCP
    D(Obst) RCOG
Miss CM Dickie SRN SCM
Miss Jennifer Dickson ARE
Mrs EG Ding
Miss Margaret Ivy Dingle
Dr Margaret Ruth Dix MD FRCS
Mrs Honor Dobbs
Mrs E Glen Dobie PHC
Miss MP Docherty
Miss Edith M Dolphin
Miss Dorothy Donaldson
Dr Honor Doyle MD BCH BAO MRCP
    DCH
Miss Evelyn M Drake-Whiteside
Miss KM Draycott
Mrs NH Drury
Miss Joseen Duncan
Mrs Kay Durrant
Ald Mrs BR Dyke MBE JP CC
Miss Sheila M Edmonds MA PhD
Miss CG Edwards BArch ARIBA
Lady Eliott of Stobs
Mrs BC Ellis LSIA
Mrs Mary Helen Ellis
Mrs Reginald Ellison BA
Miss Rosalie Emslie RBA
Miss Betty Entwistle LLB
Mrs Vivienne Entwistle
The Lady Erroll of Hale
Mrs AJ Erskine
Miss Eileen Evans MSIA
Mrs WG Evans JP
Mrs WJ Evans ARIBA BA
The Mayor of Evesham, Cllr Mrs T H
    Pitcher
Miss WM Ewing MA LLB
Miss Violet Farebrother
Miss ME Faulkner MBE
Miss Julie Felix BA
Madame L Blanche Fentiman LRAM
    ATCL MRST
Mrs Violet Field
Miss Stella P M Fisher
Mrs MCJ Fletcher ARIBA

Mrs Annabelle Forrest
Mrs Sylvia F Forster
Mrs EM Forsythe
Mrs William Foster JP OBE
Mrs Catherine Foxell SRN SCM
Miss N Franck MA
Mrs AM Frankl LLB LLD
Miss Cecilia Freeman
Mrs Eunice French MA
Miss Hermene French
Mrs JM Frisell LDS
Dr K Frith MRCOG
Mrs Joanna Gale LLB
Miss IA Gallagher SRN RFN SCM
Miss Ailsa Garland
Mrs KM Garnett
Mrs Patrick Garrett
Dr VJ Gavin JP MRCS LRCP
Mrs Doris Gerrard RBA
Mrs AL Gilby FCIB ACII
Mrs AN Gilchrist
Mrs Pamela Gilley MCSP
Dr Camilla Hay Gillies MA
Mrs Guy Gluckstein
Mrs M Glyn
Dr Etheldreda Godfrey BSc MB ChB LM
Mrs Helen May Green
Miss Pauline K Green BA LSIR
Mrs Philip Green
Miss Anna Mary Greig LDS
Miss Mary G Greysmith BSc
Ald Mrs ML Griffith OBE
Miss BJ Griffiths SRN CMB OStJ
Miss Elizabeth J Grundy ARIBA Dip Arch
Mrs ML Guays MBE
Mrs J Aylwin Guilmant
Miss Garda Hall ARAM LRAM
Mrs DJ Halley BSc MBE
Dr Margaret Hammond MB ChB
Mrs MA Hamp-Hamilton LRAM
Mrs Leslie Hardern MIPR
Miss HM Harding
Miss Patricia Hare
Miss IA Harker
Mrs MLR Harkness BSc
Miss Josephine Harris
Miss NE Harris FIPA
Miss Beryl M Harrison ARIBA
Mrs RE Harrowing JP
Mrs H Harry JP BA
Dr Margaret Hauxwell MA ChB
Mrs CM C Haynes
Miss B Heaton-Armstrong
Miss Ellen Annie Heckford BA FCIS FVI
Miss Margaret Helps

Mrs Fay Hensher
Miss JM Higgins RRC OStJ SRN SCM
Miss Gladys Hill MA MD FRCS FRCOG
Mrs Graham Hill
Miss J Ferguson Hinchliffe Dip Arch
    ARIBA
Miss Gwen Hiscocks BA
Miss Verna Hitchcock
Mrs Elsie Edna Hobday ARICS
Miss Moira Hoddell ARCA
Ald Mrs EFM Hollis MBE
Mrs Winifred Holmes
Miss Gwynneth Holt FRBS
Mrs JP Holt
Miss Mary Holt MA LLB
Miss Flora V Honywood
Miss IB Horner MA DLitt
Dr S Horner MB BS CBE
Mrs MK Horsley
Mrs M Hourigan
Mrs M Howell CBE JP MA
Miss Jennifer Howland
Mrs Dorothy Hubball
Mrs Florence Hughesdon
Mrs Gladys Humm
Cllr Miss Diana Hunter-Moody JP
Miss Joan Hurley
Mrs M Hurst
Miss Angela Huth
Miss MB Hyde MSc MIBiol
Mrs Hyde Hyde-Thomson
Mrs Paul Hyde-Thomson
Mrs Godfrey W Iredell CC
Dr Esther Jones
Cllr Mrs Marjorie E Jones
Miss Leonie Jonleigh RBA
Miss JR Joyce
Mrs PAN Keates SRN SCM
Dr ML Kellmer-Pringle BA PhD Dip Ed
    FBPSS
Mrs M Kelly Owen Dip Arch ARIBA
Mrs Mary Patricia Kendrick BA
Dr Agnes Kennedy FFA RCS
Miss NW Kennedy
Mrs Constance Kerridge JP
Lady Mary Kerr
Miss Alison King
Mrs Beryl Kitts MA
Mrs Betty Knightly
Miss Marjorie Knights OBE
Miss Dorothy Laird
Mrs Sheila Lamb
Miss Joyce FE Lang GRSM ARCM
Dr JM Langham-Hobart MB ChB
Miss Jean Lanning

Miss Eve Larsen
Miss Rosamond Lehmann
Miss Iris ME Lemare ARCM
Lady Nicholas Gordon Lennox
Miss EM Leverson MBE
Cllr Mrs Doris M Levey
Mrs EPS Lewin
Miss J Lewis SRN RFN SCM
Miss Daphne Linscott BSc
The Worshipful The Mayor of Liskeard,
    Councillor Mrs M H Nadin BA
Miss Sheila M Lloyd MA BSc
Miss Molly Lobban SRN SCM MTD
Miss Erna Low PhD MTAI
Miss Muriel Lyne MBE
The Mayor of Buxton, Cllr Mrs DI
    Ludlow JP
Miss E Lyon ARRC SRN SCM
Mrs Jack Lyons
Dr Isobel O Macalister MBE MB ChB
    DPH JP
Miss Gina Mackinnon OBE
Dr Annie D Maclaine MB LLB
Miss Emily Macmanus CBE SRN SCM
Mrs Janet W Macnaughton
Miss DH Mahanoorah-Baugh FPS
Third Officer Sheila M Malham WRNS
Mrs IME Mamik
Miss J Mann SRN
Miss Veronica Mansfield ARCM
Mrs John Mansel
Miss Marjorie Marriott OBE
Mrs Jean Marshall
Miss DE Martin
Dr Kathleen Frances Matthews MRCS
    LRCP DPH DOMS
Mrs Rachel McBryde MPS
Mrs MC McCormack BDS
Mrs CN McGeorge SRN CC
Mrs MD McHarg FCCS
Miss Maureen McKentey
Miss K McVeigh
Mrs HM Menzies
The Mayor of Merton,
Mrs Ellen V Marsh
Mrs OB Miller
Miss Margaret Mitchell MB ChB MRCS
    LRCP BSc
Miss Yvonne Mitchell
Miss Gwen Moffat
Mrs D Monard JP
Mrs AG Monk SRN CMB RST
Mrs RB Moore (Megan Moore)
Mrs F Morris
Miss Jill Morris DES RCA FRSA MSIA

Miss MR Morrison
Ald Miss Iris Helen Moseley
Dr Sylvia A Moss MB BS
Mrs Shirley Mowbray MA
Miss Jean E Muir
Dr Margit Muller MD MRCS LRCP
Miss Agnes Mulvey RGN
Miss MM Murray MBE SRN RMN
    RMPA
Miss M Murtagh ACCA ACIS
Mrs L Musson
Miss ME Myers RRC
Mrs CL Nathan
Mrs Harold Needler
Dr Dorothy F Neilan JP MB ChB DPH
Miss MB Nelson
Miss Evelyn New MSIA
Mrs VAB Newcomb FIPA
Mrs AM Newland
Mrs Laurie Newton-Sharp PRO
Miss IC Nichols MPS
Mrs Jill Nicholson BA
Miss G Niven ROI
Miss Barbara Noble
Mrs KD Nock SRN IMA
The Lady Normanbrook
The Lady Helen Nutting
Miss Eve Orme
Miss Hilda Orr
Miss ME Orr
Mrs B M Osborn JP
Miss Jean D Oswald LDS
Mrs Elizabeth Overbury
Miss Gwen Owen SRN CMB
Miss ME Owen
Mrs JRM Page BSc (Econ)
Mrs Juliet Pannett
Miss AM Parker OBE SRN SCM RST
Miss Constance-Anne Parker
Miss J Parry FCA
Miss Lily Pavey
Mrs M Peacock
Miss C Eileen Peaker MA FRCOG
The Hon Mrs Derrick Pease
Dr EL Peet MB BS MD LDS
Mrs Eric Penn
Miss Lorna Pegram BA
Miss Muriel A Pemberton ARWS FSIA
    ARCA WIAC
Miss EM Pepperell Dip Soc SI
Miss MR Peterkin DN (Lond) RMN SRN
    SCM
Mrs Margaret Peters
Mrs Doris M Phillips MBE
Miss Violet Philpin

Mrs Denise Pigott
Alderman Mrs Eva Pine MBE
Miss Anne Pitcher
Mrs Marion Plant DA LSIA
Mrs Robin Pleydell-Bouverie
Mrs Ingrid Plowright
Mrs MH Plume JP
Baroness Plummer of Toppesfield JP
Miss Gwen G Pollock
Miss MG Powell
Dr M Immes Prangnell MB ChB
Mrs Christina Press ARIBA
Miss Enid M Prevezer LLB (Lond)
Mrs MB Pritchard SRN SCM
Miss Marjorie Proops
Madame SB Prunier
Miss Laurie Purden
Cllr Miss Rabagliati MBE
Mrs L Rainer
Lady Rankin
Miss Winifred Rayment
Mrs Iris G Rayner
Miss ME Rea
Mrs WA Read
Miss Sarah M Reed
Miss EM Rees SRN SCM
Mrs E Brinley Richards
Miss Joanna Richardson MA FRSL
Mrs Norah Riley
Mrs George Ritchie
Miss Lorna Beatrix Ritchie
Brigadier Dame Jean Rivett-Drake DBE
Dr RS Rivlin MRCS LRCP CPH
Dr Margaret Jones Roberts MB ChB DPH
Miss EH Robinson
Mrs Hilda Robinson
Miss G Rodgers
Dr CM Rolant-Thomas MRCS LRCP
    LDS RCS
Cllr Mrs Monica Rowe
Mrs Hazel Rowland MCSP
Miss A Royalton-Kisch ARICS
Miss Agnes Russell
Mrs ME Ryder RMS
Miss BE Sabey BSc
Mrs Flora M Sadler MA
Mrs Denise Salem
Dr Christine F T Saville
Miss EM Scott
Mrs KM Scott-Thorburn
Miss Mabel A L Sculthorp BA FIL
Major GA Sergant AMI Mech E
Miss BM Seymour BA LSIA
Mrs FE Shaw
Miss L Shawyer

Miss Everell M Shippam MD BS FRCO
Miss JM Simpson BA FIHM
Mrs Olive Sinclair OBE MA
Miss Audrey Slaughter
Dr J Smailes MB ChB DPH
Miss Catherine Smaldon CBE
Mrs Small
Miss BE Smith
Mrs Florence Smith
Miss S Smith
Dame Nancy Snagge DBE
Mrs Sylvia Sosnow
The Mayor of South Molton, Cllr Miss
    Ada Williamson SRN SCM
Miss DM Spencer SRN SCM RSCN
Mrs Spencer-Phillips
Mrs LB Sproat MA
Mrs FC Spurgin OBE KIH JP
Mrs MJ Spurgin
Dr PC Stafford MRCS LRCP
Miss Jean Stark
Miss Sheila Stephenson BA
Mrs Jocelyn Stevens
Lady Stewart OBE JP
Mrs Stewart-Stevens
Mrs Dorothy Stone LLB
Miss Gladys Storey OBE
Mrs Eileen M Strain
Miss Patience Strong
Miss JA Stubbs MSIA
Miss E A Studley
Miss E Summers
Miss Mildred AG Sumner PHC LRAM
Mrs Bernard Sunley
Mrs Maud Swift
Mrs R Swinburne-Johnson
Dr EW Tanner MB ChB DRCOG DA
Dr NM Tattersfield MB ChB MRCS
    LRCP DCM LRAM (Music)
Miss A Adeline Taylor PHC
Miss EE M Taylor PHC
Mrs Lesley Taylor BSc AKC
Miss Odette Tchernine FRGS
Mrs PAJ Temple-Richards BA
Mrs Irene Thomas
Miss MA Thomas SRN RSCN
Miss JC Thompson MA AMIEE
Cllr Mrs ME Thompson
Mrs Kitty DV Thorp
Miss Violetta Thurstan MM FRGS LLA
Baroness Fiona Thyssen-Bornemisza
Brigadier MA Todd SRN SCM
Miss ME Tompson
Miss DE Tonge
Miss MM Torbet

Mrs AF Turner MB ChB
Brigadier Dame Margot Turner DBE RRC QHNS
Miss Theodora Turner OBE ARRC SRN SCM DN
Mrs Kathleen Tweed
Mrs Alison Uttley BSc
Mrs DW Variava BA ARIBA JP
Miss Emily Viggor
Miss BME Visick
Miss Iris Wade
Miss KM Wade SRN SCM ARRC
Miss Mabel Wakefield SRN
Mrs Richard Walker
Dr Vera B Walker MSc PhD
Miss Margaret Wallace SRN RMN SCM
Miss EK Wallen MA(Oxon)
Miss Nora Walley
Miss M Wallis MPS MRSH
Miss LM Walsh
Mrs Donald Warburg
Lady Warren CStJ JP
Mrs N Watson
Ald Mrs Winifred M Watson
The Mayor of Wallingford, Cllr Mrs Simmons
Dr Barbara Weaver PhD MRCVS
Mrs Evelyn Webster
Dr MA Webster MB ChB MRCS LRCO RCOG
Mrs A Wellington
Miss MS Wenmoth
Mrs DEL West MBE
Mrs Garfield Weston
Alderman Mrs IG Wightman MA JP
Mrs Anne Wilkie
Miss GG Williams SRN SCM RFN RNMD RMD
Miss May Williams
Miss S Garnett Williams
Mrs M Wills
Mrs CN Wimble Dipl NFU
Miss R Winslade MSIT MASEE AMBIM
Miss Hilda MM Wisdom FACCA FRVA SSStJ
Mrs Ann Wiseman SRN
Miss MM Wittich
Lady Wolfenden
Mrs CW Wood MA
Miss Cynthia Wood ARIBA AMTPI AIARB
Dr Mary Wright MB ChB
Mrs BP Wroughton Dip Arch (Lond) ARIBA
Miss M Yates SRN SCM

Professor Elezanor Zaimis MD
Miss Anna Zinkeisen ROI RDI

Monday 12th October 1966
THEME: THE BEE IN MY BONNET

Miss Ruth M Abell ARICS
Miss Sally Adams BA
Miss MKM Aitken BA LLB
Mrs Eileen Alford
Mrs Helen C Allan LDS RCS
Miss Paula Allardyce
Mrs MA Allday
Miss Diana K Allen
Mrs Margaret Amstell
Mrs Eleanor M Armitage
Dame Veronica Ashworth DBE RRC
The Viscountess Astor
Miss Vera Atkins
Mrs ILE Austin-Smith FRIBA
Mrs Charlotte Baden-Powell ARIBA AA Dipl
Mrs Aileen Ballatyne AA Dipl ARIBA
Miss Frances Barker MA
Dr Rosetta Barker BOA DPH
Miss Winifred Barker
Miss D Barratt
Mrs S Barrett SRN RCN
Miss Dorothy M Bartlett
Miss Julia Bastian
Alderman Mrs Ethel Bates SRN SCM MRCN
Miss SB Bates SRN
Mrs EJ Battey MA BSc JP
Miss Pauline Baynes MSIA
Mrs Geraldine Beamish
Mrs Ellen Belchem
Mrs Jean Blackden LRAM
Miss Lorna Blackie MA
Mrs Gillian Blacksell ARIBA
Lady Blane OBE
Mrs Paul Boissevain ARIBA
Miss H Boleyn-Smedley SRN SCM
Mrs G Book
Miss Joyce Booth MSIA AMIPA
Miss M Bosson SRN SCM
Miss Jane Bown
Miss E Bowyer SRN SCM
Miss Winifred Bowyer SRN SCM
Miss Anita Brackley
Mrs Max Braynis
Mrs Kay Brebner
Miss P Bridger MBE
Miss Vera Brittain DLitt FRSL MA (Oxon)

Lady Brocklehurst
Mrs T Broome MBE
Miss ME Brown
Mrs Margaret Philomena Bucknall-Smith BRCS
Mrs John S Budge MB ChB
Mrs M Bulpitt
Miss MR Burgess FCA
Mrs Mollie E Burgess FCA
Miss Mary Burr MA FPS
Miss G Hagar Butler SRN SCM MTD
Miss Shirley Butler
Miss Jill Butterfield
Miss AP Callender BSc FCCS
Mrs JR Callis
Miss Joan Cambridge
Miss Elizabeth Cameron LLB
Mrs Wishart Campbell MA OStJ
Miss Fanny Carby
Miss G Cardno
Miss MF Carpenter SRN SCM
Miss Ann Carroll LRAM
Mrs J Allan Cash
Miss Margaret I Chalmers BSc PhD
Lieut Col Joyce B Chambers ARRC
Mrs Mary Lumley Champion ARCA
Miss Gladys Charlton SRN SCM
Lady Chatterjee OBE MA DSc
The Viscountess Chelsea
The Lady Chesham
Mrs Francis Chichester
Mrs Mavis Ann Chipperfield
Miss MD Chorlton MA (Oxford)
Mrs JE Chrismas JP CC
Mrs Jean Christopherson ARIBA
Mrs Elsie Clarke
Mrs ML Clarke FRCVS
Miss Julia Clements (Lady Seton)
Mrs Anne Clough-Norton FCA
Miss CP Clyne SCM
Miss Anne V Coates
Mrs JC Cockroft
Miss Myrella Cohen LLB
Professor MM Cole BSc PhD
Miss Eunice L Coleman NDD CDD
Miss Patricia Galloway Coles MA
Mrs Margaret Anna Collard
Mrs Kathleen Collett
Dr Annie Collins MB BCH
Miss Jeanette Collins
Mrs Audrey Compton FRIBA AA Dipl
Miss P Comrie BA LGSM
Miss Jean Conran BSc NFF
Miss Shirley Conran
Miss Louise Cootes BA

Miss Lettice Cooper
Miss Phyllis Cooper MBE
Miss Jane Cotton
Miss Freda M Cowell BSc
Councillor Miss Clarinda Cox SRN SCM
Miss Doris L Cox
Mrs Fanny Cradock (Bon Viveur)
Miss MD Craine SRN RNM RNMS RMPA
Miss Sheila M Crane ARRC SRN SCM
Miss Mamie Crichton
Mrs PV Crook
Dr Ethel M Cruickshank BSc PhD FRSH
Miss Rosalie Crutchly
Miss Dany Culver
Mrs LM Cumbers
Miss Diana O Cundall Dipl Arch ARIBA
Mrs E Dakeyne-Cannon
Miss Jennifer Daniel
Miss Joyce M Darby
Mrs LN Darbyshire BA
Mrs EA Davenport
Miss J Eileen Davies DipEd
Mrs M Davies
Miss SA Megan Davies
Dr Veronica Frith Dawkins MD ChB
Mrs Phyllis Dawson SWA
Mrs Dorothy Day BA
Miss Beatrice de Cardi BA FSA
Councillor Mrs E M Devenay
The Mayor of Devizes, Councillor Mrs EM Payne
The Mayor of Dewsbury, Councillor Mrs A Cockroft
The Hon Lady de Zulueta
Dr Ursula M Dick MB BS MRCS LRCP D(Obst) RCOG
Miss Josephine Douglas
Mrs GE Downing Lewis
Dr Honor Doyle MD BCH BAO MRCP DCH
Miss K M Draycott
Mrs Margaret Drew HACB
Mrs N H Drury
Miss Maureen Duck
Dr Madelaine Duke BSc MB ChB
Mrs Joan Duncan
Miss Joseen Duncan
Miss Angela M Dunne
Mrs Theodora Durrant
Ald Mrs BR Dyke MBE JP
Miss Mary Eastman
Mrs HR Edwards
Lady Eliott of Stobs
Mrs Brenda Croft Ellis LSIA

Miss Mary Ellis SRN SCM
Mrs Reginald Ellison BA SRN
Miss Polly Elwes
Miss Betty Entwistle LLB
Mrs Vivienne Entwistle
Mrs Aleda J Erskine
Mrs Erica C Eske
Miss Eileen Evans MSIA
Miss Marguerite Evans PHC
Mrs Winifred Joyce Evans ARIBA BA
Miss Winifred M Ewing MA LLB
Lieut Col Marilyn Fabien ARRC
    QARANC
Miss WK Farmer MWES
Miss ME Faulkner MBE
Mrs Violet Field
Miss Stella P M Fisher
Mrs VC FitzGerald NDA NDD
Mrs MC J Fletcher ARIBA
Mrs PH Ford SSStJ
Mrs Mary I Foreman MB MS MRCS
    LRCP
Mrs Annabelle Forrest
Miss Helen Forrest
Mrs M Forsyth
Mrs Helena W Foster WRVS
Mrs W Foster CBE
Mrs Elizabeth Colwyn Foulkes BArch Dip
    CD ARIBA
Mlle Franka
Miss Judith E Frankel BSc QS ARICS
    MCQS
Mrs Anna M Frankl LLD LLB
Miss D Freeborn
Miss Cecilia Freeman
Miss Hermene French
Mrs JM Frizell LDS
Miss Phyl Fulford-Brown MIPR
Miss Monica Furlong
Miss Lilian H Gale SRN SCM
Miss IA Gallagher SRN RFN SCM
Miss Ailsa Garland
Mrs Patrick Garrett
Dr Vera J Gavin JP MRCS LRCP
Mrs CM Geary-Knox
Mrs Doris Gerrard RBA
Miss Dorothy Giles BSc
Miss VH Giles SRN SCM
Mrs Mary Gilliatt
Dr Etheldreda Godfrey BSc MB ChB LM
Col Barbara Gordon RRC QARANC
    OStJ SRN SCM
Mrs AC Gorna-Davies LLB
Miss Lilian CM Gorton LLB
Miss Susan E Graham

Mrs Helen M Green
Mrs Marjorie A Greenhough MBE
Miss Mary G Greysmith BSc
Miss Jane Griffiths BA
Mrs Katherine Grigor MBE
Miss Elizabeth J Grundy ARIBA Dipl Arch
Mrs JA Guilmant
Miss JA C Gutteridge MA CBE
Councillor Mrs G I Habershon CC
Miss Garda Hall ARAM LRAM
Mrs Doris J Halley MBE BSc
Dr Margaret Hammond MB ChB
Mrs MA Hamp-Hamilton LRAM
Miss CH Hampton
Mrs DM Hands
Miss Wendy Hanson
Miss HM Harding
Miss Phyllis Harding
Miss Elizabeth Hardman
The Mayor of Haringey, Alderman Mrs
    AF Remington JP
Miss Isabella A Harker
Mrs MLR Harkness BSc
Mrs RD Harland
Miss Josephine Harris
Miss Nellie E Harris FIPA
Mrs Beryl M Harrison ARIBA
Mrs JD Harrison
Mrs Ruth E Harrowing
Mrs Hannah Harry JP BA
Miss Winifred Hart-Davies SRN RMN
Miss Elizabeth Harvey BA
Miss MA Harwood
Mrs Gerd Hay-Edie FSIA
Mrs CMG Haynes CC
Mrs Esma M Hazelden
Miss Hy Hazell
Miss B Heaton-Armstrong
Miss Marion E Hebblethwaite
Mrs R Henderson-Howat AR HIST S
Mrs Dorothy Henry
Miss Constance H Henry MBE
Mrs FE Hensher
Miss JM Higgins RRC OStJ SRN SCM
Mrs BP Hill
Miss Mary Hill
Mrs Phyllis Hindle
Miss Gwen Hiscocks BA
Mrs Margaret Hislop RSA
Miss Vivien Hislop DA
Miss Verna Hitchcock
Mrs Elsie Edna Hobday ARICS
Miss Moira Hoddell ARCA
Miss Mary Holt MA LLB
Miss IB Horner MA DLitt

Dr Sibyl Horner CBE MB BS DPH DIH
Mrs MK Horsley
Mrs M Hourigan
Miss Mary Howard
Mrs Myfanwy Howell CBE JP MA
Mrs Jennifer Howland
Mrs Dorothy Hubball
Miss Joan LA Hughes MBE
Mrs Florence Hughesdon
Mrs G Humm
Miss Joan Hurley
Mrs LM Hutcheson ARIBA
Miss Angela Huth
Miss DD Hyams
Miss MB Hyde MSc MIBiol
Mrs Hyde Hyde-Thomson
Mrs Paul Hyde-Thomson
The Mayor of Ipswich, Alderman Mrs MJ
    Keeble JP
Mrs Ethel B Ivey
Mrs I Jack
Miss Bridget M Jackson
Mrs Dorothy Jewitt
Miss Harriette Johns
Miss EI Jones SRN OND SCM
Miss Ivy Jones
Councillor Mrs Marjorie E Jones
Dr M Jones Roberts MB ChB DPH
Miss Leonie Jonleigh RBA
Lady Joubert de la Ferté CStJ
Miss J Joyce
Dr Winifred Kane MB BS DPH DCH
Mrs Brian Keeling
Mrs Beryl Kelly
Mrs Mary P Kendrick BA
Dr Agnes Kennedy FFA RCS
Miss NW Kennedy
Lady Mary Kerr
Mrs Constance Kerridge JP
The Mayor of Kidwelly, Councillor Miss
    Charlotte L Squier JP
Mrs Clare Kipps ARCM
Mrs Betty Knightly LLB
Miss Dorothy Laird
Miss Sybil IE Lammas
Dr Jean M Langham-Hobart MB ChB
Miss Jean Lanning
Miss Isabel A Laurence FFA
Mrs Hilda Mary Laurence SRN SCM
The Duchess of Leeds
Miss Iris ME Lemare ARCM
Miss Ethel Marion Leverson MBE
Councillor Mrs DM Levey
Miss J Lewis SRN SCM RFN
Miss Lydia M Light SRN SCM

Miss Zaidee Lindsay
Miss Daphne Linscott BSc
Miss Erna Low PhD MTAI
Miss EM Lucas
Miss Muriel Lyne MBE
Dr Isobel Ord Macalister MBE MB ChB
    DPH JP
Mrs Gina MacKinnon OBE
Dr Annie D Maclaine MB ChB
Mrs Janet W Macnaughton
The Mayor of Maldon, Alderman Mrs
    EFM Brewster JP CA
Miss J Mann SRN
Miss Veronica Mansfield ARCM
Mrs Patricia P Marks LLB
Miss Marjorie Marriott OBE
Mrs CS Marsh
Miss DE Martin
Miss Mary Mason
Dr Kathleen F Matthews MRCS LRCP
    DPH DOMS
Mrs Heather Mayhew
Mrs Rachel McBryde MPS
Mrs Maeve C McCormack BDS
Mrs Kathleen V McDougal Maiden MBE
Mrs CN McGeorge SRN CC
Mrs Mary D McHarg FCCS
Miss KMcVeigh
Mrs HM Menzies
Mrs Doreen Merriman
Councillor Mrs Joan Merry
Mrs OB Miller
Mrs MJ Mitchell FRICS
Miss Gwen Moffat
Mrs Daphne Monard JP
Mrs EP Monk SRN RST CMB
Councillor Miss Diana Hunter Moody JP
Mrs Hobart Moore
Mrs Megan Moore
Miss Winifred F Morgan
Mrs F Morris
Miss Jill Morris Des RCA FRSA MSIA
Dr Constance C Morrison LRCP & S
Miss Margaret R Morrison
Mrs BC Morton-Palmer JP
Alderman Miss Iris H Moseley
Miss Jean Muir
Miss Agnes Mulvey RGN
Miss LD Murcott
Miss Margaret Macartney Murray MBE
    SRN RMN RMPA
Mrs AH Musson
Mrs Constance Nathan
Mrs Victor Neale JP
Miss Maud Neilson

Miss Evelyn New MSIA
The Mayor of Newbury, Councillor Mrs E Ganf
Mrs VAB Newcomb FIPA
Mrs AM Newland
Mrs ES Newland
Mrs Jill Nicholson BA
Mrs M Nixon
Miss MM Nobbs MIHVE MRSH
Mrs Kathleen D Nock SRN IMA
Lady Helen Nutting
Dr Margaret M O'Hare BSc MB ChB MRCP FRCP
Miss Eve Orme
Miss Hilda Orr
Miss Mary E Orr
Mrs Bessie M Osborn JP CC
Miss Jean D Oswald LDS
Mrs Elizabeth Overbury
Mrs JRM Page BSc (Econ)
Mrs Juliet Pannett SGA FRSA
Miss AM Parker OBE SRN SCM RST
Miss Constance-Anne Parker ATD SWA
Miss Elisabeth Parry
Mrs TA Parsons BSc
Mrs M Peacock
Mrs Maeve Peake
Hon Mrs Derrick Pease
Miss Muriel A Pemberton FSIA ARKIS WIAC ARCA
The Mayor of Pembroke, Mrs Margaret M Mathias
Mrs Robin Pleydell-Bouverie
Mrs Arthur Ponsonby
Miss EA Pope SRN
Mrs Emma Powell
Mrs Christina Press ARIBA
Mrs Marjorie Proops
Mme SB Prunier
Mrs AEJ Rawlinson
Mrs J Enns Read
Miss Stella Richman
Mrs George Ritchie
Councillor Mrs Monica Rowe
Miss Agnes Russell
Mrs Denise Salem
The Mayor of Saltash, Councillor Mrs Phoebe Lean MA JP
Miss Freda Sawyer SRN CMB STD
Miss Lesley Saxby
Mrs Barbara K Schmidt BA
Miss Cecil Scott
Major GA Sergant CEng AMI MechE
Miss Joan Seton
Mrs Lesley Seyd

Miss Brenda Meredith Seymour BA LSIA
Miss Dorothy Sharwood Smith
Mrs FE Shaw
The Mayor of Shrewsbury, Alderman Mrs EM Lancaster JP
Mrs Margaret H Simmons
Miss Joan M Simpson BA FIHM
Dr E Lois Skelsey MRCS LRCP
Miss Evelyn H Slarke
Miss B Smedley-Crooke OBE JP
Miss AE Smith SRN
Miss Barbara E Smith
Miss E Margaret Smith FCA
Mrs Florence Smith
Miss Rosemary Smith
Dame Nancy Snagge DBE
Dr Frances Sorrell
Mrs Sylvia Sosnow
Mrs Harry Sotnick
Miss Charlotte I Southall FI HSG MWI
Mrs June L Soutter BArch ARIBA AMTPI
Mrs Spencer-Phillips
Miss Ann Spokes MA
Mrs Sproat MA
Mrs FC Spurgin OBE JP
Miss Jean Stark
Miss Anne H Steel LLB
Miss Sheila R Stephenson BA
Miss JE Stevens
Mrs Jocelyn Stevens
Councillor Mrs Irene A Stevenson BRCS
Lady Stewart OBE JP
Mrs Stewart-Stevens
Miss MEG Stocker MBE
Miss Stockwell
Miss Helen N Stone
Dr Esme Pole Stuart JP BA PhD
Miss June A Stubbs MSIA
Miss EA Studley
Miss E Summers
Miss Rosemary Sutcliff
Mrs R Swinburne-Johnson
Dr Evelyn W Tanner MB ChB DRCOG DA
Mrs Elizabeth Taylor
Mrs Lesley Taylor BSc AKC
Mrs PHJ Temple-Richards FRGS BA
Miss Dorothy L Thomas GC
Mrs Irene Thomas
Miss MA Thomas SRN RSCN
Councillor Mrs ME Thompson
Mrs Kathleen M Scott-Thorburn
Dr Doreen M Tillotson MB ChB
Brigadier Margaret A Todd SA SRN SCM
Miss Patricia Turner Des RCA

Mrs Sarah Turner
Miss Vickery Turner
Mrs Kathleen Tweed
Mrs Alison Uttley BSc
Madame Vernier
Miss BME Visick
Mrs Ann Voelcker AA Dipl ARIBA
Miss Rena Waddell
Mrs EM Walker
Mrs Richard Walker
Dr Vera B Walker MSc PhD MRCS LRCP
Miss Margaret Wallace SRN RMN SCM
Mrs Jean Walsh FPS
Miss Jean Walwyn
Miss OH Ward
Miss Hilda Wardroper Des RCA LSIA
Lady Warren CStJ JP
Miss Olga A Warren
Alderman Mrs W M Watson
Dr Barbara M Q Weaver PhD MRCVS
Miss Maysie Webb BSc ALA
Miss Molly Weir
Mrs Pamela Westland
Mrs W Garfield Weston
Mrs Anne White BA
Dr Helen R White BSc PhD
Mrs Mary Whitehouse
Miss Evelyn MD Whiteside
Alderman Mrs IG Wightman BA
Mrs Marilyn E Wigoder Halberstam LLB
Mrs Roger Wild Dip Arch ARIBA
Mrs Cicely Williams
Miss GG Williams SRN SCM RFN
  RNMD RMN RST
Miss May Williams
Miss Annette Wilson
The Mayor of Winchester, Councillor Mrs
  WJ Carpenter Turner BA JP
Miss HM Wisdom FACCA FRVA SStJ
Mrs J Wise
Mrs Alan A Withers LLB
Lady Wolfenden
Mrs FI Wolsey-Neech
Miss Cynthia Wood AADip ARIBA
  AMTPI AIArb
Mrs Marguerite Wood MCSP
Dr Mary J Wright MB ChB
Miss M Yates SRN SCM
Miss VL Youell SRN MSR
Miss Jean Zehetmayr ARIBA

October 1968
THEME: WHATEVER NEXT?

Parlour
Miss MPA Albrecht RRC
Mrs Jean Ames
Miss Hilary Baldwin
Miss Dorian F Banister
Miss I Bannister
Miss Barbara Barrett
Miss Alexandra N Beale
Mrs Ray Bell
Mrs Constance L Beynon FRCS (Ed)
  FRCOG
Mrs Ruth Blair BVSc
Miss J Bradnock MBE
Mrs S Broad
Mrs Janet Brown AIQS
Mrs Margaret Butler
Mrs Margaret C Cameron MRCVS
Mrs C Rosemary Clarke-Smith BEM
  (Military)
Miss Elizabeth Clowes SRN SCM
Miss CP Clyne SCM
Mrs Jocelyn Cockroft
Mrs Erna Cohn FSIA
Miss EL Coleman NDD
Mrs Nina E Copp
Mrs Rosemary de Laszlo
Mrs F J Dixon, Third Officer WRNS
Mrs BA P Dobson OBE
Miss MP Docherty
Councillor Mrs F W Eske
Miss Eileen M Evans FSIA
Miss Marguerite Evans PHC
Mrs Percyval Hollyoake Ford SStJ
Mrs RG Forsyth
Mrs Helena Foster
Mrs EM Croft Foulds MBE
Mrs Anna M Frankl LLD (Prague) LLB
  (Wales)
Dr Vera Jean Gavin JP MRCS LRCP
Dr Camilla Hay Gillies MA
Miss Annabel Gosling
Mrs Eileen I Griffiths SRN SCM
Miss Irene M Grisedale MRCVS
Dr Erna Grossbard
Miss Elizabeth J Grundy ARIBA
Miss Kathleen Haacke MBE
Mrs HT Halliday
Ald Mrs Sylvia E Harris JP
Mrs Beryl Marjorie Harrison ARIBA
Miss IMS Harvey TD SRN SCM RMN
  RMPA
Mrs AH Hawley BDS LDS
Mrs EE Hobday ARICS
Miss Moira Hoddell ARCA
Mrs JP Holt

Mrs CF Hoos
Miss Mary Howard
Lady Hulton
Miss Joan Hurley
Dr Mary Jackson MB ChB DLO
Dr Catherine L Jarret BSc PhD MI INF SC
Miss Pamela Jarvis
Dr Esther Jones MRCS LPCP
Mrs Marjorie E Jones
Lady Joubert de la Ferté CStJ
Alderman Mrs Elaine Kellett MA
Miss Catherine Kelly SRN SCM
Miss Hilda Kidman SWA
Mrs Rena G Knight MA MSc DIC MI INF SC
Miss M Lawrence FCA
Miss Lysbeth Liverton Cert RAS
Mrs Dorothy M Lockwood RBSA
Miss E Lyon ARRC
Mrs IME Mamik
Mrs Winifred H Marriott SRN SCM
Mrs Jean Marshall
Mrs Constance McGeorge
Miss Isabella Main McWilliam
Miss Stella Mead
Mrs Doreen Merriman
Miss A Mulvey RGN
Mrs F Nagle
Miss Evelyn New MSIA
Miss Deirdre O'Donohoe
Miss PJ Owen AA Dip ARIBA
Miss MA Peoples
Dr JK Perkins MB BChir FFARCS
Miss Margaret Pinder
Mrs Norma Pinkerton LDS
Mrs Marion Plant DA LSIA
Miss Sheila Reid RBTCDip
Mrs E Brinley Richards
Miss Nancy Ridley LGSM (ELOC) ALCM (ELOC)
Mrs Joan Shakespeare
Mrs SJM Shaw
Miss Thurza Simmons ATD
Miss Jean M Stow FCII
Mrs Anne Summers DES RCA FRSA
Dame Margot Turner DBE RRC
Miss Harriet Turton BA
Miss BME Visick
Miss M Wallis MPS MRSH
Miss Beryl Waterson ARCA
Mrs Nellie Watson
Miss Elizabeth V Wayper MA (Edin)
Mrs Arthur White
Mrs Josephine A Williamson MD ChB

FRCOG
Miss Annette Wilson
Mrs Harold F Wilson
Mrs A Wise
Miss Rae Woodland
Mrs Barbara P Wroughton Dip Arch (Lon) ARIBA

Lancaster Room
Dr Margaret I Adamson MB CH B DPH MRSH
Mrs Alison Adburgham
Miss MKM Aiken BA LLB
Mrs DG Akroyd
Miss Margaret Alexander
Mrs Eileen Alford
Mrs Helen C Allan LDS RCS
Miss Paula Allardyce
Mrs MA Allday
Miss AMC Allen MA (Cantab) ACIS
Mrs Margaret Amstell
Mrs Lucie Arnheim FSIA
Mrs AG Asquith-Leeson
The Viscountess Astor
Mrs ILE Austin-Smith FRIBA AADipl
Mrs Charlotte Baden-Powell AADipl ARIBA
Mrs Valerie Baker
Mrs Aileen Ballantyne AADipl ARIBA
Miss Mary E Barber OBE MA
Miss Margaret Barbieri
Mrs JHJ Barford
Miss MM Bark SRN SCM MTD
Dr Rosetta Barker MB BCh BAO DPH
Mrs Doreen Bateman MRCVS
The Revd Miss M Audrey Bates
Mrs E James Battey MA BSc JP
Mrs Geraldine Beamish
Miss A Beaton SRN SCM
Mrs ECM Begg ARIBA
Mrs Zoia A Beresford Dip Arch (Oxford) ARIBA
Mrs Jean Blackden LRAM
Miss Lorna J Blackie MA
Lady Blane OBE
Mrs Muriel Blunden-Ellis
Mrs Barbara Boissevain ARIBA
Miss H Boleyn-Smedley SRN SCM
Mrs Gertrude Book
Miss Joyce Booth MSIA AMIPA
Miss Daisy T Borne ARBS RMS SWA
Mrs PM Boulton SRN
Miss E Bowen
Miss Lally Bowers
Mrs Vivienne M Bowler MRCVS

Councillor Mrs L E Bowles
Mrs Phyllis Bowman
Miss Winifred Bowyer SRN CMB
Miss Anita Brackley
Mrs Margaret Bramall MA AIMSW JP
Miss Brenda B Breakwell MBE FIHM
Mrs Kay Brebner
Mrs TV Briggs
Lady Brocklehurst
Air Commandant Dame Jean Bromet DBE
Mrs YI Brooks MRCVS
Mrs T Broome MBE
Miss Agnes Browne SRN SCM
Miss Angela Browne
Miss Kathleen Browne ATD RDS
Dr JS Budge MB ChB
Miss Patricia Callender BSc (Econ) FCCS
Mrs Jessica R Callis
Miss Diana Calvert
Miss Joan Cambridge MSc G
Miss Averil M Cameron PhD
Miss Eila MJ Campbell MA FSA
Mrs Wishart Campbell MA OStJ
Miss Fanny Carby
Miss Ann Caroll LRAM
Miss Irene EM Carpenter MBE
Mrs Marilyn Carr BArch MCD ARIBA AMTPI
Miss Joan Catesby
Alderman Mrs Ada Chadwick JP
Mrs Mary Lumley Champion ARCA
Mrs Anthea Chapman ATD (London)
Mrs Yvonne Charpentier
Miss Madeline Chase
The Lady Chesham
Miss Tsai Chin
Mrs Mavis A Chipperfield
Mrs Joan E Chrismas JP CC
Mrs Jean Christopherson ARIBA
Mrs ML Clarke FRCVS
Miss Ruth Clarke SRN RMN SCM
Miss Sheena E B Clarke
Mrs Alan Cleave
Mrs Anne Clough-Norton FCA
Prof Monica M Cole BSc PhD
Miss Muriel Cole
Miss Patricia Galloway Coles MA (Edin)
Mrs Margaret A Collard
Mrs Iris S Collenette
Mrs Kathleen Collett
Mrs Patience Collier
Miss Jeanette Collins
Mrs Audrey Compton FRIBA AADipl
Mrs Shirley Conran

Miss Joan Cooley
Miss Lettice Cooper
Miss RA Cooper SRN
Miss Wendy Cooper
Miss Anne C Corna-Davies LLB
Dame Kathleen Courtney DBE
Miss FM Cowell BSc
Councillor Miss Clarinda Cox SRN SCM
Miss Doris L Cox
Miss Elizabeth Craig FRSA
Miss Sheila-Mary Crane ARRC SRN SCM
Miss M E Craven RRC
Mrs Margaret C Creasey MRCVS
Mrs Jeanne Croft
Miss Anna Cropper
Dr Ethel M Cruickshank BSc PhD FRSH
Mrs LM Cumbers
Alderman Mrs M Cutler OBE JP
Mrs Edith Dakeyne-Cannon
Miss June Dandridge
Mrs Brenda Darling BA ARIBA
Mrs E Davenport
Miss S Megan Davies
Dr Veronica Frith Dawkins MD ChB
Mrs Dorothy Day BA
Miss Isabel Dean
Miss Beatrice de Cardi BA FSA
Miss Muriel M Deighton
Miss Angele Delanghe
Mrs Joanna Delmege
Mrs Jill Denham-Davis
Mrs MA Dennis BSc
Miss Josephina de Vasconcellos FRBS
The Hon Lady de Zulueta
Dr Ursula Dick MB MRCS LRCP Dobst RCOG
Dr Margaret Dix MD FRCS
Mrs Honor Dobbs
Miss Edith M Dolphin
Miss Anna M Donnelly SRN SCM RT
Colonel UA Dowling RRC
Miss K M Draycott
Miss Jane B Drew FRIBA FIARB FSIA AADipl Hon LLD (IBADAN)
Mrs NH Drury
Miss Maureen Duck
Miss Joseen Duncan
Miss Angela Dunne
Alderman Mrs B R Dyke MBE JP
Lady Eden
Mrs Gilbert Edgar
Miss CG Edwards BArch ARIBA
Mrs HR Edwards
Lady Eliott of Stobs

Mrs Brenda Croft Ellis LSIA
Miss Mary Ellis SRN SCM
Mrs Reginald Ellison BA Hist SRN
Miss Elsie C Ensing SRN JP
Miss Betty Entwistle LLB
Mrs Vivienne Entwistle
Mrs Aleda Erskine
Mrs Hazel Meyrick Evans
Mrs Joyce Evans ARIBA BA
Mrs Irene Everest
Miss WK Farmer MWES
Miss Hilda Fenemore
Mrs Violet Field
Mrs Vera Finlay MBE JP
Miss Stella P M Fisher
Miss Marguerite Fletcher BSc BVMS
    MRCVS
Mrs AR Flude
Mrs Ann Ford
Dr Mary I Foreman MB BS MRCS LRCP
Miss Helen Forrest
Mrs Sylvia F Forster
Mrs EM Forsythe
Mlle Franka
Mrs Gina Franklin
Miss Cecilia Freeman
Mrs JB Freeman
Mrs J M Frizell LDS
Mrs Renée Fullforth
Mrs Joanne Gale LLB
Mrs Christina Gallea-Roy
Mrs Lilian Galloway
Miss Christine Galpin
Mrs JM Gardiner
Miss Judith Gardner
Miss Ailsa Garland
Miss I Garrad SRN
Mrs Patrick Garrett
Miss Penelope Ann Geary BSc
Mrs Doris Gerrard RBA
Miss DH Gifford BA PhD
Mrs AL Gilby
Miss Dorothy Giles BSc
Mrs Mary Gilliatt
Mrs Muriel Christine Gingell
The Viscountess Glenapp
Dr Etheldreda Godfrey BSc MBChB LM
Brigadier Barbara M Gordon RRC SRN
    SCM
Mrs Lilian Carmen M Gorton LLB
Miss Muriel Gosheron RMS
Miss Edith E Gott
Mrs Mary EL Granelli ARIBA
Miss L Joan Gray SRN SCM HV Cert
    Dip Soc

Miss M Elaine Gray
Miss Elizabeth Green
Miss Mary G Greysmith BSc
Mrs Katherine Grigor MBE
Miss Louise Grose
Miss Margaret Gumuchian DA (Manc)
    ATD ATC
Miss Freda H Gwilliam CBE MA
Miss Catherine Hall
Mrs DJ Halley MBE BSc BSc(Econ)
Mrs Anne Hamilton BVMS MRCVS
Mrs MA Hamp-Hamilton LRAM (ELOC)
Miss Margaret Hancock
Miss Irene Handl
Miss Hilda M Harding
Miss Evelyn Hardy BA
Mrs MLR Harkness BSc
Mrs RD Harland
Mrs Joan Harris BSc
Miss Josephine Harris ARWS
Miss Nellie E Harris FIPA
Mrs Ruth E Harrowing
Mrs Hannah Harry JP BA
Miss Elizabeth Harvey BA (Oxon)
Miss MA Harwood
Mrs Jacqueline Haskoll
Miss Doris M Hawkins SRN RSCN SCM
    MTD
Mrs Esma M Hazelden
Miss B Heaton-Armstrong
Miss Marion E Hebblethwaite
Miss Olwen Hedley
Mrs Shirley Hedworth
Mrs R Henderson-Howat AR HIST S
Miss CH Henry MBE
Mrs Fay Hensher
Dr Josephine Heylen MBBS LRCP MRCS
Mrs Graham Hill
Miss H Hillier SRN SCM MTD
Mrs Julie F Hinchcliffe Dip Arch (Leeds)
    ARIBA
Mrs Phyllis Hindle NDD
Miss Gwen M Hiscocks BA
Miss Eileen Hitchon NDD
Mrs David Hodgson MA (TCD)
Mrs Martha A Hodgson
Dr Elizabeth Hoffa MD LRCP DCH
Miss Mary Holt MA LLB
Miss Angela Hooper
Dr Sibyl G Horner CBE MB BS DPH DIH
Mrs MK Horsley
Mrs Jennifer Howland
Mrs Betty Hunter
Mrs Sheila Hutchison
Miss MB Hyde MSc MIBiol

Mrs Hyde Hyde-Thomson
Mrs Paul Hyde-Thomson
Mrs Jacqueline Inchbald
Miss Joan Ingpen LRAM
Mrs E Ingram
Mrs JE Inson DSc Dip
Miss Ann Ivil
Miss Joy Jameson
Mrs Dorothy A Jewitt
Miss Kathleen C Johnson SRN SCM
Miss Leonie Jonleigh RBA
Miss Irene Josephy
Miss JR Joyce
The Rev Sister Jude Jude MA (Edin)
Dr Winifred Kane MBBS DPH DCH
Miss Elizabeth K Kay
Mrs Beryl A S Kelly
Mrs Mary P Kendrick BA Assoc ICE
Dr Agnes Kennedy FFA RCS
Miss NW Kennedy
Miss E M Killby OBE
Mrs Clare Kipps ARCM
Mrs Betty Knightly LLB
Mrs Jeannette C M Kruschandl
Miss Janet Lacey CBE
Dr Jean Langham-Hobart MB ChB
Miss Jean Lanning
Councillor Mrs Phoebe Lean MA
  (Cantab)
Miss Valerie Ann Leeper
Miss Florence M Legg SRN SCM RMN
Miss Iris ME Lemare ARCM
Mrs AC Lethbridge BA
Mrs DM Levey
Miss GM Lewis MBE BA
Miss J Lewis SRN SCM RFN
Miss Zaidee Lindsay
Miss Joan Loader SRN ONC
Miss Jean Lorimer
Miss Enid Love BA
Miss Erna Low PhD MTAI
Mrs Clarisse Loxton-Peacock MA
Miss EM Lucas
Miss Robina Lund
Miss Ann F Lynch
Miss Muriel Lyne MBE
Miss Penelope Lynex ARAM
Mrs Roslyn M Lyons
Mrs Carol Macartney
Miss Gillian Helen Mackay
Mrs Gena MacKinnon OBE
Dr AD Maclaine MBChB
Miss KD Maddever OBE ND
Mrs Kathleen V McDougall Maiden MBE
Mrs Donald Main JP MA (Cantab)

Miss Muriel Mallows
Miss J Mann SRN
Miss Pamela B Mann BA (Arch) ARIBA
Miss Elizabeth Manners TD MA
Mrs John Mansel
Miss Veronica Mansfield ARCM
Miss Anne Marjoribanks
Mrs Stella L Marks RMS ASMP
Miss Marjorie Marriott OBE
Miss Monica Mason
Mrs Patricia Masters BA
Mrs Rachel McBryde MPS
Mrs Maeve McCormack BDS
Dr Barbara A McGeachy MB ChB LM
Miss Teresa McGonaghle
Mrs MD McHarg FCCS
Dr Joan Menage MRCS LRCP
Miss G Mary Messer
Miss Katherine Miler
Mrs RB Moore
Miss AM Morley
Miss Jill Morris DES RCA FRSA MSIA
Miss BH Morton-Palmer JP
Alderman Miss Iris H Moseley
Miss GE Moss BA (London)
Mrs PE Mosses MSc
Miss EE Muckle LLB
Miss Jean Muir
Dr Margit Muller MD (Bratislava) MRCS
  LRCP
Miss LD Murcott
Miss Margaret Macartney Murray MBE
  SRN RMN RMPA
Mrs L Musson
Mrs Halima Nalecz
Miss Anna Neagle CBE
Mrs V Neale JP
Councillor Mrs Margaret Neep JP
Mrs Angela Newberry ARCA
Mrs VAB Newcomb FIPA
Mrs M R Newlands MA
Mrs Moya Nixon
Miss Veronica M Nolan SRN SCM
Lady Helen Nutting
Dr Margaret O'Hare BSc MBChB MRCP
  FRCP(G)
Miss Carola Oman CBE FSA FRHist Soc
  FRSL
Mrs Julia Trevelyan Oman DES RCA
  MSIA
Miss Roseanne O'Reilly
Miss Eve Orme
Miss Hilda Orr
Miss ME Orr
Mrs BM Osborn JP CC

Miss Jean D Oswald LDS
Mrs Elizabeth Overbury
Miss KN Owen FCIB
Miss Margaret E Owen SRN SCM
Mrs Norah Owen
Mrs Jane Page BSc(Econ)
Miss Jean M T Page
Mrs Fay Pannell
Mrs Juliet Pannett FRSA SGA
Miss C Parfitt SRN SCM RFN
Miss June Park ARIBA
Miss Constance-Anne Parker ATD SWA
Miss I Nora Parkinson BA (London)
Mrs Mabel Peacock
Dame Felicity H Peake DBE JP
Mrs Maeve Peake
Miss C Eileen Peaker MA FRCOG
Miss Valerie Pearlman
The Hon Mrs Derrick Pease
Miss Muriel A Pemberton FSIA ARWS
    ARCA WIAC
The Lady Pender
Mrs Eric Penn
Prof Elizabeth Perrott BSc MSc Dip Ed
    PhD FLS FInstBiol
Mrs Frances Perry MBE FLS Dip Hort
Miss MR Peterkin DN
Mrs Margaret Peters
Miss Honoria Plesch
Mrs Robin Pleydell-Bouverie
Mrs MH Plume JP
Mrs Ponsonby
Mrs Muriel B Pritchard SRN SCM
Mrs Marjorie Proops
Madame SB Prunier
Miss Laurie Purden
Lady Ralli
Lady Rankin
Miss Ann Rathbone MA BArch
Miss ME Rea
Mrs John Read
Miss EM Rees SRN SCM N Admin Cert
    (RCN)
Mrs Theresa M Reynolds BSc (Botany)
    MS (Wisconsin)
Miss Elspeth Rhys-Williams
Miss Doris Richardson (Bratislava)
Miss Joanna Richardson MA (Oxon)
    FRSL
Mrs Madeleine Riley BA (Eng)
Mrs George Ritchie
Miss Lorna B Ritchie LDS
Dr Rosa Sutton Rivlin MRCS LRCP CPH
Mrs Hilda Robinson
Mrs Peter Robinson

Miss G Rodgers
Miss Betty Rosamond
Mrs Innes Rose
Miss Rachael M T Ross JP SRN
Councillor Mrs Monica Rowe
Miss Agnes Russell
Miss H Russell-Cruise BA
Mrs Margaret E Ryder RMS
Mrs Flora M Sadler MA
Mrs Denise Salem
Mrs Gerald Samsom
Mrs Alison M Sander MA
Mrs Diane Potter Saunders
Mrs R Stewart Savill
Miss Mabel AL Sculthorp BA
Miss Brenda Meredith Seymour BA LSIA
Miss Constance Shacklock LRAM FRAM
Miss Dorothy Sharwood-Smith
Miss FE Shaw
Mrs Rose T Shaw
Miss Lois Shawyer
Miss PA Shepherdson BA
Miss Joan M Simpson BA FIHM
Dr Marie Battle Singer MA (Cantab) PhD
    (London)
The Hon Mrs Suzanne Skyrme
Miss Evelyn H Slarke NFF
Miss Barbara E Smith
Miss EM Smith FCA
Mrs Florence Smith
Mrs Mary EH Smith MBE BA FIHM
Miss PD Smith FRSH AIHM
Dr Frances Sorrell MB ChB FFARCS
Miss Irene Southall FIHM MWI
Mrs June L Soutter BArch ARIBA AMTPI
Miss Claire Spencer ARCA
Mrs Lydia B Sproat MA
Miss Freda G Spurgeon ACIS
Miss Bettie Spurling MIPR
Miss JE Stark
Miss Ann H Steel LLB
Miss Sheila R Stephenson BA
Miss Joan E Stevens
Mrs Jocelyn Stevens
Lady Stewart OBE JP
Miss Margareta Stille ATD
Mrs Dorothy Rae Stone LLB JP
Miss HN Stone Dip Soc
Miss Josephine M Storey MBE SRN CMB
Miss Joyce Stranger BSc
Miss Patience Strong
Miss June A Stubbs MSIA
Miss Rosemary Sutcliff
Mrs R Swinburne-Johnson
Mrs UH Tayler MIPA

Miss Ann Taylor
Mrs Doreen Taylor
Miss Jane Taylor MIPA
Mrs Monica Taylor
Miss RM Taylor
Miss Dorothy L Thomas GC SRN
Mrs Irene Thomas
Miss MA Thomas SRN RSCN HVCert
  Dip Soc SC
Mrs Margaret S Thompson
Mrs Kathleen M Scott-Thorburn
Mrs Kitty DV Thorp
Miss Margaret A Todd SA SRN SCM
Dr Mary Truter BSc ARCS PhD DSc
Mrs WJ Carpenter Turner BA JP
Miss Jill Tweed, SLADE Dip
Mrs Kathleen Tynan BA
Miss Jane Urquhart
Mrs Alison Uttley BSc (Physics)
Mrs Pamela Vandyke Price MA
Miss Adza Vincent
Mrs Ann Voelcker AADip ARIBA
Miss Iris Wade
The Lady Wakehurst DBE
Mrs Christine Walker
Miss Fiona Walker
Dr Vera B Walker MSc PhD
Miss Elizabeth Wallace
Miss Margaret Wallace SRN RMN SCM
Miss Jean M Walwyn MCSP
Mrs Donald Warburg
Mrs Mary Ward BArch ARIBA FSIA
Miss OH Ward
Mrs Pamela J Ward BA (Arch) ARIBA
Mrs AM Ward-Jackson MA
Miss Hilda Wardroper DES RCA ATD
  MSIA
Miss Mary E Warren MBE
Miss Olga A Warren
Mrs KJ Waxman
Miss Weaver
Dr Barbara M Q Weaver PhD MRCVS
  DVA
Miss Maysie Webb BSc ALA
Miss Joyce Weiner MA (Oxon)
Miss Gillian Weir
Miss Molly Weir
Mrs Aldyth Wellington
Mrs Pamela Westland
Mrs Frank J White BA
Miss Evelyn M Whiteside
Alderman Mrs IG Wightman BA
Miss Joan M Wild FHA
Mrs Pamela M Wilde
Mrs Anne Wilkie

Miss Gwyneth C Williams BSc DIC
  MIBiol
Miss Lena Willis FGA
Dr O Winter MD
Mrs AA Withers
Miss M M Wittich
Lady Wolfenden
Mrs FI Wolsey-Neech
Miss Cynthia Wood AADip ARIBA
  AMTPI AIARB
Miss Irene Wood
Mrs Marguerite Wood JP
Dame Ethel Wormald DBE BA JP
Dr Mary Wright MB ChB (Edin)
Miss M Yates SRN SCM
Madame Yevonde FRPS
Miss Joan Yorke
Miss VL Youell SRN MSR
Miss Jean Zehetmayr ARIBA

Monday 5th October 1970
THEME: ASPECTS OF VIOLENCE

Parlour
Mrs Margaret A Alder
Mrs Helen Allan LDS RCS
Miss Paula Allardyce BA
Mrs Helen M Allely CA
Miss Anne M C Allen MA (Cantab) ACIS
Mrs Jean Ames
Mrs Margaret Amstell
Miss Madeline E Anderson ARCA
Miss Avril Angers
Mrs Mary Attlee
Miss Barbara Bashford
Dr Mary Belton MB BCH DPH
Miss Isobel Black
Miss Marjorie Blackwood
Miss Susan Bowden
Mrs Robin Bridgeman MA
The Hon Mrs Julian Byng
Mrs Averil M Cameron MA PhD
Mrs EC Cameron LLB
Miss Wendy Campbell-Purdie
Miss Ann Carroll LRAM
Alderman Mrs Ada Chadwick JP
Miss Mary Lumley Champion ARCA
Mrs William Channing
Miss Margaret D Chorlton MA (Oxon)
Mrs Myra L Clarke FRCVS
Mrs Rosemary Clarke-Smith BEM
Miss CP Clyne SCM
Mrs Anne Coleman ACIS
Miss MJ Corcoran SRN

Mrs Mary Le Gros Corkill
Mrs R Beatrice Cowan
Councillor Miss Clarinda Cox SRN SCM
Miss Sheila-Mary Crane ARRC SRN
  SCM
Miss Anna Cropper
Dr Ethel M Cruickshank BSc PhD MRSH
Mrs Robin Dalton
Miss Zena Dare (The Hon Mrs Brett)
Miss SA Megan Davies
Mrs Jill Denham-Davis
Miss Ivey Dickson FRAM
Mrs DE Dodd JP
Miss Beryl Downing
Miss Angela Dunne
Mrs Erica G L Dunsmore ACIS
Colonel EMB Dyson OBE RRC
Miss May Elliott SRN RNMD
Mrs Barbara Ellis
Mrs Joyce Evans ARIBA BA
Mrs Irene Everest
Mrs Michael Faber
Miss Carole Ann Ford
Miss Gladys J Garjulo GSM LRAM
Dr Camilla Hay Gillies MA
Mrs Muriel C Gingell
Mrs Pauline Glass RBSA
Mrs John Glyn
Miss KO Gordon CBE
Mrs Lilian CA Gorton LLB
Miss M Elaine Gray ALA
Miss Annette Green ARCA
Miss Jane Griffiths BA
Miss Lucy Halford
Mrs Rosemary Hanby
Mrs Rita D Harland
Mrs Jill Harris MBE
Mrs Joan Harris BSc
Miss Josephine Harris ARWS NEAC
Mrs Ruth Harrowing
Miss Margaret Helps MInstM
Mrs Phyllis Hindle NDD CEAE
Miss CM Hoe PhD FRCVS
Mrs Pamela Hudson
Mrs Joan C Hughes
Lady Hulton
Miss Joan Hurley
Miss Anne Jakeways
Miss Pamela M Jarvis
Mrs Karlin Jonzen FRBS
Alderman Mrs Marjorie J Keeble
Miss Allegra Kent Taylor
Mrs JCM Kruschandl
Miss Patricia Lambert
W/Chief Inspector Vera Lee

Miss Florence M Legg SRN SCM RMN
Mrs EPS Lewin
Miss Zaidee Lindsay
Mrs Audrey I Linzell MRCVS
Mrs Muriel Littlefield
Miss Lsybeth Liverton RAS
Mrs Patricia Lloyd MPS
Mrs Dorothy Lockwood ARWS RBSA
Miss EM Lucas
Miss Anne Lynch
Miss Gillian Lyne
Miss Muriel Lyne MBE
Mrs Morris Marsham
Mrs Rachael McBryde MPS
Dr Barbara Adam McGeachy MB ChB
  LM
Mrs Stella McGrath
Mrs MD McHarg FCCS
Miss Iris H Moseley
Councillor Mrs P E Mosses MSc
Miss Eileen E Muckle LLB
Dr Margit Muller MD LRCP MRCS
Miss Agnes Mulvey RGN
Miss LD Murcott
Miss Barbara M Naish MBE
Miss Maud Neilson
Tthe Lady Helen Nutting
Councillor Mrs Athlene O'Connell
Dr Doris Odlum MA (Oxon) BA (Lon)
  MRCS LRCP DPM
Mrs Elizabeth Overbury
Miss Constance-Anne Parker
Miss Muriel A Pemberton FSIA RWS
  ARCA WIAC
Mrs Margaret Peters
Professor Mary Pickford DSc FRS
Mrs Isobel L Pocock SRN SCM
Mrs EM Jean Procter
Miss Rita J Quail CA
Lady Rankin
Miss Lorna B Ritchie LDS
Mrs Dorothy L Roberts
Lady Rose
Miss H Russell-Cruise BA
Miss Peggie D Smith FRSH AIHM
Mrs Margaret Snow Dip DOM SC
Dr Charlotte Sommer MB LRCP
Miss Jane Spriggs
Mrs Marie S Sprunt
Miss Freda G Spurgeon ACIS
Miss Jean M Stow FCII
Mrs Eileen M Strain
Mrs UH Tayler MIPA
Miss Ann Townley ACA
Mrs Monica Tyson

Mrs Edith Van Vloodorp
Miss Hilda Wardroper RCA ATD MSIA
Mrs Sadie Warr
Miss Beryl Waterson ARCA
Dr Barbara MQ Weaver PhD FRCVS
 DVA
Mrs Irene Welburn ROI RBSA
Mrs A Wellington
The Hon Mrs White OBE SRN SCM
Mrs Eileen Wild ARIBA
Mrs Denis Wilde
Miss Lena Willis FGA
Mrs Anne Wolrige-Gordon
Mrs C W Wood MA
Miss Margaret Worthington
Mrs Barbara P Wroughton Dip Arch
 ARIBA
Miss V L Youell SRN MSR

Lancaster Room
Mrs Eileen M Alford
Miss Margaret Alexander
Dr Isobel C Allardyce MB ChB DCH
Sister Helen Archer, Superior
The Viscountess Astor
Mrs Inette Austin-Smith FRIBA AA Dipl
 FSIA
Mrs Charlotte Baden-Powell ARIBA AA
 Dipl
Miss Muriel Hayler Bailey
Mrs Christine Baker JP
Mrs Hilary Baldwin
Mrs Aileen Ballantyne AA Dipl ARIBA
Miss I Bannister SRN
Mrs June Barford
Miss MM Bark SRN
Dr Rosetta Barker MB BCH BAO DPH
The Mayor of Barking, Mrs Doris Jones
Mrs Elaine Barnett
Mrs GWT Barnett CA
Mrs Jenny Barraclough BA (Oxon)
The Mayor of Barry, Alderman Mrs MR
 Gill
Mrs Doreen Bateman MRCVS
Mrs Ena Baxter DA
Miss BJ Beale BSc (Eng)
Miss Geraldine Beamish
Dr Catherine Haldane Stobe Begg MB
 ChB DPH Dip BACT OPM
Mrs Olive Belchamber ARIBA
Mrs Ray Bell
Mrs Susan J Bell
Mrs Constance L Beynon FRCS Ed
 FRCOG
Miss KM Biggin BA SRN DN

Miss Lorna Binns ARCA
Superintendent Miss Marjorie E M
 Bishop
Miss Dorothy Black FIAI
Miss Margaret M Black MA
Mrs Moira R M Blackadder BVMS
 MRCVS
Mrs Jean Blackden LRAM
Miss Lorna J Blackie MA
Mrs Muriel Blunden-Ellis
Mrs Barbara Boissevain ARIBA
Miss H Boleyn-Smedley SRN SCM
Miss Joyce Booth MSIA AMIPA
Miss DT Borne ARBS VP RMS SWA
Miss E Bowen
Mrs Vivienne M Bowler MRCVS
Miss Jane Brown
Miss Betty E Box OBE
Mrs KD Boyd (Miss Judith Gardner)
Miss Katie Boyle
Miss Anita Brackley
Mrs Patricia E M Braund
Miss P Bridger MBE
Mrs TV Briggs
Mrs Sally Broad
Lady Brocklehurst
Air Commandant Dame Jean Bromet DBE
The Mayor of Bromley, Alderman Miss
 Bertha James MA JP
Mrs Helen Brook
Mrs T Broome MBE
Miss Gillian Brown MA
Miss Janet Brown AIQS
Miss Kathleen Browne ARMS
Dr Alice E Buck MD ChB LRCP
The Mayor of Buckingham, Councillor
 Mrs ED Embleton
Mrs BJ Budgen
Mrs E Burr SRN SCM
Miss Mary Burr MA FPS
Mrs Gladys Buxton CBE JP MA
Miss Juliann M Calder BSc MEd FEIS
Miss Patricia Callander BSc (Econ) FCCS
Mrs JR Callis
Miss Joan Cambridge MSc G
Miss Margaret C Cameron MRCVS
Miss Dorothy Gordon Campbell MRCVS
Miss Elizabeth L Campbell MA OStJ
Miss Judy Campbell
Miss Fanny Carby
Mrs Marilyn Carr BArch MCD ARIBA
 AMTPI
Mrs Jean Carroll
Mrs J Allan Cash
Miss Gillian M Cazalet

Miss Judith Chalmers
Mrs Yvonne Charpentier
Miss Madeline Chase
The Lady Chesham
Lady Chichester
Mrs Mavis A Chipperfield
Mrs Jean Christopherson ARIBA
Miss Sheena Clarke NDD
Mrs Anne Clough-Norton FCA
Miss Elizabeth Clowes SRN SCM
Mrs Jan Clutterbuck
Mrs Pamela Colepodd BSc MRCVS
Miss Patience Collier
Miss JL Collins
Mrs Audrey Compton FRIBA AA Dipl
Miss R Jean Conran BSc NFF
The Mayor of Conway, Councillor Mrs EM Jones
Mrs Ida Cooke DFA
Miss EM Cooper SRN SCM RNT (Edin) RN (Lon)
Miss RA Cooper SRN
Miss Wendy Cooper
Miss Norma Corney
Miss Judy Cornwell
Miss Joan Court AAPSW MSW
Mrs Jeanne Croft
Mrs LM Cumbers
Mrs Noel Cunningham-Reid
Mrs Margaret Daglish SRN RSCN
Mrs Edith Dakeyne-Cannon
Miss June Dandridge
Miss Jennifer Daniel
Mrs LN Darbyshire BA
Miss Sylvia Darley
Viscountess Davidson DBE
Col LM Davies CBE
Mrs Margaret Maston Davies SRN
Mrs Dorothy Day BA
Miss Gertrude Dearnley MD MB BS FRCOG
Miss Jacqueline Delhaye
Mrs Joanne Delmege
Miss HM Denney MA (Oxon)
Miss Astra Desmond (Lady Neame) CBE BA RAM
Miss Josephina de Vasconcellos FRBS
The Hon Lady de Zulueta
Dr Ursula Dick MB BS MRCS LRCP D(Obst) RCOG
Sister Catherine Dineen, Superior
Dr Margaret Dix MD FRCS
Mrs Honor Dobbs
Miss Edith M Dolphin
Miss Anna M Donnelly SRN FRN SCM RT

Miss Josephine Douglas
Dr Honor Doyle MD MB BCH BAO MRCP DCH
Miss KM Draycott
Miss Jane B Drew FRIBA FIArb FSIA
Miss Maureen Duck
Miss CG Edward BArch ARIBA
Councillor Mrs D L Edwards
Miss Madeline Eidam
Mrs Brenda Ellis LSIA
Miss Mary Ellis SRN SCM
Mrs Reginald Ellison BA SRN
The Mayor of Enfield, Alderman Mrs SG Child BA
Miss Betty Entwistle LLB
Miss Vivienne Entwistle
Mrs Aleda J Erskine
Councillor Mrs FW Eske ARMS
The Countess of Euston DCVO JP
Miss Eileen M Evans FSIA
Miss Marguerite Evans PHC
Mrs Winifred Ewing MA LLB NP
Dr Letitia Fairfield CBE MD DPH
Miss WK Farmer
Miss MI Fetherston
Miss Eva Figes BA
Mrs J Vera Finlay MBE JP
Miss Marguerite Fletcher BSc BVMS MRCVS
Miss Ingrid Floering MA (Cantab)
Miss Katie Flower
Miss Janet Fooker BA MP
Mrs AM Ford SSStJ
Dr Mary I Foreman MB BS MRCS LRCP
Mrs Sylvia F Forster
Mrs Malcolm Foster
Mrs Lillian Foulkes AIB
Mrs Anna Maria Frankl LLD LLB
Dr Juliet C Frankland BSc PHD FLS
Mrs Gina Franklin
Mrs Kathleen Franklin AMPOA
Miss Cecilia Freeman
Mrs Richard Fulford-Brown
Miss Jean Overton Fuller BA
Miss Helen Galas LLB
Mrs Joanna Gale LLB
Mrs Lillian Galloway
Mrs GO Gardiner SRN SCM BTA (Cert)
Mrs J M Gardiner
Miss Ailsa Garland
Mrs Patrick Garrett
Dr V Jean Gavin JP MRCS LRCP
Miss Mabel George MBE
Mrs Doris Gerrard RBA
Mrs Audrey L Gilby FCIB

234

Miss JC Gillett BA
Miss Marion Giordan BA
Mrs Guy Gluckstein
Miss Prudence Glynn (Lady Windlesham)
Miss Renée Goddard
Miss Enid B Godwin BA
Miss Jean Gomme-Duncan MBE
Mrs Dora L Green MRCVS
Miss Elizabeth Green MInstM
Mrs M Gregory BSc
Miss Mary G Greysmith BSc
Mrs Irene M Griesdale MRCVS
Mrs CFP Griffin ACA
Miss Valerie Eaton Griffith
Miss Elizabeth J Grundy ARIBA
Miss Margaret Gumuchian DA ATD ATC
Miss Mary Gunther DES RCA
Alderman Mrs GI Habershon
Miss Judith M Hacking ACA
Mrs DJ Hailey MBE BSc (Econ)
Miss Betty E Hale
Mrs Blanche Halliday
Mrs J MacFarlane Hamlin SRN SRFN
Miss Audrey Hammond BVetMed
   MRCVS
Dr Margaret Hammond MB ChB
Mrs MA Hamp-Hamilton LRAM (Eloc)
Miss Margaret M Hancock MA RCA
Miss Hilda M Harding
Miss Phyllis Harding
Dr Rosamond E M Harding PhD LittD
Mrs MLR Harkness BSc
Miss Julie Harris
Miss Sheila Harrison
Miss Marea Hartman MBE
Miss Clare Harvey MA (Oxon)
Miss Elizabeth Harvey BA (Oxon)
Miss MA Harwood
Mrs Jacqueline Haskoll
Dr Joan Haythorne MRCS DOMS
Mrs Esma M Hazelden
Mrs M Davidson Hearn
Miss B Heaton-Armstrong
Miss Marion E Hebblethwaite
Miss Olwen Hedley
Mrs Shirley Hedworth
Mrs R Henderson-Howat ARHistS
Miss CH Henry MBE
Mrs Fay Hensher
Dr Josephine Heylen MB BS LRCP
   MRCS
Mr FM Hickson
Mrs Graham Hill
Mrs Julie Ferguson Hinchcliffe Dip Arch
   ARIBA

Miss Verna Hitchcock
Miss Jennifer Hocking
Miss Moira Hoddell ARCA
Miss Julie Hodges DES RCA
Miss Peggy Hodges MA CEng FRAES
   FIMA MWES
Mrs Martha Hodgson
Mrs SK Holmans MA (Cantab)
Miss Anne Holmes Drewry
Mrs JP Holt
Miss Angela Hooper
Miss Peggy Hooton
Dr Sibyl G Horner CBE MB BS DPH DIH
Mrs MK Horsley
Mrs VH Howarth
Miss Joan Hughes
Miss Enid Hugh-Jones BMus FRCO
   ARAM
Mrs Betty Hunter
Mrs Mary Hunter
Mrs Sheila Hutchinson
Miss Angela Huth
Mrs MB Hyde MSc MIBiol
Mrs Hyde Hyde-Thomson
Mrs Paul Hyde-Thomson
Mrs Jacqueline Inchbald
Mrs GW Iredell CA JP
Miss Jeanette Jackson SLADE Dip
Dr Mary Jackson MB ChB DLO DPH
Miss Norah C James
Mrs AW Jenkins
Miss Heather Jenner
Mrs Dorothy A Jewitt
Mrs LD Johnson BVSC MRCVS
Mrs Celia Lamont Jones
Miss Edith I Jones SRN OND SCM
Dr Esther Jones
Miss Kathleen Jones
Mrs Marjorie E Jones
Miss Leonie Jonleigh RBA
Miss MG Jordan MRCVS
Miss JR Joyce
Sister Jude MA MEd
Mrs Barbara J Kahan MA
Dr Winifred A Kane MB BS DPH DCH
Mrs Leslie Kark
Miss Moira Keenan
Mrs Elaine Kellett MA MP
Mrs Beryl Kelly MABTh
Miss C Kelly SRN
Mrs Tina EF Kelly
Mrs MO Kemp
Mrs Mary P Kendrick BA MWES ICE
Dr Agnes Kennedy FFA RCS
Miss Karen Kessey

Miss Margaret Kilkenny FCA
Mrs Betty Knightly LLB
Miss Eva M Laburn CA
Dr Jean M Langham-Hobart MB ChB
Miss Jean Lanning
Dr Elizabeth Laverick BSc PhD CEng
 FIEE FInstP SMIEE
Mrs James Lee
Miss IME Lemare
Mrs Anna C Lethbridge BA
Mrs Doris M Levy
Miss Jessie Lewis SRN SCM RFN
Miss Thyrza Anne Leyshon RMS
Mrs IR Lomax
Miss Erna Low PhD MTAI
Mrs Nina Lowry LLB
Mrs Clarisse Loxton-Peacock
Miss Janet Lyle
Mrs Jack Lyons
Miss Teresa McGonagle
Mrs Carol Macartney
Air Commandant AS McDonad ARRC
Miss Sandra MacGregor Hastie Dip SPS
Mrs May MacIntyre
Miss Gillian Mackay
Miss Anne M Mackie
Dr AD Maclaine MB ChB
Miss Elizabeth GM Macmillan BVMS
 MRCVS
Miss Janet W Macnaughton
Miss KD Maddever OBE NDD
Mrs Kathleen McDougall Maiden MBE
Mrs Donald Main JP MA (Cantab)
Miss Joy Maitland
Miss Pamela B Mann BA (Arch) ARIBA
Miss Elizabeth Manners TD MA
Mrs John Mansel
Mrs May Maple CEng FIEE
The Lady Margaret of Mar
Mrs Stella L Marks RMS ASMP
Miss Marjorie Marriott OBE
Mrs Winifred H Marriott SRN SCM
Mrs Jean Marshall
Miss Monica Mason
Mrs PA Masters BA
Alderman Mrs Margaret M Mathias
Miss Jessie Matthews OBE
Miss EG Maxey PHC
Miss Susan Mayor
Mrs TB McAleer MA
Mrs RA McAlpine
Mrs Maeve C McCormack BDS
Miss Elizabeth McLaren SRN
Miss Madeline McLauchlan BA
Mrs EMF McLean MB ChB DPH DOMS

Miss Jean McLellan MA
Dr Joan A Menage MRCS LRCP
Miss Suzy Menkes BA (Cantab)
Mrs Hilda M Menzies
Mrs KJ Merry
Miss Mary Messer MInstM
Miss Marilyn Meyer
Dame Margaret Miles BA DBE
Miss Janet Milne
Miss Gwen Moffat
Mrs Byron Moger
Mrs RB Moore
Alderman Miss GA Morgan
Miss Myfanwy Morgan
Miss Alwyne Morley
Miss Jill Morris DES RAC FRSA MSIA
Mrs E Morrish MBE
Mrs Constance Morton ARCA SWA
Miss Jean Muir
Mrs Maureen Vincent Mullally LLB
Mrs Halima Nalecz FFPS
Mrs Constance Nathan
Mrs Victor Neale JP
Miss Evelyn New MSIA
Mrs VAB Newcomb FIPA
Miss Margaret Newton MA
Mrs Moya Nixon
Mrs Vivien Noakes
Mrs Norma E Noble CA
Miss M Oakeley MA (Oxon)
Mrs ED O'Brien
Mrs Laura O'Donnell
Mrs Jean Ogden ARMCM
Dr Margaret M O'Hare BSc MB ChB
 MRCP FRGP
Miss Carola Oman (Lady Lenanton) CBE
 FRSL FRHistSoc FRSA
Mrs Sally Oppenheim MP
Miss Mary Roseanne O'Reilly
Mrs Hugh Orr-Ewing
Alderman Mrs B M Osborn JP CC BC
Miss Jean D Oswald LDS
Miss Barbara Owan BSc (Eng) ACGI
 SM(MIT)
Mrs KN Owen
Mrs Maureen Kelly Owen Dip Arch
 ARIBA
Mrs Norah L Owen
Miss PJ Owen ARIBA AA Dipl
Mrs DP Oxenham CBE JP
Mrs Jane Page BSc (Econ)
Mrs Mabel Pakenham-Walsh
Mrs Fay Pannell
Miss C Parfitt SRN SCM RFN
Miss June Park ARIBA

Miss IN Parkinson BA
Miss Phyllis Parrott FLA
Mrs Marguerite Patten
Miss Muriel Pavlow
Alderman Mrs E M Payne
Mrs Mabel Peacock
Dame Felicity Peake DBE JP
Miss C Eileen Peaker FRCOG
Mrs Naomi Pearlman BA
Miss V Pearlman
The Hon Mrs Derrick Pease
Dr EL Peet MB BS MD
The Mayor of Pembroke, Councillor Mrs MM Wrench
The Lady Pender
Miss Margaret A Peoples SRN
Professor Elizabeth Perrot BSc MSc PHD Dip Ed FLS FInstBiol
Mrs Mary Whittaker Perry MRCVS
Mrs Colette C Pickstock MB ChB DRCOG FRCS (Ed)
Miss Margaret Pinder
Miss Norma Pinkerton LDS
Mrs Psyche Pirie
Miss Honoria Plesch
Mrs MH Plume JP
Miss Gwen Pollock
Mrs W Pollock
Miss AE Porter
Miss Elizabeth V H Porter MRCVS
Miss JP Potter Dip Hort
Dr ML Kellmer Pringle BA PhD FBPS
Mrs Muriel Benjamin Pritchard SRN SCM
Mrs Marjorie Proops OBE
Madame SB Prunier
Miss Laurie Purden
Lady Ralli
Miss ME Rea
Miss EM Rees SRN SCM
Miss Beryl Reid
Mrs Theresa M Reynolds BSc MS (Wis)
Mrs E Brinley Richards
Miss Doris Richardson FIM
Mrs George Ritchie
Miss Carol Ann Robertson
Mrs Jean SS Robertson
Mrs Jean W Robertson BA
Miss Georgie Rodgers Dip HEC
Miss Muriel Rose ROI RBA
Miss Yootha Rose
Miss Rachael MT Ross JP SRN
Councillor Mrs Monica Rowe
Miss Agnes Russell
Mrs Margaret E Ryder RMS
Mrs Bertha Sack

Mrs Denise Salem
Mrs Gerald Samson
Mrs Joyce Saunders BSc AFIMA
Miss Barbara Saxon
Alderman Dr Theresa Science-Russell JP DCL
Miss Grace F Schofield SRN SCM DN
Mrs Margaret Senley
Major GA Sergant (WRAC) CEng MIMechE AMBIM
Professor Constance Shacklock LRAM FRAM
Mrs SJM Shaw
Miss Lois Shawyer
Mrs Elena Shayne-Barel
Mrs Vera Sherman NDD
Miss Irene H Short
Miss Joan M Simpson BA FIHM
Mrs EME Sims
Dr Marie Battle Singer MA (Cantab) PhD (Lon)
The Hon Mrs Suzanne Skyrme
Miss Evelyn H Slarke NFF
Miss Audrey Slaughter
Mrs Dorothy O Smith
Mrs Florance Smith
Mrs Kathleen M Smith MRCVS
Mrs Mary EH Smith MBE BA FIHM
Mrs Nina M Snook
Dr Frances Sorrell MB ChB FFARCS
Miss C Irene Southall FIHM MWI
The Mayor of Southport, Alderman Mrs Jean Leech
Mrs Joyce Spencer ATD
Mrs LB Sproat MA BEd
Miss Jean Stark
Mrs Una Steedman
Miss Anne H Steel LLB
Miss Elizabeth Steel LLB
Miss Sheila Stephenson BA
Lady Stewart OBE JP
Miss Margareta Stille NND ATD
Miss Charlotte L Stone BA Slade Dip
Miss Dorothy Rae Stone LLB JP
Miss Helen N Stone Dip Soc
Miss Joyce Stranger BSc
Miss June A Stubbs MSIA
The Mayor of Sudbury, Councillor Miss Mildred Head
Mrs Anne Summers DES RCA FRSA
Mrs R Swinburne-Johnson
Dr Jean Symington MD DPH
Mrs Doreen Taylor
Miss Eileen J Taylor BSc MBE
Mrs GC Taylor

Miss Jane Taylor FIPA
Miss D Tempest MA (Cantab)
Mrs PHJ Temple-Richards BA FRGS
Mrs Irene Thomas
Miss Millicent Thomas SRN HVCert Dip
  Soc SC
Mrs Rena Thompson
Mrs Sheila Thorns
Baroness Fiona Thyssen
Miss Margaret A Tood SRM SA
Mrs Daphne I Toseland
The Mayor of Totnes, Councillor Mrs JM
  Gilbert
Miss Christine Turnball
Alderman Mrs WJ Carpenter Turner JP
  BA
Dr Mary P Truter (Lady Cox) BSc PhD
  DSc
Miss Anna Tzelniker
Mrs DW Variava BA ARIBA JP
Miss Barbara M E Visick
Miss Iris Wade
Mrs Jean Wadland BVSC MRCVS
Lady Wakehurst DBE
Miss Elizabeth Wallace
Miss Hazel V Wallace Dip Soc SC
Miss Margaret Wallace SRN RMN SCM
Miss Nora Walley
Miss M Wallis MPS MRSH
Miss Jean Walwyn
Miss OH Ward
Lady Warren DStJ JP
Miss Molly Weir
The Mayor of Wells, Mrs W H Pinching
Mrs Pamela Wells ARIBA
Mrs Frank J White BA
Miss GC Williams
Miss LM Williams
Mrs AA Withers
Miss Margaret Wittich
Lady Wolfenden
Mrs FI Wolsey-Neech FLA FRSA
Miss Cynthia Wood AA Dip ARIBA
  AMTPI AIARB
Miss Irene Wood
Mrs Marguerite Wood JP MCSP
Miss Rae Woodland
Miss Nan P Wright CA
County Alderman Mrs Anne Yates JP
  LMRSH
Miss M Yeates SRN SCM
Yevonde (Mrs Yevonde Middleton) FRPS
Miss Jean Zehetmayer ARIBA

October 1972
THEME: FREEDOM

Parlour
Dr Margaret I Adamson MB ChB DPH
  FRSH
Miss Margaret Allen BSc
Mrs I Banham-Lee MIPR
Miss Barber
Mrs Nora Bell
Miss Margaret M Black MA
Mrs Ruth Blair BVSC
Mrs Freddy Bloom OBE BA
Mrs Julia Bradbury MIPR
Mrs Margaret E Bramall OBE MA
  AIMSW JP
Mrs Hermione Bridges ACIS
Miss Barbara M Brindle OStJ
Miss Kathleen Browne ATD
Miss Gene Buxton MIPR
Mrs Jessica R Callis
Miss Dorothy Gordon Campbell MRCVS
Miss Ann Caroll LRAM
Prof MM Cole BSc PhD
Miss Anna Coote MA
Mrs Betty Cornick JP FRSA
Mrs Jeanne Croft
Miss Teresa de Bertodano
Miss MP Docherty
Miss Katie Doyle BA
Dr Kathleen Duncan MB ChB
Mrs Armand Dutry
Alderman Mrs E D Embleton
Mrs Joyce Farnhill
Mrs Errol Flynn
Miss Carole A Ford
Miss ER Adele Gaskell BA GRAD IPM
Mrs WW Gerard
Mrs Evelyn Gibson BA
Mrs Audrey L Gilby
Miss Jean Goater
Mrs Annette Godbold
Miss Elizabeth M Grindley ARIBA
The Marchioness of Hamilton
Mrs VL Harcus
Mrs Rachael Heyhoe Flint MBE
Miss PD Hooton
Mrs Hourigan
Lady MP Hulton
Mrs Joan E Inson DSc Dip
Miss DV Johnson
Miss Shirley Kaye
Miss Margaret M Keegan
Cllr Miss ES Kidman JP
Mrs Christiane Kubrick

Miss Franka Kutlesa
Mrs Tim Lardner
Miss Thyrza A Leyshon
Mrs May Maple FIEE MWES
Mrs Heather McConnel
Mrs ME McCrory
Mrs Rhona Myers
Mrs F Nagle
Miss Maud Neilson
Mrs Hazel M Neville
Mrs CT Norman-Butler
Miss Susan Orde
Miss J Overton-Fuller BA
Miss June Park ARIBA
Miss Margaret Pinder
Mrs Ann Prattent
Dr Margherita Rendel MA PhD FRSA
Miss Shelagh Roberts
Mrs Bertha Sack
Mrs Sandra Saer
Brigadier Mary Scott
Miss Brigid Segrave
Miss PA Shepherdson BA
Mrs Mary E H Smith MBE BA FIHM
Miss Sally-Anne Stapleford
Mrs Olive Stephens
Mrs Blackie Stone
Mrs UH Tayler MIPA
Miss F Ruth Wallace
Miss Trudy West
The Hon Mrs J White
Dr A C Wilson OBE MBChB

Lancaster Room
Miss Ruth M Abell ARICS
Miss Margaret KM Aiken BA LLB
Miss Eugenie Alexander ATD
Mrs Helen Allan LDS RCS
Miss Paula Allardyce
Mrs Jean Ames
Mrs Margaret Amstell
Mrs Charles Anderson OBE
Miss Avril Angers
Mrs Hylda Armstrong
Miss Roxane Arnold BCom LLB
Mrs Laura Ashley
Mrs Barbara Attenborough
Mrs Mary Attlee
Mrs ILE Austin-Smith FRIBA AADipl
    FSIA
Mrs Ayres BSc ACA
Mrs Charlotte Baden-Powell AADip
    ARIBA
Miss Muriel Bailey
Mrs Valentine Baker BA

Miss Hilary Baldwin
Mrs Aileen Ballantyne AADipl FRIBA
Mrs J Barford
Dr Rosetta Barker MB BCh BAO DPH
Mrs Elaine J R Barnett
Mrs GWT Barnett
Mrs Doreen Bateman MRCVS
Miss DM M Baugh FPS
Mrs Ena Baxter DA
Miss Alexandra N Beale
Mrs Alfreda Bean
Miss Anne H Beattie LLB
Mrs Jennifer Begg ARIBA
Mrs Olive Belchamber ARIBA
Miss Eve Bell
Mrs Ray Bell
Mrs Susan Benjamin
Flying Officer Diana Bentley WRAF
Dr G Bergheimer MB ChB FRCGP
Miss Gillian Best
Miss AJ Billimore
Superintendent M E M Bishop
Mrs Jean Blackden LRAM
Mrs Rosamunde Blackler
Miss Marjorie Blackwood
Mrs Elaine Blower ALA
Mrs M Blunden-Ellis
Mrs Barbara Boissevain ARIBA
Mrs Joyce Bolton ARIBA BA
Miss OM Bonner SRN
Miss Susan Bowden
Miss Emily Bowen
Mrs G Mary Bowen BSc MRCVS
Mrs Vivienne M Bowler MRCVS
Cllr Mrs LE Bowles
Mrs Kenneth Boyd
Miss Katie Boyle
Mrs Patricia Bradstreet MB FRCPath
Miss WM Brancker OBE MRCVS
Mrs TV Briggs
Mrs Sally Broad
Lady Brocklehurst
Mrs Helen Brook
Miss ICS Brown
Mrs Winifred M Brown
Mrs Christine Bulmer
Mrs Mollie Elizabeth Burgess FCA
Miss MA Burr MA FPS
Miss Henrietta L Bussell
Mrs Martin Butlin
Mrs Gladys Buxton CBE JP MA
The Hon Mrs Julian Byng
Miss Juliann M Calder BSc MEd FEIS
    FSASCOT
Mrs Elizabeth Cameron BA LLB

239

Miss Margaret C Cameron MRCVS
Miss Fanny Carby RAD
Mrs Marilyn Carr Barch ARIBA
  MCDAMTPI
Mrs J Allan Cash
The Hon Mrs Isabel Catto OBE
Miss Judith Chalmers
Mrs Mary Lumley Champion ARCA
Mrs William Channing
Mrs Anthea Chapman ATD
Mrs Yvonne Charpentier
The Lady Chesham
Lady Chichester
Mrs Mavis A Chipperfield
Mrs Joan E Chrismas
Mrs Antony Christopherson ARIBA
Mrs Myra L Clarke FRCVS
Miss Sheena Clarke NDD
Miss Julia Clements
Mrs Patricia Clements
Mrs Anne Clough-Norton FCA
Miss Anne V Coates
Mrs Jocelyn Cockroft OBE
Miss Muriel Cole
Miss Patricia Galloway Coles MA
Mrs Kathleen Collett
Mrs Patience Collier
Miss Jeanette Collins
Mrs Audrey Compton FRIBA AADipl
Miss Shirley Conran
Miss A Freda Cooke MA JP
Mrs Ida Cooke DFA WIAC
Miss Doreen Cooper
Miss Joan D Cooper CB BA
Miss Heather S Coupe
Miss Joan Court MSW
Mrs RB Cowan
Miss Freda M Cowell BSc
Miss Anne Crewdson
Mrs Critchley
Mrs Brenda Croft Ellis LSIA
Miss Anna Cropper
Miss EM Cruickshank MA BSc PhD
Mrs Lois Cumbers
Mrs E Dakeyne-Cannon
Miss Margaret Dalglish SRN RSCN
Miss June Dandridge
Mrs LN Darbyshire BA
Mrs Brenda Darling BA RIBA
Mrs Joan Davidson
Miss Margaret R Davies
Mrs Alison Davis
Miss Madeline Davis SRN
Mrs Paquita Davis
Mrs Betty I Day

Mrs Dorothy Day BA
Dr Gertrude Dearnley MD BS FRCOG
Mrs Cecil Denham-Davis
Mrs J de Vasconcellos FRBS
The Hon Lady de Zulueta
Dr Ursula M Dick MB BS MRCS LRCP
  D(Obst) RCOG
Miss Ivey Dickson FRAM
Miss Mary Dilnot
Dr MR Dix MD FRCS
Mrs Honor Dobbs
Miss EM Dolphin
Dr Honor Doyle MD BCh BAO MRCP
  DCH
Air Cmdt Dame Jean Conan Doyle
  WRAF DBE
Miss Kathleen Draycott
Miss Jane B Drew FRIBA FIArb
Miss Judith Drury MA
Miss Maureen Duck
Miss Janet Dunbar
Miss Angela M Dunne
Mrs Dorothy Dunnett
Mrs EGL Dunsmore ACIS
Cllr Mrs D L Edwards
Mrs Elgood
Miss Polly Elwes
Miss Betty Entwistle LLB
Mrs Vivienne Entwistle
Cllr Mrs F W Eske ARMS SWA
Miss Eileen Evans FSIA
Mrs OW Evans MRCVS
Miss B M Eyles
Mrs Audrey Eyton
Miss Hilda Fenemore
Miss Stella PM Fisher
Miss Marguerite Fletcher BSc BVMS
  MRCVS
Mrs Percival Ford SSO StJohn
Miss Helen Forrest
Mrs Sylvia F Forster
Mrs RG Forsyth
Mrs Clarence Foster
Miss Lilian Foulkes AIB AMBIM
Miss Juanita Frances
Mrs AM Frankl LLD (Prague) LLB
  (Wales)
Mrs Kathleen Franklin AMPOA
Miss Cecilia Freeman
Miss IPM Freeston MA
Mrs P Fulford-Brown MIPR
Miss Helen Galas LLB BLitt
Mrs Joanna Gale LLB
Mrs Lilian Galloway
Mrs JM Gardiner

Miss Gladys J Garjulo GSM LRAM
Miss Ailsa Garland
Mrs Patrick Garrett
Dr V Jean Gavili JP MRCS LRCP
Mrs Doris Gerrard RBA
Mrs Janie Gibson
Miss Dorothy Giles BSc
Dr Camilla H Gillies MA
Mrs Muriel C Gingell
Mrs Guy Gluckstein
Miss Renée Goddard
Miss Enid B Godwin BA
Alderman Mrs WA Goodchild JP CC
Miss Elinor Goodman
Miss Anne C Gorna LLB
Mrs Lilian CM Gorton LLB
Mrs R S B Gray
Mrs Dora L Green MRCVS
Miss Elizabeth Green MInstM
Mrs M Gregory BSc
Miss MG Greysmith BSc
Mrs Clare Griffin FCA
Mrs Alice Griffiths
Miss Jane Griffiths BA
Mrs Irene M Grisedale MRCVS
Miss E Grundy ARIBA
Mrs Desmond Guinness
Miss Margaret Gumuchian DA ATD ATC
Mrs Mary Gunther DES RCA
Miss Judith M Hacking ACA
Miss Betty Hall
Miss Hallett
Mrs I Blanche Halliday
Miss Audrey Hammond BVetMed
    MRCVS
Miss Jane Hammond MIPR
Dr Margaret Hammond MB ChB
Mrs MA Hamp-Hamilton LRAM (Eloc)
Mrs MLR Harkness BSc
Mrs Rita D Harland
Mrs Janine Harrington
Mrs Jill Harris MBE
Miss Sheila Harrison
Miss Marea Hartman MBE BSc
Miss Elizabeth Harvey MA
Mrs Jacqueline Haskoll
Miss Alison Hawkes BA
Miss Anne Hawkins CVO
Dr Joan Haythorne MRCS DOMS
Miss Mildred Head OBE
Miss Heaton-Armstrong
Miss Marion E Hebblethwaite
Lady Hedges
Miss Olwen Hedley
Miss Margaret Helps

Mrs Jessie W Hemel SRN SCM JP
Miss Barbara Henderson
Mrs R Henderson-Howat ARHist S
Miss CH Henry MBE
Dr JCM Heylen MBBS LRCP MRCS
Mrs FM Hickson
Mrs Julie F Hinchliffe ARIBA Dipl Arch
Mrs Phyllis Hindle NDD SEA CEAE
Miss Verna Hitchcock
Miss Jennifer Hocking
Miss Moira Hoddell ARCA
Miss Peggy L Hodges OBE MA CenG
    FRAES FIMA
Mrs Martha A Hodgson
Miss DF Hollingsworth OBE BSc FRIC
    FIBiol FIFST SRD
Miss Anne Holmes-Drewry
Mrs V Holt
Mrs May K Horsley
Miss NE Caroline Hudleston
Mrs Pamela Hudson
Lady Susan Hussey CVO
Mrs Mary Hutcheson FLA
Mrs Sheila Hutchison
Mrs Elizabeth Hyde MAOT
Miss MB Hyde MSc MIBiol
Mrs Jacqueline Inchbald
Dr Mary Jackson MB ChB DLO DPH
    DIH
Miss Anne Jakeways
Miss Bertha James OBE JP MA
Miss Isabel H Jamieson MBE
Miss Pamela Jarvis
Miss Eve Johnson
Mrs LD Johnson BVSC MRCVS
Cllr Mrs Doris Jones
Dr Esther Jones
Miss Julia Jones
Miss Joy R Joyce
Dr WA Kane MB BS DPH DCH
Miss Barbara Kelly
Mrs MP Kendrick BA ICE MWES
Dr Agnes O Kennedy FFA RCS
Miss Margaret Kilkenny
Mrs Betty Knightly
Miss Wyn Knowles
Mrs JCM Kruschandl
Miss Patricia Lamburn
Miss Felicity Lane-Fox
Dr Jean Langham-Hobart MB ChB
Miss Jean Lanning JP
Lady Latey
Miss Patricia Latham
Miss Rona Laurie BA FGSM LRAM
Miss Jean S Law QPM

241

Mrs Anne Lee LLB
Mrs Cinn Lee
Miss Marjorie Lee
Mrs Jean Leech
Dr Stephanie M Leese BSc MB BS DPM
   MRCPsych
Mrs Margaret Legum MA
Miss Iris Lemare ARCM
Mrs Christine Lethbridge BA
Miss PM Lethbridge
Mrs Doris M Levey
Miss Mary Lewis MBE BA
Miss Zaidee Lindsay
Mrs Audrey I Linzell MRCVS
Mrs Muriel Littlefield
Miss Lysbeth Liverton Cert RAS NDD
Mrs C Lloyd Pack
Mrs Dorothy Lockwood ARWS RBSA
Mrs J Forbes Love
Miss Erna Low PhD MTAI
Miss EM Lucas
Miss Mollie Luke MIPR
Mrs RM Lyons
Mrs Carol Macartney
Mrs May MacIntyre
Miss Gillian H Mackay
Miss Elizabeth A MacKenzie
Miss Jacqueline MacKenzie
Miss Anne M MacKie
Dr AD MacLaine MB ChB
Miss EG Moira MacMillan BVMS
   MRCVS
Mrs Janet W MacNaughton
Miss KD Maddever OBE NDD
Mrs Kathleen Maiden MBE
Mrs Anne Maile FSDC
Miss Diana Makgill MVO
Miss Ann Mallalieu MA LLB
Mrs DM Mann
Miss PB Mann BA ARIBA
Miss Elizabeth Manners TD MA FRSA
Mrs Stella L Marks RMS ASMP
Miss Marjorie Marriott OBE
Mrs Jean Marshall
Mrs Mary Martin
Miss Millicent Martin
Mrs Blanche Marvin BA
Mrs Marian Massey
Alderman Mrs Margaret Mathias
Cllr Mrs Jean Maughan
Mrs R Alistair McAlpine
Mrs Maeve C McCormack BDS
Mrs Mary D McHarg FICS
Mrs EMF McLean MB ChB DPH DOMS
Mrs Elizabeth McLeish

Miss Jean E McLellan MA
Mrs Vernier von Meissner
Mrs Sylvia Melland ARE
Dr Jeanne Menage MRCS LRCP
Miss Suzy Menkes BA
Mrs Hilda M Menzies
Miss Mary Messer
Mrs BM Mighell BVM&S MRCVS
Miss BPJ Millar RGN SCM
Mrs I Millar
Mrs Kathryn S Miller
Miss Janet Milne
Miss Mary Mitchell FILA FFB
Miss Dolores Monreal MVO MBE
Mrs Barbara Moont BSc(Engineering)
   ACGI SM(Mit)
Mrs Iris Moreton
Alderman Miss Gwynneth Morgan
Miss Myfanwy Morgan
Miss Jill Morris DES RCA FRSA MSIA
Mrs Josephine M Morris
The Hon Mrs Charles Morrison
Miss Iris H Moseley
Councillor Mrs P E Mosses LGSM (Eloc)
   MSc
Miss EE Muckle LLB
Miss Jean Muir
Mrs Diane Munday
Miss Daisy Murcott
Mrs Halima Nalecz
Mrs Constance Nathan
Miss Jane Nelson
Mrs Laci Nester-Smith
Mrs VAB Newcomb FIPA
Dr Lotte T Newman BSc MBBS LRCP
   MRCS MRCGP
Mrs Jill Nicholson BA
Miss Anne Nightingale
Mrs M Nixon
Miss Mary Oakeley MA
Mrs Brenda Ogdon ARMCM
Dr Margaret M O'Hare BSc MBChB
   MRCP FRCPG
Dr BK Oliver FFARCS
Miss Carola Oman CBE CMA
Miss Hilda Orr
Miss Mary E Orr
Mrs Hugh Orr-Ewing
Mrs BM Osborn JP
Mrs Elizabeth Overbury
Mrs Aron Owen
Miss Dilys Owen SRN
Mrs Maureen Kelly Owen ARIBA
Mrs Norah Owen
Mrs JRM Page BSc

Mrs Fay Pannell
Mrs Juliet Pannett FRSA SGA
Miss Constance A Parker ATD
Miss IN Parkinson BA
Miss LAC Peachey
Miss Clarisse L Peacock MA
Mrs Leonard Pearl
Mrs Naomi Pearlman BA
Miss Valerie Pearlman
The Hon Mrs Derrick Pease
Miss Muriel A Pemberton FSIA ARWS
  ARCA WIAC
Lady Pender
Lady Penn
Dr Elsa E Perls MD LRCS LRCP
Mrs Margaret Peters
Professor M Pickford DSc FRS
Mrs Norma Pinkerton LDS
Mrs Psyche Pirie
Mrs Patricia Player
Miss Honoria Plesch
Mrs Margaret H Plume JP
Mrs Edna M Podmore BA Dip Ed
Miss Gillian Pollard BA
Miss AE Porter
Mrs P Potiphar
Miss Evadne Price
Madame SB Prunier
Miss Laurie Purden
Miss RJ Quail
Lady Ralli
Miss Margaret E Rea
Mrs John Read
Miss Mary Redcliffe
Miss Anne Redmile
Mrs George Ritchie
Mrs Elisabeth Rivers-Bulkeley
Miss Rachel Roberts BA
Mrs Jean Robertson MRCVS
Mrs Jean W Robertson BA
Mrs Joan Robins OBE
Mrs H Robinson
Miss Mary C Robinson MBE
Miss Georgie Rodgers
Miss Jacqueline Rose MIPR
Miss Annie Ross
Mrs BP Ross-Esson
Mrs Margaret E Ryder RMS SWA
Mrs Flora M Sadler MA
Mrs Denise Salem
Dame Barbara Salt DBE
Mrs Joyce Saunders BSc AFIMA
Miss Barbara Saxon
Miss Grace F Schofled SRN SCM DN
Mrs MW Scott

Major GA Sergant WRAC CEng
  MIMECHE AMBIM
Miss Elena Shayne-Barêl
Miss Joan M Simpson BA FIHM
Mrs EME Sims
Dr Marie Singer MA PhD
The Hon Mrs Suzanne Skyrme
Mrs DO Smith
Miss EM Smith FCA
Miss Mary Smith LLB
Miss PD Smith FRSH AIHM
Mrs Nina Marguerite Snook
Miss Gay Soper
Dr Frances Sorrell MB ChB FFARCS
Mrs Sylvia Sosnow
Mrs Honor Southern
Mrs P Spencer-Phillips
Mrs LB Sproat MA BED
Mrs MJ Spurgin
Miss Prunella Stack
Miss Jean Stark
Mrs Pamela Stark FCA
Miss Sheila Stephenson BA
Lady Stewart OBE JP
Miss Gloria Stewart BA
Dame Muriel Stewart MA MED
Miss Margareta Stille ATD
Mrs Edna M Stokes
Miss Jean M Stow FCII
Mrs Joyce Stranger BSc
Miss June A Stubbs MSIA
Mrs Anne Summers DES RCA FRSA
Mrs R Swinburne-Johnson CBE
Mrs Alexander Taft
Miss Alannah Tandy
Mrs Ashena Tapster
Mrs GC Taylor
Miss Molly Taylor
Mrs Monica Taylor
Miss Doris Tempest MA
Miss Gwen Thomas Dip PE
Mrs Irene Thomas
Miss Marjorie Thomson
Mrs Rena Thompson
Mrs Kitty DV Thorp
Miss Rosemarie Timmis Dip BYAM
  SHAW
Mrs Ethel L Tonkin
Mrs Daphne Toseland
Miss Ann Townley ACA
Miss Joan Turner
Miss Sylvia Tutt
Miss Pauline Viola
Miss BME Visick
Mrs Edith van Vloodorp

Miss Iris Wade
Mrs Helen Wakeford
Dame Margaret Wakehurst DBE LLD
Miss Nicolette Milnes Walker BSc MSc
  MBE
Dr Vera Walker MSc PhD
Miss Elizabeth Wallace
Mrs Elizabeth Wallace SRN
Miss Hazel V Wallace OBE
Miss Nora Walley
Miss M Wallis MPS MRSH
Miss OH Ward
Mrs Pamela J Ward BA (Arch) RIBA
Miss Mary Gordon-Watson
Dr Barbara MQ Weaver PhD FRCVS
  DVA
Miss Julia Weaver
Miss Molly Weir
Mrs Penelope A Wellington
Mrs Bernice Weston
Miss Margaret E Whitbread
Mrs Maureen White LLB JP
Mrs Evelyn Whiteside
Mrs Margaret Wigley
Mrs Marilyn E Wigoder-Halberstam LLB
Mrs Zena AP Williams LLCM
Miss Diane Winsor
Mrs AA Withers
Miss Margaret Wittich
Lady Wolfenden
Mrs FI Wolsey-Neech FLA FRSA
Miss Cynthia Wood AADip ARIBA FFB
  AMRTPI AIARB
Miss Irene Wood
Mrs Marguerite Wood JP MCSP
Miss Rae Woodland
Mrs Margaret M Wrench
Miss Nan Wright
Mrs BP Wroughton Dip Arch
Miss VL Youell SRN DSR

Monday 6th October 1975
THEME: IMAGE OR REALITY?

Parlour
Miss Ames
Miss Barber BA
Mrs D Bateman MRCVS
Flt Lt Diana Bentley WRAF
Miss J Calder BSc MEd FFIS
Mrs AG Christopherson ARIBA
Mrs Kay Clay
Miss C Clyne SCM
Mrs Ida Cooke DFA WIAC

Miss Sylvia Darley
Dr A Rosalie David BA PhD
Mrs Jean Denton BSc (Econ)
Mrs Dermot de Trafford
Dr Ursula Dick MBBS MRCS LRCP
  M(Obst) RCOG
Dr Margaret Dix MD FRCS
Mrs Maureen Dobkin
Miss Caroline Dobson Dip Soc SC
Miss Mary Docherty
Miss P Downs BA BComm MIPM
Miss Janet Dunbar
Mrs Erica Dunsmore FCIS
The Countess of Effingham
Miss Audrey Emerton
Miss Betty Eyles
Mrs AM Frankl LLB
Mrs Joanna Gale LLB
Mrs P Garrett
Miss Marion Giordan BA
Mrs Helen Glover MA
Miss Patricia Gordon
Mrs Lilian Gorton LLB
Miss Kate Greenwood
Miss Margaret Gumuchian DA(Manc)
  ATD ATC FRSA
Miss Audrey Hammond BVetMed MRCVS
Miss Irene Harris
Mrs Harwood
Dr Joan Haythorne MRCS DOMS
Mrs AMD Henderson-Howat ARHist S
Mrs VH Howarth
Mrs Elizabeth Hyde BMAOT
Mrs Madeleine Jinkinson BA
Mrs Doris Jones
Miss Shirley Kaye
Mrs Mary Kendrick BA MWES
  Companion ICE
Mrs Christine Lethbridge BA
Miss Priscilla Lethbridge
Mrs Carol Macartney FAHE
Miss Elizabeth G M Macmillan BVMS
  MRCVS
Councillor Mrs T Mallinson JP
Mrs Jean M McCorry
Mrs Anthea Meldrum
Mrs Pauline Molnar MA
Miss Pat Montagu
Miss Patricia Morgan
Miss Barbara Morrison
Mrs Nicholas Mountain
Mrs Diana Napier Tauber
Miss Maud Neilson
Miss Sue Nichols
Mrs Laura M O'Donnell

Miss Rhylva Offer
Miss Constance-Anne Parker ATD
Mrs Peter Parsons
Hon Mrs D Pease
Dr EL Peet MBBS MD
Professor Mary Pickford DSc FRS
Mrs PG Rabjohn ARIBA
Mrs Ruth Reynolds
Mrs George Ritchie
Miss Kathleen M Robinson MD FRCS
    FRCOG
Mrs Beatrice Ross-Parkinson BA
Mrs Bertha Sack FPS
Miss OE Senior SRN SCM ONC RCNT
    HV AMBIM
Miss J Shales
Miss Elizabeth Sidney MA
Mrs EM Sims
Mrs I Skillen
Mrs Mary EH Smith MBE BA FIHA
Miss Margareta Stille ATD
Mrs Alexander Taft
Mrs UH Tayler MIPA
Miss Jane Taylor FIPA
Miss Honor Thackrah
Mrs Irene Thomas
Mrs Rena Thompson
Miss Hilda Wardroper DES RCA ATD
    MSIA BSc
Mrs Della Walters
Mrs Bernice T Weston
Miss Margaret EA Whitbread
Mrs Berenice S Whiteman
Mrs Marie R Wilbraham SRN SCM
    RMN RMPANS DIN

Press
Miss Jean Carr
Miss Shirley Davenport
Miss Carole Dawson
Miss Phillipa Kennedy
Miss Silvia Margolis
Miss Janice Morley
Miss Elizabeth Morris
Miss Ann Redmile
Miss Gillian Strickland
Miss Joan Thompson
Miss Francesca Turner
Miss Jane Walmsley
Miss Valerie Webster

Lancaster Room
Miss Heather Ablard
Dr Margaret T Adamson MB ChB DPH
    FRSH

Miss Margaret Aiken BA LLB
Mrs Margaret Alder
Miss Eugenie Alexander NDD ATD
Miss Margaret Alexander
Mrs Betty Allan
Mrs Helen Allan LDS RCS
Mrs J Allan Cash ARPS
Miss Paula Allardyce
Miss Sheila Allen
Mrs Margaret Amstell
Miss Pamela Anderson
Miss Silvia Anderson
Miss Marina Andrews
Miss W A Andrews
Lady Elizabeth Anson
Miss Val Arnison
Miss Diana Athill BA (Oxon)
Mrs Inette Austin-Smith RIBA AADipl
    FSIA
Mrs Charlotte Baden-Powell AADipl
    RIBA
Mrs Frances Bailey JP
Mrs GA Baker
Miss Loretta Balfour
Mrs Sue Bancroft
Mrs Iris Banham-Lee MIPR
Miss Dorian Banister
Mrs June Barford
Mrs Maggie Barge
Mrs Elaine Barnett
Mrs Joan Barrell
Mrs IM Barrett
Miss Anne Basser
Miss Dorothy Baugh
Miss Nancy Beaty
Mrs R Bell
Mrs Susan Benjamin
Miss Deborah Bennett
Miss Elizabeth Beresford
Mrs Constance Beynon FRCSEd FRCOG
Miss Marjorie Bidmead
Miss Suzie Biggs
Mrs Jean Blackden LRAM
Miss Lorna Blackie MA
Mrs F Bloom OBE
Mrs CE Blow
Mrs Adrien Blunt
Mrs D Bolingbroke-Kent
Miss Eve Bonham
Mrs Nansie Boston FSA SCOT
Miss E Bowen
Miss Betty Box OBE
Miss Patricia Boxall
Mrs RD Boyd MECI
Miss Katie Boyle

Mrs Anita Brackley-Shield
Mrs Julia Bradbury
Mrs Helen Bradley
Mrs Melody Bradley
Mrs Christine Brady
Mrs Margaret Bramall OBE MA AIMSW JP
Mrs Harriet Bridgeman MA
Miss Barbara Brindley
Lady Helen Brook
Miss ICS Brown
Mrs Sandra Brown
Miss Kathleen Browne
Mrs Maurice Bulpitt
Mrs Mollie Burgess FCA
Miss Mary Burr OBE MA FPS
Miss Gene Buxton MIPR
Mrs Ingela Byng BA
Mrs Kathleen Caddick NDD
Miss Patricia Callender BSc (Econ)
Mrs J Callis
Mrs Libby Calvert
Miss Joan Cambridge MSc
Mrs Myar Campbell Fraser
Miss Fanny Carby RAD
Mrs Marilyn Carr BArch ARIBA AMTPI
Brigadier Helen Cattanach RRC QHNS
Mrs Janet Chadwick BSc MBE
Miss Judith Chalmers
Mrs Mary Lumley Champion ARCA
Mrs Anne Channing
Mrs Yvonne Charpentier
Miss Joan Chaumeton
The Lady Chesham
Lady Chichester
Ms Lisa Childs LRAM
Mrs Mavis Chipperfield
Mrs Joan Chrismas JP
Mrs Elizabeth Christie LLB
Miss Jill Churchill
Mrs Julia Clements VMH
Mrs Jan Clutterbuck
Miss Joan Cole CBE
Professor Monica M Cole BSc PhD (Lond)
Mrs Peggy Cole
Mrs Patience Collier
Miss Jeanette Collins
Mrs Audrey Compton AADipl FRIBA
Miss Sylvia Compton-Miller
Mrs Joan Cook
Miss Cynthia Cooke CBE RRC QHNS
Miss Jean Cooke RA
Miss Doreen Cooper
Miss Joan D Cooper CB BA FR ANTHOP I

Mrs Wendy Cooper
Miss Judy Cornwell
Mrs Q Cotton
Miss Joan Court
Mrs R Cousens
Miss R Cowan
Miss Brenda Cowderoy MA MBIM
Miss F Cowell BSc (Lond) SRD
Mrs Felicity Hampden Cowley JP
Mrs Molly Cox
Mrs Mary Craig MA (Oxon)
Miss Anne Crewdson
Mrs Brenda Croft Ellis LSIA
Miss Eileen Crone
Mrs Gwenda Crone BA
Miss Anna Cropper
Miss Ethel Cruickshank MA BSc PhD
Mrs L Cumbers
Miss D M Cutcliffe SRN
Mrs E Dakeyne-Cannon
Mrs S Kenneth Davies
Mrs Alison Davis
Mrs Paquita Davis
Mrs Jill Denham-Davis
The Hon Lady de Zulueta
Miss Anne Dickinson
Miss Ivey Dickson FRAM
Miss Mary Dilnot
Miss Vivien Dinham
Mrs Honor Dobbs
Miss Edith M Dolphin
Mrs Elsie Donald
Miss Natalie Donay
Miss Kathleen Draycott
Miss Judith Drury MA ATC
Sister Ruth Duckworth
Dr Kathleen Duncan MB ChB
Miss Angela Dunne
Miss Jane Durham Dipl Arch (UCL) FRIBA FRAIA
Madame T Dutry
Miss Sally Dymott
Miss Barbara Edwards
Mrs SA Emerson
Mrs J Enever
Mrs Erica Eske RMS
Miss Christine Evans
Mrs E Evans
Mrs I Evans MPS PH C
Mrs Olive Evans MRCVS
Miss Lindsay Fairgrieve
Miss Hilda Fenemore
Miss Peggy Fenner
Miss Stella Fisher
Miss Marguerite Fletcher BSc BVMS

MRCVS
Miss Brenda Flower
Miss Joan Forbes
Mrs J Forbes Love
Miss Carole Ann Ford
Mrs RG Forsyth
Mrs Anthea Fortescue
Miss Lilian Foulkes AIB AMBIM
Miss Barbara Franc
Miss Juanita Frances
Miss Gladys Francis BEM
Miss Franka
Mrs Kathleen Franklin
Mrs Marilyn Freedman
Miss Cecilia Freeman
Miss IPM Freeston MA (Oxon)
Mrs Erika Frei
Miss Helen Galas LB BLitt
Mrs LG Galloway
Miss Eve Gardiner
Miss Gladys Garjulo GSM LRAM
Miss Ailsa Garland
Mrs Ruth Gaunt
Mrs H Gestetner OBE
Miss Roberta Gibbs
Miss Joy Gibson LRAM ALAMDA
Miss Dorothy Giles BSc
Mrs Muriel Gingell
Miss Shirley Giovetti
Miss Janet Girsman
Miss Renée Goddard
Mrs EM Goodwin
Miss Mary Gordon-Watson
Miss Anne Gorna-Davies LLB
Mrs Irene Grandison-Clark
Miss Patricia Grant-Wilson
Miss Dulcie Gray
Mrs RSB Gray
Miss Elizabeth Green M Inst M
Mrs Margaret Green
Miss Patricia Gregory
Miss Andree Grenfell
Miss Elizabeth Grey
Miss Freda Grove
Mrs D Guinness
Miss Elizabeth Gyngell BSc
Mrs I Blanche Halliday
Dr Margaret Hammond MB ChB
Mrs MA Hamp-Hamilton LRAM (Eloc)
Miss Doris Hare MBE
Mrs MLR Harkness BSc
Mrs Harrington
Mrs Jill Harris MBE
Miss Diane Hart
Miss Marea Hartman BSc (Econ) MBE

Miss Elizabeth Harvey MA (Oxon)
Miss MA Harwood
Miss Olwen Hedley FRSL
Miss Shirley Hedworth
Miss Marie Helvin
Miss CL Henley
Miss CH Henry MBE
Mrs GFW Heycock
Mrs Joan Hillaby
Mrs Phyllis Hindle NDD
Mrs Myrtle Hirsh BSc (Econ)
Miss Jennifer Hocking
Miss Moira Hoddell ARCA
Miss Anne Holmes Drewry
Mrs Vesey Holt JP
Miss Gloria Hooper
Miss Peggy Hooton
Miss Jan Hopcraft
Mrs MK Horsley
Mrs GA Howard CEng MIMechE
    AMBIM
Mrs Pamela Hudson
Lady Susan Hussey CVO
Mrs Mary Hutcheson FLA
Mrs Sheila Hutchison
Miss MB Hyde MSc MI Biol
Mrs Zoe Hyde-Thomson JP
Miss Joy Hyman NFFC (Froebel)
Mrs Douglas Jack
Miss Margaret M Jackson MP
Dr Mary Jackson MB ChB DLO DPA DIH
Miss Winefride Jackson
Miss Anne Jakeways
Alderman Miss Bertha James OBE MA JP
Miss Nancy Jarrett
Miss Pamela Jarvis
Miss Judy Jay
Miss Alison D Jennings
Miss Marie Jennings
Sister John SND BA MA (USA) PhD
Dr Margaret Gwyneth Jones MP PhD
Miss Joyce
Mrs E Kasket MA
Mrs Maureen Kelly Owen JP Dip Arch
    ARIBA
Miss Anne Kent
Mrs Allegra Kent-Taylor
Dame Marion Kettlewell DBE
Miss Margaret Kilkenny
Mrs Henny King RA
Mrs Betty Knightly
Miss Wyn Knowles
Miss Nancy Kuo Dip Art
Miss Maureen Laker
Mrs Margaret Lampard JP

Mrs Tina Lanfranchi
Miss Henrietta Langdale-Bussell
Miss Jean Lanning JP
Miss R Laredo MA
Miss Patricia Latham
Miss Rona Laurie BA FGSM LRAM
Miss Sue Lawley BA
Mrs Day Lawson
Miss Marjorie Lee
Miss Valerie A Leeper
Mrs Lynda Lee-Potter
Mrs Jean Le Fevre
Miss Moira Leggatt
Miss Suzanna Leigh
Miss Iris Lemare ARCM
Lady Lenanton
Mrs Joanna Lewis
Miss Mary Lewis MBE BA
Miss Thyrza A Leyshon
Miss Jackie Lindhurst
Miss Zaidee Lindsay
Mrs Audrey I Linzell MRCVS
Miss Moira Lister
Mrs Muriel Littlefield
Mrs Patricia Lloyd MPS
Mrs Dorothy Lockwood RWS RBSA
Mrs Norah Lofts
Miss Frederica Lord BA
Miss Margot Lovell MIPR
Miss Erna Low PhD MTAI
Miss Clarisse Loxton Peacock MA
Miss Rhona Lyle
Lady Lyons
Mrs May MacIntyre
Mrs Janet Macnaughton
Miss KD Maddever OBE NDD
Mrs Anne Maile FSDC
Mrs Elizabeth M Main JP MA (Cantab)
Miss Diana Makgill MVO
Miss Patricia Malley MBE
Miss Patricia Mann MCAM FIPA
Miss Elizabeth Manners TD MA FRSA
Miss Pamela Manson
Mrs Terry Marsland
Mrs Mary Martin
Miss Irene Massarella
Councillor Mrs Margaret M Mathias
Miss Wendy Matthews FAHE BSc
Miss Lindsay Maxwell BSc ACGI
Mrs Rachel McBryde
Mrs S McCombe
Miss Heather McConnell
Mrs Maeve C McCormack BDS
Miss Teresa McGonagle
Miss Stella McGrath MAIE

Mrs Mary D McHarg FICS
Mrs EMF McLean MB ChB DPH DOMS
Mrs Elizabeth McLeish
Miss M McLeod Black MA
Ms Bettina McNulty
Miss Brenda Mee
Ms Suzy Menkes BA (Cantab)
Mrs HM Menzies
Miss G Mary Messer
Mrs BM Mighell BVMS MRCVS
Dame Margaret Miles BA DCL DBE
Mrs Doreen Miller
Mrs Kathryn S Miller
Miss Rosemary Miller
Miss Janet Milne
Mrs Iris Minard JP ALCM
Miss Mary Mitchell FILA
Mrs Cecile Moon
Cllr Miss Gwynneth A Morgan
Mrs JT Morgan MBE JP
Miss Jill Morris DES RCA FRSA MSIA
Miss Jean Morton
Cllr Mrs PE Mosses MSc LGSM (Eloc)
Mrs Barbara M Moullin ACCA FTII
Miss Jean Muir RDI
Miss Gabriella Mustillo
Mrs Halima Nalecz FPS WIAC APA
Mrs Gillian Nester-Smith JP
Mrs Hazel M Neville
Mrs VAB Newcomb FIPA
Mrs CE Nichols
Mrs Muriel Nissel JP MA (Oxon)
Mrs Moya W Nixon
Brigadier Eileen J Nolan ADC
Dr Barbara Oliver FFA RCS
Miss Susie Orde
Miss Jean D Oswald LD
Mrs Aron Owen JP
Miss Norah Owen
Mrs Christina E Page
Mrs Jane Page
Mrs Fay Pannell
Mrs Juliet Pannett
Miss June Park ARIBA
Miss Lucretia M Parker
Ms Molly Parkin
Mrs Marguerite Patten
Miss Margaret A Pattle
Miss Muriel Pavlow
Miss Ruby Payne
Miss Louise A C Peachey
Mrs Leonard Pearl
Miss Valerie Pearlman
Lady Pender
Lady Penn

Miss Sandie Perrins BA
Dr Elizabeth Perrott BSc Dip Ed MSc PhD
 FIBiol
Mrs Margaret Peters
Mrs Mary Davis Peters MA (Oxon)
Mrs K Phillips
Mrs Lucienne Phillips
Mrs Norma Pinkerton LDS
Mrs Psyche Pirie
The Lady Pitt
Mrs Pamela C Podd BSc MRCVS
Mrs Mollie Porter
Miss Rosamund Powner BA
Mrs Anne Prattent
Miss Evadne Price
Miss AM Prime OBE
Dr Mia Kellmer Pringle CBE PhD DSc
Miss Alison Pritchard
Mrs Gloria Proops
Madame SB Prunier
Mrs Laurie Purden MBE
Miss Rita J Quail
Mrs Mark Quin
Miss Florence Quinlan
Lady Ralli
Miss Esther Rantzen
Miss Jill Raymond
Mrs John Read
Lady Anne Redmayne
Miss Eirlys M Rees SRN SCM
Miss Elizabeth Rees-Jones BA
Mrs Nancy Richards
Mrs Valerie Riches CSW
Miss Joyce C Riddiough
Mrs Eva M Rigg JP LRAM
Mrs Pida Ripley
Miss Angela Rippon
Miss Elizabeth I Ritchie
Miss MC Ritchie BSc
Miss Alma E Robbins FCIS
Mrs Jean Robertson MRCVS
Mrs Jean W Robertson BA
Mrs H Robinson
Miss Zsuzsi Roboz
Miss Caroline Roney
Miss Gillian Roscoe SRN CMB HN
Miss Muriel Rose RBA ROI
Mrs Valerie Rouse
Mrs RE Russell BA Commercial Art KU
Dr Josephine Rutter MBBS MRCPsych
 DPM
Miss Winifred Sainer
Mrs Denise Salem
Mrs Thelma Saul QBT
Mrs Joyce Saunders BSc

Mrs A Scott-Gard
Mrs Margaret Senley BA
Miss Candy Seymour-Smith
Mrs Serena Shaffer
Mrs Susan JM Shaw
Miss Elena Shayne-Barel
Mrs Belle Shenkman
Mrs David Sheppard
Mrs M Sigler
Miss Phyllis Sigsworth
Mrs JA Simons
Miss Lydia Simpson
Miss Auriol Sinclair
Dr Marie Singer MA (Cantab) PhD
 (Lond)
The Hon Mrs Suzanne Skyrme
Miss Audrey Slaughter
Mrs Dorothy O Smith
Miss Mary Smith LLB
Miss Maureen Smith
Mrs Sylvia L Sosnow
Miss Eileen B Sowerbutts BA
Mrs Audrey Sowrey
Miss Maude Spector
Mrs Ivor Spencer
Mrs P Spencer-Phillips
Mrs LB Sproat MA BEd
Miss Sally-Anne Stapleford
Miss Jean Stark
Mrs Ivy Starkie
Miss Arianna Stassinopoulos MA
 (Cantab)
Miss Jean Stead
Lady Stewart OBE JP
Miss Gloria Stewart BA (Russian)
Mrs Wendy Stewart-Robertson
Miss Helen Stone
The Hon Mrs Julia Stonor Saunders
Dr Miriam Stoppard MB BS MD MRCP
Miss Maude Storey SRN SCM RCI (Edin)
 RNT
Ms Heidi Stransky
Miss Patience Strong
Miss June A Stubbs MSIA
Mrs R Subba Row
Mrs Anne Summers DES RCS FRSA
Mrs Elaine Sunderland JP MA FIPM
Mrs KM Sykes
Miss Cleo Sylvestre
Miss Mary Talbot CB ADC BA
Miss Alannah Tandy
Ms Ann Taylor
Mrs GC Taylor
Mrs Mary Taylor
Lady Tewson JP

249

Miss Mary Thomas
Mrs Netta Thomas
Miss Rachael M Thomson-Ross JP SRN
Miss Wendy Thorogood
Mrs Kitty DV Thorp
Mrs Jacqueline Thwaites
Miss Kaye Tompkins
Mrs Margaret Toms
Ms Pamela Townshend
Miss Sheila Tracy
Mrs Nancy Tuft
Miss Frances Tulloch BA (Oxon) DipTh
  (London)
Dr Prudence Tunnadine MB BS
Mrs Audrey L Turner
Miss Kathleen Turner
Miss Sylvia I M Tutt
Miss Anne Tyrrell DES RCA
Miss Tamara Ustinov
Mrs Jane Venner-Pack LLB MIPR
Mrs Gerda Visconti
Miss Iris Wade MIPR
Mrs Anne Wall
Miss Elizabeth Wallace
Miss Nora Walley
Miss OH Ward
Mrs Merecia Watkins
Dr Barbara MQ Weaver PhD FRCVS
  DVA
Miss Mary Wedlake
Miss Molly Weir
Miss Trudy West
Mrs Huw Wheldon
The Hon Mrs White
Mrs Evelyn M Whiteside
Mrs Marjorie Wickham JP
Mrs Margaret Wigley
Mrs Katie M Wilde MHCIMA
Miss Catrin M Williams FRCS BSc MB
  BCh
Miss Gwyneth C Williams BSc DIC
  MIBiol
Miss May Williams
Mrs Sandra Williams BA MA
Miss Shirley Garnett Williams
Cllr Mrs Zena Williams
Mrs Josephine A Williamson MDChB
  FRCOG
Mrs Bella Wingate
Miss Margaret M Wittich
The Lady Wolfenden
Mrs FI Wolsey-Neech FLA FRSA
Miss Cynthia Wood AADip ARIBA
  AMRTPI FFB AIARB
Miss I Wood

Mrs Muriel Wood
Miss Rae Woodland

Monday 20th October 1980
THEME: 25 YEARS BACK – 25 YEARS ON

Dr Aileen Adams MA MB ChB FF ARCS
Dr Margaret I Adamson MB CHB DPH
  FRSH
Mrs Joan Agar
Miss Margaret KM Aiken OBE BA LLB
Miss MJ Aitkin NDDF FSA (Scot)
Miss Eugenie Alexander NDD ATD
Mrs Isobel Allan
Miss Monica C Allanach FIA
Mrs Margeret Amstell
Sister Mary Andrew SRN SCM
Mrs I Archer
Miss Val Arnison
Mrs Anne C Arnold-Silk FADO
Miss Ruth M Ashton SRN SMC MTD
Mrs Charlotte Baden-Powell AADip
  RIBA
Mrs Frances Bailey JP
Miss Margery Baker
Mrs Mary Baker MA
Miss Loretta Balfour
Ms Nancy Balfour MA OBE
Lady Banks
Mrs Maggie Barge
Ms Denise Barnes
Miss Mary Barnes
Mrs Joan Barrell
Mrs Irene M Barrett
Mrs Doreen Bateman MRCVS
Mrs Patricia Batty Shaw
Miss Dorothy Baugh
Miss Beatrice J Beale BSc (Eng)
Miss Nancy Wolcott Beaty
Ms Olive Belchamber ARIBA
Miss Edith Graeme Bell
Miss Judith H de M Bell
Mrs RF Bell
Miss Pennie Bellas BA
Mrs Doreen Bellerby JP
Dr Mary Belton MB BCh DPH
Mrs Susan Benjamin
Miss Mary Berry
Mrs Pamela Bevan Funnell
Mrs Constance L Beynon FRCSEd
  FRCOG
Miss Elizabeth O Black MChS
Mrs Freddy Bloom OBE
Ms Patsy Bloom

Mrs Adrien Blunt
Mrs Nansie M Boston FSA (Scots)
Miss Anne Boutwood MBBS
Miss Jane Bown
Mrs Celia Bowring
Miss Betty E Box OBE
Mrs KD Boyd MIEC
Mrs Gwendoline M Boyle
Mrs M Bremner
Ms Edith Le Breton FIAL
Mrs Harriet Bridgeman MA
Miss Geraldine D N Bridgewater
Miss PJ Brigstocke
Miss Betty Brittain
Mrs Sally Broad
Lady Brook
Miss Faith Brown
Miss Agnes Browne SRN SCM
Ms Tanya Bruce-Lockhart
Miss Betty I Burkitt Dip Theology
Mrs Christabel Burniston MBE LRAM
    ALAM FRSA GODA FESB
Mrs Mary A Burr OBE MA FPS
Mrs Christina Burton
Mrs Esme P Busby MALTDS
Mrs Joyce Butler
Ms E Byrne
Mrs Elizabeth Cadwallader JP
Ms Joan Cambridge
Mrs Gloria Cameron MBE JP
Miss Winnie Cameron
Mrs Shirley Cameron Becke OBE OStJ
Professor Eila MJ Campbell MP
The Hon Mrs John Campbell
Dr Suzanne Campbell-Jones BA MPhil
    PhD
Mrs Rae Campbell-Tanner BSc
Miss Jennifer M Capon Dipl Arch ARIBA
Miss Fanny Carby
Mrs David Carr
Mrs Janet Chadwick BSc
Miss Judith Chalmers
Miss Sandra Chalmers BA
Mrs Mary Lumley Champion ARCA
Mrs W Channing
Mrs Margaret Charrington
Mrs Erika Cheetham MA
Lady Chichester
Mrs AG Christopherson ARIBA
Miss Jill Churchill
Miss Felicity Clark
Ms Anne Claxton Dip WCF
Ms Lucie Clayton
Miss C P Clyne
Mrs Rosalie Cody

Mrs Loretta Cohen
Her Honour Judge Myrella Cohen QC
Ms Patience Collier
Miss Jeanette Collins
Mrs Audrey Compton RIBA AADip
Mrs Dorothy Cook MPS
Mrs Ida Cooke DFA
Miss Doreen Cooper
Miss Robyn Cooper
Mrs Norma Corney
Ms Judy Cornwell
Miss Heather S Coupe
Mrs Ruth M Cousens FSAI
Miss FM Cowell BSc SRD FHCIMA
Mrs Sandra Coxe Madden
Mrs Mary Craig MA (Oxon)
Mrs MC Craig BSc (Econ)
Ms Anna Cropper
Mrs Elspeth Cross BArch
Dr Ethel M Cruickshank MA BSc PhD
Mrs Edith Dakeyne-Cannon
Miss Sylvia Darley
Mrs Brenda Darling BA RIBA
Rev Jean Darnall
Mrs Margaret Davidson Hearn MBE FIH
Dr Louise Davies BSc PHK FAHE
Mrs Myriel Davies MBE
Mrs Alison Davis
Mrs Paddy Davis SRN RFN
Ms Nicole Davoud
Ms Sue Dawson
Dr José Day MBBS MRCEP
Mrs Elaine J Dean
Mrs Dermot De Trafford
Mrs Tarn Dearden
Dr Susan Dev
Dr Josephina De Vasconcellos DLitt FRBS
Mrs Elizabeth de Winter FAMU
Miss Anne Dickinson
Miss Mary Dilnot
Dr Margaret Dix MD FRCS
Miss Mary P Docherty
Mrs J D'Olier BA
Miss Natalie Donay BA
Ms Christine Doyle BSc
Miss Kathleen Draycott
Mrs Hazel Duffy
Dr Kathleen Duncan MB ChB
Mrs Dorothy Dunnett
Lt Col Irene Durmam
Miss Eugenia C Dyess
Miss Sally Dymott SRN OHNC ONC
The Hon Mrs Honor Earl
Mrs Phyliss Earl BA
Ms Elizabeth Ellett

Miss Jasmin Elliot
Miss Susan Elliot
Miss Carol Ellis LLB QC
Miss Polly Elwes
Mrs Erica Eske RMS
Mrs Helen Ettles BEM
Ms M Evans MPS PhC
Mrs OW Evans MRCVS
Ms Susan Jane Exley
Madame Robbert Fack
Mrs Sheila Faith JP LDS MP
Miss Susan Farmer
Miss Hilda Fenemore
Mrs N Fenn
Mrs Peggy Fenner
Miss Gillian E Fisher BA
Miss Marguerite Fletcher BSc BVSMS
    MRCVS
Mrs Flower
Miss Janet Fookes BA MP
Mrs Annabelle Forrest
Mrs RW Forrester
Ms Lois Franklin
Ms Gilly Fraser
Ms Joan Freeman BSc Dip Ed Guid MEd
Ms Ylva French
Mrs AM Frisby BA (Durham) DPA
    (Oxon)
Ms Audrey Gale
Mrs Joanna Gale LLB
Ms Helen Gales LLB BLitt
Miss G Ganderton-Forsyth
Miss Eve Gardner
Mrs Trixie Gardner
Mrs Hilda Garfield
Miss Ailsa Garland
Mrs Ruth Gaunt
Miss D Rosslyn Gibbs
Miss Roberta Gibbs
Ms Marcia Gibson-Watt BA
Mrs BA Gilroy MA Dyp Psy ACP
Mrs Muriel C Gingell
Dr GMA Gledhill PhD
Dr Jane Glover MA DPhil (Oxon)
Miss Renée Goddard
Ms Jessica Goldsmith MB CBH FRCS
    FRACS
Miss Maggie Goodman
Lady Alastair Gordon
Miss Mary Gordon-Watson MBE
Mrs Mirette Gore JP
Miss Christina Gorna LLB
Mrs Joyce Gould
Miss GM Grant
Miss Dulcie Gray

Miss Elizabeth Green MInstM
Miss Patricia Gregory
Mrs RSB Grey
Miss Elizabeth J Grundy ARIBA
Mrs D Guinness
Miss Janet Gulland MA MRAES
Miss Elizabeth Gyngell BSc
Miss JM Hadley
Lady Raina Haig
Miss Griselda Hamilton-Baillie
Mrs Daphne Hamilton-Fairley LLS T
Mrs MA Hamp-Hamilton SSStJ LRAM
    (Eloc)
First Officer R N Hancock
Mrs HH Handyside OBE
Miss Kay Harding BA
Mrs MLR Harkness BSc (Chem)
WPC Mrs Monica Harris
Miss Diane Hart
Miss Rosemary Hart BA (London)
Miss Marea Hartman CBE
Miss Elizabeth Harvey MA (Oxon)
Mrs Muriel Hayler Wood
Ms Suzanne DL Hayman BA
Dr Joan Haythorne MRCS DOMS
Miss Anne Haywood
Miss Joan B Headlen
Mrs Margaret Davidson Hearn
Miss Edith Hedger
Mrs Diana Henderson
Mrs Rachael Heyhoe Flint
Miss Elizabeth Hill
Mrs June F Hinchliffe Dip Arch (Leeds)
    RIBA
Mrs Phyllis Hindle NND
Miss Hermione Hobhouse ModHist
    (Oxon)
Miss Jennifer Hocking
Miss Angela Holder MA (Cantab)
Miss Thelma Holt
Miss Victoria Holt
Ms Jan Hopcraft
The Rt Hon Baroness Hornsby-Smith
Mrs MK Horsley
Ms Barbara Hosking
Miss Elizabeth Jane Howard
Mrs Judith Hudson
Mrs Mary Hutcheson FLA
Miss Angela Huth FRSL
Mrs Janet Jack AADipl RIBA ALI
Ms Winefride M Jackson
Miss Betty Jakens FAHE
Dr Marjorie L James MB BOh BSc
Miss Pamela Jarvis Dip AD MSIAD
Mrs Mary Jay

Miss Sheelagh Jefferies MA (Cantab) MA
    (Smith USA)
Mrs Daphne E Jordan
Mrs Nicky Joyce
Mrs Esther Kasket MA (Cantab) ASIA
Mrs Katz
Miss Barbara Kelly
Miss Penelope H Kemp
Mrs Mary P Kendrick BA MWES Comp
    ICE
Miss Tessa Kennedy
Miss Elizabeth Kerr BSc
Miss Margeret Kilkenny FCA
Mrs FL King Lewis
Mrs D Kingston
Miss Simone A Klass MIPR
Mrs Jill Knight MP
Mrs Betty Knightly
Miss Wyn Knowles
Mrs Koppel
Ms Hilary Laidlaw Thomson
Miss Phylis Lake MAMS
Ms Katie Lander
Miss Jean Lanning JP
Miss Patricia Latham FJI
Mrs Harold Leake
Mrs Sheila Leaning
Mrs Lynda Lee-Potter
Miss Moira Leggat
Miss Lyn Leigh
Ms Mary D Leigh
Miss Iris Lemare ARCM
Ms Ann Leslie BA (Oxon)
Mrs Charlotte Lessing
Ms Harriette Lewis
Miss Thyrza A Leyshon ASFA
Miss Yvonne Littlewood
Ms Kate Littner
Mrs Patricia Lloyd MPS
Miss MJ Long MArch
Dr Lavina Loughridge MB FRCP
Dr Erna Low PhD
Miss Clarisse Loxton-Peacock MA
Mrs Josephine Lundberg
Mrs Barbara Lynch
Lady Lyons
Miss Anthea Lyons AFPhys
Councillor Mrs May Macintyre
Miss Maureen MacLaine
Mrs Kenneth Macmillan
The Hon Diana Makgill MRVO
Miss Dorothea M P Malley MBE
Miss Anne Mansel
The Countess of Mar and Kellie JP
Miss MF Markes BSc FRGS

Sister Mary Perpetua FC
Miss Monica Mason
Mrs IEA Matthews
Mrs Celia Maxwell BCS Dipl Arch
Mrs S McAlpine
Ms Nancy B McConkey
Mrs Maeve C McCormack BDS
Miss Norah McEllistrim
Miss T McGonagle
Mrs Stella McGrath FAIE IPR
Professor Naomi McIntosh BA
Miss Julia McKenzie
Mrs EMF McLean MB ChB DPH DOMS
Mrs Betty McLeish
Mrs Ann McMullan
Mrs Rosemary McWhirter
Ms Jill McWilliam
Lady Medawar MA BSc
Miss Leonie Mellinger
Ms Suzy Menkes MA (Cantab)
Mrs Eleanor Michell AADip RIBA
Ms BM Mighell BVMS MRCVS
Dame Margaret Miles DBE
Ms Doreen Miller JP
Mrs Kathryn S Miller
Miss Janet Milne
Mrs Iris Minard JP
Mrs Inge Mitchell
Ms Mary Mitchell FLI FFB
Miss Marjorie E Monks OBE
Miss D Monreal MVO MBE
Ms Bel Mooney BA
Miss Stella Moore
Miss Ingrid Morris AADip RIBA
Miss Jill Morris DES RCA FRSA FSIAD
Miss Judith A Morris BSc MSc FBCO
Miss Jean Morton
Mrs M Moutain
Mrs Halima Nalecz FPS NS APA HAC
Mrs Felicity Nellen
Dr Elizabeth Nelson BA PhD
Mrs L T O'Brien
Miss Kay O'Dwyer
Mrs Jane Olivier
Miss M Roseanne O'Reilly MBE
Mrs Elizabeth Ormiston JP
Miss Jean Orr BA
Mrs Eoleen O'Sullivan
Miss Jennifer A Over
Captain Elizabeth Overbury
Mrs MA Overton
Mrs Norah Owen FIPR
Mrs J Page
Ms June Park RIBA AADip
Mrs Betty Parsons

Mrs L Pearl SStJ
Dr EL Peet MD
Ms Mary Perigoe
Professor Elizabeth Perrott BSc MSc PhD
  FInsBiol
Mrs David Pettifer
Mrs Lucienne Phillips
Miss Marita Phillips
Mrs ST Phoenix MBE
Dr Mary Pickford DSc FRCPE FRSE FRS
Mrs Norma Pinkerton LDS (Dunelm)
Mrs JS Pitman
Mrs Louise Pleydell-Bouverie
Mrs Pamela C Podd BSc MRCVS
Ms Diana Potter
Mrs M Powell
Mrs Sheila M Pragnell SRN CMB
Mrs Elizabeth A Prattent
Dr Mia Pringle BA PhD DSc CBE
Mrs Valerie Profumo
Miss Laurie Purden MBE
Miss Rita Quail
Miss MJ Quinault
Lady Ralli
Mrs Susan Raven BA
Miss Jill Raymond
Miss Santa Raymond Dip Arch RIBA
Lady Rayner
Ms Claire Rayner SRN
Mrs Eric Rayner
Mrs EV Rayner BSc
Lady Read
Mrs Eva Redfern
Miss Jane Reed
Miss Angharad Rees
Professor Lesley Rees MSc MD MRCPath
  FRCP
Ms Elizabeth Rees-Jones BA
Mrs Diana Reid JP
Dr Margaret Reinhold MD FRCP
Air Commodore H F Renton ADC MA
Miss Leila Restan MChS SRCH
Miss Elspeth Rhys-Williams
Mrs Nancy Richards
Mrs Joan Richardson FInstTM
Miss Stella Richman
Miss Joyce C Riddiough
Mrs Eva M Rigg JP LRAM
Miss Elizabeth I Ritchie
Mrs G Ritchie
Miss Jean H Ritchie LLM LLB AKC
Miss Lorna Ritchie LDS RFPSG
Miss J Robertson ARRC
Ms Zsuzsi Roboz
Miss Adel Rootstein

Ms Annie Ross
Mrs Janet W Ross
Miss Ann Rossiter MA
Ms Bridget Rowe
Dr Salmons MB ChB DCH MRCPsych
Mrs Josephine Sandilands
Miss Carol Sarler
Mrs Joyce Saunders OBE BSc MInstE
  AFIMA
Ms Barbara Saxon
Miss Annabel Schild
Mrs Daphne Schild
Mrs Mary Service
Miss Faith M Seward BA
Mrs Margaret Seward MDS FDS
Dr Jean Shanks BA BM BCh
Mrs Jean Shapiro
Mrs Susan J M Shaw
Mrs Shirley Shelton
Miss Carlo Sheppard
Miss D Sheppard
Mrs AIM Shield
Miss DA Shipsey SRN SCM
Mrs Elizabeth Sigmund
Miss Phyllis Sigsworth QPM
Ms Janet Silver MPhil FBC'O MBIM
Miss Elizabeth Simons
Dr Marie Singer MA (Cantab) PhD (Lon)
Ms Valerie Singleton
Ms Petra Von Siniawski RAD ISTD
Miss Jane Sketchley BSc
Miss Kathleen D Skillern QPM
The Hon Mrs Suzanne Skyrme
Miss Yasmine Smart
Mrs Dorothy O Smith RSA
Dr Joan Smith MA LLB HhD
Ms Valerie Smith
Mrs Sallie Snowman
Miss Anna M Soubry LLB
Mrs Audrey Sowrey
Mrs Peggy Spencer MBE FISTD
Mrs Lydia B Sproat MA BED
Ms Meryl Stannard
Miss Arianna Stassinopoulos MA
  (Cantab)
Mrs Denise St Aubyn Hubbard
Lady Stewart OBE JP
Mrs Floi Stewart-Murray
Mrs Wendy Stewart-Robertson
Ms Greville Stewart-Stevens
Miss Helen Stone DipSoc
Miss Janet Stone FBOA HD FSMC DCLP
Mrs Valerie P M Strachan BA
Miss June A Stubbs MSIAD
Ms Mollie Sugden

Ms Anne Summers DES RCA FRSA
Dr Mary Sutherland MRCS LRCP JP
Dr Rosa Sutton Rivlin MRCS LRCP CPH
Mrs JC Swallow BSc
Dr Marjorie Sweeting MA PhD (Cantab)
Mrs Barbara Taylor
Miss Doris Tempest MA (Cantab)
Mrs HM Temple-Richards
Ms Honor Thackrah
Mrs Irene Thomas
Mrs Netta Thomas MBE
Mrs Margaret Tierney
Miss Tryphena Todd
Ms Vivienne Tomei
Mrs Margaret Toms
Miss Sheila Tracy
Miss Joyce Trotman BA MLitt
Miss Frances Tulloch MA Bio (Oxon) Dip
    Th (Lon)
Ms Sue Turner BA
Miss Sylvia IM Tutt
Miss Lucia Van Der Post BA (Eng & Pol
    Phil)
Mrs Betty Van Gelder
Miss Jessica Van Hall
Mrs Jean Venables MSC BSc (Eng) MICE
    ACGI
Mrs David Verey
Baroness Vickers DBE MBE
Miss Eliane Vogel BA MA
Ms Petra Von Siniawski
Miss Hazel Vincent Wallace OBE
Miss Elizabeth Waller MA BLitt
Ms Nora Walley
Ms Jane Walmsley BA MA
Miss Marcia Warburton
Mrs Elizabeth Ward MBE
Miss MF Ward
Ms Shirley Ward
Miss Hilda Wardroper DES RCA MSIA
    BSc
Mrs S Wayne
Dr BMQ Weaver PhD FRCVS DVA
Miss Molly Weir
Ms Rosemary Whiffen AIMSW
Mrs LF Whitaker FADO
The Hon Mrs White
Mrs Maureen White LLB
Mrs ECJ Whitmarsh
Mrs Lilian Wick LRAM LGSM
Ms Claire Wickham
Mrs Marjorie Wickham JP
Miss Gillian Widdicombe
Mrs Betty Wight SRN FPA
Mrs Olive M Wightman

Mrs Katherine Wilde MHICMA
Lady Elizabeth Williams JP
Colonel Violet Williams
Councillor Mrs Zena Williams
Miss EF Willis FGA
Ms Helen Wilson
Miss Vivian Wilson
Mrs Margaret Wingfield CBE
Lady Wonter
Mrs Elizabeth Wood ARMS SWA
Mrs Marguerite Wood JP MCSP
Miss Rae Woodland
Mrs Muriel G Woods
Miss Rosalind Woolfson
Mrs Anna Wyner
Councillor Pennie Yaffé Dip Ed
Councillor Mrs Joan Yates
Miss Penny Yates
Mrs Deirdre Yeats-Brown

Monday 25th October 1982
THEME: LIFE BEGINS AT...

Dr Margaret I Adamson MB ChB DPH
    FRSH
Ms Kate Adie
Mrs Bandana Ahmad BA
Sister Ahrou
Miss Margaret KM Aiken BA LLB OBE
Miss MJ Aitken NDD FSA
Miss Eugenie Alexander NDD ATD
Mrs Josephine Della Alvarez
Miss Margaret Amstell
Cllr Pamela Anderson
Miss Marina Andrews
Lady Anson LLB
Mrs Leana Arain
Miss Val Arnison
Mrs Anne Ashby SRN SCM
Miss Ruth M Ashton SRN SCM MTD
Mrs Jane Atkinson
Mrs Charlotte Baden-Powell AA Dip
    RIBA
Mrs Mary Baker
Mrs Anne Ballard MA
Ms Maggee Barge
Mrs JS Barrell
Mrs Gay Barrett
Mrs Shirley Comerson Becke OBE OStJ
    QPM
Miss Lillian Beckwith
Miss Judith H de M Bell
Mrs Mary Belsham
Sqn Ldr Diana Bentley

Ms Mary Berry
Mrs Wendy J Bevan
Mrs Bevan Funnell
Mrs Constance Lang Beynon JP FRCS Ed
  FRCOG
Dr Ann Birchall BA PhD FSA
Miss Elizabeth O Black
Miss Lorna Blackie MA
Mrs Freddy Bloom OBE
Mrs Constance Blow
Mrs Adrien Blunt
Mrs B Bobath MBE FCSP APTA
Mrs Margaret Bowden
Ms Betty Box OBE
Mrs Judith Mary Boyd MEIC
Mrs GM Boyle FInstD
Ms S H Brickett
Mrs Harriet Bridgeman MA
Mrs Heather Brigstocke MA
Miss Joyce Brigstocke
Lady Brook
Ms Faith Brown
Miss Iona Brown
Mrs Sandra Brown
Miss Tanya Bruce-Lockhart
Miss Christine Bruell
Ms Helen Brunner ARCM
Mrs Joy Bryer BA
Mrs J Bunge
Miss Betty I Burkitt Dip Th
Ms Christabel Burniston MBE LRAM
  FRSA FESB
Ms M A Burr OBE MA FPS
Miss Suzy Burston
Joyce Butler
Ms Joan Cambridge
Professor EMJ Campbell MA
Paddy Campbell
Mrs Rae Campbell-Turner
Miss Fanny Carby
Mrs Margaret Chadd JP AIMSW
Mrs Janet Chadwick BSc MBE
Dr Penny A Chaloner BA MA PhD
Mrs William E Channing
Mrs Margaret Charrington
Mrs Wen-Ying Hsiung Chen
Ms Audrey Chessell AInst TT
Lady Chichester-Clark
Mrs Lisa Childs
Miss Joan Chrismas BA
Mrs Jean Christopherson ARIBA
Miss Jill Churchill
Miss Felicity Clark
Ms Anne Claxton
Ms Julia Cleverdon

Miss Cecilia Clyne
Mrs Rosalie Cody
Mrs Loretta Cohen
Mrs Pauline Cohen BA
Prof Monica Cole BSc PhD
Mrs Stephanie Coles
Mrs Patience Collier
Miss Collins RRC QHNS
Ms Marilyn Collyer BA Dip Soc Admin
Mrs Audrey Compton FRIBA AA Dip
Miss Doreen Cooper
Mrs Winefride Coulson OBE
Miss Heather Coupe
Mrs Ruth M Cousens FSAI
Miss Freda Marion Cowell BSc SRD
Mrs Mary Craig MA
Miss Christodoulou LLB
Miss Anna Cropper
Miss Susan Crowson
Mrs Jennifer d'Abo
Miss Judith Dagworthy
Mrs Ellen Dahrendorf BA MSc
Mrs Edith Dakeyne-Cannon
Mrs Carol Dalrymple
Miss Sylvia Darley
Mrs BP Darling BA RIBA
Dr AR David BA PhD
Mrs S Davidson
Ms Alison Davies
Dr Louise Davies BSc PhD
Mrs Myriel Davies MBE
Mrs Paddy Davies SRN RFN
Mrs Nicole Davoud
Mrs Tarn Dearden
Mrs Caroline de Courcy Ireland
Sister Marie De Lourdes-McLoughlin
  SRN SCM
Mrs Jean Denton BSc (Econ) FInst
Prof Susan Dev MSc FCCA AITI
Mrs Elizabeth de Winter FAMU
Miss Anne Dickinson
Dr MR Dix MD FRCS
Mrs Joan d'Olier BA
Mrs Greta R Drinkwater MBE
Dr Madelaine Duke MB ChB
Mrs Sheila Dunmore
Miss Sarah Dunn MA
Mrs Dorothy Dunnett
Mrs Raymonde Dunster
Mrs Catherine Dupre
Miss Elena Duran
Lieut Col Irene Durman
Miss Lois Dyer MCSP
Miss Sally Dymott SRN OHNC ONC
Mrs Phyllis Earl BA

Mrs Anthea Moore Ede
Dr Marta Elian MD
Ms Elizabeth Elleit
Miss Susan Elliot
Mrs Ruth Elliott MA
Miss Polly Elwes
Mrs Elizabeth Emanuel MA DES RCA
Miss MR Emslie LCST MCST Dip IPA
Mrs Helen Ettles BEM
Mrs Marguerite Evans MPS PhC
Mrs Olive Evans MRCVS
Mrs Susan Exley
Mrs Audrey Eyton
Mrs Sheila Faith JP LDS
Miss Susan Farmer
Ms Jean Farrall
Ms Carolyn Faulder BA Phil
Miss Hilda Fenemore
Mrs Peggy Fenner MP
Ms Ann Field
Lady Fisher
Ms Gillian E Fisher BA
Miss Marguerite Fletcher BSc BVMS
   MRCVS
Mrs Vivienne Flower
Miss Janet Fookes BA
Mrs RW Forrester
Mrs Helen Fovargue BSc
Ms Decima Francis
Lady Sheila Francis-Chichester
Dr Winifred Francis MD FRCAS
Mrs KV Franklin
Ms Helen Franks
Dr Joan Freeman PhD MEd BSc
Mrs Erika Frei
Miss Anne Frost
Ms Helen Galas LLB BLitt
Miss Jocelyn Galsworthy
Miss Eve Gardiner
Mrs Hilda Garfield
Miss Ailsa Garland
Miss Pat Garratt MA
Ms Catherine Gaskin
Mrs Ruth Gaunt
Mrs Dorothy Genn FInstIC
Miss Roberta Gibbs
Mrs Marcia Gibson-Watt BA
Dr Alison FZ Giles MD
Mrs Muriel Gingell
Dr GMA Gledhill PhD LLB
Mrs Helen Glover MA
Mrs Renée Goddard
Mrs Muriel Elva Gollan
Miss Mary Gordon-Watson MBE
Miss A Christina Gorna LLB

Mrs Donald Graham
Miss Elizabeth Green MInstM
Miss Felicity Green
Mrs Maggie Green
Miss Jenny Greene MA
Miss Patricia Gregory
Miss Janet Gulland MA
Mrs E Gullick BA MA (Oxon)
Ms Betty Margaret Guyatt
Ms Lucille Hall
Mrs Muriel Hamilton
Miss Griselda Hamilton-Baillie
Mrs D Hamilton-Fairley LCST MCST
Mrs MA Hamp-Hamilton SSSt LRAM
   (Eloc) FSA Scot
Miss Margaret Hampshire MA
Miss L Ann Hansen
Miss Doris Hare MBE
Mrs Susan Harley MA
Mrs Anne Harris
Miss Mollie Harris ACIS
Ms Venessa Harrison
Miss Rosemary Hart
Mrs Beryl Hartland
Miss Marea Hartman CBE
Miss Elizabeth Harvey MA (Oxon)
Ms Carol Haslam
Mrs Tamara Hassani
Mrs Muriel Hayler Wood
Dr Joan Haythorne MRCS DOMS
Miss Joan B Headlen
Mrs Margaret Davidson Hearn MBE FIH
Miss Edith Hedger
Mrs Diana Henderson
Ms Angela Heylin
Miss Betty Hicks MA BA
Mrs EVR Hillier
Mrs Phyllis Hindle NDD
Miss Jennifer Hocking
Ms Alison Hogan BA MPhil (Oxon)
Mrs Wendy M Hogg BSc BEd
Mrs LJ Holdaway
Mrs Sheila Holland
Lady Holland-Martin OBE
Miss Thelma Holt MA
Miss Victoria Holt
Miss Angela Hooper
Ms Hopcroft
Miss Jill M Hopkins
Miss Pamela Horner MCAM
Miss Hannah Horovitz
Mrs MK Horsley
Ms Barbara Hosking
Miss Verity Hudson
Dr Fay Hutchinson MB BS

Mrs Cynthia I Iliffe BA MA
Ms Pippa Isbell
Mrs Amy Isherwood FBCO
Ms Janet Jack AA Dip RIBA ALI
Mrs Lindsay Jacobs
Miss Betty Jakens FIHEc
Dr ML James
Miss Pamela Mary Jarvis SIAD
Mrs Mary Jay
Mrs Muriel Johnston
Ms Joyce Jones
Ms Penny Jones MDes RCA
Miss Sarah Jones BA
Mrs Daphne Jordon
Mrs Nicky Joyce
Mrs Leslie Kark
Mrs E Kasket BA MA
Mrs Jennifer Katz
Mrs Wendy Keith
Miss Penny Kemp
Mrs Mary Kendrick BA MWES
Miss Mary Kenny
Mrs Lionel King-Lewis
Mrs JA Kirkpatrick BEd
Miss Simone Klass
Mrs Betty Knightly
Miss Wyn Knowles
Mrs Nita Koppel
Ms Dorothy Kuya
Ms Jacqui Lait
Miss Phylis Lake MAMS
Ms Verity Lambert
Miss Patricia Lamburn
Miss Jean Lanning JP
Miss Patricia Latham FJI
Miss Diana Law MBE
Mrs Lawrence
Mrs Harold Leake
Mrs Jane Leaver
Ms Edith Le Breton
Mrs Noa Lee-Potter
Miss Moira Leggat
Miss Faith Legh FInstD MInstSP MInstM
Miss Lyn Leigh
Councillor Mary Leigh
Miss Iris Lemare ARCM
Mrs Charlotte Lessing
Mrs Harriette Lewis
Mrs WE Lindsay
Ms Adella Lithman
Miss Yvonne M P Littlewood
Ms Kate Littner
Mrs Amber Lloyd
Mrs Patricia Lloyd MPS
Marie Lloyd-Evans

Dr J Lomas-Simpson MRC Psych MB
    CHB DPM
Miss Frederica Lord BA
Mrs Jennifer Loss
Miss Felicity Lott BA ARAM
Dr Erna Low PhD
Miss Clarisse Loxton-Peacock
Ms Eve Lucas
Mrs Mary Lumley Champion ARCA
Mrs Josephine Lundberg
Lady Lyons
Cllr May MacIntyre
The Hon Diana Makgill MVO
Ms S Malin
Miss DMP Malley MBE
Sister Mary Perpetua
Miss Marguerite Markes BSc
The Countess of Mar and Kellie JP
Mrs Sara Mason-Pearson
Mrs Irene Elizabeth Matthews
Ms Nancy McConkey
Mrs Maeve C McCormack BDS
Miss Ada McDonald
Mrs Kay McDonald
Miss Norah McEllistrim
Mrs Stella McGrath Wardell FAIE MIPR
Mrs FJ McIvor LLB BL
Miss Julia McKenzie
Mrs Betty McLeish
Mrs Teresa McManus
Mrs Ann McMullan
Mrs Rosemary McWhirter
Miss Jill McWilliam
Dr Jeanette Meadway MB ChB MRCP
    (UK)
Lady Medawar MA BSc
Mrs BM Mighell BVM & S MRCVS
Mrs Doreen Miller JP
Mrs Kathryn S Miller
Miss Janet Milne
Mrs Iris Minard JP ALCM
Miss Frances Minogue
Miss Mary Mitchell FLI FFB
Mrs Pauline Molnar MA
Miss Dolores Monreal MVO MBE
Miss Marion Montgomery
Ms Bel Mooney BA
Miss Stella Moore
Miss Lucy E Morgan
Miss Ingrid Morris AA Dip RIBA
Miss Jill Morris DES RCA FRSA FSIAD
Miss Judith A Morris BSc MSc FBCO
Miss Jean Morton
Begum Sara Seyid Muhammad
Miss Jean Muir Hon DR RCA RDI

Mrs Lillian Muller
Miss Mary Murphy MBE SSStJA
Mrs Halima Nalecz FFPS AP
Mrs VT Nathanson
Miss Sheila J Needham
Mrs Felicity Nellen
Dr Elizabeth H Nelson BA PhD
Miss Caroline Neville
Ms Susan Hilary Nixon BA Econ
Miss Kay O'Dwyer
Mrs Eileen O'Sullivan
Miss Jennifer Ann Over
Captain Elizabeth Overbury
Mrs Page
Ms June Park AA Dip RIBA
Miss Constance-Anne Parker ATD ARBS
Mrs Vivienne Mary Hunt Parry BSc
Mrs Audrey Parsons
Miss Judith Patten
Miss Claudia Payne
Mrs Rivka Pearl
Mrs Sue Pearson
Miss Mary Perigoe
Professor Elizabeth Perrott MSc PhD
　FRSA FIBiol
Ms Ann Pettitt BA
Mrs Lucienne Phillips
Dr Mary Pickford DSc FRCPE
Mrs Norma Pinkerton LDS
Mrs Pamela Cole Podd BSc MRCVS
Councillor Mrs Shirley Porter JP
Mrs Elizabeth Anne Prattent
Miss Anne Sheila Price
Dr Mia Pringle BA PhD DSc CBE
Ms Gloria Ann Proops
Miss Laurie Purden MBE
Miss Rita June Quail
Miss MJ Quinault
Miss Wendy Ramshaw
Mrs Susan Raven
Miss Jill Raymond Dip Lon Drama
Miss Santa Raymond RIBA
Lady Read
Mrs Eva Redfern
Miss Jane Reed
Mrs Geraldine Rees
Miss Elizabeth Rees-Jones BA
Mrs Diana Reid JP
Dr Margaret Reinhold MB FRCP
Air Cdre HF Renton CB ADC MA LLD
Miss Leila Restan MChS SR Ch
Mrs Nancy Richards
Mrs Joan Richardson
Ms Fiona Richmond
Miss Angela Rippon

Miss Elizabeth Ritchie AIB (Scot)
Dr Rosa Sutton Rivlin MRCS LRCP CPH
Brigadier VM Rooke CBE RRC QHNS
　SRN RSCN
Miss Adel Rootstein
Ms Wendy Rose-Neil BA
Mrs Janet W Ross
Miss Ann Rossiter MA
Mrs Joan Rothschild
Ms Bridget Rowe
Miss Janine Roxborough Bunce
Mrs Barbara Rutherford
Mrs Jehan el-Sadat Osman
Mrs K Sadeck
Ms M Sanderson
Lady Saunders (Katie Boyle)
Ms BC Scott
Mrs Barbara J Searle BSc ALCM
Mrs Ian Service
Miss Faith Seward MBE BA
Mrs Margaret Seward BDS MDS FDS
Mrs Phyllis May Seymour
Ms Jean Shapiro
Mrs Shirley Shaw
Mrs Susan Shaw
Mrs D Sheppard
HE Mrs Maudline Shillingford
Ms Elizabeth Sidney MA BA AB Psys
Lady Sieff BA
Ms Janet Silver MPhil FBCO MBIM
Miss EH Simons
Miss Jane Sketchley BSc CEng MICE
The Hon Mrs Suzanne Skyrme
Mrs Dorothy Octavia Smith RSA
Dr Joan Smith MA LLB PhD
Miss Liz Smith
Mrs Mary Smith MBE BA FIH
Mrs Sallie Snowman
Mrs A Sowrey
Miss Min Sowrey
Mrs Peggy Spencer MBE FISTD
Mrs Sproat MA BED
Mrs Denise St Aubyn Hubbard
Miss Suzanne Stanton
Miss Daphne Steele SRN SCM
Ms Carolyn Stephan NIA
Sister Stevens
Lady Stewart JP OBE
Mrs FE Stewart-Murray
Miss Susanne Stoessl BA Econ
Ms Carole Stone
Miss Helen Stone Dip Sociol
Miss Moira Stuart
Miss June Ann Stubbs MSIAD
Ms Una Stubbs

Ms Norma Sullivan
Mrs J Anne Summers DES RCA FRSA
Dr Mary Sutherland MRCS LRCP JP
Mrs JC Swallow BSc
Miss Cleo Sylvestre
Mrs Taylor SRN SCM
Mrs Aileen Taylor BA PGCE
Mrs Wyn Taylor BA
Mrs Honor Thackrah
Miss Carol Thatcher LLB
Mrs Irene Thomas
Mrs Netta Thomas MBE
Miss Angela Thorne
Miss Terry Todd
Mrs Noemi Tomba
Ms Vivienne Tomei
Mrs Margaret Toms
Miss Sheila Tracy LRAM
Mrs Jane Tridgell
Miss Joyce Trotman BA MLitt
Miss Frances Tulloch MA (Oxon) Dip Th
  (Lon)
Alderman Miss Florence Tunniecliffe
Mrs PD Turk
Ms Sue Turner BA
Miss Sylvia IM Tutt
Miss Taufa Vakatale BA
Miss Lucia Van der Post BA
Mrs Betty Van Gelder
Miss Elizabeth Vaughan
Miss Petra von Siniawski RAD ISTD
Mrs Jean Wadlow
Ms PM Walker
Mrs Sheila Walker CBE JP
Miss Elizabeth Wallace
Miss Hazel Vincent Wallace OBE
Ms Jane Walmsley BA MA
Miss Marcia Warburton
Mrs Elizabeth Despard Ward MBE
Miss MF Ward
Ms Shirley Ward
Miss Hilda Wardroper DES RCA MSIA
  BSc
Dr Barbara M Q Weaver PhD FRCVS
  DVA
Miss Dorothy May Webster CBE SRN
  SCM MTD
Mrs Alison Weir (Oxon) Dip Ed
Miss Molly Weir
Mrs LF Whitaker FADO
Mrs AM White MInstM
Mrs Maureen White LLB JP
Mrs B Whiteman
Mrs E C J Whitmarsh
Mrs Lilian Wick LRAM LGSM

Mrs Marjorie Wickham JP
Miss Gillian Widdicombe
Miss Doris Anne Wilkinson BA
Mrs Roma Wilkinson
Mrs Colonel Violet Williams
Cllr Zena Williams
Mrs EM Wilson
Ms Jenny Wilson BSc
Miss Sheila Wilson MA
Ms Nancy Wise LRAM LGSM ALAM
Mrs Marguerite Wood JP BA MCSP
Miss Rae Woodland
Dr Jules Wright PhD
Mrs Anna Wyner
Mrs JG Yates
Miss Joanna Zlotnik (Jessica Goldsmith)
  MB CHB FRCS FRACS
Mrs Susan Zwinoira

Monday 22nd October 1984
THEME: HOW TO BE FIRST

Dr Fiona Acheson FFARCS
Ms Jan Adams
Ms Margaret Alexander
Mrs Clementine Allen
Miss Murial Allen
Mrs JD Alvarez
Mrs Pamela Anderson
Ms Sylvia Anderson
Ms Elizabeth Anioniou SRN
Miss Val Arnison MIPR
Ms Anne Ashby SRN SCM
Miss Jane Asher
Mrs Jane Atkinson MIPR
Mrs Charlotte Baden-Powell AA Dip
  RIBA
Mrs Susie Banks
Miss Mary Barnes
Miss Ann Barr
Mrs JS Barrell
Miss Jocelyn Barrow OBE
Dr Yvonne Barton PhD MPhil BSc
Ms Lindsay Bates
Miss Napine Beddington MBE FRIBA
  FSIAD
Miss Jennifer Beeston MA (St Andrews)
Mrs Mary Belsham
Ms Floella Benjamin
Mrs Susan Benjamin
The Countess Jill Bernadotte of Wisberg
  BA
Ms Mary Berry
Mrs Constance Beynon FRCS Ed FRCOG JP

Dr Ann Birchall BA PhD FSA
Ms Lorna Blackie MA
Mrs Freddy Bloom OBE
Ms Susan Bloom
Miss Joyce Blow MA FIPR FRIM
Ms Stefanie Blower BA Dip CAM
Professor Margaret Boden MA (Cantab) PhD (Harvard) FBA
Mrs SI Bondie-Arning BSc MA
Miss Iris Borton
Mrs Mary Bottaro
Miss Katie Boyle
Miss Suzanne Brickett
Mrs Fiona Brothers BSc
Miss Iona Brown
Miss Janet Brown
Mrs Sandra Brown
Dr SA Bucknall BSc MSc MIBiol PhD
Miss Patience Bulkeley
Miss Janine Roxborough Bunce MIPR
Mrs AEL Burleigh MCSP
Ms Suzy Burston
Ms Sarah Burton
The Hon Cindy Buxton
The Hon Paddy Campbell
Mrs Rae Campbell-Tanner BSc
Miss Fanny Carby
Miss Marcia Carlowe
Mrs Margaret Chadd AIMSW JP
Mrs K Chamberlain
Mrs WE Channing
Ms Adele Cherreson
Lady Caroline Chichester Clark
Mrs Jane Christopherson ARIBA
Ms Jill Churchill
Miss Felicity Clark
Mrs Georgina Clark
Mrs Olive Clark MBE JP
Mrs Siobhan Clark
Mrs Rosalie Cody
Mrs Pauline Cohen BA
Miss Eileen Cole BA (Cantab) MIOD CBIM Mem MRS
Professor Monica Cole BSc PhD
Miss Gill Coleridge
Ms Dianne Coles
Mrs Patience Collier
Mrs Anne Collins BSc
Ms Marilyn Collyer BA Dip Soc Admin
Mrs Yvonne Conolly BED
Ms Conran
Miss Doreen Cooper
Mrs Lucy Cooper
Mrs Norma Corney
Ms Edith Coulson BA

Mrs Winifred Coulson OBE
Mrs Tricia Court
Mrs Valerie Cridland
Miss Anne Cropper
Miss EB Cullen
Mrs Frances Dagg
Mrs Edith Dakeyne-Cannon
Mrs Lucy Darwall-Smith
Mrs Judith Davenport
Dr A Rosalie David BA PhD
Mrs Bridget Davies
Mrs Dorothea Davies FHCIMA LCG
Mrs Lillian Davies SRN RFN
Mrs Alison Davis
Miss Jane Davis
Mrs Elaine Dean
Sister Marie Delourdes
Miss Denavane
Ms Celia Denton LLB FCA
Mrs Jean Denton BSc (Econ) F Inst M FIMI
Mrs Esther de Waal
Professor Susan Dev MSc FCCA ATII
Ms Pamela Dimmock
Ms Sue Dobson BA
Miss Zuleika Dobson
Mrs Mary Caroline Donlan BA
Mrs Mikki Doyle
Ms Jane Drew FRIBA
Mrs Dorothy Dunnett
Mrs Elena Duran-Emmerson
Miss Sally Dymott SRN OHNC ONC
Mrs Laura Edwards MA
Dr Marta Elian MD
Mrs EWL Elliot ACIS
Miss Susan Elliott
Miss Polly Elwes
Mrs Elizabeth Emanuel MA (RCA)
Miss Christine Evans
Miss Patricia Ewing
Mrs Audrey Eyton
Ms Enid Falaschi JP BA MPhil
Miss Susan Farmer
Miss Eleanor Fazan
Mrs Helena Felix
Miss Hilda Fenemore
Mrs Peggy Fenner MP
Mrs Jane Ferguson
Mrs Susan Fieldman LLB
Mrs Karen Finch OBE
Lady Fisher
Mrs Janet Fitch
Councillor Mrs Joan FitzWilliams
Mrs PJ Fleming BA
Lady Fletcher-Cooke BA MA

Mrs Angela Flowers
Ms Jo Foley
Miss Janet Fookes MP BA
Mrs Nancy Forrester
The Hon Mrs Olga Polizzi Forte
Miss Mary Frampton MBE
Ms Decima Francis
Dr Winifred Francis MD FRCOG
Lady Sheila Francis-Chichester
Ms Lynne Franks
Mrs Susanne Frei
Mrs Ann Freud BA
Mrs Jill Freud
Ms Helen Galas LLB BLitt
Mrs Christine Gallie
Baroness Gardner of Parkes BDS/Life Peer
Miss Roberta Gibbs
Mrs Marcia Gibson-Watt BA
Mrs Beryl Gilroy MA
Ms Elizabeth Gluck BA
Mrs Maggie Goldsmith
Ms Hannah Gordon
Mrs Jenny Gray
Miss Elizabeth Green MInstM
Miss Janet Green
Mrs Maggie Green
Miss Patricia Gregory
Miss Janet Gulland Ma CEng MRAeS
Mrs Trish Gullett
Mrs Mary Gunther DES RCA MIPR
Ms Betty Guyatt AIB
Miss Katherine Hadley BA
Mrs D Hamilton-Fairley MCST
Ms Susan Hampshire
Mrs Barbara Hardwick
Miss Doris Hare MBE
Lady Harlech BA
Ms Irene Harris
Miss Margaret Harris MA
Mrs Beryl Hartland
Miss Marea Hartman CBE BSc Econ
Mrs Tamara Hassani
Miss Joyce Hawkins MA
Ms Suzie Hayman
Mrs Pauline Hedges AIB
Mrs Diane Henderson
Mrs Miriam Henderson
Ms Angela Heylin
Miss Jennifer Hilton BA MA Dip Crim
    Dip Hist Art
Mrs Phyllis Hindle NDD CEAE
Miss Jennifer Hocking
Miss Min Hogg
Lady Holland-Martin DBE DL
Miss Victoria Holt

Miss Angela Hooper
Mrs Cherry Hopkins
Miss Barbara Hosking
Miss Margaret Howard
Mrs Caryl Hubbard BA (Oxon)
Mrs M Hudson
Miss Verity Hudson
Miss Carole Hunt BEd
Miss Sarah Hunt BEd
Dr Mollie Hunton MBBS MF Hom
Lady Susan Hussey DCVO
Dr Fay Hutchinson MBBS
Mrs Ethel Imber
Mrs Amy Isherwood FBCO
Mrs Janet Jack RIBA ALI
Mrs Elaine Jackson JP SRN SCM HV
    DNED RNT RN
Miss Helen Jackson MA LLB
Miss Betty Jakens FInstHE
Mrs Carolyn James
Miss Pamela Jarvis SIAD
Dr Marcelle Jay PhD
Mrs Mary Lavinia Jay
Mrs Pansy Jeffrey JP
Mrs Zoë Jenkinson
Miss Beryl Johns
Ms Penny Jones MDes FCA
Miss Sarah Jones
Miss Leela Kapila FRCS
Mrs Ishbel Kargar
Mrs E Kasket MA
Miss Hilary Kay
Mrs Jacqueline Kehoe SR CH
Ms Linda Kelsy
Miss Mary Kenny
Miss Sheila Kerr
Mrs Mandy Ketchin RIBA ARIAS
Squadron Leader Jo Kingston MBBS
    LRCP MRCS Dip Ave Med
Ms Jenny Kirkpatrick
Miss Penny Kitchen
Mrs Betty Knightly
Miss Wyn Knowles
Dr Eva Kohner MD FRCP
Mrs Janet Kurta MA (Cantab) BSc Agrig
Miss Ann Ladbury
Ms Jacqui Lait
Miss Maureen Laker
Miss Patricia Lamburn
Miss Jean Lanning JP
Miss Jane Lapotaire
Mrs Mary Law
Mrs Harold Leake
Ms Edith Lederer
Mrs Lynda Lee-Potter

Miss Moira Leggat
Ms Joy Leitch BSc Dip Ed
Ms Ann Leslie BA (Oxon)
Mrs Avril Lethbridge
Dr Rosa Letts LLB MPhil
Miss Mary Lewis
Ms Adella Lithman
Miss Yvonne Littlewood
Ms Kate Littner
Mrs Janet Lloyd LLB
Mrs Marie Lloyd-Evans
Dr JM Lomax-Simpson FRCPsych MB
  ChD DPM
Miss Pamela Long
Miss Frederica Lord BA
Ms C Loxton-Peacock MA
Ms Josephine Lundberg
Ms Luciana C Lynch
Ms Sue MacGregor
Ms Elaine M Maclean
Ms Fiona Maddocks MA (Cantab)
Mrs Bo Maggs
The Hon Miss Diana Makgill MVO
Miss DMP Malley MVO MBE
Miss Patricia Mann FCAM FIPA
The Countess of Mar and Kellie OBE
  OStJ JP
Mrs Stella Margetts
Mrs Joy Martin
Sister Mary Perpetua
Miss Betty Masters OBE BA FSA
Mrs YM Mazur
Dr Alison McCartney MA MB BChir
  MRCPath
Mrs Desmie McClean
Ms Nancy McConkey
Mrs Anna McCurley MP
Ms Anne McDermid
Mrs Jill McIvor LLB
Ms Hilda McKerral
Mrs Betty McLeish
Mrs Ann McMullan Dip CAM
Ms Brigid McMullen
Ms Althea McNish CMT DesRCA FSIAD
Mrs Wendie McWatters
Ms Leonie Mellinger
Miss June Mendoza
Mrs Suzy Menkes MA (Cantab)
Lady Micklethwait
Dr Rosalind Miles MA (Oxon) PhD JP
Ms Ann Miller BA
Mrs Kathryn Miller
Ms Fran Minogue
Mrs Pauline Molnar MA
Miss D Monreal MVO MBE

Ms Bel Mooney BA
Ms Patricia Mordecai DipEd
Mrs Jan Morgan
Dr Jane Morgan MA (Wales) PhD (Leic)
Miss Janice Morley
Mrs Frances Morrell
Miss Jill Morris DES RCA FRSA FSIAD
Ms Fran Morrison MA
Mrs Nicholas Mountain
Dr Sasai Mpuchane BSc MSc PhD
Mrs JRL Mukerji BA MHCI MA MRSH
Miss Clare Mulholland MA
Mrs Lynn Murdoch BEd (Cantab)
Miss Gabriella Mustillo
Dr Elizabeth Nelson BA PhD
Miss Caroline Neville
Rabbi Julia Neuberger
Ms Emma Nicholson LRAM ARCM
Mrs Brigid Norris BSc (Aero Eng) Cert Ed
  (Cantab) CTB
Miss Dett O'Cathain BA
Ms Kay O'Dwyer
Ms Sally O'Sullivan
Miss Jennifer Oyer
Miss Jane Pannel
Miss Constance-Anne Parker FRBS ATD
Miss Jane Parker-Smith ARCM LTCL
Mrs Elizabeth Parkinson JP
Ms Sue Parrish BA Eng (UCL)
Mrs Vivienne Parry BSc
Miss Saidie Patterson MBE MA
Miss Claudia Payne MVO
Lady Penn
Ms Victoria Pepys BA
Miss Mary Perigoe
Mrs Harold Phillips
Reverend Sybil Phoenix MBE
Mrs Dorothy Pinker SRN
Ms Jenny Pitman
Miss Priscilla Playford
Mrs Louise Pleydell-Bouverie
Ms Eve Pollard
Lady Popplewell JP MA (Cantab)
Mrs Anthony Post
Miss Jane Procter
Ms Gloria Proops
Miss Mavis Quinault
Mrs Lois Ramphal SRN
Mrs Yvonne Randall
Miss Esther Rantzen
Mrs Claire Rayner SRN
Lady Read
Miss R W Read FLCM LLCM (TD)
  ALAM
Miss Jane Reed

Miss Elizabeth Rees-Jones BA
Dr Margaret Reinhold MD FRCP
Air Commodore H F Renton CB ADC MA LLD
Mrs Donald Rich MIEC MICFM
Miss Fiona Richmond
Miss Joyce Riddiough
Mrs Inger Riley SRN
Mrs Lois Roberts MA
Ms Patricia Roberts
Mrs Patsy Robertson BA
Ms Jancis Robinson MA MW
Mrs Marion Roe MP
Miss Diana Rookledge MA
Mrs Diana Rose LSE
Ms Wendy Rose-Neil BA
Miss Ann Rossiter MA
Ms Bridget Rowe
Mrs Ann Rudd
Mrs Barbara Rutherford
Mrs E Safronova
Mrs Harry Sager
Mrs Anne Sargent
Ms Anna Scher
Miss Barbara Scott
Mrs Charlotte Scott, Freeman of the City of London
Mrs Constance Seifert
Mrs Ian Service
Dr Chandra Sethurajan MBBS DCH (Lon)
Miss Faith Seward MBE
Mrs Susan Shaw
Miss Caroline Sheppard
Mrs Mary Seton Sheppard
Ms Janet Silver MPhil FBCO FBIM
Councillor Mrs Lydia Simmons
Miss Hazel Sims
The Hon Mrs Suzanne Skyrme
Ms Audrey Slaughter
Ms Anne Sloman BA
Miss Maureen Smith
Mrs Sallie Snowman
Mrs Greville Spratt
Ms Patricia Speirs
Ms Sally-Anne Stapleford
Mrs Denise St Aubyn Hubbard MRIN
Miss Daphne Steele SRN SCM HV
Miss A J Stephany
Lady Stewart OBE JP
Mrs Floi Stewart-Murray
Mrs Caryl Stockham
Mrs Katharine Stockley BA (Oxon)
Miss Susanne Stoessl BA Econ
Miss Carole Stone
Miss Helen Stone Dip Soc

Miss Anne Stonehill BA
Ms Moira Stuart
Mrs E Ann Stubbs
Ms Clare Stubbs
Miss Sara Sugarman
Ms Morma Sullivan
Ms Cleo Sylvestre
Ms Wendy Taylor LDAD
Mrs Honor Thackrah
Miss Allison Thomas
Mrs Netta Thomas MBE
Mrs Hilary Laidlaw Thomson
Ms Victoria Thornton
Miss Tryphena Todd
Miss Sheila Tracy
Miss Joyce Trotman BA MLitt
The Right Hon Baroness Trumpington
Mrs Lorraine Tuckey BA
Miss Frances Tulloch MA Dip Th (Lon)
Miss Flo Tunnicliffe
Mrs Phyllis Turk
Mrs Muriel Turner
Miss Jenny Turton
Miss Sylvia Tutt
Mrs Rita Udall
Ms Arline Usden
Dame Olga Uvarov DBE DSc FIBio FRCVS
The Lady Vaizey
Mrs Rosemary Van Musschenbroek BSc
Mrs Gina Vanning
Mrs Jean Vine
Miss Sally Voak
Ms Isabel Walker BA
Miss Marjorie Walker
Mrs Owen Walker CBE JP
Miss Elizabeth Wallace
Miss Marcia Warburton
Miss MF Ward
Mrs Stella Wardell FAIE
Ms Diana Warwick
Miss Frances L Watt
Ms Kathie Webber
Miss Molly Weir
Ms Katharine Whitehorn
Miss Gillian Widdicombe
Ms Shireen Williams
Ms Stephanie Williams BA
Miss Joan Wills SWA UA MH (Paris) FRSA
Mrs Wilmot-Sitwell
Ms Dorienne Wilson-Smillie
Mrs Margaret Wingfield CBE
Ms Nancy Wise
Lady Wolfson
Councillor Mrs Margaret Wood

Mrs Marguerite Wood JP BA MCSP
Mrs Gillian Woolcock MBIM DInstM
Mrs Anna Wyner
Miss Dorothy Young

Monday 28th October 1985
THEME: HOPE

Dr Fiona Acheson FFARCS
Ms Linda Agran
Mrs Clementine Allen
Miss Muriel Rose Allen
Mrs Pamela Anderson
Ms Sylvia Anderson
Miss Val Arnison
Mrs Joanna Ashbourne BA
Mrs Anne Ashby SRN SCM
Miss Ruth Ashton SRN SCM MTD
Mrs Elizabeth Aziz
Mrs Charlotte Baden-Powell AA Dip
  RIBA
Mrs Anne Ballard MA
Mrs Iris Banham-Lee MIPR
Mrs Susie Banks
Ms Margie Barbour BA
Miss Joanna Barlow
Mrs Joan Barrell
Dr Yvonne Barton PhD MPhil BSc
Ms Marianne Bates JP
Miss Nadine Beddington MBE FRIBA
  FSIAD
Miss Jennifer Beeston MA (St Andrews)
Mrs Mary Belsham
Ms Floella Benjamin
Ms Sandra Benjamin
Mrs Susan Benjamin
Mrs WE Bennett
Countess Jill Bernadotte of Wisberg BA
Ms Mary Berry
Miss Anne Berthoud
Mrs Mary Beverley BA Dip Ed
Mrs Constance Beynon FRCS FRCOG JP
Mrs Gay Biddlecombe
Mrs Joan Bingley MA FCIS
Miss Lorna Blackie MA
Professor Margaret Boden MA PhD FBA
Mrs Sandra Bonadie-Arning BSc MA
Mrs Georgina Boosey
Mrs Mary Bottaro
Miss Janet Brown
Mrs Sandra Brown
Ms Tanya Bruce-Lockhart
Miss Patience Bulkeley
Mrs Kate Bunn

Miss Penelope Burder-Andrews BA
Mrs AE Burleigh MCSP SRP
Ms Suzy Burston
Miss Iris Burton
Ms Cindy Buxton
Ms Ivy Cameron
The Hon Mrs Paddy Campbell
Mrs Rae Campbell-Tanner BA BSc
Miss Fanny Carby
Ms Marcia Carlowe
Mrs Margaret Chadd AIMSW JP
Miss Sandra Chalmers BA
The Hon Mrs Rhiannon Chapman LIB
  AKC FIPM
Ms Caroline Charles
Mrs Margaret Charrington
Mrs Jean Christopherson ARIBA
Ms Jill Churchill
Mrs Georgina Clark
Mrs Olive Clarke MBE JP
The Hon Mrs Gervas Clay
Ms Amanda Cochrane
Mrs Rosalie Cody
Mrs Pauline Cohen BA
Miss Eileen Cole BA
Ms Marilyn Collyer BA Dip Soc
Miss Joyce Conwy Evans DES RCA FSIAD
Mrs Coode
Miss Doreen Cooper
Ms Sara Mai Cordelia BA
Mrs Mary Craig MA
Miss Susan Crowson
Miss Eileen Cullen MA
Miss Adrienne de Trey-White
Mrs Edith Dakeyne-Cannon
Ms Sarah Dallin
Mrs Judith Davenport
Dr Rosalie David BA PhD
Dr Sally Davies MB MSc MRCP MRC
  Path
Ms Alison Davis
Miss Jane Davis
Mrs Lillian Davis SRN RFN
Mrs Elaine Dean
Ms Alyn de Casembroot MA
Ms Trudi de Haney
Sister Marie de Lourdes SRN SCM
Ms Susan Denny
Ms Celia Denton LLB FCA
Professor Susan Dev MSc FCCA ATII
Ms Sue Dobson BA
Miss Zuleika Dobson NDD ATD
Ms Mikki Doyle
Ms Jane Drew FRIBA LLD IBADAM
Mrs Dorothy Dunnett

Ms Sophie Dupre
Ms Elena Duran-Emmerson
Ms Jennifer Durrant Dip FA
Miss Sally Dymott SRN OHNC ONC
Mrs Laura Edwards MA
Dr Marta Elian MD
Miss Polly Elwes
Mrs Elizabeth Emanuel MA (RCA)
Miss Christine Evans
Dr Elizabeth Evans BSc PhD
Mrs Audrey Eyton
Ms Siobhan Fahey
Mrs Enid Falaschi JP BA MPhil
Miss Susan Farmer
Mrs Helena Felix
Miss Hilda Fenemore
Mrs Peggy Fenner MP
Mrs Maralyn Fichte
Mrs Susan Fieldman LLB
Ms Karen Finch OBE
Mrs Janet Fitch
Councillor Mrs Joan Fitzwilliams
Mrs PJ Fleming BA
Ms Susan Fletcher BA
Lady Alice Fletcher-Cook MA
Mrs Vivienne Flower
Mrs Angela Flowers
Mrs Joanna Forrester
Mrs Nancy Forrester
Mrs Anthea Fortescue
Mrs Molly Fox BSc
Miss Mary Frampton MBE
Ms Decima Francis
Dr Winifred Francis MD FRCOG
Ms Lynne Franks
Ms Daphne Fraser BA CRNA
Mrs Susanne Frei
Mrs Ann Freud BA His
Ms Anne Frye BA
Ms Helen Galas LLB BLitt
Dr Janet Gale-Grant BA MSc PhD
Ms Divina Galica MBE
Miss Jocelyn Galsworthy
Baroness Gardner of Parkes BDS JP
Mrs Janet Gaymer MA LLM
Mrs Pam Gems BA Psy
Ms Nicola Gerrard MA
Ms Rosslyn Gibbs
The Hon Mrs Marcia Gibson-Watt BA
Miss Maureen Gillespie BSc
Mrs Beryl Gilroy MA Dip Psy
Mrs Renée Goddard
Ms Maggie Goodman
Professor Margaret Gowing CBE FBA
    DLitt DSc BA

Miss Elizabeth Green MInstM
Ms Felicity Green
Miss Janet Green
Miss Jennefer Greenwood BSc ARICS
Miss Patricia Gregory
Miss Janet Gulland MA CEng MRAES
Ms Betty Guyatt AIB
Miss Katharine Hadley BA
Mrs Pauline Halliday
Ms Susan Hampshire
Ms Barbara Hardwick
Lady Pamela Harlech BA
Miss Diane Hart
Miss Patricia Hart BA
Miss Marea Hartman CBE BSc
Mrs Tamara Hassani
Ms Suzie Hayman
Ms Dianne Hayter
Miss Audrey Head
Pte Annette Heaton WRAC
Mrs Diana Henderson
Mrs Miriam Henderson
Mrs Elizabeth Higgs
Mrs Phyllis Hindle NDD CEAE
Mrs Jennifer Hocking
The Hon Mrs Sarah Hogg MA
Lady Holland-Martin DBE DL
Ms Pam Holmes BSc SRN
Mrs Sylvia Holmes
Miss Thelma Holt MA
Miss Victoria Holt
Miss Angela Hooper CBE
Mrs Cherry Hopkins
Miss Hannah Horovitz
Ms Freda Horrocks
Miss Rosamund Horwood-Smart
Ms Barbara Hosking OBE
Ms Jane Howard BHC Econ HCIMA
Ms Rosalind Howells
Mrs Caryl Hubbard BA
Mrs Margaret Hudson
Miss Verity Hudson
Ms Jane Humphrey
Miss Gayle Hunnicutt UCLA BA
Dr SL Hurley BPhil DPhil
Ms Susie Hush BA
Dr Fay Hutchinson MB BS
Mrs Amy Isherwood FBCO
Ms Janet Jack RIBA ALI
Mrs Elaine Jackson JP SRN SCM HV D
    NED RNT RN
Miss Betty Jakens FInst HE
Ms Geraldine James
Mrs Peggy Jansz BA
Dr Marcelle Jay PhD

Mrs Mary Jay
Ms Zoë Jenkins
Mrs Zoë Jenkinson
Ms Penny Jones MDes FCA
Miss Sarah Jones BA
Miss Leela Kapila FRCS
Mrs E Kasket MA
Ms Penelope Keith
Miss Frances Kelly
Miss Jane Kelly LLB
Ms Penny Kemp
Mrs Glenys Kinnock BA
Mrs Jennifer Kirkpatrick BEd
Miss Cherry Kisch
Mrs Betty Knightly
Miss Wyn Knowles
Dr Eva Kohner MD FRCP
Mrs Janet Kurta MA (Cantab) BSc
Miss Ann Ladbury
Ms Jacqui Lait
Mrs Marjorie Langford
Mrs Lucille Langley-Williams
Miss Deborah Langslow MA
Miss Jean Lanning JP
Ms Di Latham MPhil
Mrs Mary Law
Ms Felicity Lawrence BA
Mrs Audrey Lawson Johnston
Mrs Jennifer Leader
Mrs Dorothy Leake
Mrs Linda Lee-Potter
Ms Joy Leitch BSc DipEd MA
Ms Ann Leslie BA
Mrs Charlotte Lessing
Mrs Avril Lethbridge
Mrs Carrie Lewis
Ms Adella Lithman
Miss Yvonne Littlewood
Mrs Svetlana Lloyd
Mrs Marie Lloyd-Evans
Miss Pamela Long
Ms Maureen Longley BA
Ms Frederica Lord BA
Ms Jennifer Loss
Ms Josephine Lundberg
Ms Kerry MacKenzie MA
Mrs Alison Mackonochie
Ms Fiona Maddocks MA (Cantab)
The Hon Miss Diana Makgill LVO
Miss Suzi Malin
Ms Jacqueline Malton
Miss Patricia Mann FCAM FIPA CBIM
Ms Anne Manson BA
The Countess of Mar & Kellie JP OBE
   OStJ

Mrs Constance Mark
Miss Marguerite Markes BSc FRGS
Mrs Caroline Marland
Ms Janette Marshall BA
Mrs Terry Marsland
Mrs Elizabeth Martin BSc ACA ATII
Sister Mary Perpetua
Ms Anastasia Mattheson
Ms Angela McArthur
Dr Margaret McCann MB BCh BAO
Dr Alison McCartney MA MB BChir
   MRC Path
Ms Nancy McConkey
Mrs Heather McConnell FIPR
Ms Anne McDermid BA
Mrs Barbara McDermott
Ms Hilda McKerral
Mrs Ann McMullan MBE Dip Cam
Ms Althea McNish CMT DesRCA FSIAD
Mrs Robert Maxwell MA DPhil
Lady Medawar MA BSc
Ms Leonie Mellinger
Mrs Suzy Menkes MA (Cantab)
Ms Vida Menzies
Miss Doris Mercer
Lady Micklethwaite
Dr Rosalind Miles MA PhD JP
Ms Jacqueline Miller
Mrs Kathryn Miller
Ms Sheila Ming
Ms Frances Minogue
Ms Bel Mooney BA
Mrs Diana Moran
Mrs Jan Morgan SRN ANAEA
Dr Jane Morgan MA PhD
Miss Janice Morley
Lady Morris of Kenwood
Miss Jill Morris DES RCA FRSA FSAID
Ms Maria Morris
Ms Fran Morrison MA
Mrs M Morrison BEM
Mrs Penelope Mountain
Dr Sisai Mpuchane BSc MSc PhD
Mrs Lynn Murdock BEd (Cantab)
Mrs Leila Murison
Miss Gabriella Mustillo
Ms Sheila Needham
Dr E H Nelson BA PhD
Miss Caroline Neville
Miss Emma Nicholson LRAM ARCM
Miss Detta O'Cathain OBE BA
Ms Prue O'Day
Miss Kay O'Dwyer
Mrs Jane Olivier
Miss Jennifer Over

Ms Michaela Pain
Miss Jane Parker-Smith ARCM LTCL
Ms Susan Parrish BA AGSM
Mrs Betty Parsons
Ms Elizabeth Parsons FCII MInstM DMS
Miss Rowanne Pasco CBE
Miss Claudia Payne MVO
Mrs Elizabeth Peacock MP JP
Mrs Sue Pearson MIH Ec
Lady Penn
Miss Mary Perigoe
Mrs Harold Phillips
Ms Sue Phipps BA
Reverend Sybil Phoenix MBE
Mrs Jenny Pitman
Lady Pitt
Baroness Platt of Writtle CBE MA C Eng MR AES
Mrs Louise Pleydell-Bouverie
Ms Brenda Polan BA
The Hon Mrs Olga Polizzi
Mrs Anthony Post
Mrs N Prevett BSc (Econ)
Miss Anne Price
Ms Gloria Proops
Miss Laurie Purden MBE
Miss Dorothy Quick LLB
Miss Mavis Quinault
Ms Toni Racklin
Mrs Lois Ramphal SRN
Miss Wendy Ramshaw
Mrs Yvonne Randall
Miss Rosemary Ransome-Wallis BA FRSA
Lady Dorothy Read
Miss Rosalie Read FLCM LLCM(TD) ALAM
Ms Geraldine Rees
Miss Elizabeth Rees-Jones BA
Air Commodore Helen Renton CB ADC MA LLD
Mrs Donald Rich MIEC MICFM
Miss Fiona Richmond
Ms Caroline Riley BSc Geology
Mrs Inger Riley SRN
Miss Angela Rippon
Miss Patricia Roberts
Mrs Helen Robinson
Mrs Marion Roe
Miss Diana Rookledge MA
Miss Adel Rootstein
Mrs Diana Rose LSE
Ms Wendy Rose-Neil BA
Miss Ann Rossiter MA
Miss Patricia Routledge BA
Ms Bridget Rowe

Miss Janine Roxborough Bunce MIPR
Mrs Barbara Rutherford
Mrs Anne Sager
Ms Josephine Sandilands
Ms Carol Sarler
Ms Anna Scher
Mrs Allison Scott
Mrs Charlotte Scott
Mrs Mary Service
Dr Chandra Sethurajan MBBS DCH
Miss Faith Seward MBE BA
Miss Henrietta Shaw BA (Cantab)
Ms Hillary Shaw
Mrs Susan Shaw
Miss Caroline Sheppard
Mrs Mary Sheppard
Ms Janet Silver MPhil FBCO MBIM
Ms Prudence Skene
The Hon Mrs Suzanne Skyrme
Ms Audrey Slaughter
Mrs Anne Sloman BA (Oxon)
Mrs Frances Smith BA
Mrs Sallie Snowman
Ms Patricia Speirs
Ms Sally-Anne Stapleford
Mrs Denise St Aubyn Hubbard MRIN
Mrs Stenhouse
Miss AJ Stephany
Mrs Joan Stephens BA
Miss Mary Stevens BA (Cantab) MA
Lady Stewart OBE JP
Mrs F Stewart-Murray
Mrs KM Stockley BA (Oxon)
Miss Carole Stone
Miss Helen Stone Dip Soc
Miss Anne Stonehill BA
Ms Moira Stuart
Ms Clare Stubbs
Ms Una Stubbs
Ms Wendy Taylor LDAD Dist
Miss Kerry ten Kate
Mrs Netta Thomas MBE
Miss Sue Thorne
Ms Victoria Thornton
Miss Tryphena Todd
Miss Sheila Tracy LRAM
Miss Joyce Trotman BA MLitt
Miss Frances Tulloch MA DipTh
Miss Jenny Turton
Miss Sylvia Tutt
Ms Arline Usden
The Lady Vaizey
Miss Marjorie Walker
Mrs Sheila Walker CBE JP
Miss Elizabeth Wallace

Ms Noelle Walsh BA
Miss Marcia Warburton
Miss MF Ward
Mrs Stella Wardell FAIE
Ms Diana Warwick BA
Miss Frances Watt HND ONA
Miss Molly Weir
Miss Katharine Whitehorn BA LLD
Mrs Mary Whitehouse CBE
Miss Stephanie Williams BA
Mrs Violet Williams
Ms Chrissy Wilson
Mrs Margaret Wingfield CBE
Mrs Andrea Wonfor BA (Cantab)
Mrs Marguerite Wood BA MCSP JP
Ms Keren Woodward
Mrs Anna Wyner

Monday 27th October 1986
THEME: VISION

Ms Jan Adams
Mrs Caroline Agar
Ms Linda Agran
Miss Muriel Allen
Mrs Pamela Anderson
Lady Anson LLB JP DL
Miss Sarah Arkel BA (Cantab)
Miss Val Arnison MIPR
Mrs Joanna Ashbourn BA
Mrs Anne Ashby SRN SCM
Miss Ruth Ashton SRN SCM MTD
Lady Attenborough
Mrs Elizabeth Azis
Mrs Charlotte Baden-Powell AA Dip RIBA
Miss Linda Bailey
Miss Loretta Balfour
Mrs Susie Banks
Miss Joanna Barlow
Miss Ann Barr
Mrs Joan Barrell
Dr Yvonne Barton BSC MPhil PhD CEng
    MICE
Miss Joyce Beak
Mrs Helen Beard
Mrs Patricia Beecham
Miss Jennifer Beeston MA
Ms Floella Benjamin
Mrs Susan Benjamin
Miss Sally Berner
Miss Mary Berry
Miss Babs Beverley
Miss Joy Beverley
Mrs Mary Beverley MA
Miss Teddie Beverley

Dr Beulah Bewley MD FFCM
Lady Rachel Billington MA
Mrs Jennifer Birch BSc MPhil FBCOO
    SMSA DIC
Miss Marie-Claire Black
Ms Lorna Blackie MA
Dr Tessa Blackstone BSc PhD
Professor Margaret Boden MA DPhil FBA
Mrs Sandra Bonadie-Arning BSc MA
Mrs Georgina Boozey
Miss Stella Boyce
Mrs Diana Britten
Ms Faith Brown
Miss Iona Brown OBE
Mrs Sandra Brown
Miss Tanya Bruce-Lockhart
Miss Christl Bruell SRCN
Miss Patience Bulkeley
Mrs Kate Burgess
Mrs Rose Marie Burrow
Ms Suzy Burston
Mrs Gwendoline Butler BA
The Hon Victoria Buxton
Mrs Mary Calland ADI RAC
Ms Ivy Cameron
Ms Hilary Caminer BA BPhil
Mrs Paddy Campbell
Miss Fanny Carby
Ms Margaret Chadd UP AIMSW
Mrs Rhiannon Chapman LLB
Ms Caroline Charles
Mrs JL Clanchy MA
Miss Felicity Clark
Ms Chris Clyne
Miss Emma Cochrane
Mrs Rosalie Cody
Ms Stephanie Cole
Mrs Ariadne Collier BA BSW MSW
Mrs Anne Collins BS
Ms Doreen Cooper
Ms Judy Cornwell
Ms Heather Couper BSc FRAS
Mrs RM Cousens FSAI
Mrs Mary Craig MA (Oxon)
Miss Annabel Croft
Mrs Rose Cunningham
Mrs Dorothea Davies FHCIMA Cert Ed
Dr Sally Davies MB MSc RCP MRCPath
Ms Alison Davis
Mrs Elaine Dean
Miss JA Deeley FCIS
Sister M de Lourdes
Ms Janet Demain
Ms Elaine Denby Dipl Arch ARIBA
Mrs Jean Denton BSc Econ

Professor Susan Dev MSc FCCA ATII
Ms Sue Dobson BA
Ms Susan Downe
Mrs Mikki Doyle
Miss Pauline Doyle
Miss Sophie Dupre
Ms Elena Duran-Emmerson
Dr Marta Elian
Miss Jessica Elliott BA MIPA
Mrs Lyn Ellis SEN
Miss Polly Elwes
Miss Julia Ernst
Dr Elizabeth Evans BSc PhD
Mrs Pennie Evans BA
Captain Alison Ewan WRAC
Mrs Audrey Eyton
Ms Sonia Falaschi BSc Hons CEng
   MIMechE
Miss Lynn Farleigh
Mrs Susan Faux
Mrs Helena Felix
Mrs Peggy Fenner MP
Mrs Karen Finch OBE FRSA FIIC
Lady Patricia Fisher
Mrs V G Fitzgerald
Mrs Susan J Fletcher BA
Miss Jo Foley BA
Mrs Nancy Forrester
Mrs Joan Forsberg
Mrs Betty Foster
Miss Josephine Fowler BEd
Ms Decima Francis
Mrs Linda Francis
Ms Lynn Francis
Dr Winifred Francis MD FRCOG
Ms Flora Fraser MA
Mrs Ann Freud BA
Ms Ann Frye BA MCIT
Ms Davinia Galica MBE
Miss Jocelyn Galsworthy
Mrs Cordelia Gara-George
Baroness Gardner of Parkes BDS
Mrs Janet Gaymer MA LLM
Ms Nicci Gerrard BA MA MPhil
Mrs Ann Gibson Dip Arch RIBA
Ms Anne Gibson BA
Mrs Marcia Gibson-Watt BA
Mrs Rosalind Gilmore MA
Mrs Gail Girling
Miss Sheila Gish
Lady Glendyne
Ms Diana Goodman
Mrs Patricia Grant
Mrs Lorna Gratton MPS
Mrs Mary Grayson

Miss Elizabeth Green MInstM
Ms Felicity Green
Miss Janet Green
Mrs Mary Greenland
Miss Jennefer Greenwood BSc ARICS
Miss Patricia Gregory
Miss Katharine Hadley BA
Mrs Pauline Halliday
Mrs Barbara Hardwick
Miss Doris Hare MBE
Pamela, Lady Harlech BA
Miss Patricia Hart BA
Miss Marea Hartman CBE
Mrs Tamara Hassani
Miss Joyce Hawkins MA
Mrs Isobel Hay
Mrs Diana Henderson
Mrs Gill Hewitt
Mrs Phyllis Hindle
Miss Isabel Hitchman BA
Ms Jennifer Hocking
Surgeon Commander A Elizabeth Hodges
   RN MA MB BChir MFOM Dip Av
   Med
Miss Min Hogg
Lady Holland Martin DBE DL
Dr Sheila Hollins MB BS MRCPsych
Miss Elizabeth Hobbs MBE
Ms Pamela Holmes BSc SRN
Mrs Sylvia Holmes
Miss Thelma Holt
Miss Victoria Holt
Miss Rosamund Horwood-Smart
Miss Barbara Hosking OBE
Mrs Ros Howells
Mrs Caryl Hubbard BA (Oxon)
Miss Verity Hudson
Miss Gayle Hunnicutt BA
Ms Susi Hush
Miss Gwendoline Hutchings
Mrs Cynthia Iliffe BA MA
Mrs Ethel Imber Lithman
Ms Jocasta Innes BA (Cantab)
Mrs Elaine Jackson JP SRN SCM HV RN
   Dip NE RNT
Miss Betty Jakens FInst H Ec
Ms Geraldine James
The Lady Janner CBE JP
Mrs Mary Jay
Mrs Pansy Jeffrey JP
Mrs Zoe Jenkinson
Ms Eva Jiricna RIBA Dipl Arch
Miss Greta Jones BA
Miss Sarah Jones BA
Miss Hazel Kay BA

Ms Ann Keast BSc FBIM
Mrs Jennifer Keaveney BA
Miss Jane Kelly LLB
Miss Penelope Kemp
Mrs Thora Ker
Mrs Griselda Kerr
Ms Naseem Khan MA (Oxon) FRSA
Mrs Kingman Brewster
Wing Commander Jo Kingston MB BS
  LRCP MRCS Dip Av Med
Ms Glenys Kinnock
Miss Simone Klass MIPR
Miss Wyn Knowles
Dr Eva Kohner MD FRCP
Mrs Sonia Kurtam BSc MA (Cantab)
Ms Dorothy Kuya
Miss Maureen Laker
Miss Patricia Lamburn CBE
Ms Di Latham MPhil
Ms Felicity Lawrence
The Hon Pearl Lawson Johnston JP
Miss Gillian Lawton
Miss Barbara Lee MBE
Mrs Lynda Lee-Potter
Miss Moira Leggat LBIPP
Miss Victoria Legge-Bourke LVO
Ms Joy Leitch BSc Dip Ed MA
Ms Ann Leslie BA (Oxon)
Mrs Charlotte Lessing
Ms Olivia Lichtenstein BA MA
Miss Pat Liddiard
Mrs Judi Linney SRN SCM HV Dip HEd
Ms Maureen Lipman
Mrs J Lister-Boyd MCSD
Ms Adella Lithman
Miss Pamela Long
The Countess of Longford CBE MA DLitt
Mrs Ann Longley MA
Miss Maureen Longley BA
Miss Frederica Lord BA
Lady Lovell-David MA
Dr Erna Low PhD
Miss Alexandra Loyd
Lady Lyons
Mrs Barbara Macdermott HNC
Ms Sue MacGregor
Ms Kerry Mackenzie MA
Ms Shonaig MacPherson LLB
Mrs Bo Maggs
Ms Suzi Malin
Ms Anne Manson BA
Mrs Caroline Marland
Miss Janette Marshall BA
Mrs W Marshall-Foster
Mrs Joy Martin

Sister Mary Perpetua
Miss Barbara Maxwell BA
Miss Angela McArthur
Dr Margaret McCann MB BCW BAD
Dr Alison McCartney MA MB BChir
  MRCPath
Miss Emma McClure BA MA
Mrs Jill McIvor LLB BL
Miss Julia McKenzie
Ms Hilda McKerral
Mrs Betty McLeish
Miss Sheila McLeish
Mrs Ann McMullan MBE OStJ
Ms Althen McNish
Miss June Mendoza RP ROI DLitt
Mrs SP Menkes MA (Cantab)
Lady Micklethwait
Dr Rosalind Miles MA PhD
Miss Alwyn Miller MSF
Mrs Kathryn Miller
Miss Simone Mirman
Miss Sophie Mirman
Ms Hy Money
Ms Patricia Mordecai DipEd
Mrs Janice Morley
Lady Morris of Kenwood
Ms Fran Morrison MA
Mrs Margaret Morrison BEM
Miss Jean Morton
Ms Clare Mulholland MA
Ms Marie Mullarney
Miss Sheila Needham
Rabbi Julia Neuberger
Ms Sonia Newhouse
Mrs Geraldine Norman MA
Ms Prue O'Day
Mrs Jill Oddy
Ms Meryl O'Keefe BA
Ms Sally O'Sullivan
Miss Jennifer Over
Miss Dianne Oxley
Miss 'P'
Miss Jane Packer
Miss Claudia Payne MVO
Miss Sylvia Pearce BA (Cantab) MA
Lady Penn
Ms Penny Perrick
Mrs Nora Perry
Mrs Diana Phillips
Mrs Georgina Phillips
Ms Sue Phipps BA
Mrs JS Pitman
Lady Pitt
Mrs Louise Pleydell-Bouverie
The Hon Mrs Olga Polizzi

Miss Eve Pollard
Ms Nyree Dawn Porter OBE
Mrs Nana Prevett BSc (Econ)
Mrs Margaret Prosser
Mrs Elizabeth Proudlock
Ms JB Provost
Miss Laurie Purden MBE
Miss Wendy Ramshaw FSIAD FRSA
Miss Jean Rankine BA MPhil
Mrs Diana Rau BA
Lady Read
Miss Jane Reed
Miss Elizabeth Rees-Jones BA
Miss Betty Richardson Soc SC Cert FIPM
Mrs Gillian Rides
Mrs Pida Ripley MA DICP AKC
Mrs Anita Roddick
Mrs Marion Roe
Mrs J Rosenberg
Miss Bridget Rowe
Miss Janine Roxborough Bunce MIPR
Ms Sue Roxburgh
Mrs JL Sage
Miss Judith Salinson
Ms Josephine Sandilands
Lady Saunders
Ms Anna Scher
Dr Julia Schofield BSc PhD MBCS
Mrs Ian Service
Miss Faith Seward MBE BA Adv Dip Ed
Miss Henrietta Shaw BA
Miss Caroline Sheppard
Mrs Mary Seton Sheppard
Miss Pauline Shuker
Ms Janet Silver MPhil FBCO MBIM
Mrs Anthony Skyrme
Ms Audrey Slaughter
Miss Maureen Sleeman BA
Ms Sue Slipman
Mrs Anne Sloman BA
Mrs Frances Smith BA
Ms Maureen Smith
Mrs Nicola Smith
Miss Sonja Smith
Mrs Sallie Snowman
Lady Charles Spencer-Churchill
Ms Rosemary Squire BA
Mrs Joan Stephens BA
Lady Stewart OBE
Ms Daphne Stewart MA
Mrs F E Stewart Murray
Mrs Gerald Stockley MA
Ms Sue Stoessl BA
Mrs Doris Stokes
Miss Veronica Stokes BA DipEd DArch

Ms Moira Stuart
Miss Claire Stubbs
Ms Una Stubbs
Ms Norma Sullivan
Miss Liz Sutherland
Mrs Barbara Switzer
Ms Cleo Sylvestre
Mrs Barbara Tate PSWA RMS SBA FRSA
Mrs G Tebape
Mrs Netta Thomas MBE
Ms Valerie Thompson
Dr Ruth Thomson MB ChB DCH
    DRCOG FRCP
Ms Sue Thorne
Ms Tryphena Todd
Mrs Claire Tomlinson BA
Miss Sheila Tracy
Baroness Trumpington
Miss Frances Tulloch MA Dip Theol
Baroness Turner of Camden
Lady Vaizey
Mrs JM Viall
Ms Caroline Walker BSc MSc
Mrs Christine Walker
Miss Janet Walker PPE
Mrs Sheila Walker CBE JP
Miss Elizabeth Wallace
Ms Noelle Walsh BA
Dame Anne Warburton DCVO CMG MA
Miss Marcia Warburton
Mrs Stella Wardell
Miss Frances Watt HND OND
Miss Molly Weir
Dr Susan Wharton BA PhD
Mrs Lucia White BA MA
Mrs Susan White
Miss Katherine Whitehorn MA LLD
Lady Wilcox
Ms Shireen Williams
Miss Stephanie Williams BA
Ms Susan Williams
Miss Joan Wills VPSWA ASAF FRSA
Ms Helen Willsher-Powlette
Mrs Margaret Wingfield CBE
Ms Nancy Wise
Mrs Leila Wishart
Ms Andrea Wonfor BA
Mrs Anna Wyner
Ms Paula Yates

26th October 1987
THEME: SURVIVAL

Miss Diane Abbot

272

Ms Kate Adie
Mrs Caroline Agar
Miss Muriel Allen
Lady Anson
Mrs Margaret Anstey
Mrs Christina Appleyard
Miss Sarah Arkle
Miss Joan Armatrading
Mrs J Ashbourn
Mrs Anne Ashby
Miss Jane Asher
Mrs Elizabeth Aziz
Mrs Charlotte Baden-Powell
Ms Mary Baker
Mrs Iris Banham-Lee
Ms Joanna Barlow
Miss Wendy Barnes
Miss Ann Barr
Mrs Joan Barrell
Dr Yvonne Barton
Dr Catherine Baudino
Mrs Helen Beard
Mrs Jillian Becker
Miss Vivienne Becker
Mrs Patricia Beecham
Ms Floella Benjamin
Mrs Susan Benjamin
The Countess Jill Bernadotte of Wisborg
Miss Mary Berry
Miss Babs Beverley
Miss Joy Beverley
Mrs Mary Beverley
Miss Teddie Beverley
Dr Beulah Bewley
Mrs Jennifer Birch
Mrs Georgina Boosey
Miss Jane Bown
Mrs Evette Branson
Miss Katie Boyle
Viscountess Bridgeman
Miss Jill Bristow
Mrs Diana Britten
Miss Janet Brown
Ms Sandra Brown
Miss Tanya Bruce-Lockhart
Mrs Kate Burgess
Mrs Ann Burleigh
Mrs Susanna Burr
Mrs Rosemarie Burrow
Miss Maggie Butler
The Hon Victoria Buxton
Ms Janice Cairns
Mrs Paddy Campbell
Miss Bunny Campione
Miss Annabel Carter

Ms Sally Cartwright
The Hon Rhiannon Chapman
Mrs Margaret Charrington
Mrs Madeline Chase-Thomas
Ms Jill Churchill
Miss Lindka Cierach
Miss Felicity Clark
Ms Margaret Clark
Mrs Olive Clarke
Mrs Stella Clarke
Miss Melanie Clore
Mrs Anne Collins
Mrs Rosita Conway
Mrs Margaret Cooper
Ms Judy Cornwell
Mrs Winifred Coulson
Miss Marilyn Cox
Mrs Mary Craig
Professor Rosemary Cramp
Miss Annabel Croft
Dr Sally Davies
Mrs Sue Davies
Ms Alison Davis
Mrs Lillian Davis
Miss Alison Dean
Ms Brenda Dean
Mrs Elaine Dean
Mrs Caroline de Courcy-Ireland
Mrs Sylvia Denman
Mrs Jean Denton
Ms Sally Dexter
Miss Anne Dickinson
Ms Pamela Dimmock
Mrs Julie Donnelly
Mrs Mikki Doyle
Ms Lindsay Duncan
Ms Sophie Dupre
Mrs Elena Duran-Emmerson
Mrs Sheila Edwards
Dr Marta Elian
Mrs Joan Ellerton
Ms Jessica Elliott
Mrs Lyn Ellis
Mrs Sheilah Ellis
Dr Elizabeth Evans
Mrs Eria Evans
Mrs Pennie Evans
Mrs Audrey Eyton
Ms Sonia Falaschi
Ms Susan Farmer
Mrs Helena Felix
Miss Penny Ffitch-Heyes
Mrs Karen Finch
Miss Allison Fisher
Mrs Shreela Flather

Ms Jo Foley
Miss Annette Fookes
Mrs Emma Ford
Mrs Nancy Forrester
Mrs Betty Foster
Miss Mary Frampton
Dr Winifred Francis
Ms Lynne Franks
Mrs Erika Frei
Ms Dawn French
Miss Elizabeth Gage
Miss Davinia Galica
Miss Jocelyn Galsworthy
Mrs Vera Gandy
Mrs Cordelia Gara-George
Mrs Hilda Garfield
Mrs Janet Gaymer
Miss Phyllis George
Mrs Ann Gibson
Mrs Anne Gibson
Mrs Rosalind Gilmore
Ms Ruth Glick
Mrs Elspeth Goodchild
Ms Maggie Goodman
Professor Margaret Gowing
Mrs Ann Green
Miss Elizabeth Green
Ms Felicity Green
Miss Janet Green
Miss Jennefer Greenwood
Miss Patricia Gregory
Miss Katherine Groves
Mrs Tricia Guild
Miss Katherine Hadley
Miss Judith Hall
Ms Maggi Hambling
Ms Barbara Hardwick
Miss Doris Hare
Pamela, Lady Harlech
Mrs Ann Harris
Mrs Jackie Harris
Ms Josephine Hart
Miss Lesley Hart
Miss PM Hart
Mrs Romaine Hart
Miss Marea Hartman
Mrs Tamara Hassani
Miss Felicity Hawkins
Miss Joyce Hawkins
Miss Anna Healey-Fenton
Mrs Frances Heaton
Mrs Kate Herbert-Hunting
Mrs Cathleen Herring
Mrs Gill Hewitt
Miss Angela Heylin

Miss Janet Hildreth
Mrs Phyllis Hindle
Miss Isabel Hitchman
Mrs Clare Hoare
Ms Jennifer Hocking
Surgeon Commander Elizabeth Hodges
Miss Min Hogg
Lady Holland-Martin
Dr Sheila Hollins
Ms Holmes
Ms Nichola Hood
Miss Rosamund Horwood-Smart
Ms Barbara Hosking
Miss Verity Hudson
Ms Susi Hush
Miss Diana Hutchinson
Mrs Cynthia Iliffe
Mrs Susan Iwanek
Lady Jacomb
Mrs Carolyn James
Ms Geraldine James
Miss Elly Jansen
Lady Jay
Dr Marcelle Jay
Mrs Zoë Jenkinson
Ms Brenda Jones
Miss Greta Jones
Miss Sarah Jones
Ms Clare Kahtan
Miss Hilary Kay
Ms Ann Keast
Miss Jane Kelly
Ms Linda Kelsey
Miss Penny Kemp
Ms Helena Kennedy
Wing Commander Kingston
Mrs Jenny Kirkpatrick
Miss Gillian Kitching
Simone Klass
Dame Jill Knight
Miss Wyn Knowles
Miss Maureen Laker
Mrs Marjorie Langford
Ms Di Latham
Ms Felicity Lawrence
Miss Ann Lawson
Miss Gillian Lawton
Miss Barbara Lee
Mrs Lynda Lee-Potter
Miss Moira Leggat
Miss Victoria Legge-Bourke
Ms Joy Leitch
Ms Ann Leslie
Miss Pat Liddiard
Ms Maureen Lipman

Ms Rosie Logan
Miss Frederica Lord
Miss Erna Low
Lady Lyons
Mrs Mary Lyons
Ms Kerry Mackenzie
The Hon Diana Makgill
Miss Anne Manson
Mrs Caroline Marland
Mrs Genet March
Mrs Wenche Marshall Foster
Mrs Eve Martin
Sister Mary Perpetua
Ms Barbara Maxwell
Dr Zena Maxwell
Ms Angela McArthur
Dr Alison McCartney
Mrs Heather McConnell
Ms Anne McDermid
Ms Frankie McGowan
Ms Hilda McKerral
Mrs Suzy Menkes
Miss Vida Menzies
Lady Micklethwait
Ms Lori Miles
Dr Rosalind Miles
Miss Simone Mirman
The Hon Rosamond Monckton
Ms Hazel Montague
Mrs Diana Moran
Ms Patricia Mordecai
Mrs Jan Morgan
Ms Janice Morley
Lady Morris of Kenwood
Mrs Margaret Morrison
Mrs Patricia Morrison
Ms Clare Mulholland
Miss Sheila Needham
Miss Caroline Neville
Ms Sonia Newhouse
Dr Lotte Newman
Brigadier Shirley Nield
Miss Dee Nolan
Mrs Geraldine Norman
Ms Prue O'Day
Mrs Jane Olivier
Miss Dian Oxley
Miss Jennifer Over
Miss Jane Packer
Mrs Jane Mancroft Page
Mrs Alix Palmer
Miss Jane Parker-Smith
Ms Ruth Parr
Mrs Elizabeth Parsons
Mrs Lyndy Payne

Lady Penn
Ms Sue Phipps
Miss Fiona Pitt-Kethley
The Hon Mrs Olga Polizzi
Mrs AAB Poole
Mrs Nana Prevett
Miss Laurie Purden
Mrs Elaine Quigley
Ms Toni Racklin
Miss Wendy Ramshaw
Miss Prudence Raper
Ms Elizabeth Rees-Jones
Miss Betty Richardson
Miss Fiona Richmond
Mrs Paula Ridley
Miss Angela Rippon
Miss Pat Roberts
Ms Patricia Roberts
Mrs Marion Roe
Mrs Jennifer Rosenberg
Miss Ann Rossiter
Miss Bridget Rowe
Miss Janine Roxborough-Bunce
Ms Susan Roxburgh
Councillor Mrs Elizabeth Russell
Mrs Elizabeth Rutherford
Mrs Susan Ryan
Mrs Peggy Sage
Miss Judith Salinson
Lady Saunders
Miss Jennifer Saunders
Ms Anna Scher
Dr Julia Schofield
Miss Emma Sergeant
Mrs Mary Service
Dr Chandra Sethurajan
Miss Faith Seward
Miss Linda Sharp
Mrs Susan Shaw
Mrs Louise Sheaves
WPC Sheehan
Dr Shirley Sherwood
Ms Janet Silver
Ms Posy Simmonds
Miss Deborah Simms
Mrs Caro Skyrme
Miss Maureen Sleeman
Miss Mara Smit
Mrs Elizabeth Smith
Miss Sonja Smith
Mrs Sallie Snowman
Ms Sally Soames
Miss Shirley St Claire-Smith
Mrs Irene Stein
Mrs Joan Stephens

Mrs Pamela Stevens
Mrs Floi Stewart-Murray
Mrs Kathy Stockley
Miss Sue Stoessl
Miss Carole Stone
Mrs Ann Stubbs
Mrs Clare Stubbs
Miss Una Stubbs
Mrs Barbara Switzer
Miss Cleo Sylvestre
Mrs Nancy Tait
Mrs Barbara Tate
Mrs Aileen Taylor
Miss Jane Taylor
Ms Annette Taylor-Schofield
Miss Carol Thatcher
Miss Heidi Thomas
Mrs Netta Thomas
Ms Valerie Thompson
Mrs Sue Thomson
Miss Angela Thorne
Miss Sue Thorne
Miss Tryphena Todd
Mrs Tessa Traeger
Lieutenant Leisa Tucker
Baroness Turner of Camden
Mrs Jean Tyrrell
Lady Vaizey
Mrs Mary Van Reyk
Ms Dena Vane
Ms Caroline Walker
Miss Janet Walker
Mrs Sheila Walker
Ms Susan Walker
Miss Elizabeth Wallace
Miss Vivien Wallace
Miss Carol Wallis
Miss Noelle Walsh
Miss Marcia Warburton
Mrs Marion Ward
Mrs Stella Wardell
Ms Diana Warwick
Mrs Anna Waters
Ms Janice Watson
Miss Frances Watt
Mrs Shirley Webster-Jones
Miss Ceri Weeks
Miss Molly Weir
Miss Laura Wells
Dr Susan Wharton
Miss Jayne White
Mrs Lucia White
Mrs Susan White
Mrs Mary Whitehouse
Lady Wilcox

Miss Sally Ann Wilkinson
Ms Jennifer Williams
Miss Stephanie Williams
Miss Jeanne Wills
Miss Joan Wills
Miss Anna Wing
Miss Marguerite Wood
Miss Annette Worsley-Taylor
Mrs Hannah Wright
Mrs Anna Wyner

Monday 24th October 1988
THEME: GIVE ME TIME

Mrs Caroline Agar
Mrs Anne Ainsley MIPR
Miss Muriel Allen
Mrs Ameera Alli
Mrs Hazel Ampaw
Mrs Margaret Anstey LLB
Ms Aileen Armitage
Ms Pamela Armstrong
Mrs Anne Ashby SRN
Miss Ruth Ashton SRN SCM MTD
Ms Marilyn Aslani
Mrs Glenda Aussenberg
Miss Zeinab Badawi BA
Mrs Charlotte Baden-Powell AA Dip
  RIBA
Miss Heather Baillie BSc
Miss Marilyn Baker
Mrs Mary Baker
Mrs Susie Banks
Miss Elizabeth Barker
Ms Joanna Barlow
Dame Josephine Barnes OBE FRCP
  FRCOG
Miss Ann Barr
Miss Danielle Barr
Mrs Joan Barrell
Ms Lynn Barton
Mrs Helen Beard
Mrs Patricia Beecham
Miss Jennifer Beeston MA
Ms Vastiana Belfon BA
Ms Floella Benjamin
Miss Babs Beverley
Miss Joy Beverley
Mrs Mary Beverley BA
Miss Teddie Beverley
Mrs Gay Biddlecombe
Miss Mhairi Black
Mrs Jenny Blanc
Mrs S Bonadie-Arning MA BSc

Miss Jane Bown MBE
Viscountess Bridgeman MA
Miss Geraldine Bridgewater
Ms Sarah Brightman
The Hon Jaqumine Bromage
Mrs MW Bromiley SRP MCSP
Mrs Jennifer Bryant-Pearson
Mrs Norma Buckle
Mrs Rosemary Bugden
Mrs Katie Bunn
Mrs Rose-Marie Burrow
Ms Iris Burton
Miss Maggie Butler Dip AD
The Hon Cindy Buxton
Miss Ivy Cameron
Ms Paddy Campbell
Miss Bunny Campione
Ms Marcia Carlowe
Ms Sally Cartwright
Cathryn Countess Cawdor
Sandra Chalmers
Mrs Margaret Jean Chambers ALCN
Mrs Judith Chaplin MA
The Hon Rhiannon Chapman LLB AKC
  FIPM
Ms Caroline Charles
Mrs Madeline Chase Thomas
Dame Elizabeth Chesterton DBE ARIBA
  FRTPI
Miss Rosalind Christie
Felicity Clark
Ms Chris Clyne
Mrs Peggy Cole
Ms Gill Coleridge
Mrs Judy Cornwell JP
Miss Gillian Craig BA
Mrs Mary Craig MA
Miss Annabel Croft
Ms Penny Croft
Mrs Susan Crook
Miss Dorothy Cumpsty
Ms Sinead Cusack
Mrs Tessa Dahl
Miss J A Deeley FCIS
Sister Marie DeLourdes
Professor Juliana DeneKamp BSc PhD
  DSC
Mrs Jean Denton BSc FINST M FIMI
  FRSA
Lieut L M Derben
Ms Michele Deverall MSC BSc
Miss Anne Dickinson FIPR CBIM
Ms Sue Dobson BA
Mrs Elizabeth C Docherty
Sister Winifred Dolan

Ms Mikki Doyle
Ms Gillian DuCharme MA
Mrs Dorothy Dunnett
Ms Sophie Dupre
Ms Ann-Marie Dyas BA
Ms Dorothea Edwards
Mrs Elkan
Ms Patricia Ellis BA
Mrs Sheilah Ellis BEM
Miss Elizabeth Emanuel
Miss Roslyn Emblin
Mrs Gillian Eustace
Dr Elizabeth Evans BSc PhD
Mrs Audrey Eyton
Miss Ailsa Fairley
Mrs Susie Faux
Miss Penny Ffitch-Heys
Ms Helen Field
Mrs Janet Filderman
Mrs Karen Finch OBE FRSA
Mrs Janet Fitch
Ms Jo Foley
Mrs Emma Ford
Mrs Nancy Forrester
Mrs Betty Fox
Miss Ruth Fox BSc
Dr Winifred Francis MD FRCOG
Miss Rosemary French MA
Mrs E C Fulthorpe LLB
Miss Davinia Galicia MBE
Mrs Janet Gaymer MA LLM
Miss Rosslyn Gibbs
Ms Sheila Gish RADA Diploma
Ms Ruth Glick
Miss Anne Godfrey BA
Mrs Elspeth Goodchild BSc
Ms Maggie Goodman
Miss Hannah Gordon
Mrs Joan Grahame
Mrs Mary-Anne Grant
Mrs Theresa Grant Peterkin
Ms Elizabeth Green
Miss Janet Green
Mrs Judi Green BA
Miss Penny Green
Miss Jennefer Greenwood BSc
Miss Patricia Gregory
Ms Tricia Guild
Mrs Joan Gunn
Dr Jennifer Gunning PhD
Mrs Beverley Haig AVA
Miss Judith Hall
Mrs Pauline Halliday
Mrs Sue Hammerson OBE
Miss Doris Hare MBE

Pamela Lady Harlech BA
Lady Harris
Mrs Ann Harris
Mrs Loelia Harris
Miss Mollie Harris ACIS
Ms Karen Harrison
Ms Josephine Hart
Ms Nicola Hart BA
Dr Marea Hartman CBE
Ms Marjorie Hayter
Mrs Frances Heaton BA LLB
Mrs Diana Henderson
Ms Sandra Hepburn
Mrs Kate Herbert-Hunting
Miss Melanie Herfet
Mrs Charlotte Hilton
Ms Jennifer Hocking
Miss Victoria Holt
Miss Nichola J Hood AISTD
Ms Barbara Hosking OBE
Ms Ros Howells
Ms Janet Hull MA
Ms Andrea Hulmes
Lady Hulton
Ms Diana Hutchinson
Dr Fay Hutchinson MB BS
Miss Margaret Hyde
Ms Sheila Innes MA CBIM FRSA
Miss Eve Jackson
Mrs Carolyn James
Lady Jay
Margaret Jay
The Viscountess Jellicoe SRN
Ms Susi Jenkins
Ms Kay M Jones BA
Miss Margaret Jones
Miss Sarah Jones BA
Ms Grace Jordan
Ms Linda Kelsey
Ms Felicity Kendal
Ms Helena A Kennedy
Mrs Marjorie Kenning OBE
Mrs Etta Imogene Khwaja BED
Mrs Georgina Kirby JP
Mrs Ann M Kitching
Miss Simone Klass
Miss Wyn Knowles
Miss Enriqueta Koch De Godreynd
Professor Eva M Kohner MD FRCP
Ms Dorothy Kuya
Mrs Hilary Laidlaw Thomson
Miss Verity Ann Lambert Doc LAW
Lady Lucinda Lambton
Commandant Anthea Larken ADC
  WRNS

Ms Felicity Lawrence
Miss Judy Leden
Miss Victoria Legge-Bourke LVO
Mrs Charlotte Lessing
Mrs Patricia Lewis-Graham
Ms Maureen Lipman
Miss Frederica Lord BA
Miss Jeanette Lovell
Dr Erna Low PhD
Mrs Anthony Lyle Skyrme
Lady Lyons
Ms Mary Lyons
Miss Eleanor MacDonald MBE BA
Mrs Julia MacDougall
Ms Sue MacGregor
Ms Kerry MacKenzie
Mrs Alison MacKonochie
Ms Kirsty MacMaster LLB Dip BA
Mrs Bo Maggs
Lady Olga Maitland
The Hon Diana Makgill LVO
Ms Suzi Malin
Dr Anna Mann PhD BA
Ms Anne Manson BA
Ms Janette Marshall BA
Ms Anne McCaffrey BA
Dr Joy McCalman SRN
Ms Frankie McGowan
Professor Susan McKenna Lawlor
Ms Julia McKenzie FGSM
Mrs Betty McLeish BA
Miss Shelagh McLeish
Ms Anna McNair-Scott
Lady Medawar BSc MA
Ms Leonie Mellinger
Mrs Doreen Miller JP
Madame Simone Mirman
Mrs Diana Ruth Moran
Lady Morris of Kenwood
Mrs C E Morris
Mrs Margaret Morrison BEM
Mrs Patricia Morrison BA
Professor Elaine Murphy MD FRC Psych
Ms Jenni Murray
Mrs Lynette Murray RN RM
Ms Angela Neustatter
Mrs Carolyn Newman
Dr Lotte Newman BSc MBBS LRCP
  MRCS FRGCP
Miss Emma Nicholson
Brigadier Shirley P Nield ADC BA
Ms Barbara Nokes
Miss Detta O'Cathain OBE BA
Mrs Jill Oddy
Ms Rita O'Regan

Miss Jane Packer
Ms Elaine Page
Miss Michaela Pain
Mrs Betty Parsons MBE
Mrs Elizabeth Parsons BSc
Miss Sally Pasmore
Miss Deirdre Louise Patten
Dr June Paterson-Brown MB ChB
Ms Sheilagh Patterson
Lady Penn
Mrs RT Perera
Ms Penny Perrick
Mrs Pauline Perry MA FRCP FRSA
Ms Barbara Peters
Mrs Harold Phillips D of OStJ
Ms Sue Phipps
Mrs S Phoenix MBE MS
Miss Susan Pike SRN
Miss Fiona Pitt-Kethley BA
Mrs O Polizzi
Ms Toni Racklin
Miss Leela Ramdeen MA BED
Ms Wendy Ramshaw
Ms Esther Rantzen
Miss Prudence Raper
Ms Susan Raven BA
Ms Susan Read BA
Ms Jane Reed
Mrs June Rees
Ms Sheila Reiter
Mrs L Reveley BPharm
Mrs Nancy Richards
Miss Fiona Richmond
Ms Pida Ripley MA AKC
Ms Patricia Roche
Ms Su Rogers BSc
Ms Elizabeth Rorison
Ms Wendy Rose-Neil BA
Mrs Jenifer B Rosenberg
Ms Bridget Rowe
Miss Janine Roxborough Bunce MIPR
Mrs Elizabeth Rutheford JP BA
Mrs Doris Saatchi BA
Mrs Suzy Sainsbury
Ms Jennifer Saunders
Ms Anna Scher
Miss Caroline Schicht
Dr Julia Schofield BSc PhD
Ms Clare Selerie-Grey
Mrs Mary Service
Miss Faith M Seward MBE BA
Mrs MR Seymour MISPE MBIM
Miss Linda Sharp
Mrs Felicia Sharples
Dr Shirley Sherwood MA DPhil

Dr Janet Silver MPhil FBIM
Miss Deborah Simms
Ms Alison Smith BA
Mrs Elizabeth Smith MA
Mrs Kay Smith
Ms Patricia Smith
Mrs Sallie Snowman
The Hon Emma Soames
Lady Charles Spencer-Churchill
Mrs Leone Stanhouse
Miss Fiona Staniland MA
Mrs Joan Valerie Stephens MA
The Hon Francesca Sternberg
Ms Pamela Stevens
Mrs Floi Stewart-Murray
Ms Gerald Stockley
Ms Sue Stoessl
Miss M Veronica Stokes BA
Miss Carole Stone
Miss Alison Streeter
Cristina Stuart
Ms Moira Stuart
Ms A Stubbs
Miss Clare Stubbs
Miss Una Stubbs
Mrs Elaine Sunderland JP MA BSc
Mrs Barbara Switzer
Mrs Barbara Tate PSWA RMS ASAF
    FSBA FRSA
Ms Terry Tavner
Mrs Aileen Taylor BA PGCE
Diane Taylor
Ms Annette Taylor-Schofield
Dr Ruth B Thompson MB ChB FRCP
    DRCOG DCH
Uta Thompson
Ms Valerie Thompson
Miss Sue Thorne
Mrs Joy Thorpe
Mrs Sue Tinson BA
Mrs Tryphena Todd SRN
Miss Pamela Townley
Ms Margaret Townshend
Miss Helen Tridgell
Baroness Trumpington
Miss Frances Tulloch MA
Baroness Turner of Camden
Miss Dorothy Tutin CBE
Mrs Sarah Jacqueline Tyacke BA
Dr JM Tyrell OBE LLD DL
The Lady Marina Vaizey
Mrs Rosemary Van Musschenbroek BSc
Mrs Rosemary Verey
Mrs Deirdre Vine
Mrs Jean Wadlow

Mrs Daphne Wakefield FSCT
Mrs Kim Walker
Mrs Owen Walker CBE JP
Miss Elizabeth Wallace
Miss Vivien Wallace
Miss Phyllis Walters
Miss Brenda Warburton ACIB
Miss Marcia Warburton
Mrs Elizabeth D Ward BEM
Mrs MO Ward
Ms Diana Warwick BA
Mrs Rachel Waterhouse CBE MA PhD
Miss Frances L Watt
Ms Lizzie Webb
Mrs Shirley Webster-Jones
Miss Molly Weir
Ms Bernice Weston
Mrs Betty I Weston
Dr Susan Wharton BA PhD
Mrs Susan White
Miss Katharine Whitehorn MA LID
Mrs EA Why BA
Mrs Anne Wicks BSc Soc
Miss Sally Ann Wilkinson
Colonel Violet Williams
Ms Jeanne Mary Willis
Ms Russell Willis Taylor
Mrs Peter Wilmot-Sitwell
Mrs Rahera Windsor
Miss Anna Wing
Mrs Margaret Wingfield CBE
Miss Nancy Wise
Mrs Anna Wyner
Mrs Marguerite Wood JP BA MCSP
Mrs Claire Woodroffe
Ms Bridget Woods
Miss Vicki Woods
The Lady Young of Graffham

Monday 16th October 1989
THEME: HELP

Ms Lesley Abdela
Ms Linda Agran
The Countess of Airlie CVO
Ms Maggie Alderson MA
Miss Muriel Allen
Mrs Jill Allen-King MBE
Mrs Ameera Alli
Ms Brenda Almond BA MPhil
Ms Valerie Amos BA MA
Professor Kathleen Anderson OBE BSc
    PHD CChems FRSC
Miss Moira Anderson OBE Dip RSAM

Ms Susan Angoy BA MA
Dr Barbara Ansell CBE MD FRCS FRCP
Mrs Margaret Anstey LLB
Mrs Anne Antoszewska
Mrs Aileen Armitage
Miss Pamela Armstrong
Mrs Anne Ashby SRN SCM
Miss Jane Asher
Miss Ruth Ashton RGN RM MTD
Mrs Vivienne Ashworth FInst LEx
Ms Marilyn Aslani
Mrs Barbara Attenborough
Ms Claire Attenborough
Mrs Liz Attenborough
Miss Tracy Axten
Mrs Elizabeth Azis
Mrs Charlotte Baden-Powell AA Dip
    RIBA
Miss Glenda Bailey BA
Miss Elizabeth Barker
Ms Joanne Barlow FRGS
Mrs Belinda Barnes
Miss Marisol Barnes MECI
Mrs Mary Barnes
Mrs Rosie Barnes BA
Miss Danielle Barr
Mrs Joan Barrell
Miss Jocelyn Barrow OBE BA MA
Ms Lynn Barton
Dr Catherine Baudino BA PhD
Ms Marilyn Baxter
Mrs Helen Beard
Ms Vastiana Belfon BA
Mrs Sally Bell
Ms Floella Benjamin
Mrs Rosemary Berry
Mrs Elsie Bertram MBE
Ms Penny Bickerstaff LLB ACA
Ms Charlotte Bingham
Ms Ann Blackburn
Mrs Mary Bottara
Mrs Louise Botting BSc
Miss Jane Bown MBE DLitt
Mrs Ann Bowtell BA CB
Ms Jenny Bradley
Miss Margaret Brain OBE
Mrs Rosalind Brent BA MSc
Mrs Mary Bromiley MCSP RPT
Mrs Pauline Brown
Ms Tanya Bruce-Lockhart
Mrs Rosebud Bruney
Dr Margaret Buckler MB ChB DRCOG
Mrs Rosemarie Burrow
Ms Iris Burton
The Hon Victoria Buxton

Ms Ivy Cameron
Ms Paddy Campbell
Ms Sarah Campbell BA
Miss Lynn Carmichael ACMA
Miss Sally Cartwright
Lady Cave BA
Miss Judith Chalmers
Miss Sandra Chalmers BA
Ms Caroline Charles
Dr Anne Charlton BA MEd PhD
Mrs Sharon Christians
Miss Lindka Cierach
Miss Felicity Clark
Mrs Olive Clark MBE JP
Ms Chris Clyne
Mrs Peggy Cole
Ms Susan Collier
Mrs Ivor Connick
Ms Shirley Cooklin
Mrs Maria Coombs
Ms Judy Cornwell
Mrs Edwina Coven CBE JP DL
Mrs Mary Craig MA
Ms Janet Crawford
Miss Annabel Croft
Mrs Tessa Dahl
Mrs Elizabeth Davys Wood PSLm SWA
Miss Linda Day
Sister Marie de Lourdes
Mrs Sylvia Denman LLM
Mrs Jean Denton BSc CBIM FIMI
    FCInstM
Miss Anne Dickinson FIPR CBIM
Mrs Elizabeth Docherty
Ms Mikki Doyle
Mrs Dorothy Dunnett
Miss Ann-Marie Dyas BA
Miss Karen Earl
Ms Patricia Ellis BA
Mrs Sheilah Ellis BEM
Mrs Elizabeth Emanuel
Miss Roslyn Emblin
Ms Amanda Evans
Dr Elizabeth Evans BSc PhD
Dr Susannah Eykyn MB BS MRCP
    FRCPath
Mrs Audrey Eyton
Miss Ailsa Fairley
Ms Lynda Farran
Mrs Roma Felstein
Dame Peggy Fenner DBE MP
Mrs Anne Ferguson BA
Miss Penny Ffitch-Heyes
Mrs Janet Filderman
Mrs Janet Fitch

Mrs Elizabeth Flach
Mrs Angela Flowers
Ms Jo Foley
Miss Annie Fooks
Mrs Betty Fox
Ms Lynne Franks
Mrs Elizabeth Freeman
Mrs Cordelia Gara-George
Mrs Linda Garbutt
Mrs Janet Gaymer MA LLM
Mrs Marcia Gibson-Watt BA
Mrs Brenda Giles
Ms Sheila Gish
The Lady Glendyne
Mrs Renée Goddard
Miss Anne Godfrey BA
Miss Hannah Gordon FRSA MA
Lady Graham BA MA
Mrs Yvonne Gray
Miss Elizabeth Green
Miss Janet Green
Miss Patricia Gregory
Ms Susan Griggs BA
Miss Patricia Guild
Dr Jennifer Gunning BA PhD
Ms Marney Hague BA MA
Miss Julia Hailes
Mrs Lois Hainsworth
Ms Judith Hall
Ms Unity Hall
Mrs Susan Hammerson OBE
Ms Susan Hampshire DLitt
Miss Christine Hancock BSc
Miss Tina Hancock
Pamela, Lady Harlech BA
Lady Harris
Mrs Susan Harris
Ms Karen Harrison
Ms Josephine Hart
Ms Patricia Hart
Mrs Jocelyn Hay BA
Ms Suzie Hayman
Miss Marjorie Hayter BA
Mrs Edna Healey
Mrs Diana Henderson
Mrs Sandra Hepburn
Miss Caroline Herbert DHist
Mrs Kate Herbert-Hunting
Miss Melanie Herfet
Ms Jane Hewland
Ms Denise Hickling
Mrs Ann Hithersay
Mrs Clare Hoare
Ms Jennifer Hocking
Miss Beverley Hodson BA

Mrs Anona O'Sullivan
Ms Sally O'Sullivan
Ms Elaine Page
Ms Michaela Pain
Mrs Juliet Pannett
Dr June Paterson-Brown MB ChB
Ms Sheilagh Patterson BA
Miss Collette Paul
Mrs Lyndy Payne
Lady Penn RCM
Dr Myrtle Peterkin MB BS(UWI) MRC
    Path
Mrs Georgina Phillips OStJ
Miss Sue Phipps
Mrs ST Phoenix MBE
Miss Susan Pike
Ms Fiona Pitt-Kethley BA
Mrs Sarah Pohlinger BSc
Mrs Olga Polizzi
Councillor Lady Porter
Ms Usha Prashar
Miss Judith Prendergast BA
Mrs Louise Purvis BA
Mrs Elaine Quigley BA
Mrs Ann Rachlin MBE
Ms Toni Racklin
Ms Leela Ramdeen BEd MA
Miss Mary-Elizabeth Raw BVSc FRCVS
    DVR
Miss Jane Reed
Ms Elizabeth Rees-Jones BA
Miss Penny Reid
Miss Eurwen Richards MSc NDD FIFST
Mrs Nancy Richards
Ms Fiona Richmond
Miss Diana Rigg CBE
Miss Angela Rippon
Mrs Ann Roberts
Ms Jackie Roberts
Ms Patricia Roche
Mrs Kathy Rodger
Her Excellency Dr Patricia Rodgers PhD
    MA
Ms Liz Rorison BMus
Miss Patricia Routledge BA
Miss Bridget Rowe
Miss Janine Roxborough Bunce MIPR
Ms Kathryn Samuel
Mrs Yvonne Sarch MA
Mrs Sy Sayer BSc
Ms Anna Scher
Dr Julia Schofield BSc PhD MBCS
Miss Joan Scott MIPR
Dr Lorna Secker-Walker MA PhD
Ms Clare Selerie-Grey BA

Ms Ashleigh Sendin
Mrs Ian Service
Mrs Susan Shaw
Mrs Gillian Shephard
Dr Janet Silver MPhil FBCO FBIM
Ms Petronilla Silver
Miss Liz Skinner
Ms Sue Slipman
Mrs Elizabeth Smith MA
Miss Patricia Smith
Dr Sheila Smith
Mrs Wendy Smyth
Ms Julia Somerville BA
Lady Charles Spencer-Churchill
Dr Margaret Sprackling MB BS FRCP
    FRSA
Mrs Wendy Stephenson
Dr Lindsay Stevens
Ms Pamela Stevens BA BI Dip
Mrs Daphne Stewart JP MA Dip CG
Ms Moira Stuart
Miss Vivien Stuart BA
Miss Clare Stubbs
Miss Una Stubbs
Miss Sherry Suett NDSF
Miss Mollie Sugden MGSM
Miss Liz Sutherland
Pastor Betty Swarbrick Dip Ed
Mrs Barbara Tate PSWA RMS SBA FRSA
Mrs Diana Taylor
Mrs Sue Taylor
Ms Annette Taylor-Schofield
Mrs Netta Thomas MBE
Mrs Valerie Thompson
Dr Ruth Thomson MB ChB
Miss Sue Thorne
Mrs Elizabeth Tilberis BA
Ms Heather Tilbury
Ms Tryphena Todd
Mrs Tessa Traeger
Ms Di Trevis
Miss Helen Tridgell
The Baroness Trumpington
Mrs Winifred Tumim JP MA FRSA
Mrs Myra Turnball JP
Baroness Turner of Camden
The Lady Vaizey MA
Miss Lucia Van der Post BA
Mrs Jean Varnam JP
Ms Deirdre Vine BA
Mrs Anna Vinton
Miss Virginia Wade OBE BSc D Laws
Mrs Daphne Wakefield FSCT
Ms Kim Walker
Mrs Owen Walker CBE JP

Ms Ann Wallace
Miss Elizabeth Wallace
Miss Brenda Warburton ACIB
Mrs Brenda Ward MBE
Mrs Camilla Warner
Miss Janice Watson AGSM
Miss Frances Watt
Ms Ruth Watts-Davis
Mrs Shirley Webster-Jones
Miss Molly Weir
Mrs Betty Weston
Miss Sally Whitaker
Miss Jayne White FBAPT
Ms Kim Whiteford Dip Art
The Hon Mrs Whitehead
Ms Maggie Whitlum
Mrs Anne Wicks BSc
The Lady Wilcox
Ms Sally Ann Wilkinson
Colonel Violet Williams
Ms Helen Willsher
Ms Colleen Wilson LLB
Miss Nancy Wise
Mrs Kath Worrall MA
Mrs Anna Wyner
Mrs Patsy Yardley
Dr Kate Young PhD
Mrs Jennie Younger
Miss Carrie Zetter

Monday 15th October 1990
THEME: CHALLENGE OF THE 90S

Ms Lesley Abdela MBE
Ms Louise Adams BA
Mrs Bandana Ahmad BA
Mrs Matti Alderson
Ms Valerie Amos BA MA
Mrs Aileen Armitage BA
Ms Pamela Armstrong
Mrs Romi Arora Dip SW CQSW
Miss Jane Asher
Miss Ruth Ashton SRN SGM MTD
Mrs Jane Atkinson MIPR
Mrs Liz Attenborough
Ms Tracy Axten
Miss Alison Backhouse
Mrs Charlotte Baden-Powell AADip RIBA
Ms Glenda Bailey
Ms Heather Baillie
Mrs Mary Baker
Mrs Belinda Barnes
Mrs Mary Barnes
Mrs Rosie Barnes BA

Major Allison Barnett MB BS DIH
   DAvMed
Miss Ann Barr
Mrs Joan Barrell
Miss Joan Bartlett OBE
Miss Jenifer Bate BA FRCO LRAM
   ARCM
Mrs Helen Beard
Ms Linda Beard MDes (RSA)
Ms Barbara Beck-Coulter BSc
Miss Anne Beckwith-Smith
Mrs Patricia Beecham
Ms Floella Benjamin
Rev Rachel Benson MA
Lady Bidwell
Mrs Christabel Bielenberg
Ms Maria Bjornson MA
Mrs Sandra Bonadie-Arning BSc MA
Dame Margaret Booth DBE
Miss Jane Bown MBE DLitt
Ms Susan Bradbury
Ms Jenny Bradley
Miss Margaret Brayton MBE FWACN
   FRSA SRN SCM RSC
Mrs Rosalind Brent BA MSc
Miss Emma Bridgewater
Lady Geraldine Brocas, Viscountess
   Jellicoe
Miss Christine Brodie-Cooper BA
Mrs Rory Brookman
Miss Janet Brown
Ms Tanya Bruce-Lockhart
Mrs RT Bruney
The Duchess of Buccleuch
Ms Sally Burgess
Mrs Rosemarie Burrow
Ms Iris Burton
Ms Margaret Busby BA
Captain Victoria Buxton
The Hon Mrs Nona Byrne
Mrs Barbara Calvert QC BSc Econ
Mrs Blythe Campbell
Miss Ffiona Campbell
Ms Paddy Campbell
Miss Bunny Campione
Ms Aileesh Carew
Mrs Anne-Marie Carter HND Electronic
   Eng
Dr Marion Carter BSc PhD
Ms Sally Cartwright
Miss Judith Chalmers
Miss Sandra Chalmers BA
Dr Sandra Chapman DIC PhD
Miss Caroline Chard LLB
Mrs Rosemary Cheetham BA (Cantab)

Ms Tsai Chin MA
Mrs Sharon Christians BA
Miss Lindka Cierach
Ms Felicity Clark
Mrs Gill Clark FCII MCIM DipM
Canon Margaret Clarke
Sister Sarah Clarke
Ms Melanie Clore BA
Ms Chris Clyne
Ms Ellen Cogut
Her Honour Judge Myrella Cohen QC
  LLB
Ms Judith Collins MA PhD
Ms Elizabeth Connell B Mus (Rand)
Ms Kathryn Cooper BA
Miss Heather Couper BSc FRAS
Miss Romy Crewe DipCOT SROT DUS
  MBES
Miss Barbara Crickmore
Ms Katy Cropper
Baroness Cumberledge of Newick CBE
  DL
Mrs Edwina Currie MA MSc
Miss Jilly Curry
The Countess of Dalkeith
Dr Avril Dankworth Doc in Music Ed
Mrs Gloria Davies BA
Ms Louise Davis
Mrs Rosemary Day BA
Mrs Anna de Bailetti
Sister Marie de Lourdes SRN SCM
Mrs Sylvia Denman LLM
Dr Diane Dickens MB CLB FRCPsych
  DPM DCH
Miss Evelyn Dickey BSc
Miss Anne Dickinson FIPR CBIM
Fiamma di San Giuliano
Ms Sue Dobson BA
Sister Winifred Dolan BEd MED
Miss Helene Donnelly BA
  Eng.Degree(PC)
Mrs Sarah Doukas
Ms Joanna Downs BCOM
Mrs Mikki Doyle
Mrs Gillian du Charme MA (Cantab)
Mrs Vivien Duffield CBE MA DLitt RCM
Mrs Ann Duncan
Ms Lindsay Duncan
Ms Sarah Duncan BA
Ms Jennifer Durrant DipFA
Ms Ratna Dutt BA MA CQSW
Ms Anne-Marie Dyas BA
Dr Marta Elian MD
Mrs Jenny Elkan
Mrs Ann Elliot Dip AD Dip ED

Miss Roslyn Emblin
Miss Lesley Exley BA
Mrs Audrey Eyton
Miss Susan Farmer FRSA MIPR
Ms Angela Farrell MA (Cantab)
Ms Roma Felstein
Dame Peggy Fenner DBE MP
Mrs Janet Filderman
Mrs Philippa Finch
Miss Allison Fisher
Miss Julie Fisher
Dr Melissa Fitzgerald
Miss Louise Fitzroy
Ms Jo Foley BA
Miss Annette Fooks
Mrs Emma Ford
Mrs Gillian Ford
Mrs Joanna Foster
Mrs Sandra Fox JP
Ms Jenni Francis DipCAM MIPR
Miss Wynnette Freedman
Miss Emma Freud BA
Ms Lesley Garrett LRAM ARAM
Mrs Jane Garside JP
Mrs Janet Gaymer MA LLM
Miss Phyllis George FRCS
Mrs Margaret Ghilchik BSc MS FRCS
Miss Maggie Gibbon BA
Mrs Ann Gibson Dip Arch
Mrs Zerbanoo Gifford
Ms Sheila Gish ALAM
Ms Renée Goddard
Ms Georgina Godley MA
Mrs Fay Godwin
Ms Maggie Goodman
Miss Hannah Gordon
Ms Christina Gorna
Miss Jane Grantham BEng
Mrs Theresa Grant-Peterkin
Miss Kathleen Grasham
Mrs Clare Graydon-James
Miss Elizabeth Green
Miss Janet Green
Miss Jennefer Greenwood BSc ARICS
Miss Patricia Gregory
Ms Debbie Gresty
Mrs Alison Griffith BSc
Ms Avril Groom MA
Mrs Joan Gunn JP
Dr Jennifer Gunning PhD BA
Ms Betty Guyatt ACIB
Ms Unity Hall
Mrs Daphne Hamilton-Fairley OBE
  MCST LCST
Mrs Sue Hammerson OBE

Mrs Madeline Hamper
Ms Brenda Hancock JP BA Ext Dip Ed
Miss Judith Hanratty LLB LLM
Pamela, Lady Harlech BA
Mrs Karen Harper BEd
Lady Harris
Miss Mollie Harris ACIS
Miss Marea Hartman CBE
Ms Sylvia Heal MP BSc (Econ)
Mrs Edna Healey
Mrs Sandra Hepburn
Ms Carole Herbert
Miss Caroline Herbert DHist
Miss Thena Heshel
Ms Jane Hewland
Ms Angela Heylin
Ms Patricia Hodge
Miss Kate Hoey MP BEd
Professor Sheila Hollins MBBS FRCPsych
Miss Thelma Holt MA
Miss Victoria Holt
Baroness Hooper BA (Laws)
Mrs Joyce Hopkirk
Ms Barbara Hosking OBE
Mrs Sheila Hourston
Ms Margaret Howard
Prof Celia Hoyles BSc MEd PhD
Mrs Caryl Hubbard BA
Ms Gill Hudson
Mrs Greta Hughes BA
Ms Janet Hull MA
Mrs Jean Hunt
Miss Gillian Hush BA
Ms Diana Hutchinson BA
Dr Fay Hutchinson MBE MB BS
Ms Nicola Jacobs
Mrs Barbara Jacquesson
Miss Margery Jagger BSc
Mrs Annette James
Ms Catherine James BA
Ms Geraldine James
Ms Sue James
Lady Jay
Dr Margaret Johnson MD MRCP
Dame Gwyneth Jones
Ms Kay Jones BA
Miss Sarah Jones BA
Mrs Grace Jordan
Ms Linda Kelsey
Ms Helena Kennedy
Ms Nasseem Khan MA FSA
Mrs E Khwaja BEd
Mrs Chrissie Kimmons BA Law
Ms Henny King
Miss Simone Klass MIPR

Mrs Tina Knight
Professor Eva Kohner MD FRCP
Ms Dorothy Kuya Dip Ed
Miss Hilary Laidlaw Thomson
Miss Maureen Laker
Mrs Diana Lamplugh Dip Ed AE/FE
Commandant Anthea Larken ADC
   WRNS
Miss Joanne Lawrence BA MA NBA
Mrs Lynda Lee-Potter
Miss Santina Levey BA AMA FMA
Miss Elizabeth Licence BA
Mrs Janie Lightfoot
Dr Kate Loewenthal BSc PhD ABPS
Miss Jeanette Lovell
Mrs Katharine Lovett
Miss Erna Low PhD MCIM
Her Honour Judge Nina Lowry QC LLB
Professor Christina Lyon LL BS
Miss Morag MacDonald LLB
Ms Kirsty MacMaster LLB BA
Mrs Christine MacNulty FRSA
Ms Bo Maggs
Miss Sarah Mahaffy BA
The Hon Diana Makgill CVO
Ms Suzi Malin
Miss Avril Mansfield MB ChM FRCS
Miss Marguerite Markes BSc FRGS
Mrs Patricia Marshall MSc
Mrs Wenche Marshall-Foster
Ms Pearl McCafferty
Ms Frankie McGowan
Professor Susan McKenna-Lawlor PhD
Miss Julia McKenzie FGSM
Mrs Betty McLeish
Mrs Anna McNair Scott MA
Miss June Mendoza AO RP ROI
Miss Rosemary Michael
Dr Rosalind Miles MA PhD FRSA
Mrs Kathryn Miller
Mrs Barbara Mills QC
Mrs Simone Mirman
Ms Sophie Mirman
Air Commodore RMB Montague ADC
   BSc
Ms Jan Morgan FNAGA
Mrs Katherine Morgan
Mrs Victoria Morgan
Lieutenant Sarah Morley
Lady Morris of Kenwood
Dr Jackie Morris
Miss Sally Morris
Mrs Margaret Morrison BEM
Ms Karen Morse
Ms Kate Moseley MIHE

Ms Rosa Mota
Mrs Jane Muir MA
Ms Carmen Munroe
Mrs Lynne Murphy
Miss Marie Murray
Miss Georgina Nayler
Miss Vee Neild Dip NEBSS
Dr Elizabeth Nelson BA PhD FRSA
Rabbi Julia Neuberger MA (Cantab)
Ms Caroline Neville MIPR
Mrs Yvette Newbold LLB
Dr Lotte Newman BSc MBBS LRCP
    MRCS FRCGP
Mrs Thi Be Nguyen
Ms Caroline Nicholson
Miss Emma Nicholson MP LRAM
    ARCM
Miss Dee Nolan
Ms Prue O'Day
Ms Maria Oshodi
Mrs AVM Palmer MBE
Mrs Juliet Pannett
Ms Sara Parkin RGN
Mrs Georgina Paterson
Mrs Diana Paterson-Fox BSc
Mrs Jean Paton
Ms Ruth Patterson BA
Ms Sheilagh Patterson BA
Mrs Rowena Paxton
Lady Penn RCM
Ms Nadine Peppard CBE BA
Dr Myrtle Peterkin MB BS (UWI) MRC
    Path (Haem)
Mrs Harold Phillips D of OStJ
Miss Anne Pitcher
Ms Fiona Pitt-Kethley BA
Ms Eve Pollard
Ms Usha Prashar BA
Miss Judith Prendergast BA
Mrs Mandy Price
Miss Jane Proctor
Miss Gloria Pullan
Mrs Kailash Puri
Miss Anne Rafferty QC
Ms Leela Ramdeen BEd MA
Miss Esther Rantzen BA MA
Miss Mary-Elizabeth Raw BVSc FRCVS
    DVR
Miss Jane Reed
Ms Helen Rees MA (London) MA
    (Camb)
Dr Margaret Rees MA MB BS BSc DPhil
    MRCOG
Ms Penny Reid BSc
Dr Barbara Reynolds BA

Miss Eurwen Richards MSc NDD FIFST
Miss Ilona Richards
Ms Marcia Richards
Miss Fiona Richmond
Miss Diana Rigg CBE
Miss Angela Rippon
Mrs Carole Roberts NDA
Her Exc Dr Patricia Rodgers PhD MA
Frau Gonke Roscher
Miss Bridget Rowe HND
Miss Janine Roxborough-Bunce MIPR
Mrs Marie Rubin BA
Ms Marcelle Saad
Mrs Shahwar Sadeque MPhil MSc
Ms Joanne Salazar BA
Ms Arundhati Sanyal MSc Psych
Mrs Wendy Savage BA MB FRCOG BCh
Ms Anna Scher
Dr Julia Schofield BSc PhD MBSC
Dr Anne Scott PhD BSc
Ms Patricia Scott
Mrs Myra Scullion SRN SCM
Ms Clare Selerie-Grey BA
Mrs Mary Service
Mrs Susan Shaw
Miss Shirli-Ann Siddall
Ms Elizabeth Sidney
Ms Janet Silver MPhil FBCO FBIM
Ms Posy Simmonds
Mrs Heather Slade-Lipkin BMus GRSM
    ARMCM
Mrs Sallie Snowman
Ms Julia Somerville BA
Mrs Estella Spencer
Dr Sarah Springman MA MPhil MICE
    PhD CEng
The Countess of St Andrews BA MA
Mrs Marcia Stanton
The Hon Francesca Sternberg
Dr Lindsey Stevens MA MB BChir MRCP
Mrs Valerie Stewart
Ms Linda Stoker
Miss Carole Stone
Dr Miriam Stoppard BA
Ms Moira Stuart
Ms Vivien Stuart BA
Mrs Barbara Switzer
Miss Cleo Sylvestre
Ms Elizabeth Symons MA
Ms Muriel Tabinor Dip Ed
Mrs Kathleen Tacchi-Morris
Mrs Barbara Tate PSWA RMS FSBA
    FRSA
Mrs Satinder Taunque BA BABT
Ms Kathy Tayler

Mrs Aileen Taylor BA PGCE
Mrs Diane Taylor
Ms Annette Taylor-Schofield
Dr Ruth Thomson MB ChB SCH FRCP
Miss Angela Thorne
Miss Sue Thorne
Rana Thukral BDS
Mrs Elizabeth Tilberis
Ms Heather Tilbury FISTD MIPR
Ms Tryphena Todd
Mrs Anne Toler BA MIPM
Miss Helen Tridgell
Miss Rhona Tridgell
The Rt Hon Baroness Trumpington
Miss Yuen Har Tse
Mrs Dinah Tuck MA FRSA
Miss Frances Tulloch MA Dip Th
Baroness Turner of Camden
Miss Angela Turner BEd
Mrs Sarah Tyacke BA
Rev Sister Monica Tywang
Miss Caroline Upcher
Lady Marina Vaizey MA
Ms Deirdre Vine BA
Mrs Anna Vinton
Miss Virginia Wade OBE BSc D Laws
The Hon Mrs Caroline Waldegrave
Mrs Christine Walker
Mrs Margaret Walker MSc FCST
Mrs Owen Walker CBE JP
Mrs Grace Walmsley
Ms Noelle Walsh BA
Ms Harriet Walter
Miss Marcia Warburton
Ms Deborah Warner
Ms Diana Warwick BA
Miss Frances Watt HND ONA
Prof D Wedderburn MA (Cantab) DLitt
Mrs Sandy Weinbaum
Miss Molly Weir
Mrs Bernice Weston
Mrs Karen Weston
Mrs Andrea Whalley JP BA
Dr Susan Wharton BA PhD
Miss Fatima Whitbread MBE
Mrs Julie Whiting BSc PGCE
Mrs Lilian Wick LRAM LGSM
Lady Wilcox
Mrs Diane Williams CChem MRSC
Mrs Freya Williams
Miss Lorna Wing
Miss Marion Woodard DipCST FETC
Mrs Claire Woodroffe
Miss Anna Worrall QC LLB
Mrs Kath Worrall MA

Mrs Anna Wyner
Dr Kate Young PhD
Mrs Jennie Younger BA Psych

Monday 28th October 1991
THEME: HARMONY

Ms Lesley Abdela MBE
Ms Jenny Abramsky BA
Ms Louise Adams BA
The Countess of Airlie CVO
Mrs Louise Aitken-Walker
Mrs Matti Alderson
Ms Dounne Alexander-Moore
Miss Charmian Ali
Mrs Ameera Alli
Ms Aileen Armitage BA
Mrs Romi Arora DipSW CQSW
Miss Jane Asher
Mrs Margaret Asher RAM ARCM
Miss Ruth M Ashton OBE
Mrs Jane Atkinson MIPR
Mrs Elizabeth Attenborough
Ms Alison Backhouse
Mrs Charlotte Baden-Powell AADip
  RIBA
Ms Glenda Bailey
Mrs Jane Bailey BEng
Miss Margaret Bailey
Ms Heather Baillie
Mrs Mary Baker MA
Miss Fay Ballard BA
Ms Elizabeth Bargh BA
Mrs Belinda Barnes
Mrs Mary Barnes
Mrs Rosie Barnes MP
Miss Ann Barr
Mrs Joan Barrell
Miss Joan Bartlett MBE OBE
Dr Yvonne O Barton BSc MPhil PhD
  CEng MICE
Miss Jennifer Bate BA FRCO LRAM
  ARCM
Mrs Barbara Beck-Coulter BSc
Mrs Iris Beckham
Mrs Patricia Beecham
Mrs Veronica Benjamin
Ms Martha Bennett MA
Mrs Moira Bennett
Rev Rachel Benson JP MA
Ms Lynne Berry BA MPhil CQSW DipSS
Rev Esme Beswick DipTh
Ms Reena Bhavnani BSc MEd
Miss Maria Björnson MA

Miss Katie Boyle
Ms Susan Bradbury BSc
Ms Jenny Bradley
Miss Margaret Brain OBE SRN SCM
  MTD FBIM FRCOG
Miss Margaret Brayton MBE SRN SCM
  RSCN FWACN FRSA
Miss Cristina Brodie Cooper BA
Mrs Mary Bromiley FCSP RPT (USA) SRP
Miss Janet Brown
Ms Tanya Bruce-Lockhart
Mrs Rosemarie Burrow
Miss Maggie Butler
Captain Victoria Buxton
Ms Carmen Callil BA
Mrs Barbara A Calvert QC BSc AIntArb
Ms Cheryl E Cameron
Ms Ivy Cameron
Mrs Paddy Campbell
Mrs Bunny Campione
Mrs Rosi Capper MA AMA
Ms Sally Cartwright
Dame Beatrice Cayzer DStJ MA
Miss Judith Chalmers
Mrs Judith Chaplin
Mrs Rhiannon Chapman LLB AKC FIPM
Dr Sandra Chapman PhD DIC
Miss Caroline Chard LLB
Ms Hannah Charlton BA MA
Ms Nikki Cheetham BA (Oxon)
Mrs Rosemary Cheetham BA (Cantab)
Dame Elizabeth Chesterton DBE AADipl
  ARIBA Dist TP FRTPI
Miss Tsai Chin
Miss Rosalind Christie
Miss Lindka Cierach
Miss Felicity Clark
Mrs Gillian Clark FCII MCIM DipM
Mrs Jean Clark
Ms Melanie Clore BA
Mrs Hazel Clowes
Ms Chris Clyne
Mrs Nicola Coe
Miss Eileen Cole CBE BA
Professor Dulcie Coleman MBBS MD
  FRCPath FIAC
Dr Judith Collins MA PhD FRSA
Ms Madeleine Colvin
Mrs Rosemary Conley
Ms Susie Constantinides BA
Miss Sarah Cook BA
Ms Sue Cook BA
Dr Heather Couper BSc Hon DLit FRAS
Miss Romy Crewe DipCOT SROT DUS
  MBES

Mrs Susan Crewe
Mrs Ann Crichton BA
Mrs Eliza Crisp
Miss Annabel Croft
Ms Katy Cropper
Ms Dorothy Cumpsty
Miss Phyllis Cunningham
Mrs Edwina Currie MP MA MSc
Dr Julie Curtis MA DPhil (Oxon)
Mrs Janet Daley BA
Miss Phyllis Dalton
Ms Barbara Daly
Dr Avril Dankworth BMus GTCL LRAM
  ARCM
Ms Marcelle D'Argy Smith
Mrs Wendy Davidson BA
Dr Brenda Davies MB ChB MRCS LRCP
  BSc MPS MRCPsych
Mrs Gloria Davies BA (PPE)
Mrs Eileen Day Kilcourse, Kentucky
  (USA) Colonel
Miss Patricia Day BA FCIS
Ms Brenda Dean BA
Sister Marie de Lourdes SRN SCM
Mrs Sylvia Denman LLM
Dr Janet Dewdney BVSc MRCVS PhD
  FIBiol CBiol
Dr Diana Dickens FRCPsych DPM DCH
Miss Anne Dickinson FIPR CBIM
Miss Barbara Dickson
Ms Sue Dobson BA
Miss Emily Donnelly BSc
Miss Helene Donnelly BA
Ms Margaret Douglas
Mrs Mikki Doyle
Mrs Vivien Duffield CBE MA (Oxon)
  DLitt RCM
Miss Jennifer Durrant DipFA (Lond)
Mrs Tracey Edwards MBE
Dr Marta Elian MD
Miss Roslyn Emblin
Miss Ruth Etchells MA BD
Miss Amanda Evans BEd
Miss Lesley Exley BA
Mrs Audrey Eyton
Miss Susan Farmer FRSA MIPR
Rev Christine Farrington BA Dip ASS MA
Mrs Susie Faux
Ms Sally Feldman
Dame Peggy Fenner MP DBE
Mrs Janet Filderman
Miss Philippa Finch
Mrs Judy Finnigan BA
Miss Louise Fitzroy
Miss Jo Foley BA

Ms Sheila Forbes MA (Oxon) MPM
Miss Anna Ford BA
Mrs Emma Ford
Miss Giancarla Forte
Ms Lynne Franks
Mrs Margaret Frearson
Ms Fiona Fullerton
Mrs Clare Fulthorpe LLB
Mrs Jane Garside JP
Miss Phyllis George FRCS
Ms Anne Gibson BA
Mrs Ann Gibson DipArch RIBA
Ms Renée Goddard
Ms Georgina Godley MA
Ms Maggie Goodman
Miss Hannah Gordon
Miss Christina Gorna LLB
Miss Glenis Graham BSc ARICS
Ms Rosamund Grant
The Lady Grantchester MA (Cantab)
Miss Elizabeth Green MInstM
Miss Janet Green
Miss Patricia Gregory
Mrs Joan Gunn JP
Ms Betty Guyatt ACIB
Mrs Lois Hainsworth
Mrs Jan Hall BA
Miss Judith Hall
Miss Maggi Hambling
Ms Clare Hambro
Miss Sarah Hamilton-Fairley MA
Mrs Sue Hammerson OBE
Miss Julia S Hammond BCE
Ms Brenda Hancock BA JP
Ms Susannah Harker
Pamela, Lady Harlech BA
Miss Mollie Harris ACIS
Mrs Jacqueline Harris
Lady Pauline Harris
Mrs Fiona Harrison BSc
Miss Marea Hartman CBE
Miss Anna Harvey
Ms Julie S Hasler
Miss Brenda Haywood
Dr Deborah Hennessy DPhil
Mrs Sandra Hepburn
Miss Caroline Herbert BA (Oxon)
Ms Maria Herron
Miss Thena Heshel BA
Ms Patricia Hewitt MA (Cantab) AMusA
    (Sydney)
Miss Patricia Hodge
Professor Sheila Hollins MBBS FRCPsych
Miss Thelma Holt MA
Mrs Joyce Hopkirk

Ms Lis Howell BA
Professor Celia Hoyles BSc MEd PhD
Mrs Greta Hughes BA MSc
Ms Janet Hull MA DEML
Mrs Jean Hunt
Mrs Diane Hunter CertEd
Ms Pamela Hunter CIBiol MIBiol
Miss Gillian Hush BA MA
Ms Susi Hush BA
Ms Judy Hutcheson MA FCMA
Ms Diana Hutchinson BA
Dr Fay Hutchinson MBE MBBS
Ms Sheila Innes MA CBIM FRSA FITD
Mrs Betsy Innes-Smith
Miss Margery Jagger BSc
Mrs Annette James ACIB
Miss Catherine James MA
Ms Geraldine James
Mrs Mary James
Ms Sue James
Dr Ruth Jarrett MBChB
Lady Jay
Miss Eva Jiricna DipArch RIBA
Miss Sarah Jones BA
Mrs Grace Jordan
Miss Kazia Kantor BSc
Ms Adah Kay MA
Mrs Linda Kelly BPharm MRPS
Ms Linda Kelsey
Ms Helena Kennedy QC
Miss Patricia Kerr MBE
Miss Simone Klass MIPR
Ms Evelyn Knowles BA
Professor Eva M Kohner MD FRCP
    FCOPhthalm
Ms Kate Kumah BSc MPhil MA
Ms Dorothy Kuya SEN DipEd
Ms Hilary Laidlaw Thomson
Miss Jennifer C E Laing
Miss Maureen Laker
Ms Verity Lambert
Mrs Diana Lamplugh DipEd AE FE
Miss Patricia Latham FJI
Ms Helen Lederer BA
Mrs Lynda Lee-Potter
Mrs Arabella Lennox-Boyd
Ms Charlotte Lessing
Mrs Janie Lightfoot
Mrs Ann Lindsay
Ms Frances Line
Mrs Veronica Linklater
Miss Tasmin Little ARCM DipGSM
Surgeon Captain Vanessa Lloyd-Davies
    BA MBBS
Miss Nicola Loud

Dr Erna Low PhD MInstTT MCIM MBIM
Her Honour Judge Nina Lowry QC
Ms Margaret Lundin MBA
Professor Christina Lyon LLB FRSA SSC
Miss Morag MacDonald LLB FRSA
Ms Sue MacGregor
Ms Shauna J MacKenzie MA
Ms Kirsty Macmaster LLB DipBA
Ms Bo Maggs
Miss Carol A Makin MBBch PhD FRCS
Miss Suzi Malin
Ms Jacqueline Malton
Mrs Caroline Marland
Mrs Eve Martin
Mrs Irene Marvin FECI
Miss Sally Mason BA
Miss Wendy Matthews MBE BSc FIHEC FRSH FKC
Ms Mary McAnally
Miss Nichola McAuliffe
Mrs Heather McConnell
Sister Marie McDonald
Ms Geraldine McEwan
Mrs Jill McIvor LLB BL
Professor Susan McKennar-Lawlor PhD
Captain Julia McLardy
Mrs Betty McLeish
Miss June Mendoza AO DLitt RP ROI
Dr Heather Milburn MBBS MSc MD MRCP
Ms Caroline Millington BA
Mrs Barbara Mills QC MA (Oxon)
Ms Sophie Mirman
Dr Jacqueline Mitton MA PhD ARCM FRAS
Miss Emma Molesworth-St Aubyn
Air Commodore Ruth Montague ADC BSc
Mrs Jan Morgan SRN FNAGA
Mrs Victoria Morgan
Lady Morris of Kenwood
Mrs Patricia Morrison BA
Mrs Beryl Morton
Mrs Jane Muir MA
Ms Carmen Munroe
Ms Evelyn Murray BA (Oxon) MA (Lond)
Miss Georgina Nayler BA
Dr Elizabeth Nelson BA PhD FRSA
Dr Lotte Newman OBE FRCGP BSc
Miss Helen M Newport
Mrs Thi Be Nguyen
The Rt Hon Baroness Oppenheim-Barnes
Miss Jennifer Page
Mrs Veronica Palmer MBE
Mrs Juliet Pannett FRSA

Ms Diana Parker MA MPhil
Mrs Betty Parsons MBE
Dr June Paterson-Brown CBE DL MB ChB
Lady Penn Hon RCM
Dr Margaret Penston FRAS DPhil
Ms Nadine Peppard CBE BA
Dr Myrtle Peterkin MB BS MRCPath
Mrs Olive Peters
Miss Anne Pitcher
Ms Fiona Pitt-Kethley BA
The Lady Plowden DBE
Miss Laura Ponsonby AGSM
Ms Rachel Portman BA
Ms Usha Prashar BA
Miss Judith Prendergast BA
Mrs Mandy Price
Ms Jane Priestman OBE FCSD FRIBA
Lady Prior
Miss Jane Procter
Ms Margaret Prosser
Mrs Kailash Puri
Mrs Koshii Quarcoopome-Harper BEd
Miss Anne Rafferty QC
Ms Leela Ramdeen MA BEd
Brig Gael Ramsey MBE ADC
Miss Wendy Ramshaw FSIAD FRSA
Mrs Yvonne Randall BSc NDA NDD BEd
Miss Esther Rantzen BA MA
Miss Mary-Elizabeth Raw MBE BVSc MSC FRCVS DVR
Miss Patricia Rawlings BA LSE IntlDip
Ms Carol Reay BA
Miss Jane Reed
Dr Margaret Rees MB BS BSc DPhil MRCOG MA
Ms Elizabeth Rees-Jones BA
Ms Penny Reid BSc
Miss Ilona Richards
Miss Eurwen Richards MSc Ndd FIFST
Ms Caroline Richards
Miss Fiona Richmond
Miss Angela Rippon
Mrs Shireen Ritchie
Mrs Hope Rixson BA
Miss Pat Roberts
Dr Ann Robinson
Ms Patricia Roche
Mrs Joyce Rose CBE JP DL
Ms Marcelle Saad
Ms Joanne Salazar BA IPFA
Ms Yvonne Sarch MA
Ms Anna Scher
Dr Julia Schofield BSc PhD MBCS
Miss Anne Scott-James

Mrs Myra Scullion SRN SCM
Ms Clare Selerie BA
Mrs Mary Service
Mrs Geraldine Sharpe-Newton
Mrs Susan Shaw
Mrs Elizabeth Sidney BA MA ChPsy
Ms Janet Silver MPhil FBCO FBIM
Miss Prudence Skene
Mrs Heather Slade-Lipkin BMus GRSM
  ARMCM ARCM
Flying Officer Fiona Smith BEng
Miss Jan E Smith BA
Mrs Pat Smith
Mrs Caroline Snow
Ms Sally Soames
Ms Julia Somerville BA
Ms Patricia Spallone BSc MA
Mrs Estella Spencer
Miss Rosemary Spencer CMG BA
Dr Sarah Springham MA MPhil PhD
  CEng MICE
The Countess of St Andrews BA MA
Mrs Marcia Stanton
The Hon Francesca Sternberg
Ms Daphne Stewart JP MA
Mrs Phyllida Stewart-Roberts JP DL
Ms Sue Stoessl BA
Miss Carole Stone
Mrs Linda Stone BPharm MRPharm
Ms Kathryn Stott ARCM
Miss Anne Stotter MA PhD (Cantab)
  MBBS FRCS
Ms Moira Stuart
Miss Vivien Stuart
Ms Sarah Suttor Key DipPhys MSJ (Aust)
Mrs Elizabeth Svendsen MBE
Mrs Barbara Switzer
Ms Elizabeth Symons MA (Cantab)
Ms Muriel Tabinor DipEd
Mrs Judith Tarlo BA
Mrs Elisabeth Taylor MA
Councillor Mrs Frank Taylor
Ms Annette Taylor-Schofield
Dr Ruth B Thomson MBChB FRCP
Miss Angela Thorne
Miss Sue Thorne
Dame Sue Tinson DBE BA
Ms Yvonne Todd
Miss Emily Todhunter
Miss Helen Tridgell
Miss Rhona Tridgell
The Lady Tyron
Mrs Christine Tulloch BA
Miss Frances Tulloch MA DipTh
The Hon Provost Mrs Myra Turnball JP

The Baroness Turner of Camden
Mrs Sarah Tyacke BA
Mrs Veronica Uchendu
Mrs Arline Usden
Lady Marina Vaizey MA
Mrs Ayesha Vernon BA
Mrs Deirdre Vine BA
Mrs Anna Maria Vinton
Ms Virginia Wade OBE BSc
Mrs Veronica Wadley
The Hon Mrs Caroline Waldegrave
Miss Janet Walker MA (Oxon)
Mrs Sheila Walker CBE JP
Ms Marjorie Wallace BA
Mrs Grace Walmsley
Mrs Camilla Warner
Ms Diana Warwick BA
Miss Frances L Watt
Mrs Gail Webster MA (Cantab)
Miss Jane Webster DesRCA FGE
Miss Molly Weir
Mrs Bernice Weston LLB MPA
Ms Vivienne Westwood
Dr Susan Wharton BA (Lond) PhD
  (Cantab)
Mrs Susan White
Miss Faye Whittaker
Mrs Rahera Windsor
The Hon Mrs Joanna Wood
Mrs Marion Woodard DipCST FETC
Mrs Claire Woodroffe
Mrs Patsy Woodward
Miss Anna Worrall QC LLB
Mrs Elizabeth Wright
Ms Anna Wyner
Mrs Christine Young
Mrs Jennie Younger BA

Monday 26th October 1992
THEME: COMMUNITY

Miss Jenny Ackroyd MChir FRCS
The Countess of Airlie CVO
Mrs Matti Alderson
Ms Dounne Alexander-Moore
Mrs Jill Allen-King MBE
Mrs Ameera Alli
Ms Moira Anderson OBE
Ms Christine Angell BA DMS(PA)
Ms Alyson Anstey
Miss Isabel Appio
Ms Aileen Armitage BA
Miss Val Arnison
Mrs Romi Arora DipSU CQSW

Miss Jane Asher
Mrs Liz Attenborough
Ms Alison Backhouse
Mrs Charlotte Baden-Powell AADip RIBA
Ms Glenda Bailey
Miss Margaret Bailey
Ms Beryl Bainbridge
Mrs Gilly Baker BEd
Dr Frances Balkwill PhD
Mrs Margaret Bamford
Mrs Carol Banfield
Mrs Iris Banham-Lee
Mrs Jane Barker BSc FCA FCT
Mrs Mary Barnes
Mrs Rosie Barnes
Miss Ann Barr
Mrs Joan Barrell
Mrs Helen Beard
Mrs Barbara Beck-Coulter BSc
Mrs Margaret Beckett MP
Mrs Joan Belcher JP MA FRSA
Miss Lia Belli
Miss Floella Benjamin
Mrs Joan Bennett
Ms Martha Bennett MA
Mrs Moira Bennett
Ms Lynne Berry BA MPhil CQSW FRSA
Ms Reena Bhavnani BSc MEd
Ms Jane Bilcock BA
Dr Diana Birch MBBS DCH MRCP MSc
    MFCH MD
Miss Maria Bjornson MA
Ms Carole Blake
Mrs Susan Bonnici
Miss Jane Bown MBE DLitt
Miss Katie Boyle
Mrs Jane Bradford ACIB
Mrs Valerie Bragg BSc
Miss Margaret Brain OBE SRN SCM
    MTD FBIM FRCOG
Miss Margaret Brayton MBE SRN SCM
    RSCN FWACN FRSA
Mrs Yvonne Brewster LRAM
Miss Emma Bridgewater BA
Miss Janet Broad FCIS
Ms Tanya Bruce-Lockhart
Mrs Hebe Buckley-Sharpe
Sister Lavinia Byrne IBVM
Ms Karen Caines BA
Ms Ivy Cameron
Ms Blythe Campbell
Mrs Hilary Campbell BA MA
Mrs Paddy Campbell
Miss Rebecca Campbell
Ms Susanna Capon

Mrs Margaret Carey JP
Ms Sally Cartwright
Mrs Cynthia Casey LTCL CMTA
Miss Judith Chalmers
Miss Sandra Chalmers BA
Cllr Mrs Lurline Champagnie SRN NDN
Miss Ann Chant
Ms Elizabeth Chapman OBE BA MEd
Mrs Rhiannon Chapman LLB AKC FIPM
Dr Sandra Chapman PhD DIC
Ms Hannah Charlton BA MA
Mrs Madeline Chase Thomas
Dr Penny Childs PhD MSc FCII
Miss Rosalind Christie
Cllr Miss Elizabeth Christmas MBE
Mrs Hilary Christodoulou BSc
Miss Lindka Cierach
Miss Felicity Clark
Mrs Jean Clark
Ms Melanie Clore BA
Ms Madeline Close
Ms Chris Clyne
Miss Hilary Cochran JP BA
Ms Marie Colvin BA
Mrs Rosemary Conley
Mrs Rosita Conway BA
Ms Sue Cook BA
Miss Winsome Cornish
Miss Kay Coward
Dr Harriet Crabtree BD ThM ThD
Ms Christine Crawley MEP
Ms Elspeth Crichton Stuart BA MA
Mrs Eliza Crisp
Ms Katy Cropper
Ms Maureen Cropper
Mrs Sunny Crouch MA FCIM FTS
Ms Dorothy Cumpsty
Miss Phyllis Cunningham
Mrs Jo Cutmore
Mrs Tessa Dahl
Miss Hilary Dart
Dr Brenda Davies MB ChB MRCS LRCP
    BSc MPS MRCPsych
Mrs Ruth Deech BA MA
Mrs Helen Delnevo BSc
Miss Mary Dent BSc MPhil
Dr Marie de Lourdes SRN SCM
Ms Charlotte De Rothschild ARCM
Dr Janet Dewdney BVSc MRCVS PhD
    FIBiol CBiol
Miss Anne Dickinson FIPR CBIM
Miss Barbara Dickson
Brigadier Hilary Dixon-Nuttall RRC
    QHNS
Ms Sue Dobson BA

Miss Emily Donnelly BSc MPSI MRPharms
Mrs Moira Dower MA
Mrs Mikki Doyle
Miss Philippa Drew MA
Ms Deborah Ellwood
Miss Roslyn Emblin
Ms Eldred Evans OBE SADG RIBA AADip DiplTP
Mrs Sue Evans BA
Dr Maya Even BA DPhil
Miss Lesley Exley BA
Mrs Audrey Eyton
Dr Elizabeth Fagan AKC MBBS BSc MSc MD MRCP
Miss Susan Farmer FRSA MIPR
Ms Irene Fick BA PGCG MA
Miss Shirley Ann Field
Miss Philippa Finch
Ms Fiona Finlay BA
Mrs Judy Finnigan BA
Miss Louise Fitzroy
Miss Jo Foley BA
Mrs Emma Ford
Ms Elaine Foster BEd MPhil
Ms Dawn French
Mrs Tonia Fulford
Miss Jocelyn Galsworthy
Miss Lorella Galvani
Mrs Hilda Garfield
Mrs Jane Garside JP
Mrs Marie Gerritty
Ms Anne Gibson BA
Ms Eile Gibson
Miss Caroline Gledhill
Miss Kate Glover
Ms Renée Goddard
Ms Georgina Godley MA
Ms Maggie Goodman
Mrs Glynne Gordon-Carter BA MSc
Dr Nori Graham BM BCh FRCPsych
Ms Rosamund Grant
The Lady Grantchester MA (Cantab)
Miss Elizabeth Green MInstM
Ms Sally Anne Greene
Miss Patricia Gregory
Dr Jennifer Gunning PhD BA
Ms Fazilet Hadi BA
Mrs Lois Hainsworth
The Baroness Hamwee MA
Ms Brenda Hancock MBE JP BA
Lady Harlech BA
Mrs Fiona Harrison BSc
Miss Diane Hart
Miss Marea Hartman CBE

Miss Anna Harvey
Miss Jan Harvey
Mrs Monique Heald BSc
Mrs Frances Heaton BA LLB
Mrs Josephine Henderson
Mrs Sandra Hepburn
Miss Caroline Herbert MA (Oxon)
Ms Kathy Heseltine
Miss Thena Heshel BA
Ms Patricia Hewitt MA (Cantab) AMusA
Councillor Mrs Barbara Hillier
Professor Sheila Hollins MBBS FRCPsych
Miss Victoria Holt
Baroness Hooper BA
Mrs Joyce Hopkirk
Mrs Alison Horler BA
Ms Barbara Hosking OBE
Mrs Linda Huett BA MA
Mrs Greta Hughes BA MSc
Ms Janet Hull MA DEML
Reverend Vera Hunt
Mrs Diane Hunter
Ms Diana Hutchinson BA
Dr Fay Hutchinson MBE MB BS
Mrs Betsy Innes-Smith
Mrs Sally Irvine MA (Cantab)
Ms Elizabeth Irwin
Miss Betty Jackson MBE RDI
Miss Brenda Jackson JP
Mrs Carolyn James
Mrs Mary James
Ms Sue James
Dr Ruth Jarrett MBChB
Lady Jay
Miss Sarah Jones BA
Ms Adah Kay MA
Ms Jane Kelly LLB
Ms Jude Kelly BA
Ms Linda Kelsey
Ms Helena Kennedy QC
Ms Mary Kenny
Ms Sarah Key DipPhys MSJ
Mrs Etta Khwaja BEd
Miss Simone Klass MIPR
Ms Liz Knights BA
Mrs Ann Knowles BA
Ms Evelyn Knowles BA
Ms Dorothy Kuya SEN DipEd
Miss Mei Sim Lai FCA FCCA
Ms Hilary Laidlaw Thomson
Miss Maureen Laker
Ms Verity Lambert
Ms Caroline Langridge MPPS
Ms Patrona Lashley
Ms Di Latham MPhil

Miss Patricia Latham FJI
Dr Ghislaine Lawrence MSc MBBS MRCS LRCP
Mrs Maureen Leach MBE
Ms Edith Lederer
Mrs Lynda Lee-Potter
Miss Prue Leith OBE
Mrs Charlotte Lessing
Mrs Ann Lindsay
Surgeon Major Vanessa Lloyd-Davies MA MBBS
Miss Julia Lloyd Williams
Mrs Clare Longman
Miss Nicola Loud
Dr Erna Low PhD MInstTT MCIM MBIM
Mrs Ruth Lowe NDO
Her Honour Judge Nina Lowry QC LLB LLD
Mrs Josephine Lundberg
Ms Margaret Lundin MBA
Professor Christina Lyon LLB FRSA SSC
Flt Lt Karen Macaulay WRAF BA
Ms Sue MacGregor OBE
Ms Bo Maggs
Miss Sarah Mahaffy BA
The Hon Diana Makgill CVO
Miss Suzi Malin
Mrs Caroline Marland
Lady Marre CBE BA
Mrs Peter Marsh
Ms Terry Marsh BEd MSc
Mrs Patricia Marshall MSc
Miss Sally Mason BA
Ms Barbara Maxwell BA
Ms Mary McAnally
Ms Oveta McInnis MA
Mrs Jill McIvor LLB
Mrs Victoria McKee MA FRSA
Ms Jean McKelvey BA
Professor Susan McKennar-Lawlor PhD
Ms Pamela Meadows BA MSc
Ms Leonie Mellinger
Ms Barbara Melunsky MA
Ms Susan Milan ARCM
Dr Heather Milburn MBBS MSc MD MRCP
Dr Rosalind Miles MA PhD FRSA
Miss Tracey Miles
Mrs Liz Mills
Mrs Christine Milton
Mrs Gladys Mitchell BA PGCE
Mrs Marguerite Mitchell
Dr Jacqueline Mitton MA PhD ARCM FRAS
Mrs Marion Montgomery

Mrs Lesley Moore
Lady Morris of Kenwood
Mrs Patricia Morrison BA
Mrs Beryl Morton
Ms Kate Moseley
Dr Marjorie Mowlam MP
Ms Carmen Munroe
Ms Nathalie Murcott
Ms Evelyn Murray BA MA
Mrs Leith Myerson MBE
Ms Nina Myskow
Dr Elizabeth Nelson BA PhD FRSA
Ms Lisa Nelson
Ms Caroline Neville
Mrs Romy Newell DipCot SROT DUS MBES
Dr Lotte Newman OBE FRCGP BSc
Mrs Thi Be Nguyen
Miss Wendy Nicholls
Miss Emma Nicholson MP LRAM ARCM
Flt Lt Sally Ockwell-Page HND
Mrs Julia Ogilvy MA
Mrs Susan Oglethorpe BA
Ms Sally O'Sullivan
Mrs Allwyn Owen
Mrs Angela Palmer
Mrs Juliet Pannett FRSA
Mrs Gil Parker
Ms Beverley Parkin MA
Dr Margaret Penston FRAS DPhil
Ms Nadine Peppard CBE BA
Dr Myrtle Peterkin MB BS MRCPath
Ms Fiona Pitt-Kethley BA
Mrs Louise Pleydell-Bouverie
Miss Laura Ponsonby AGSM
Ms Jennifer Potter
Ms Usha Prashar BA
Miss Judith Prendergast BA
Mrs Rosalind Preston
Mrs Diana Pride RGN
Lady Prior
Miss Jane Procter
Mrs Kailash Puri
Mrs Koshii Quarcoopome-Harper BEd
Miss Carol Quirk
Ms Sarah Radclyffe
Ms Leela Ramdeen MA BEd
Miss Wendy Ramshaw FSIAD FRSA
Miss Esther Rantzen BA MA
Miss Ruth Rattenbury
Miss Mary-Elizabeth Raw MBE BVSc MSc FRCVS DVR
Mrs Elizabeth Ray JP
Ms Carol Reay BA

Miss Jane Reed
Ms Elizabeth Rees-Jones BA
Ms Penny Reid BSc
Ms Fiona Reynolds MA MPhil (Cantab)
Miss Anneka Rice
Miss Caroline Richards
Dr Heather Richardson FRCP MRCP
   FCCH DCH
Reverend Kathleen Richardson
Ms Gloria Ricks BA
Miss Angela Rippon
Miss Pat Roberts
Dr Ann Robinson
Brigadier Joan Roulstone ADC
Dr Rhiannon Rowsell MB BCh MRCP
Ms Marina Salandy-Brown BA
Mrs Janet Salt
Ms Jennifer Saunders
Ms Anna Scher
Dr Julia Schofield MBE BSc PhD MBCS
Mrs Julie Scott-Bayfield
Ms Christine Searle FRGS
Mrs Tamar Segal
Mrs Mary Service
Professor Dorothy Severin AB AM PhD
Mrs Brenda Sharp BEd FRSA
Mrs Geraldine Sharpe-Newton BA
Mrs Susan Shaw
Miss Tina Shaw
Miss Dorothy Shipsey MVO RGN
Miss Alexandra Shulman
Ms Janet Silver MPhil FBCO FBIM
Mrs Mary Simpkins GRSM LRAM
   ARCM MIACT
Ms Freya Slade
Ms Anne Sloman BA
Mrs Elizabeth Smith MA
Flying Officer Fiona Smith BEng
Ms Sally Soames
Commandant Anne Spencer ADC WRNS
   HCIMA
Mrs Estella Spencer
Ms Marcia Spencer BA
Miss Stevie Spring
The Countess of St Andrews BA MA
Mrs Anna Stewart BA
Ms Christine Stewart-Munro
Mrs Phyllida Stewart-Roberts JP DL
Ms Barbara Stocking BA MSc
Ms Susan Stockley
Ms Elizabeth Stokes RICS
Miss Carole Stone
Miss Anne Stotter MA PhD MBBS FRCS
Ms Moira Stuart
Mrs Veronica Sutherland CMG BA MA

Mrs Ann Swain LRSC FRSA
Ms Alison Swan Parente BA MACP
Councillor Mrs Gill Sweeting
Mrs Barbara Switzer
Ms Elizabeth Symons MA
Ms Catherine Syron BSc
Miss Jane Tabor
Mrs Elizabeth Taylor MA
Mrs Annette Taylor-Schofield
Ms Jane Thompson
Dr Ruth B Thomson MBChB FRCP
Miss Sue Thorne
Mrs Patricia Thornton
Commissioner Maude Tillsley
Dame Sue Tinson BA
Ms Yvonne Todd
Miss Emily Toddhunter BA
Ms Sandi Toksvig MA
Mrs Sue Treagus
Ms Di Trevis
Miss Helen Tridgell
Ms Fleur Tukham
Miss Frances Tulloch MA
Inspector Shirley Tulloch
The Hon Provost Mrs Myra Turnball JP
Baroness Turner of Camden
Ms Debbie Tweedi
Mrs Veronica Uchendu
Ms Bernadette Vallely
Mrs Ayesha Vernon BA
Ms Deirdre Vine BA
Dr Gail Vines BA PhD
Mrs Anna Maria Vinton
Mrs Veronica Wadley
Ms Elizabeth Wakeford
Ms Christine Walker BA
Mrs Sheila Walker CBE JP
Dr Louise Wallace PhD
Miss Fiona Watson
Ms Judith Watson
Miss Frances Watt
Miss Molly Weir
Ms Candida Wenham
Mrs Bernice Weston LLB MRA
Mrs Veronica Whelan
Miss Fatima Whitbread MBE
Mrs Julie Whiting BSc JNT PGCE
Mrs Teresa Wickham FRACS
Lady Wilcox
Mrs Verna Wilkins
Professor Dianne Willcocks BSc
Dr Eve Wiltshaw OBE MD FRCP
   FRCOG
Ms Anne Winder
Mrs Rahera Windsor

Ms Tess Woodcraft
Miss Vicki Woods
Mrs Patsy Woodward
Ms Anna Worrall QC
Ms Annette Worsley-Taylor
Miss Jean Worth
Dr Anne Wright BA PhD
Mrs Liz Wright
The Rt Hon Baroness Young DL MA
Dr Kate Young PhD
Mrs Jennie Younger BA

Monday 25th October 1993
THEME: BRINGING DOWN BARRIERS

Ms Linda Agran
The Lady Alexander of Tunis
Dr Jean Alexander BSc PhD FRPSL
Ms Dounne Alexander-Moore
Mrs Frances Allen
Ms Mary Allen MA
Miss Marjorie Allthorpe-Guyton BA
Mrs Beverly Anderson
Professor Kathleen Anderson OBE BSc
    PhD FRSC
Mrs June Anstey
Ms Anne Anstice BPharm MRPharm
Mrs Aileen Armitage BA
Ms Carolyn Armstrong
Miss Val Arnison
Miss Joyce Arram FInst LEx MBIM FRSA
Mrs Ann Ashfield
Captain Rose Ashkenazi BSc
Miss Ruth M Ashton OBE RN RM MTD
Mrs Peggy Aylen MA
Mrs Charlotte Baden-Powell AADip RIBA
Ms Liz Badowska
Miss Glenda Bailey BA
Miss Margaret Bailey
Mrs Mary Baker MA
Ms Melanie Baker
Dr Frances Balkwill PhD
Mrs Carol Banfield
Ms Eleanor Barger
Mrs Jane Barker BSc FCA FCT
Ms Sue Barnard BEd FIHEC
Miss Ann Barr
Mrs Joan Barrell
Mrs Sue Barrett
Miss Jennifer Bate BA FRCO LRAM
    ARCM
Miss Michelle Beaconsfield MRCS LRCP
    MBBS DO FRCS FCOPhth
Miss Helen Beard

Miss Debbie Beaumont-Howell
Mrs Barbara Beck-Coulter BSc
Mrs Joan Belcher JP MA FRSA
Miss Floella Benjamin
Mrs Susan Benjamin MVO
Ms Martha Bennett MA
Ms Rosalind Beveridge MA
Dr Manju Bhavnani MBChB MRCPath
Mrs Joan Bingley MA FCIS
Ms Wendy Birnie BA
Mrs Patsy Bloom
Ms Doreen Boulding
Mrs Ann Bowtell BA CB
Miss Karen Brady
Ms Rosa Branson
Mrs Voirrey Branthwaite BA
Ms Wendy Braverman
Ms Cella Brayfield
Ms Rita Britton
Miss Linda Brown BEd
Mrs Marion Brown BA PGCE PhD
Mrs Joy Bryer BA
Miss Dinah Bulstrode
Mrs Rosemarie Burrow
Mrs Joan Burstein
Ms Janet Bush BA
Miss Ffyona Campbell
Ms Diane Canady BA MA
Ms Susanna Capon
Mrs Lida Lopes Cardozo
Mrs Louise Carstairs
Ms Evelyn Carter BA
Ms Sally Cartwright
Lady Cass JP BA
Mrs Julia Cassel
Mrs Honor Chapman BSc MPNI
Ms Caroline Charles
Dr Anne Charlton BA MEd PhD
Ms Hannah Charlton BA MA
Mrs Doreen Cherry JP SRN
Ms Margaret Childs LLB
Mrs Pat Chrisfield CQSW
Miss Lindka Cierach
Miss Felicity Clark
Ms Audrey Clarke MA BSc
Canon Margaret Clarke
Mrs Olive Clarke MBE JP DL
Ms Katie Clemson BA PGCE
Mrs Lorraine Clinton MA DMS FRSA
Mrs Della Clyne
Her Honour Judge Myrella Cohen QC
    LLB
Professor Dulcie Coleman MBBS MD
    FRCPath FIAC
Mrs June Collins

Mrs June Collins FHCIMA
Ms Lin Collins BA
Miss Susie Constantinides MA
Miss Sarah Cook MA MHort
Ms Elizabeth Cooke
Mrs Diana Coombs
Mrs Fiona Corby
Ms Marsha Corper
Professor Heather Couper BSc DLitt FRAS
Mrs Linda Crossland
The Baroness Cumberledge of Newick
    CBE DL JP
Ms Joanne Curin BCom ACA
Miss Jilly Curry
Ms Jo Cutmore BSc FCCA
The Countess of Dalkeith BSc
Mrs Christine Dare
Ms Marcelle D'Argy-Smith
Ms Marian Darke
Miss Hilary Dart
Mrs Betty Davies JP LGSM MBIM
Miss Pamela Davies BA FCIS
Sister Marie De Lourdes SRN SCM
Mrs June De Moller
Miss Nicki Denaro
Ms Kathy Denton BA
Dr Janet Dewdney BVSc MRCVS PhD
    FIBiol CBiol
Dr Neena Dhoat MB BS
Dr Diana Dickens FRCPsych DPM DCH
Miss Anne Dickinson FIPR CIM
Ms Sue Dobson BA
Ms Claire Dove MBE BA
Mrs Moira Dower MA
Mrs Mikki Doyle
Mrs Marjorie Drawbell FRBS
Ms Sarah Ebanja
Mrs Linda Edwards BA MIPR
Mrs Sheilah Ellis BEM
Ms Jane Ellison BA
Ms Elizabeth Emanuel
Miss Roslyn Emblin
Ms Deborah Evans BA
Ms Eldred Evans OBE SADG RIBA
    AADipl DiplTP RWA
Miss Jean Faulkner
Dr Jane Feely BPharm PhD MRPharms
Miss Mercy Fenton
Ms Elizabeth Filkin BSocSC
Mrs Dawn Fitt HNCEng
Ms Lorna Fitzsimons
Mrs Angela Flowers
Ms Julia Flynn BA MS MBA
Miss Jo Foley BA
Dr Susan Forda BPharm PhD

Dr Greta Forster MB ChB MRCOG
Ms Elaine Foster BEd MPhil
Ms Liz Francis BA
Dr Winifred Francis MD FRCOG
Miss Carol Galley BA
Miss Patricia Gallimore ALAM
Ms Sharon Gamsin
Ms Sally Gardner BA
Mrs Jane Garside JP
Miss Samantha Gemmell BA
Mrs Marcia Gibson-Watt BA
Dr Clare Gilbert MB ChB FRCS FCOPath
Mrs Shirley Gillingham
Dr Jean Ginsberg MA DM FRCP
Ms Renée Goddard
Ms Jeanette Golding
The Hon Lady Goodhart MA
Miss Val Gooding
Ms Maggie Goodman
Miss Hannah Gordon FRSAMD DLitt
Miss Christina Gorna LLB
Lady Graham MA FSA
Dr Jill Graham MB ChB MRCGP
Ms Marianne Gray BA
Mrs Rose Gray
Miss Elizabeth Green MInstM
Miss Susan Green
Ms Tracie Greenfield
Miss Dina Gregory
Miss Patricia Gregory
Miss Rosabella Gregory
Mrs Rosemarie Griffith
Ms Ann Hall BA
Mrs Jan Hall BA
Miss Heather Hallett QC MA
Miss Jennie Halsall
Mrs Mary Halsall
Ms Clare Hambro
Ms Kate Hampton MA
Miss Marea Hartman CBE
Miss Anna Harvey
Ms Julie Hasler
Miss Linda Haye MA DSoc
The Lady Healey BA
Mrs Renske Heddema
Miss Gill Hedley BA FRSA
Mrs Sandra Hepburn
Miss Caroline Herbert MA
Ms Norma Heyman
Professor Marian Hicks OBE PhD DSc
    FRCPath
Mrs Christian Hill ICSF
Dame Thora Hird DBE OBE DLitt
Mrs Clare Hoare
Ms Tracy Hofman BA

Miss Edith Holland MBE
Mrs Jenny Hoon ARCA
Miss Emma Hope
Mrs Eunice Hopkins
Mrs Joyce Hopkirk
Mrs Alison Horler BA
Mrs Nicola Horlick BA
Mrs Mary Horner
Ms Jane Howard
Mrs Norma Huddy
Ms Janet Hull MA
Miss Jennifer Hunt BA MPhil RGN FRCN
Ms Susi Hush BA
Ms Diana Hutchinson BA
Miss Jacqueline James
Miss Caroline Janzen LLB
Mrs Gillian Jason
Sergeant Alison Jenkins
Mrs Rosemary Jenkins RGN RM DMS
    MTD MBIM
Ms Marie Jennings
Ms Sue Johnston
Professor Ludmilla Jordanova MA PhD
    FRHS
Miss Jill Keen BA
Miss Jane Kelly LLB
Mrs Marjorie Knightley Day RGN
Ms Debra Kocher
Ms Nancy Koot
Ms Dorothy Kuya SEN DipEd
Miss Mei Sim Lai FCA FCCA
Miss Maureen Laker
Ms Verity Lambert
Dr Erika Langmuir BA MA PhD
Mrs Pamela Langworthy BA
Ms Tory Laughland MA
Mrs Maureen Leach MBE
Ms Helen Lederer BA
Mrs Lynda Lee-Potter
Miss Victoria Legge-Bourke LVO
Miss Jenny Leggott
Miss Prue Leith OBE
Mrs Charlotte Lessing
Mrs Annabel Lewis
Ms Sue Limb BA
Ms Frances Line
Miss Tasmin Little ARCM
Mrs Vicki Lloyd BSc
Miss Julia Lloyd Williams
Ms Margaret Lochrie BA
Mrs Joy Loyla BA
Ms Rosalina Luis
Ms Joanna Lumb BSc
Mrs Josephine Lundberg
Miss Anne Mace MA

Ms Shelagh Mackay BSc CA
Ms Shauna MacKenzie MA
Ms Rosemarie MacQueen BSc DipArch
    DMS
Mrs Bo Maggs
The Hon Diana Makgill CVO
Mrs Elizabeth Malden MA
Miss Patricia Mann FCAM FIPA CBIM
Ms Miriam Margoyles BA LBSM
Dr Gillian Markham MB ChB DObst
    RCOG FRCR
Mrs Kathryn Marsden
Mrs Wenche Marshall Foster
Ms Mary McAnally
Ms Cathy McCargow MBA
Ms Teresa McCarthy
Dr Alison McCartney MA MD FRCPath
    FCOphth
Mrs Margaret McClean
Mrs Anne McElvoy BA
Mrs Morag McGilp Rosie MBE FRSA
Miss Sylvia McInnes
Mrs Betty McLeish
Ms Shelagh McLeish BA
Mrs Janet McMorran
Ms Helen McMurray BA
Miss Rebecca Meitlis BA MA
Dr Maureen Michaelson PhD
Mrs Linda Miney
Miss Frances Minogue
Ms Anne Minto LLB DPM NP FRSA
    MBIM
Ms Alison Mitchell BA
Mrs Marguerite Mitchell
Ms Mary Mitchell
Dr Suzanne Mitchell MB BS FRCS
    FRCOphth DO
Dr Jacqueline Mitton MA PhD ARCM
    FRAS
Ms Judy Moate
Air Commodore Ruth Montague ADC
    BSc
Mrs Gail Moore
Mrs Diana Moran
Lady Morris of Kenwood
Mrs Patricia Morris-Thompson BA MBA
Mrs Betty Mulcahy BA LRAM
Miss Clare Mulholland MA
Mrs Minna Nathoo MA MIPM
Miss Lesley Neil MA
Ms Caroline Neville
Mrs Yvette Newbold LLB
Ms Frances Newell BA FRSA FCSD
Miss Sara Nicholson BSc
Mrs Vivien Nookes MA

Miss Adele Nozedar
Ms Wendy Oberman
Mrs Farquhar Ogilvie
Lady Elizabeth Ogilvy
Miss Emma O'Gorman
Ms Jane Packer
Ms Jill Palmer
Dr Katerine Panter MA MBBS
Ms Jane Parker-Smith ARCM LTCL
Mrs Stephanie Parkes-Crick MBA RGN
  RM RHV OND
Lady Penn RCM
Ms Polly Perkins
Miss Pauline Peters
Mrs Jenny Pitman
Mrs Carolyn Plunkett
Professor Marcia Pointon BA MA PhD
Miss Eve Pollard
Miss Susannah Pollen BA
Mrs Madeleine Ponsonby
Ms Janet Porter BSc
Ms Jennifer Potter BA
Mrs Julia Prescot MA
Ms Wendy Proctor BA
Ms Heather Rabbatts BA MSc
Miss Anne Rafferty QC FRSA
Miss Wendy Ramshaw OBE FSIAD FRSA
Mrs Yvonne Randall BSc NDA NDD BEd
Miss Esther Rantzen OBE BA MA
Dr Jessica Rawson LittD FBA
Mrs Elizabeth Ray JP
Ms Carol Reay BA
Dr Margaret Rees MB BS BSc DPhil
  MRCOG MA
Mrs Elizabeth Rees-Jones BA
Miss Penny Reid BSc
Miss Ilona Richards
Mrs Paula Ridley JP MA DL
Miss Angela Rippon
Miss Pat Roberts
Mrs Katy Rodger
Lady Ruth Rogers
Ms Andrea Rose BA MA
Mrs Anthea Rose MA
Miss Janine Roxborough Bunce MIPR
Mrs Amanda Royce
Dame Rosemary Rue DBE MA MB BS
  FRCP FFPHM
Mrs Sophie Ryder
Ms Marina Salandy-Brown BA
Professor Naomi Sargant BA
Mrs Jennifer Savage FInst FRSA
Miss Rosalind Savill BA FSA FRSA
Ms Deborah Saybolt BSME MSME MBA
  RPE

Ms Sophie Schellenberg
Dr Julia Schofield MBE BSc PhD MBCS
Ms Hilary Sears BSc MBA
Mrs Patsy Seddon
Ms Marguerite Sells
Mrs Brenda Sharp BEd FRSA
Mrs Susan Shaw MSI
Miss Dorothy Shipsey MVO RGN
Dr Evelyn Silber PhD
Ms Janet Silver MPhil FBCO FBIM
Mrs Catherine Simon Bell
Mrs Marjorie Simonds-Gooding
Miss Susannah Simons AGSM FRSA
Ms Audrey Slaughter
Ms Sue Slipman BA
Mrs Patricia Smith
Flt Lieut Nicky Smith
Ms Julia Somerville BA
Professor Lesley Southgate FRCGP
  MClinSci
Miss Barbara Speake
Miss Estella Spencer
Lady Charles Spencer-Churchill
Ms Barbara Spittle BA DCG MSc
Miss Stevie Spring LLB
Mrs Toushy Squires BA
The Countess of St Andrews BA MA
Mrs Judy Stammers MA FCMA
Ms Deirdre Stamp BA ALI
Mrs Zoe Stamper BA
Ms Naomi Stanford BA MEd MSc
Ms Gail Stephenson DBO
The Hon Francesca Sternberg
Mrs Marie Stevens LLB
Mrs Sheena Stewart
Mrs Floi Stewart-Murray
Ms Susan Stroman
Ms Moira Stuart
Miss Vivien Stuart BA
Miss Una Stubbs
Miss Mollie Sugden MGSM
Dr Elisabeth Svendsen MBE DVMS
Mrs Ann Swain LRSC FRSA
Pastor Betty Swarbrick
Ms Barbara Switzer
Miss Naomi Tarrant BA
Ms Maureen Theobald SRN RNT MA
Mrs Jennifer Thomas
Ms Jane Thompson
Dame Sue Tinson DBE BA
Dr Maria Tippett BA PhD FRS
Miss Helen Tridgell
Mrs Jane Tridgell
Mrs Elizabeth Tuke BSc
Mrs Katy Turner

Ms Sylvia Tutt FCIS
Rev Sister Monica Tywang
Lady Marina Vaizey MA
Dr Elizabeth Vallance JP MA MSc PhD
Ms Bernadette Vallely
Miss Lucia Van Der Post BA
Ms Elizabeth Vann
Mrs Anna Maria Vinton
Ms Virginia Wade OBE BSc
Ms Christine Walker BA
Mrs Jean Walker
Mrs Sheila Walker CBE JP
Ms Marjorie Wallace BA
Miss Brenda Wallam RGN RM MTD
   ADM
Ms Claire Walmsley
Miss Johannah Walton BA
Ms Deborah Warner
Miss Frances Watt HND
Mrs Shirley Webster-Jones
Miss Molly Weir
Mrs Zelda West Meads
Mrs Bernice Weston LLB MPA
Mrs Susan White
Ms Kate Whiteford BA
Ms Rebecca Whitfield
Miss Faye Whittaker
Mrs Lilian Wick LRAM LGSM
Mrs Anna-Katarina Wild
Mrs Verna Wilkins
Ms Hilary Williams BA MBA MIMgT
Mrs Patricia Williams MA
Ms Deanna Wilson BA
Mrs Sylvia Wilson BSc
Miss Nancy Wise
Mrs Marion Woodard DipCST FETC
Miss Vicki Woods
Ms Annette Worsley-Taylor
Dr Iffat Yazdani MBBS MD MACP
Mrs Jennie Younger BA
Mrs Mary Yule MA

Monday 31st October 1994
THEME: WHAT MATTERS MOST

Ms Jenny Abramsky BA
Ms Dawn Airey MA
The Countess of Airlie CVO
Mrs Val Aisher
Mrs Rosemary Alexander
Ms Mary Allen MA
Miss Hilary Allison
Mrs Julia Allison
Mrs Marjorie Allthorpe-Guyton BA FRSA

Professor Kathleen Anderson OBE BSc
   PhD FRSC
Ms Moira Anderson OBE RSAM
Miss Joan Armatrading
Miss Val Arnison
Miss Jane Asher
Ms Yvette Asscher
Ms Zeinab Badawi BA MA
Mrs Charlotte Baden-Powell AADip RIBA
Ms Vivien Baeza BSc DMS
Miss Margaret Bailey
Mrs Mary Baker MA
Mrs Lorraine Baldry
Mrs Lesley Balls
Mrs Carol Banfield
Ms Liz Bargh BA
Mrs Joy Barling Loyla BA
Miss Denise Barnes BA
Ms Shirley Barnett
Miss Ann Barr
Mrs Joan Barrell
Mrs Peggie Barry
Mrs Annette Barwick
Miss Jennifer Bate BA FRCO LRAM
   ARCM
Floella Benjamin
Ms Barbara Bennett BA
Mrs Sonia Benster
Mrs Viorica Bergman BDS LDS RCS
Ms Pascale Bernard
Mrs Sharon Beuthin
Miss Charlotte Black
Ms Malorie Blackman
Mrs Sandra Boler
Miss Camilla Boodle MA
Ms Colette Bowe PhD
Ms Penny Boyd
Miss Katie Boyle
Ms Wendy Braverman
Mrs Rita Britton
Ms Lesley Brown MA
Ms Tanya Bruce-Lockhart
Mrs Anne Bruh
Mrs Joy Bryer BA
Dr Jill Bullimore MB BS MRCS LRCP
   DMRT FRCR
Mrs Joan Burstein
Ms Diane Canady BA MA
Ms Alison Canning MBA BA
Ms Susanna Capon
Mrs Lida Lopes Cardozo
Mrs Louise Carstairs
Mrs Evelyn Carter BA
Ms Sally Cartwright
Miss Louise Casey BA

Mrs Julia Cassel
Mrs Catherine Cecillon
Ms Anna-Mei Chadwick BA
Miss Judith Chalmers OBE
Miss Jane Cheffings
Viscountess Chelsea MVO RGN
Ms Emma Chichester Clark MA
Mrs Catherine Churchard LLB
Miss Felicity Clark
Ms Katie Clemson BA PGCE
Mrs Lorraine Clinton MA DMS FRSA
Ms Melanie Clore BA
Mrs Della Clyne FECI
Ms Liza Cody
Mrs Janet Cohen
Dr Beverly Collett MBBS FRCA
Miss Deborah Collett LLB
Mrs June Collins
Miss Sue Colwill
Mrs Rosemary Conley
Ms Imogen Cooper
Ms Winsome-Grace Cornish
Ms Linda Cowie BPharm MBA
Miss Elizabeth Crotty BSc
The Baroness Cumberlege CBE DL
Miss Jilly Curry
Mrs Tessa Dahl
Mrs Janet Daley BA
Ms Marcelle D'Argy Smith
Mrs Betty Davies JP LGSM MBIM
Ms Emma Davies BA
Ms Judith Deeble BA MA
Mrs June De Moller
Ms Kathy Denton BA
Dr Janet Dewdney BVSc MRCVS PhD
    FiBiol CBiol
Miss Anne Dickinson FIRP CIM
Ms Michele Dimitri
Mrs Georgina Donnelly BA
Ms Helene Donnelly BA Dip Con
Mrs Diana Donovan
Ms Caroline Douglas
Ms Claire Dove MBE BA
Professor Ann Dowling MA PhD CEng
    FIMechE
Ms Mikki Doyle
Mrs Julie Drabble
Mrs Marjorie Drawbell FRBS
Mrs Shirley Dunster
Ms Georgina East DMS MSc
Mrs Linda Edwards BA MIPR
Ms Marian Elliott (Poly Styrene)
Miss Jane Ellison BA
Miss Roslyn Emblin
Miss Lesley Exley BA

Miss Jean Faulkner BA
Mrs Julia Feast
Mrs Janet Fitch
Mrs Dawn Fitt AMIEIE HNC
Ms Siobhan Fitzpatrick BA
Miss Louise Fitzroy
Miss Elizabeth Floyd
Ms Jo Foley BA
Ms Barbara Follett BSc
Mrs Emma Ford
Dr Greta Forster MB ChB MRCOG
Miss Nicola Foulston
Group Captain Cynthia Fowler ADC
Dr Winifred Francis MD FRCOG
Ms Lynne Franks
Captain Jenny Fray BA
Mrs Clara Freeman MA
Professor Joan Freeman PhD FBPS
Ms Dawn French BA
Ms Maria Friedman
Mrs Pamela Funnell
Mrs Jean Gaffin JP MSc BSc
Miss Helen Galbraith
Miss Jocelyn Galsworthy
Ms Sharon Gamsin
Mrs Jane Garside JP
Miss Heather Gething BA
Mrs Joy Gilchrist
Dr Jean Ginsburg MA DM FRCP
Mrs Philippa Gitlin
Mrs Renée Goddard
The Hon Lady Goodhart MA
Miss Valerie Gooding BA
Ms Elinor Goodman
Ms Maggie Goodman
Miss Janet Gough MA
Mrs Eirwyn Goule
Dr Nori Graham BM BCh FRCPsych
Mrs Eileen Gray OBE
Miss Elizabeth Green MInstM
Dr Elaine Griffiths MBBS FRCS
Mrs Lindy Grobler
Mrs Muriel Hackland BA
Mrs Kate Hallatt BSc
Miss Jennie Halsall
Ms Sarah Hamilton-Fairley MA
Ms Sandra Hampson
Ms Kate Hampton BA
Mrs Cheryl Hampton-Coutts BA FCIS
Ms Margaret Harbury
Ms Alison Hargreaves
Miss Barbara Harmer
Mrs Patricia Harris
The Lady Healey BA
Mrs Frances Heaton BA LLB

Mrs Sandra Hepburn
Ms Maria Herron
Miss Thena Heshel BA
Ms Norma Heyman
Professor Marian Hicks OBE PhD BSc
    PhD DSc FRCPath
Ms Nicola Hicks MA
Mrs Gina Higginbottom BA RN RM
    RHV
Mrs Christian Hill NDSE FSF
Mrs Grete Hobbs
Ms Beverley Hodson BA
Miss Min Hogg MBE
Mrs Helen Holmes
Mrs Irene Holmes
Ms Judith Holmes Drewry BFA
Ms Mary Honeyball MA
Mrs Jenny Hoon ARCA
Mrs Joyce Hopkirk
Mrs Nicola Horlick BA
Ms Anna Horsbrugh-Porter BA
Ms Jane Howard BSc
Mrs Norma Huddy
Ms Janet Hull MA
Miss Diana Hutchinson BA
Mrs Bernadette Igboaka BSc
Mrs Gillian Jason
Mrs Rosemary Jenkins RGN RM DMS
    MTD MBIM
Ms Norma Johnston BA
Miss Sarah Jones BA
Dr Carole Jordan BSc PhD FRS
Dr Frances Jowell PhD BA
Ms Adah Kay MA
Mrs Anne Kelley
Dr Deidre Kelly MD FRCPI
Ms Linda Kelsey
Ms Patricia Kenna
Mrs Joanna Kennedy MA DSc CEng
    FICE
Miss Philippa Kennedy BA
Miss Janet Kerr
Captain Yvonne Kershaw
Mrs Gayle King BA
Ms Denise Kingsmill MA
Dr Judith Kingston FRCP BSc
Mrs Marjorie Knightley Day RGN
Mrs Ann Knowles
Ms Dorothy Kuya
Mrs Jacqui Lait MP
Dr Joanna Lambert FRCOG FRCR
Ms Verity Lambert
Mrs Diana Lamplugh OBE
Dr Nancy Lane OBE DPhil ScD LLD
    FIBiol

Dr Erika Langmuir BA MA PhD
Ms Jane Lapotaire
Mrs Elizabeth Lawrence FHCIMA
Mrs Zara Lazenby-Field
Ms Helen Lederer BA
Mrs Lynda Lee-Potter
Ms Sue Leggate
Miss Jenny Leggott
Mrs Anthea Lemonheigh
Mrs Arabella Lennox-Boyd
Mrs Evelyn Le Roex
Mrs Charlotte Lessing
Mrs Annabel Lewis
Miss Ann Lewis
Ms Rita Lewis BSc
Ms Frances Line
Dr Kristen Lippincott
Miss Tasmin Little ARCM
Lady Jane Lloyd MA CQSW
Mrs Ursula Lloyd MBBS FRCOG
Miss Julia Lloyd Williams BA MA
Mrs Angela Lovering-Moon
Dr Erna Low PhD MInstTT MCIM
    MBIM
Miss Emma Lumsden
Miss Kate Lumsden
Ms Shelagh Mackay BSc CA
Miss Diana Mackie BS MS MBA
Lady Deborah Macmillan
Ms Rosemarie MacQueen BSc Dip Arch
    DMS
Dr Jane Maher MRCP FRCR
The Hon Diana Makgill CVO
Professor Averil Mansfield MD ChM FRCS
Mrs Cheryl Marcus
Dr Gillian Markham MB ChB DObst
    RCOG FRCR
Mrs Ann Marks JP BA
Mrs Caroline Marland
Miss Joan Martin
Miss Monica Mason
Dr Lindsey Matheson MB BS MRCP
Ms Mary McAnally
Ms Cathy McCargow MBA
Ms Anne McElvoy BA
Ms Frankie McGowan
Mrs Victoria McKee BA MA FRSA
Ms Judy McKnight BSocSc
Miss June Mendoza AO DLitt RP ROI
Ms Linda Miller BA
Miss Sophie Miller
Mrs Barbara Mills QC MA
Mrs Beth Milsom
Ms Suzanne Mitchell MB BS FRCS
    FRCOphth DO

Lady Montagu
Ms Maggie Monteith BA
Ms Gillian Moore MBE GSM BMus MA
Lady Morris of Kenwood
Mrs Patricia Morrison BA
Mrs Margaret Mountford MA
Mrs Betty Mulcahy BA LRAM
Ms Clare Mulholland MA
Ms Claire Myerscough
Mrs Minna Nathoo MA MIPM
Dr Elizabeth Neville MA PhD
Miss Pauline Neville-Jones CMG MA
Ms Helen Newman LLB AKC
Ms Jane Newman
Mrs Ruth Newton Jones BA
Miss Emma Nicholson MP LRAM ARCM
Mrs Judith Nicol
Ms Judy Niner
Mrs Vivien Noakes MA
Lady Celestria Noel
Miss Adele Nozedar
Ms Wendy Oberman
Ms Barbara Obstoj
Mrs Renate Olins JP MA
Mrs Sally O'Sullivan
Mrs Jo Ouston
Ms Jane Packer
Ms Jill Palmer
Mrs Eileen Parker
Ms Jo Parker BSc MBA CEng MICE
Dr Valerie Payne PhD MSc ARCS
Her Honour Judge Nasreen Pearce
Dr Irene Peat FRCP FRCR
Ms Eileen Pembridge BA
Lady Penn RCM
Ms Polly Perkins
Mrs Sybil Phoenix MBE
Miss Melanie Pini
Miss Amanda Platell BA
Miss Katy Plater
Ms Eve Pollard
Ms Janet Porter
Mrs Julia Prescot MA
Miss Fay Presto
Mrs Rosalind Preston OBE
Miss Jane Procter
Ms Paula Pryke
Ms Josephine Pullein-Thompson MBE
Mrs Patience Purdy MA
Mrs Kailash Puri BA
Mrs Karen Pusey
Mrs Koshii Quarcoopome-Harper BEd
Miss Carol Quirk
Ms Sarah Radclyffe
Miss Leela Ramdeen MA BEd

Mrs Joan Rampton
Miss Wendy Ramshaw OBE FSIAD FRSA
Mrs Gwen Randall BA
Miss Esther Rantzen OBE BA MA
Dr Gillian Rathbone MB BS MRCGP
Ms Carol Reay BA
Ms Gail Rebuck BA
Dr Margaret Rees MB BS BSc DPhil
    MRCOG MA
Professor Felicity Reynolds MBBS FRCA
    MD
Mrs Jan Reynolds
Miss Angela Rippon
Mrs Lynda Robbins BA
Ms Pat Roberts
Ms Sue Robertson BA
Ms Jancis Robinson MA
Ms Lois Rogers
Ms Sandra Rogers
Mrs Morag Rosie MBE FRSA
Ms Bridget Rowe
Mrs Amanda Royce
Mrs Pamela Saint
Mrs Ann-Marie Salmon
Ms Judith Sample BA
Ms Yvonne Sarch MA
Professor Naomi Sargant BA
Miss Jennifer Saunders
Miss Vivien Saunders BSc MSc PhD
Miss Rosalind Savill BA FSA FRSA
Ms Deborah Saybolt BSME MSME MBA
    PE
Dr Julia Schofield MBE BSc PhD MBCS
Miss Patricia Scotland QC LLB
Mrs Jill Scott JP
Dr Katharine Scott PhD DPhil
Ms Denine Searle BSc
Mrs Carolyn Sears
Mrs Patsy Seddon
Mrs Jean Seeley
Ms Anne Seymour BA
Mrs Fiona Shackleton LLB
Mrs Geraldine Sharpe-Newton BA
Mrs Susan Shaw MSI
Mrs Vicki Sheen
Miss Caroline Sheppard
Mrs Helen Sher
Mrs Stephanie Shirey OBE
Miss Julie Shrimpton BA
Ms Janet Silver MPhil FBCO FBIM
Ms Josette Simon
Mrs Catherine Simon Bell
Captain Julia Simpson ADC RN BSc
Dr Catherine Smith BSc MSc PhD FCIBS
    FRSA

Dr Lynne Smith BSc PhO
Mrs Nicola Smith
Mrs Wendy Smyth BA
Mrs Cilla Snowball BA
Ms Emma Soames
Mrs Sally Soames
Ms Julia Somerville BA
Mrs Estella Spencer
Ms Lisa Spiro
Ms Barbara Spittle BA DCG MSc
Ms Stevie Spring LLB
The Countess of St Andrews BA MA
Mrs Fianne Stanford MA
Mrs Margaret Staple BA
Ms Peggy Staples
Miss Rebecca Starks
Ms Gail Stephenson DBO(T) SRO
Mrs Marie Stevens LLB
Mrs Anna Stewart BA
Miss Margaret Stockwell
Ms Sue Stoessl BA
Miss Carole Stone
The Hon Georgina Stonor
The Hon Julia Stonor
Ms Moira Stuart
Dr Elisabeth Svendsen MBE DVMS
Ms Ann Taylor
Mrs Susan Taylor
Ms Maureen Theobald MA RGN RCNT
   RNT
Mrs Elizabeth Thom BSc
Ms Jane Thompson
Ms Caroline Thomson
Ms Phillippa Toomey
Mrs Trudy Towell
Miss Helen Tridgell
The Rt Hon Baroness Trumpington
Mrs Jennifer Turco BSc FLIA
Mrs Katy Turner
Ms Sylvia Tutt FCIS
Ms Elizabeth Tyson
Ms Bernadette Vallely
Mrs Gilly Vincent
Ms Deirdre Vine BA
Mrs Anna Maria Vinton
Ms Virginia Wade OBE BSc
Mrs Anna Walker
Miss Janet Walker MA
Mrs Jean Walker
Miss Marjorie Walker
Mrs Sheila Walker CBE JP
Ms Marjorie Wallace MBE BA
Miss Brenda Wallam RGN RM MTD
   ADM
Ms Claire Walmsley

Miss Johannah Walton BA PGCE
Miss Deborah Ward
Ms Deborah Warner
Ms Diana Warwick BA
Miss Frances Watt HND
Councillor Miss Doreen Weatherhead
Miss Molly Weir
Mrs Ann Wheatley-Hubbard OBE FRAgS
Mrs Janet Whitaker
Miss Isabelle White
Mrs Anna Whitehead
Ms Lucinda Whiteley
Mrs Penelope Whitelock BEd
Miss Faye Whittaker
Mrs Louise Wigley
Dr Sheila Willatts MD FRCP FRCA
Ms Hilary Williams BA MBA MIMgT
Miss Nicola Williams
Mrs Sylvia Wilson BSc
Ms Marlene Winfield BA
Ms Nancy Wise
Ms Tanya Wiseman
Ms Jean Wood MA
Ms Annette Worsley-Taylor
Mrs Aida Young
Mrs Jennie Younger BA

Monday 30th October 1995
THEME: 40 YEARS ON – HAVE WE COME A
LONG WAY, BABY?

Ms Diane Abbott MP MA
Ms Lesley Abdela MBE
Ms Jan Adams
Ms Linda Agran
Mrs Valerie Aisher
Mrs Rosemary Alexander
Ms Britt Allcroft
Miss Marjorie Allthorpe-Guyton BA
Dr Barbara Ansell CBE MD FRCS FRCP
Mrs Alyson Anstey
Mrs Aileen Armitage BA
Miss Val Arnison
Mrs Joyce Arram FInst LEx MIMgt FRSA
Miss Jane Asher
Mrs Lucy Atkins BA MA
Mrs Jane Atkinson
Ms Zeinab Badawi BA MA
Mrs Charlotte Baden-Powell AADip RIBA
Ms Glenda Bailey BA
Miss Margaret Bailey
Mrs Gail Johnstone Baldwin
Ms Alison Ball QC LLB
Mrs Carol Banfield

Mrs Margaret Banks MEd
Ms Ann-Marie Baptiste
Mrs Margaret Barbour CBE DL
Ms Liz Bargh BA FRSA
Mrs Elsie Baring RD
Miss Ann Barr
Mrs Joan Barrell
Ms Lynda Bass
Miss Jennifer Bate BA FRCO LRAM
    ARCM
Miss Susan Batey
Dr Christina Baxter BA CertEd PhD
Ms Jane Beechey
Mrs Joan Belcher JP MA FRSA
Mrs Kim Bell BA
Floella Benjamin
Mrs Susan Bennett
Miss Mary Biggart
Ms Carole Blake
Ms Patsy Bloom
Mrs Irene Bloor MEd
Miss Camilla Boodle MA
Mrs Marian Bosall MA
Ms Doreen Boulding
Ms Lynette Bowen
Ms Candida Boyes BA
Ms Jenny Bradley
Mrs Wendy Brandon MA
Ms Celia Brayfield
Mrs Rita Britton
Dr Gill Burrington MA(Econ) PhD FLA
Mrs Joan Burstein
Ms Jean Butler BA Theatre Arts
Ms Sandra Campbell BA MA DMS FIPD
    FRSA
Mrs Susanne Campbell MA
Ms Diane Canady BA MA
Ms Susanna Capon
Mrs Lida Lopes Cardozo
Ms Jean Carr BA
Ms Kate Carr BA
Mrs Louise Carstairs
Mrs Penelope Cavenagh BSc MSc DMS
    LCST
Dr Jean Chadha PhD MED
Miss Tracey Chadwell
Ms Anna-Mei Chadwick BA
Miss Judith Chalmers OBE
Mrs Sheila Chapman BA
Viscountess Chelsea MVO RGN
Mrs Doreen Cherry JP SRN
Mrs Catherine Churchard LLB
Ms Nikki Clare BA
Miss Felicity Clark
Mrs Olive Clarke OBE JP DL

Mrs Lorraine Clinton MA DMS FRSA
The Viscountess Cobham
Dr Beverly-Jane Collett MBBS FRCA
Mrs June Collins
Ms Rosemary Conley
Mrs Margaret Cooper
Miss Sue Cooper
Ms Val Corbett
Mrs Tessa Dahl
Mrs Janet Daley BA
Miss Hilary Dart
Mrs Betty Davies JP LGSM MBI
Ms Caroline Dawnay
Ms Susan Dean
Ms Kathy Denton BA
Ms Janet Dicks
Mrs Kay Doe
Ms Moya Doherty
Ms Diane Dollery BSc
Ms Margaret Donnelly BSc
Mrs Diana Donovan
Mrs Marjorie Drawbell FRBS
Lady Eames LLB MPhil
Mrs Christina E Edwards MBA
Mrs Linda Edwards BA MIPR
Mrs Theo Ellert
Mrs Rebecca Elliott
Ms Jane Ellison BA
Miss Roslyn Emblin
Ms Ireen Esmann
Ms Sophia Fairclough
Mrs Yvonne Farlam MBE
Miss Susan Farmer FRSA MIPR
Mrs Carolyn Faulder BA
Miss Jean Faulkner BA
Mrs Jane Ferguson BA
Ms Angela Finbow
Dr Ilora Finlay MBBS FRCGB
The Lady Finsberg MA
Janet Fitch
Mrs Diane Fitchett
Mrs Dawn Fitt Eng Tech AMIEIE
Ms Siobhan Fitzpatrick BA
Miss Louise Fitzroy
Mrs Caroline Flint SRN SCM ADM
Miss Elizabeth Floyd
Ms Jo Foley BA
Ms Barbara Follett BSc
Mrs Emma Ford
Mrs Daphne Foulsham
Ms Celestia Fox
Dr Winifred Francis MD FRCOG
Mrs Clara Freeman MA
Professor Joan Freeman PhD FBPS
    CPsychol

Ms Ylva French
Mrs Nini Fuller
Ms Cathy Galvin BA
Dr Cathy Garner MA PhD
Dr Selina Gellert MB MRCGP DRCOG
Miss Vera Gilbert BA
Dr Vivette Glover MA PhD DSc
Mrs Renée Goddard
Mrs Jane Gogan
Miss Valerie Gooding BA
Mrs Doreen Goodman BA MPhil
Ms Maggie Goodman
Mrs Hilary Gough
Mrs Anita Gracie BSc
Mrs Icilda Graham
Ms Lorna Graham
Mrs Patricia Grant OBE DBA FInstD FRSA
Mrs Eileen Gray OBE
Professor Susan Greenfield MA DPhil
Dr Elaine Mary Griffiths MBBS FRCS
Ms Miriam Gross
Mrs Olwyn Gunn Dip Ed (Adv)
Ms Kim Haddaway BA
Dr Neva Haites MB ChB PhD
Miss Jennie Halsall
Miss Maggi Hambling OBE
Mrs Cheryl Hampton-Coutts BA FCIS
Ms Margaret Hanbury
Ms Kleshna Handel
Miss Judith Hanratty LLB LIM
Mrs Juliet Harbutt
Miss Barbara Harmer
Ms Dragana Hartley BSc
Lady Healey BA
Mrs Kim Hemstead
Mrs Sandra Hepburn
Mrs Maria Herron
Mrs Norma Heyman
Cllr Mrs Rosemarie Higham
Mrs Christian Hill NDSE FSF
Ms Tessa Hilton
Miss Min Hogg MBE
Lady Holland BA MBE
Ms Moira Holmes MPhil
Ms Judith Holmes Drewry BFA
Ms Mary Honeyball MA
Ms Emma Hope
Mrs Joyce Hopkirk
Ms Lisbeth Howell BA
Miss Margaret Howell DipAD Fine Arts
Mrs Ros Howells OBE
Ms Janet Hull MA
Ms Judith Hunt BA
Princess Shahnaz Husain
Miss Gillian Hush BA MA

Ms Diana Hutchinson BA
Mrs Ann Hutley
Ms Darryl Jaffray BA PGCE PDTA FRSA
Ms Val James BA
Professor Lisa Jardine MA PhD FRSA
Mrs Gillian Jason
Miss Sarah Jones BA
Dr Carole Jordan BSc PhD FRS
Professor Ludmilla Jordanova MA PhD
  FRHS
Ms Lesley Joseph
Dr Frances Jowell PhD BA
Ms Florence Kay
Mrs Frances Kelly LLB
Ms Linda Kelsey
Dr Olga Kennard OBE ScD FRS
Mrs Ann Kennedy
Ms Helena Kennedy QC LLD
Mrs Joanna Kennedy MA DSc CEng FICE
Miss Philippa Kennedy BA
Ms Anne Keogh RGN DipN
Mrs Betty Kershaw
Captain Yvonne Kershaw
Dr Julia King MA PhD FIM CEng
Miss Irina Kirillova
Ms Anne Klahn
Mrs Marjorie Knightley Day RGN
Maggie Koumi
Ms Dorothy Kuya DipEd
Dr Erika Langmuir OBE
Mrs Kathryn Langridge MA
Mrs Sally Larkin MBE
Miss Francine Lawrence
The Hon Mrs Carole Lawson
Mrs Zara Lazenby Field
Ms Helen Lederer BA
Mrs Liz Lee-Kelly FCIS FCMA FRSA
Ms Janet Leeming
Ms Lynda Lee-Potter
Miss Victoria Legge-Bourke LVO
Dr Angela Lennox MBS MRCP
Mrs Katy Lennox
Mrs Charlotte Lessing
Ms Kathy Lette
Ms Karen Levi
Miss Ann Lewis LLB FRPharms MCPP
  HSM
Mrs Bunty Lewis
Ms Gill Lewis BA
Ms Sue Limb BA
Ms Frances Lincoln MA
Ms Maureen Lipman DLitt
Miss Julia Lloyd Williams MA
Mrs Jennifer Lonsdale
Ms Heather Love

Dr Erna Low PhD MInstrT MCIM MBIM
Miss Nagadya-Miriam Lwanga
Ms Juliet Lysons
Mrs Lesley MacDonagh
Ms Sue MacGregor OBE MRCP
Ms Shelagh Mackay BSc CA
Lady Deborah Macmillan
Miss Fiona Macpherson MA BEd
The Hon Diana Makgill CVO
Ms Anjum Malik
Dr Neeta Manek MBChB HRCPath
Dr Anna Mann PhD BA
Professor Averil Mansfield ChM FRCS
Mrs Ann Marks JP BA
Mrs Caroline Marland
Ms Penny Marshall BA
Mrs Alison Maslen LLCN (Eloc)
Mrs Sue Mason
Ms Sheila Masters LLB FCA ATII
Dr Lindsey Matheson MBBS MRCP
Dr Anne E May
Ms Carolyn McCall BA MA
Dr Alison McCartney MA MD FRCPath
   FCOphth
Ms Polly McDonald
Miss Heather McGlone
Ms Frankie McGowan
Mrs Victoria McKee BA MA FRSA
Ms Judy McKnight BSoc Sc
Ms Patricia McLean
Mrs Betty McLeish
Mrs Christine McMillen
Mrs Deborah McNicol
Dr Ann McPherson MBBS DCH FRCGP
Ms Leonie Mellinger
Miss June Mendoza AO RP ROI
Ms Margaret Michie
Mrs Barbara Mills QC MA
Miss Jenna Mistry
Mrs Manjula Mistry
Belinda Lady Montagu
Ms Maggie Monteith BA
Lady Morris of Kenwood
Mrs Patricia Morris-Thompson RGN RM
   BA MBA
Mrs Patricia Morrison BA
Miss Clare Mulholland MA
Lady Mary Mumford
Mrs Hazel Murphy
Ms Claire Myerscough
Mrs Minna Nathoo MA MIPD
Dr Elizabeth Nelson BA PhD FRSA
Dr Elizabeth Neville MA PhD
Mrs Yvette Newbold LLB
Mrs Patricia Newman LLB

Mrs Olive Newton JP BA
Mrs Vivien Noakes BA
Ms Christina Noble
Miss Dee Nolan
Miss Erica Norton OBE BA
Ms Wendy Nugent
Ms Wendy Oberman
Ms Denise O'Donoghue BA
Mrs Renate Olins JP MA
Ms Susie Orbach BA MSW PhD
Ms Sally O'Sullivan BA
Mrs Jane Packer
Ms Jill Palmer
Janet Paraskeva BA
Mrs Betty Parsons MBE
Miss Barbara Patterson BA
Mrs Lynette Patterson BA
Mrs Lyndy Payne
Miss Anthea Pelham Burn
Ms Eileen Pembridge BA FRSA
Ms Lorie Peters Lunn BA
Ms Sarah Petitt BA
Mrs Lilian Phillips JP DL
Mrs Sybil Phoenix MBE MS
Ms Sylvie Pierce LLB
Ms Anne-Marie Piper LLB
Mrs Beverly Piper
Baroness Platt of Writtle CBE DL FEng
   FRAS
Mrs Yvette Price-Mear
Mrs Margaret Pritchard
Mrs Karen Pusey
Mrs Koshii Quarcoopome-Harper BEd
Ms Anne Quigley BA
Dr Jennifer Raiman
Mrs Nicola Ralston BA
Miss Wendy Ramshaw OBE FSIAD FRSA
Ms Beverley Randall
Ms Paulette Randall
Esther Rantzen OBE BA MA
Ms Caroline Raphael
Lady Read
Ms Carol Reay BA
Ms Gail Rebuck BA
Ms Alexis Redmond BA ACA
Ms Sharon Reed
Mrs Jan Reynolds
Ms Sally Anne Roberts BA
Ms Pat Roberts Cairns
Mrs Merigold Robertson-Saul
Dr Ann Robinson MA MA Phd
Dr Anna-Maria Rollin
The Hon Mrs Felicity Rollo
Mrs Gail Ronson
Mrs Helen Rosbottom MBE

Mrs Patricia Rothman
Miss Janine Roxborough Bunce MIPR
Mrs Amanda Royce
Ms Galina Samsova
Professor Naomi Sargant BA
Miss Jennifer Saunders
Miss Vivien Saunders BSc MSc PhD
Cllr Mrs Sheila Schaffer
Ms Anna Scher
Dr Julia Schofield MBE BSc PhD
Ms Betty Scott
Ms Jacqueline Sealey-Benn MA(Ed)
   GRSM LRAM LGSM FRSA
Miss Elsie Sebastian MA
Mrs Patsy Seddon
Mrs Fiona Shackleton LLB
Mrs Iris Shanahan JP BA
Mrs Susan Shaw MSI
Miss Janet Silver MPhil FBCO FBIM
Mrs Catherine Simon Bell
Captain Julia Simpson DC RN BSc
Ms Christine Smith
Miss Jan Smith BA
Mrs Nicola Smith
Miss Valerie Smith
Lady Smith-Gordon BEd
Ms Sally Soames
Mrs Elizabeth Sobczynski BA
Ms Julia Somerville BA
Miss Barbara Speake
Mrs Estella Spencer
Dr Margaret Spittle FRCR FRCP AKC
Ms Stevie Spring LLB
The Countess of St Andrews BA MA
Mrs Margaret Staple BA DipEd
Miss Rebecca Stephens BSc
Ms Gail Stephenson DBO(T) SRO
Mrs Jane Stevens
Mrs Anna Stewart BA
Miss Carole Stone
The Hon Georgina Stonor OSJ
The Hon Julia Stonor
The Hon Sophie Stonor
Ms Moira Stuart
Ms Serena Sutcliffe
Miss Janet Suzman DLitt
Miss Cleo Sylvestre
Mrs Sonia Taha
Pauline Tambling CertEd
Mrs Susan Taylor
Ms Maureen Theobald MA
Ms Theresa Thomas
Mrs Lynda Myles Till
Ms Daphne Todd PRP NEAC
   HDFA(Lond)

Mrs Claire Tomalin MA FRSL
Ms Philippa Toomey
Dr Janet Treasure PhD MRCP FRCPsych
The Rt Hon The Baroness Trumpington
Miss Dorothy Tutin CBE DLitt
Miss Debbie Tweedie
Dr Elizabeth Vallance JP MA MSc PhD
Ms Bernadette Vallely
Mrs Patricia Vaz
Mrs Pauline Vernon
Ms Penny Vincenzi
Miss Sophie Vincenzi
Ms Deirdre Vine BA
Ms Bettina Von Hase MA
Ms Virginia Wade OBE BSc
Mrs Sheila Walker CBE JP
Mrs Pamela Wall
Miss Brenda Wallam RN RM MTD
Ms Claire Walmsley
Ms Jane Walmsley BA
Dr Julia Walsh BSc PhD
Dr Roberta Ward PhD MPhil
Ms Shaa Wasmund BSc
Mrs Charlotte Watcyn Lewis
Ms Neslyn Watson-Druee MSc BA
Miss Frances Watt
Miss Molly Weir
Ms Natalie Wheen BMus ARCM
Mrs Ann White
Mrs Anna Whitehead
Ms Irene Whitehead BA
Miss Faye Whittaker
Dr Helen Whitwell MB ChB MRCPath
   DMJPath
Ms Toyah Willcox
Ms Jayne Willetts LLB
Ms Hilary Williams BA MBA MIMgt
Miss Louise Woolcock
Ms Annette Worsley-Taylor
Dr Jules Wright PhD
Mrs Karen Wright MA MBa
Mrs Margaret Wright
Yazz
The Rt Hon The Baroness Young DL MA
Mrs Aida Young
The Hon Mrs Jennie Younger BA

Monday 7th October 1996
THEME: BALANCE

Miss Diane Abbott MA
Ms Lesley Abdela MBE
Ms Jan Adams
Professor Judith Adams MBBS FRCR
   FRCP

Ms Sandra Addae LLB
Ms Linda Agran
Dr Anjana Ahuja PhD BSc
The Countess of Airlie DCVO
Mrs Louise Aitken-Walker MBE
Miss Sonita Alleyne MA
Miss Moira Anderson OBE RSAM
Mrs Eleanor Angel
Mrs Alyson Anstey
Miss Melinda Appleby BSc
Mrs Aileen Armitage BA
Miss Val Arnison
Miss Joyce Arram FInst LEx FRSA
Mrs Dora Asgeirsdottir
Miss Caroline Atkins BA
Ms Zeinab Badawi BA MA
Mrs Charlotte Baden-Powell AADip RIBA
Ms Pam Bader OBE
Ms Sally Baffour
Ms Kamlesh Bahl LLB
Ms Margaret Bailey
Mrs Mary Baker MBE BA AIMSW
   FCSLT
Mrs Carol Banfield
Mrs Margaret Banks MBE MEd
Mrs Kareni Bannister BA
Ms Ann-Marie Baptiste
Mrs Margaret Barbour CBE DL
Ms Margie Barbour BA
Mrs Anita Barnard BA JP
Miss Ann Barr
Mrs Joan Barrell
Mrs Sue Barrett
Ms Liz Barron
The Hon Lady Barttelot OStJ
Mrs Liz Bavidge JP BA
Lady Bellinger
Mrs Veronica Benjamin
Ms Glenwyn Benson
Miss Mary Biggart
Miss Charlotte Black
Ms Ingrid Bleichroeder
Mrs Janet Boateng MA
Professor Margaret Boden MA ScD PhD
   FBA
Ms Bibiana Boerio MBA BS
Colonel C R Bolland ADC
Dr Margaret Bone MB CMB FRCA
Josephine Lady Bonfield
Miss Camilla Boodle MA
Mrs Ann Botwell BA CB
Ms Rosie Boycott
Ms Jenny Bradley
Ms Gabriele Bramante BA M(ARCH)
Mrs Wendy Brandon MA

Ms Tanya Bruce-Lockhart
Dr Mary Buchanan MRCS LRCP DFFP
Miss Anne Buddle
Mrs Jessica Burley BA
Ms Gill Burns BEd
Ms Iris Burton
Miss Maggie Butler DiPAD
Mrs Dorothy Calder
Ms Diane Canady BA MA
Ms Susanna Capon
Mrs Lida Lopes Cardozo
Mrs Gloria Carnevali-Hawthorn
Mrs Evelyn Carter OBE BA
Mrs Margaret Carter-Pegg NFF
Ms Sally Cartwright
Mrs Jenne Casarotto
Mrs Cynthia Casey LTCL CMTA
Lady Olwen Cass JP BA
Ms Anna-Mei Chadwick BA
Ms Lesley Chalmers BA FCIH
Ms Melinda Chandler
Dr Qudsia Chandran MBBS DRCOG
Mrs Hannah Charlton BA MA
Mrs Anne Murray Chatterton BA
Ms Lois Cheesman
Miss Margie Clark
Ms Nicola Clark BA
Mrs Elaine Clarke LCGI
Mrs Olive Clarke OBE JP DL
Dr Lisa Clayton
Ms Rita Clifton
Viscountess Cobham
Dr Beverly-Jane Collett MBBS FRCA
Ms Ann Colligan
Ms Teresa Collings
Mrs June Collins
Mrs Carole Collins-Deamer
Ms Rosemary Conley
Ms Helen Conn Fifst FIFST BSc
Mrs Susan Conrad
Mrs Pamela Cooper
Ms Val Corbett
Mrs Vivian Cotterill
Ms Lynn Cox
Mrs Bridget Cracroft-Eley
Dr Yvonne Cripps PhD
Miss Beverley Cuddy BA
Ms Jo Cutmore BSc FCCA
Ms Joan DaCosta-Robinson
Mrs Janet Daley BA FRCA
Dr Avril Dankworth BMus GTCL LRAM
   ARCM
Ms Carol Darby-Darton
Miss Hilary Dart
Miss Rita Dattani BA AGS

Mrs Philomena Davidson Davis
Mrs Corinne Davis
Mrs Leanda De Lisle
Mrs Marie Devlin BComm HDE ACCA
Mrs Janet Dicks
Ms Judy Dobias BA MA
Mrs Kay Doe
Ms Margaret Donnelly BSSc
Mrs Diana Donovan
Mrs Linda Downey
Ms Fiona Driscoll MA
Mrs Ann Driver RN RMW
   DipNursing(Lond)
Mrs Anne Dunham
Mrs Elizabeth Earnshaw
Mrs Sue Ellen BSc DHSM
Dr Michele Elliott PhD
Ms Jane Ellison BA
Miss Roslyn Emblin JP
Mrs Pauline Emburey BA ACA
Lady Euston BA MA
Mrs Kit Evered
Mrs Eileen Ewers
Mrs Audrey Eyton
Miss Diana Faber LLB
Dr Jan Fairley
Mrs Sue Farrell Dip BSCPsych
Mrs Helena Felix
Mrs Julian Fellowes
Ms Suzanne Finch
Miss Louise Fitzroy
Miss Elizabeth Floyd
Ms Jo Foley BA
Ms Barbara Follett BSc
Mrs Emma Ford
Miss Antonia Forster BSc
Mrs Joanna Foster
Mrs Vivien Fowle
Mrs Marjorie Francis
Ms Carole Franco MPhil
Miss Liz Fraser
Ms Ylva French
Ms Leisha Fullick
Ms Cathy Galvin BA
Mrs Maria Gardener
Ms Diana Garnham BA MA
Dr Selina Gellert MB MRCGP DRCOG
Ms Susan Gernaey
Mrs Susan Gibbons
Ms Jane Gill
Mrs Rita Gill
Ms Maggie Giraud
Mrs Renée Goddard
Ms Margaret Godfrey
Mrs Jane Gogan

Mrs Dilys Goggins NFF
Miss Janet Goldsmith
Ms Joanna Goldsworthy
Miss Valerie Gooding BA
Miss Patricia Gregory
Ms Miriam Gross MA
Miss Jennie Halsall
Ms Margaret Hanbury
Miss Judith C Hanratty LLB LIM
Mrs Juliet Harbutt
Ms Belinda Harley
Mrs Susan Harmsworth
Vicky Harper
Miss Mollie Harris ACIS
Ms Tanya Harrod BA DPhil
Ms Dragana Hartley BSc
Mrs Christine Hartopp
Mrs Anna Harvey
Mrs Khanam Hassan
Lady Healey BA
Mrs Maria Herron
Professor Julia Higgins FRS CBE
Mrs Jenny Hoon ARCA
Ms Premilla Hoon BSc MBA
Mrs Joyce Hopkirk
Mrs Judith Howard
Professor Judith Howard BSc DPhil DSc
   FRSC CBE
Mrs Ros Howells OBE
Mrs Deborah Hudd, Queen Ratling,
   Grand Order Lady Ratlings
Mrs Norma Huddy FRSA
Ms Janet Hull MA DIDM FRSA
Ms Sally Hunter
Ms Diana Hutchinson BA
Ms Blossom Jackson
Mrs Wendy Jacobs BA
Ms Darryl Jaffray BA PGCE PDTA RSA
Miss Jacqueline James
Dr Susan James
Miss Sarah Jones BA
Professor Carole Jordan BSc PhD FRS
Mrs Florence Kay
Mrs Bronagh Kennedy BA
Mrs Deirdre Kennedy
Ms Philippa Kennedy BA
Ms Mary Kenny
Captain Yvonne Kershaw
Mrs Arabella Killander BA
Ms Rachael King
Ms Denise Kingsmill MA
Ms Hazel Kirkham BA
Mrs Jenny Kirkpatrick BEd MIPR FRSA
Mrs Anne Klahn
Ms Laura Knapp

Professor Eva M Kohner MD FRCP
FCOphtalm
Ms Maggie Koumi
Ms Dorothy Kuya CertEd SEN
Miss Jennifer Laing
Miss Sue Laing
Dr Nancy Lane OBE BSc MSc DPhil PhD
ScD
Miss Janet Langdon MA BSc
Mrs Doreen Lawrence BA
Mrs Jean Lawrence FHCIMA
Dr Annette Lawson BSc PhD
The Hon Mrs Carole Lawson
Ms Helen Lederer BA
Miss Elizabeth Lee
Ms Lynda Lee-Potter
Ms Vanessa Leeson
Miss Victoria Legge-Bourke LVO
Miss Jenny Leggott
Mrs Bunty Lewis
Ms Mary Lewis BA
Mrs Ursula Lloyd MBBS FRCOG
Ms Sue Lloyd-Roberts MA
Mrs Jennifer Lonsdale
Mrs Pamela Lonsdale
Ms Heather Love
Dr Erna Low PhD MInstrT MICM MBIM
Mrs Joy Loyla BA
Miss Michelle Lucarotti MB ChB FRCS
MD
Miss Nagadya-Miriam Lwanga LLB
Captain Jenny Lyons
Ms Juliet Lysons
Ms Sue MacGregor OBE MRCP DLitt
Miss Alison Macho
Ms Fiona Macpherson MA BEd
Ms Rosemarie Macqueen BScSoc
DipArch AADipURP
Ms Avril Mair MA
The Hon Diana Makgill CVO
Professor Averil Mansfield ChM FRCS
MD FRACS
Mrs Caroline Marland
Dr Caroline Marriott MB BCL MRCPsych
Ms Penny Marshall BA
Dr Monica Mason Hon Doct Surrey Uni
Ms Sally Mason
Dame Sheila Masters DBE LLB FCA ATII
Ms Terry Matthews
Mrs Theresa May MA
Mrs Margaret McAllister BA MEd
CPsychol AFBPsS
Ms Mary McAnally
Miss Jane McCloskey
Miss Sheena McDonald MA

Miss Linda McDougall
Miss Heather McGlone BA
Ms Frankie McGowan
Professor Rosamond McGuiness BA MA
DPhil FSA
Ms Judy McGuire
Miss Jean McIntosh
Mrs Victoria McKee BA MA FRSA
Mrs Judith McKenzie MIPR
Miss Julia McKenzie FGSM
Ms Judith McKnight BSocSc
Mrs Monica McWilliams BSSc Dip TP MSc
Mrs Eileen Meadmore
Mrs Jennifer Medd
Miss June Mendoza RP ROI AO
Ms Margaret Michie
Mrs Lesley Millar BSc PGCE MBA
Mrs Patricia Miller
Mrs Dawn Mitchell
Mrs Gill Monk
Ms Catalina Montesinos
Miss Sue Moore
Dr Yvonne Moores DSc DCL
Ms Joanna Moorhead BA
Lady Morris of Kenwood
Ms Roz Morris
Mrs Patricia Morris-Thompson BA MBA
RGN RM
Miss Janet Morrison
Mrs Patricia Morrison BA
Ms Kate Mosse BA MA
Miss Clare Mulholland MA
Mrs Heather Muncey
Ms Janice Munday
Lady Heather Murray
Mrs Tamlyn Nall MA
Ms Sara Nathan BA
Mrs Minna Nathoo MA MIPD
Mrs May Naylor
Mrs Olive Newton JP BA
Mrs Ruth Newton-Jones BA
Ms Julia Nolan
Mrs Karen Norman
Ms Wendy Oberman
Ms Denise O'Donoghue BA
Mrs Renate Olins JP MA
Ms Anne Olorun-Rinu BSc
Ms Barbara Osborn
Miss Sade Oshinusi BA LLM
Ms Sally O'Sullivan BA
Ms Jane Packer
Mrs Elli Panteli
Mrs Lyndy Payne
Mrs Carole Phillips
Ms Fiona Phillips LLB

Dr Ann Phoenix MA PhD
Miss Anne-Marie Piper LLB
Mrs Beverley Piper
Ms Jane Platt
Ms Eve Pollard
Mrs Julia Prescot MA
Mrs Margaret Pritchard
Dr Penny Probert MA PhD MIEE CEng
Mrs Kailash Puri BA
Ms Alison Pylkkanen
Ms Mary Quicke BA FRAgs FAgrM DipFM
Ms Anne Quigley BA
Miss Jane Rabagliati MA
Mrs Nicola Ralston BA
Mrs Gwen Randall BA
Miss Esther Rantzen OBE BA MA DLitt
Mrs Marsha R Ratcliff
Mrs Julia Rayer Rolfe
Mrs Alexis Redmond BA ACA
Mrs Elizabeth Rees-Jones BA
Mrs Carole Regan
Professor Felicity Reynolds MBBS FRCA MD
Miss Alexandra Rhodes
Miss Linda Rhodes
Miss Stephanie Rice BA
Mrs Louise Riley-Smith
Ms Sharon Ring
Mrs Sally Anne Roberts BA
Ms Pat Roberts Carins
Mrs Rosena Robson BA
Dr Anna-Maria Rollin MB BS FRCA
Miss Janine Roxborough Bunce MIPR
Ms Angela Royal
Mrs Brenda Ryan
Mrs Sophie Ryder ARBS
Mrs Pearl Sagar
Edna Lady Samual
Ms Sue Saville
Dr Julia Schofield MBE BSc PhD FRSA MBCS
Miss Patricia Scotland QC LLB
Mrs Irene Scott
Mrs Julie Scott-Bayfield
Dr Chandra Sethurajan
Mrs Fiona Shackleton LLB
Mrs Iris Shanahan JP BA
Mrs Susan Shaw MSI
Mrs Vicki Sheen MCSP DipPT
Mrs Missouri Sherman-Peter BA MIA
Ms Mary Ann Sieghart MA
Dr Janet Silver OBE MPhil FBCO FBIM
Captain Julia Simpson ADC RN BSc
Mrs Joginder Singh BA

Ms Jenny Singleton BA
Mrs Barbara Smith
Mrs Elizabeth Smith MA
Dr Susan Smith
Ms Susy Smith BA
Mrs Valerie Smith
Ms Emma Soames
Ms Sally Soames
Dr Jane Somerville
Miss Barbara Speake
Dr Margaret Spittle FRCR FRCP AKC
The Countess of St Andrews BA MA
Ms Fianne Stanford MA
Ms Linda Stevens
Dr Marie Stewart
Ms Julie Stokes BSc MSc
Miss Carole Stone
Ms Moira Stuart
Ms Rachel Sullivan
Mrs Nicola Swan
Mrs Barbara Switzer
Mrs Elizabeth Sydney
Miss Cleo Sylvestre
Ms Yuki Tanaka
Mrs Susan Taylor
Ms Barbara Thomas BA
Miss Pat Thomas MA
Ms Theresa Thomas
Ms Jane Thompson
Mrs Rosemary Thomson
Mrs Francesca Tiffin MA
Ms Ann Todd BA MBA
Ms Philippa Toomey
The Rt Hon The Baroness Trumpington
Mrs Nanette Tyrrell
Ms Priscilla Vacassin
Mrs Pauline Vernon
Mrs Penny Vincenzi
Miss Sophie Vincenzi
Mrs Sheila Walker CBE JP
Ms Claire Walmsley
Ms Jane Walmsley BA
Dr Roberta Ward PhD MPhil
Ms Diana Warwick BA
Miss Tricia Warwick
Mrs Susan Wates
Miss Frances Watt
Ms Molly Weir
Mrs Janet Weitz
Ms Jill White FRAM FBSM
Mrs Anna Whitehead
Miss Jane Whittaker LLB
Mrs Barbara Whittome
Ms Toyah Wilcox
Miss Lindsay Wilkinson

Miss Jayne Willetts LLB
Mrs Shirley Williams
Ms Stephanie Williams BA
Mrs Janet Williamson
Mrs Russell Willis-Taylor AB
Ms Marlene Winfield BA
Rev Dr Janet Wootton MA PhD
Mrs Karen Wright MA (Cantab) MBA
Miss Rosamund Wynn-Pope MBE
Yazz
Mrs Aida Young
The Hon Mrs Jennie Younger BA

Monday 6th October 1997
THEME: MAKING A DIFFERENCE

Ms Lesley Abdela MBE
Ms Sandra Addae LLB
Professor Jean Aitchison MA AM
Ms Jean-Marion Aitken BA MA
Dr Jane Anderson PhD FRCP
Professor Kathleen Anderson OBE FRSE
    PhD DSc(H) FRSC
Mrs Eleanor Angel
Mrs Carmel Angrave RGN RM
Ms Anne Applebaum BA MSc
Miss Val Arnison
Mrs Pamela Arnold
Ms Sally Arnold
Ms Sue Arnold MA
Miss Joyce Arram FInst LEx FRSA
Ms Zenna Atkins MSc
Ms Zeinab Badawi BA MA
Mrs Charlotte Baden-Powell AADip RIBA
Ms Pam Bader OBE
Miss Margaret Bailey
Mrs Vicky Bailey RGN RM MSc
Mrs Carol Banfield
Miss Ann Barr
Ms Liz Barron
The Hon Lady Barttelot OStJ
Ms Sandra Barwick
Miss Jennifer Bate BA FRCO LRAM
    ARCM
Miss Kate Battersby
Mrs Liz Bavidge OBE JP BA
Mrs Joan Belcher MA JP FRSA
Miss Kim Bell BA
Ms Margaret Bennett BA
Mrs Susan Bennett
Ms Pascale Bernard
Miss Danielle Bernstein
Mrs Pek Yeong Berry BSc MSc Dip Ed
    MBE

Dr Dora Black MB FRCPsych FRCPCH
    DPM
Ms Earlette Blake IPD DMS
Mrs Bridget Blow MBCS MBIM
Ms Anna Blundy
Ms Bronwyn Gold Blyth
Mrs Janet Boateng
Professor Margaret Boden ScD PhD FBA
Colonel Caroline Bolland
Dr Margaret Bone MB CMB FRCA
Lady Boothby
Miss Lindsay Boswell QC
Mrs Helen Bouch
Mrs Karen Bradburn
Mrs Wendy Braverman
Ms Kate Bravery
Ms Annie Brough BA MA
Dr Doreen Browne MB BS MSc FRCA
Ms Tanya Bruce-Lockhart
Professor Judith Bryce MA PhD
Mrs Sharon Buckle BSc
Miss Anne Buddle
Miss Deborah Bull
Ms Jackie Burdon
Mrs Susan Burnell
Ms Rosemary Burnett
Miss Gill Burns BEd
Mrs Paddy Burt
Ms Amanda Burton
Mrs Jackie Butterworth RGN ONC ENB
Ms Jayne Buxton BA MBA
Dr Louise Byles
Dr Lavinia Byrne
Mrs Kate Caddy
Paddy Campbell, Fellow of RSA
Mrs Pat Campbell
Ms Diane Canady BA MA
Ms Lynda Cantor
Mrs Lida Lopes Cardozo
Mrs Louise Carstairs
Mrs Evelyn Carter OBE BA
Ms Sally Cartwright
Miss Caroline Cassels
Ms Andre Chadwick BA
Ms Anna-Mei Chadwick BA
Professor Anne Charlton BA MEd PhD
    PGCE
Mrs Catherine Churchard LLB
Mrs Pauline Clare QPM BA CIM Mgt
Miss Felicity Clark
Ms Nicola Clarke BA MBA
Mrs Olive Clarke OBE JP DL
Mrs Lorraine Clinton MA
The Viscountess Cobham DSc
Mrs Elsie Coghlan

Dr Beverly-Jane Collett FRCA MBBS
Mrs June Collins
Mrs Martina Coombs
Ms Val Corbett
Mrs Jennifer P Corbin
Mrs Vivian Cotterill
Dr Yvonne Cripps PhD LLM LLB
Dr Louise Culham PhD MPhil BSc
Mrs Clare Cunningham-Hill MCSP
Mrs Hilary Curry
Mrs Janet Daley BA FRCA
Mrs Maria Dalrymple BEd
Ms Barbara Daly
Miss Jill Dando
Mrs Ann Daniels
Dr Avril Dankworth BMus FTCL ARCM
Dr Robyn Dasey PhD
Mrs Karlene Davis BEO
Baroness Dean of Thornton-Le-Fylde BA
Mrs Ruth Deech MA
Mrs Lucille De Zalduondo Briance BA
Miss Anne Dickinson FIPR CIBM
Mrs Janet Dicks
Mrs Patricia Dilley FInstL Exs
Miss Ann Donkin
Mrs Diana Donovan
Professor Ann P Dowling BA MA PhD
   FEng FIMech
Mrs Kay Dunbar
Ms Liz Earle
Mrs Beryl Easton
Ms Imogen Edwards-Jones
Mrs Sue Ellen BSc
Mrs Rebecca Elliott BA MIPS MBIM
Ms Jane Ellison BA
Miss Roslyn Emblin DN JP
Mrs Pauline Emburey BA ACA
Miss Brenda Emmanus BA
Ms Libbie Escolme-Schmid OAM JP
The Countess of Euston BA MA
Miss Valerie Evans CBE BSc FIBiol
Ms Caroline Eversfield BA
Mrs Audrey Eyton
Miss Diana Faber LLB
Mrs Sue Farr
Ms Lynda Farran
Ms Carolyn Faulder BA
Ms Jean Faulkner BA
Dame Peggy Fenner DBE DL
Ms Anne Fenton BSc MIPD MBKS
Ms Helen Fielding BA
Ms Suzanne Finch
The Lady Finsberg MA
Mrs Lindsay Firth-McGuckin BA MBA
   ACII MCIM

Mrs Dawn Fitt Eng Tech AMIEIE HNC
Miss Amelia Fitzalan Howard BA
Miss Louise Fitzroy BA
Miss Elizabeth Floyd
Mrs Jo Foley BA
Ms Barbara Follett BSc
Mrs Emma Ford
Mrs Joanna Foster
Miss Emma Freud
Lady Jill Freud
Miss Sue Fullilove MA FRCS
Ms Catherine Galvin BA
Ms Diana Garnham BA MA
Mrs Janet Gaymer MA LLM
Dr Selina Gellert MB MRCGP
Ms Jane Gill LLB
Mrs Janet Gillman
Dr Vivette Glover MA PhD DSc
Ms Janet Goldsmith
Mrs Joanna Goldsworthy
Mrs Mari Markus Gomori
Mrs Diana Good
Miss Valerie Gooding BA
Ms Pamela Gordon MA
Miss Mandy Graham
Mrs Moira-Ann Grainger
Betty, Lady Grantchester MA
Mrs Tonia Green BAC
Professor Susan Greenfield BA DPhil
Miss Patricia Gregory
Dr Elaine Griffiths MBBS FRCS
Ms Miriam Gross MA
Mrs Muriel Hackland BA
Mrs Harfiyah Abdel Haleem BA
Ms Moira Hallberg
Miss Jennie Halsall
Mrs Barbara Hamilton MA OM
Ms Eng Juan Han SRN
Mrs Linda Hanford RN BN MSc(A)
   FRSH
Miss Judith Hanratty LLB LLM
Miss Jane Hanson BEd MA
Miss Michele Hanson BA MA
Miss Barbara Harmer
Mrs Susan Harmsworth BA MILAM
Ms Jacqui Harper BA MA
Dr Tanya Harrod BA DPhil
Mrs Dragana Hartley BSc
Mrs Khanam Hassan
Mrs Eileen Hayes MSc BSc
Ms Josephine Hayes MA LLM
Mrs Alma Headland
Mrs Arabella Heathcoat Amory
Mrs Thyra Heaven BA MSc
Mrs Sandra Hepburn

Mrs Maria Herron
Dr Joan Hester MBBS FRCA
Ms Patricia Hewitt MP MA
Mrs Margaret Ann Hickish
Miss Tessa Hilton
Mrs Jeanette Hobart
Mrs Maria Holton HNC
Mrs Jenny Hoon ARCA
Mrs Joyce Hopkirk
Mrs Nicola Horlick BA
Mrs Ros Howells OBE
Ms Zoe Hudson
Miss Ella Hughes
Dr Mary-Lorraine Hughes BSc MBA PhD
Ms Janet Hull MA DIDM FRSA
Ms Gay Hutchings BA
Ms Diana Hutchinson BA
Mrs Rosa Iken
Ms Vicky Ireland
Dr Jean Irvine FBCS OBE
Dr Pam Johnson MD MRCGP MRCOG
Miss Sarah Jones BA
Ms Sarah-Louise Jones BA
Dr Jeannette Josse MBBS MRCPsych
Professor Annette Karmiloff-Smith PhD
   FBA FRSA CPsychol
Ms Adah Kay MA
Ms Caroline Kellett
Mrs Avril Kennedy
Ms Bronagh Kennedy BA MA
Ms Helena Kennedy LLD
Ms Philippa Kennedy BA
Ms Anne Keogh BA RGN DipN
Dr Betty Kershaw
Captain Yvonne Kershaw
Miss Linda Key
Mrs Marjorie Knightley Day RGN
   Him(Dip)
Mrs Sandra Knowles
Professor Eva Kohner OBE MD FRCP
   FCOphthalm
Ms Maggie Koumi
Ms Dorothy Kuya CertEd SEN
Ms Nancy Lam
Ms Verity Lambert BA
Dr Nancy Lane OBE DPhil SCD LLO
Miss Janet Langdon MA BSc
The Hon Mrs Carole Lawson
Mrs Christina Lebus
Ms Helen Lederer BA
Ms Lynda Lee-Potter
Mrs Charlotte Lessing
Dr Elizabeth Letsky MB BS FRCPath
   FRCOG FRCPCH
Ms Mary Lewis BA

Dr Tasmin Little DLitt ArcM DipCSM
Mrs Ursula Lloyd MBBS FRCOG
Sylvia Loch
Mrs Jennifer Lonsdale
Miss Heather Love
Dr Erna Low PhD MCIM MBIM
Miss Michelle Lucarotti MD FRCS
Mrs Anne Luther BSc
Professor Christina Lyon LLB FRSA
Mrs Amanda Macandrew JP
Ms Shelagh MacLeod MA
Ms Rosemarie Macqueen BScSoc
   DipArch Cons DMS MRTPI
The Hon Diana Makgill CVO
Lady Marina Marks BA MA FRAS OM
   KM
Mrs Caroline Marland
Ms Helen Marriage BA
Dr Caroline Marriott MB BCh
   MRCPsych
Ms Penny Marshall BA
Mrs Ilana Martin BA FCIS
Ms Juliette May BA MA
Ms Sue McAinsh
Mrs Antonia McAlindin LLB LLM BA
Mrs Margaret McAllister BA MEd
   CPsychol AFBPsS
Mrs Primrose McCabe CA
Ms Carolyn McCall BA MA
Ms Janet McCormac
Mrs Bridget McCrum ARBS
Miss Linda McDougal
Ms Anne McElvoy BA
Dr Helen McEwan MD FRCOG FRCS
   FRCP
Professor Baroness McFarlane of Llandaff
   BSc MA FCN FRCN
Miss Heather McGlone BA
Ms Frankie McGowan
Mrs Ann McIntyre BA DBOT
Ms Victoria McKee BA MA FRSA
Mrs Judith McKenzie BA
Ms June McKerrow MPhil
Miss Judy McKnight BSocSc
Mrs Patricia McLean BEd MA
Mrs Betty McLeish
Ms Nancy Meckler BA
Mrs Janice Meek
Miss June Mendoza AO RP ROI
Mrs Penny Methuen
Ms Sarah Miller
Dame Barbara Mills DBE QC
Ms Sophie Mirman
Mrs Dawn Mitchell FMRS
Ms Anna Moffat

Dr Anne Molyneux OBE MA MB BCHIR
Mrs Yvonne Moores DSc DCL
Lady Morris of Kenwood
Ms Roz Morris BA
Mrs Patricia Morris-Thompson BA MBA RGN RM
Mrs Jean Mossman BSc
Mrs Elizabeth Murdoch BA
Ms Ann Murray Chatterton
Mrs Minna Nathoo MA MIPD
Dr Ann Naylor MB BS FRCA
Dr Elizabeth Neville QPM MA PhD
Mrs Olive Newton BA JP
Mrs Esme Newton-Dunn
Ms Mary Nicholson BA BAOG(dip)
Mrs Elaine Noad
Ms Barbara Nokes
Miss Dee Nolan
Miss Sally Jane O'Neill QC LLB
Dr Marilyn Orcharton BDS DipM MCIM
Mrs Helen O'Shea BA
Dr E C Osmond MBBS MRCP DRCOG MRCGP
Miss Catherine Ostler MA
Ms Sally O'Sullivan BA
Mrs Sylvia Owen BSc DipEd
Mrs Jane Packer
Ms Elaine Paige OBE
Ms Michaela Pain
Ms Jill Palmer
Mrs Elli Panteli
Ms Janet Paraskeva BA JP
Mrs Alison Parry LLB ALA FRSA
Miss Jennifer Paterson
Mrs Lyndy Payne
Miss Maggie Philbin BA
Dr Ann Phoenix MA PhD
Dr Jayshree Pillaye MB ChB MSc
Ms Anne-Marie Piper LLB
Det Constable Catherine Plummer
Ms Eve Pollard
Miss Paula Power
Mrs Marian Pringle BA DipLib ALA
Mrs Margaret Pritchard
Mrs Kailash Puri BA
Ms Alison Pylkkanen
Miss Jane Rabagliati MA
Ms Heather Rabbatts BA MA
Mrs Nicola Ralston BA
Mrs Marsha R Ratcliff
Mrs Shashi Rattan BSc
Dr Jessica Rawson CBE DLitt
Mrs Susan Read BA
Ms Carol Reay BA
Ms Gail Rebuck BA

Mrs Alexis Redmond BA ACA
Ms Elsa Redwood
Ms Marie Restori BSc MSC
Professor Felicity Reynolds MBBS MD FRCA FRCOG
Mrs Gillian Reynolds MA
Miss Anneka Rice
Dr Ann Richardson BA MA PhD
Mrs Susan Riches
Ms Victoria Riches BA
Ms Sharon Ring
Miss Lucy Roberts
Mrs Sally Anne Roberts BA
Mrs Pat Roberts Cairns
Dr Ann Robinson MA
Ms Zsuzsi Roboz
Dr Anna-Maria Rollin MBBS FRCA
Ms Patricia Rothman BSc
Ms Bridget Rowe
Miss Jan Rowland LLB
Mrs Chinwe Roy BA
Ms Susan Rozsnyai BA
Mrs Jill Ruddock
Dr Philippa Russell OBE DSocSc BA
Mrs Brenda Ryan
Miss Sophie Ryder
Lady Samuel
Miss Tessa Sanderson MBE
Mrs Angela Sarkis
Ms Tanya Sarne
Ms Anna Scher
Ms Jenny Seagrove
Ms Hilary Sears BSc MBA
Mrs Geraldine Sharpe-Newton BA
Mrs Pam Shaw
Mrs Susan Shaw MSI
Ms Caroline Shott
Dr Janet Silver OBE DSc MPhil FBCOpton
Miss Ashley Simpson
Miss Rosemary Anne Sisson BA MLitt
Miss Prudence Skene
Mrs Sue Skeen BAA
Mrs Elizabeth Smith MA
Mrs Valerie Smith
Ms Sally Soames
Lady Solti
Miss Barbara Speake ARAD MISTD MIDTA
The Countess of St Andrews BA MA
Mrs Ann Stanway MCSP SRP
Mrs Jenny Staples MA
Mrs Gai Stephenson DBO(T) SRO
Ms Zoe Stravrinidis BSc MA
Ms Moira Stuart

Miss June Stubbs MCSD
Mrs Annie Subba Row
Ms Janis Susskind BA
Mrs Barbara Switzer
Mrs Judy Tarlo
Mrs Peta Tayler BA
Miss Pamela Thayer OBE ISO MA
Ms Cathy Thomas MSc
Ms Dianne Thompson
Dr Janet Thompson DPhil BSc
Mrs Patricia Thompson MA GRNCM
  ARMCM PGCE FRSA
Miss Shirley Thompson BA
Ms Sandi Toksvig MA
Ms Jill Tookey
Ms Philippa Toomey
Dr Lina Toukan
Dr Christina Townsend PhD
Miss Helen Tridgell
The Rt Hon The Baroness Trumpington
Baroness Turner of Camden
Miss Dorothy Tutin CBE DLitt
Mrs Beryl Vertue
Ms Deirdre Vine BA
Mrs Anuradha Vittachi-Armstrong BA MA
Miss Shelley Von Strunckel
Mrs Bharti Vyas MBABTAC
Mrs Pamela Maunsell Wall
Ms Emma Walmsley BA
Ms Alice Walters BA Anthropology
Mrs Liz Warom
Miss Joan Webster QPM BA
Mrs Grace Wedekind
Ms Molly Weir
Mrs Janet Whitaker MA FRSA
Mrs Ann White
Miss Jill White FRAM FBSM FRSA
Ms Katherine Whitehorn LLD
Mrs Jan Whitehouse CIPFA ILAM MIM
  IOD
Miss Jane Whittaker LLB
Ms Esme Winch BA ACMA
Ms Annette Worsley-Taylor
Ms Dorothy Wright MA

Monday 12th October 1998
THEME: TOMORROW'S CHILDREN

Ms Maureen Adamson
Tinu Adele
Ms Niki Akhurst
Ms Clare Alexander
Ms Pam Alexander
Ziggi Alexander

Ms Britt Allcroft
Ms Sue Altschuler
The Countess of Ancram
Mrs Eleanor Angel
Mrs Carmel Angrave RGN RM
Ms Yasmin Anwar
Miss Joan Armatrading DLitt
Ms Sylvia Armistead
Miss Val Arnison
Mrs Romi Arora Dip SW CQSW
Miss Joyce Arram FInst LEx FRSA
Miss Jane Asher
Ms Helen Ashton
Ms Rosie Atkins
Mrs Liz Attenborough
Miss Pam Ayres
Ms Zeinab Badawi BA MA
Mrs Charlotte Baden-Powell AADip RIBA
Ms Sally Balfour
Angela Banfield
Mrs Carol Banfield
Mrs Karen Bannister BA
Dr Sue Barnes
Miss Ann Barr
Mrs Jayne Barr
Mrs Joan Barrell
Ms Beth Barry
Mrs Helen Barton
Mary Baskin
Ms Sarah Bates
Ms Marilyn Baxter
Mrs Irene Beard
Ms Lynda Bellingham
Ms Sarah Benioff
Mrs Veronica Benjamin
Ms Margaret Bennett BA
Ms Pascale Bernard
Dr Mary Berry MA PhD MusB
Helena Best
Mrs Jane Betts
Ms Diana Billingham
Miss Charlotte Black
Ms Elizabeth Blackburn
Mrs Janet Boateng
Dr Adrianne Booth MA MB BChir
Mrs Claudia Borchard
Miss Jane Bown MBE
Ms Candida Boyes BA
Ms Katie Bradford
Ms Greta Bradley MA
Ms Barbara Braithwaite
Dr Margaret Branthwaite MA
Ms Faith Brown
Miss Maggie Butler Dip AD
Ms Pia Buxton

Ms Sue Cameron BA
Paddy Campbell
Ms Janet Canetty-Clarke
Mrs Lida Lopes Cardozo
Ms Lavinia Carey
Ms Gill Carrick
Ms Sally Cartwright
Miss Caroline Cassels
Ms Maureen Castens
Miss Judith Chalmers OBE
Dr Mohan Kawal Chandok MBBS
Dr Qudsia Chandran MBBS DRCOG
Ms Enid Chanelle
Ms Lesley Chapman
Ms Pat Chapman-Pincher BA
Maya Cheetham
Dr Miriam Chung PhD
Miss Lindka Cierach
Ms Jane Clarke
Ms Judi Clements
Mrs Penny Cleobury
Ms Mary Cockroft
Dr Beverly-Jane Collett FRCA MBBS
Ms Carole Collins
Mrs June Collins
Mrs Lynn Collins
Ms Phillipa Colloby
Annette Collymore
Ms Marion Colomb Kermanshahchi
Ms Sarah Connolly
Mrs Shirley Conran
Ms Geraldine Cooke
Martina Coombs
Dr Griselda Cooper
Ms Ann Copeland
Ms Val Corbett
Ms Hazel Courteney
Ms Ros Coward BA PhD
Ms Diane Creightmore
Ms Katy Cropper
Dr Louise Culham PhD MPhil BSc
Ms Chloe Cunningham
Ms Jo Darbyshire
Ms Ginny Darley
Dr Clare E Davies PhD
Ms Isabel Davies
Ms Katie Derham
Professor Ann P Dowling BA MA PhD
    FEng FIMech
Mrs Fiona Driscoll
Ms Joyce d'Silva
Ms Anne Dudley
Mrs Julia Duffield
Ms Heather du Quesnay CBE
Mrs Beryl Easton

The Hon Mrs Cathy G Edwards
Ros Edwards BA
Mrs Sandra Edwards
Mrs Tracy Edwards MBE
Mrs Sue Eleen BSc
Ms Di Ellis
Ms Clare Elsby
Ms Katie Elsom
Miss Roslyn Emblin DN JP
The Countess of Euston BA MA
Miss Valerie Evans
Ms Caroline Eversfield BA
Mrs Audrey Eyton
Adelaien Farhey
Mrs Sue Farr
Ms Lynda Farran
Ms Helen Faulkner
Mrs Helena Felix BA
Ms Vanessa Feltz MA
Dame Peggy Fenner DBE DL
Miss Shirley Ann Field
Ms Emily Fitzroy
Miss Louise Fitzroy BA
Miss Elizabeth Floyd
Miss Antonia Forster BSc
Mrs Vivien Fowle
Ms Daphne Fowler
Ms Sue Fox
Ms Jane Frost
Ms Leisha Fullick
Sonja Garsvo
Ms Pat George
Ms Lizi Gill
Ms Mandy Gillespie
Mrs Leni Gillman BA
Miss Caroline Gledhill
Dr Vivette Glover MA PhD DSc
Mrs Renée Goddard
Mrs Doreen Goodman BA MPhil
Ms Julia Goodman
Ms Maggie Goodman
Mrs Jane Gordon-Clark
Ms Jacquie Granditer
Ms Jane Grant
Ms Anne Gray
Ms Allison Green
Miss Susan Green
Miss Patricia Gregory
Olwyn Gunn
Ms Ursula Guy
Mrs Lois Hainsworth FCIJ FRSA
Miss Jennie Halsall
Ms Kleshna Handel
Ms Susan Hardwick BA
Mrs Coleen Harris

Ms Lucile Harris
Dr Tanya Harrod BA DPhil
Dr Agnes Hauck
Miss Linda Haye MA DSoc
Ms Patty Healey
Ms Lorraine Heggesey
Ms Lindy Hemming
Mrs Sandra Hepburn
Mrs Maria Herron
Mrs Norma Heyman
Ms Caroline Hickman
Dr Rowan Hillson
Commodore Muriel Hocking
Ms Anna Hodson-Pressinger
Miss Thelma Holt MA CBE
Mrs Joyce Hopkirk
Mrs Nicola Horlick BA MD
Ms Simonette Hornby
Mrs Ros Howells OBE
Professor Celia Hoyles PhD BSc MED
Miss Ella Hughes
Ms Nerys Hughes
Ms Janet Hull MA DIDM FRSA
Ms Sally Hunter
Mrs Elizabeth Innes-Smith
Ms Judy Ironside
Dr Jean Irvine FBCS OBE
Mrs Pat Jackson
Ms Sian James
Professor Lisa Jardine MA PhD (Cantab)
    FRHistS FRSA
Mrs Caroline Jeremy
Mrs Mimi Johnson BCom FRSA
Dr Pam Johnson MD MRCGP MRCOG
Ms Patricia Jones BA MA ACA
Miss Sarah Jones BA
Ms Susie Kaufman
Ms Martha Kearney
Ms Marie-Claire Kerr
Ms Diana Kingdon
Ms Denise Kingsmill MA
Ms Maggie Koumi
Ms Dorothy Kuya CertEd SEN
Dr Ann Lackie PhD
Miss Sue Laing
Ms Alison Lambert
Ms Anne Lambert
Dr Nancy Lane OBE DPhil SCD LLO
Ms Claire Lavin CertCIB
Ms Alison Lawrence
Mrs Doreen Lawrence BA
The Hon Mrs Carole Lawson
Ms Sheryl Leach
Ms Helen Lederer BA
Ms Lynda Lee-Potter

Mrs Charlotte Lessing
Ms Amanda Levete AA Dip RIBA
Ms Sue Limb BA
The Baroness Linklater
Ms Dorothy Livingston
Ms Margaret Lochrie BA
Ms Christina Lomas
Ms M J Long
Ms Lizanne Macgregor
Ms Sarah Mackay Whitley MA
Mrs Gilly Mackwood
Ms Yvette Mahon
The Hon Diana Makgill CVO
Miss Suzi Malin
Professor Averil Mansfield ChM FRCS
    MD FRACS
Ms Bernadette Marjoram
Mrs Caroline Marland
Ms Jayne Marsden
Mrs Ilana Martin BA FCIS
Miss Joan Martin
Ms Noreen Martin
Ms Helen Mather
Ms Terry Ann Matthews
Ms Anna Maxwell
Ms Maria McAulay
Helen McDermott
Ms Margaret McDonagh
Miss Sheena McDonald MA
Ms Anne McElvoy BA
Ms Jacqui McGlade
Ms Judy McGuire
Ms Joy McKenzie
Mrs Judith McKenzie BA
Ms Chris Meaden
Ms Leonie Mellinger
Miss June Mendoza AO RP ROI
Ms Margaret Michie
Mrs Lesley Millar BSc PGCE MBA
Ms Sarah Miller
Dame Barbara Mills DBE QC
Ms Helen Mirren
Ms Anna Moffatt
Ms Galina Molchanov
The Hon Mrs Anne Money-Coutts
Belinda Lady Montagu
Mrs Yvonne Moores DSc DCL
Ms Margaret Morgan
Lady Morris of Kenwood
Ms Roz Morris BA
Mrs Patricia Morris-Thompson BA MBA
    RGN RM
Ms Margaret Morrisey OBE
Ms Marie Morrow MBE
Mrs Jane Muir

Mrs Jane Muir MA
Ms Ann Murray Chatterton
Ms Nina Myskow
Mrs Minna Nathoo MA MIPD
Dr Elizabeth Nelson BA PhD FRSA
Mrs Penny Newman
Ms Linda Norris
Miss Deborah Oliver TD MA
Mrs Sally O'Sullivan BA
Mrs Jane Packer
Ms Jill Palmer
Mrs Elli Panteli
Vigdis Parkins
Ms Clare Paterson
Mrs Georgia Paterson
Mrs Lynette Patterson BA
Mrs Liz Paver FCollP FRSA
Ms Cynthia Payne
Ms Jean Penny
Ms Fiona Phillips
Ms Penny Phipps
Mrs Sybil Phoenix MBE MS
Ms Sylvie Pierce LLB
Ms Anne-Marie Piper LLB
Ms Judith Pipes
Ms Susan Jennifer Pipes
Mrs Jenny Pitman OBE
Ms Jane Platt
Ms Eve Pollard
Mrs Julia Prescot MA
Mrs Joan Price
Mrs Marian Pringle BA DipLib ALA
Mrs Margaret Prosser
Ms Geraldine Proudler
Ms Alison Pylkkanen
Miss Jane Rabagliati MA
Ms Heather Rabbatts BA MA
Ms Amanda Randle
Miss Esther Rantzen OBE MA DLitt FRTS
Ms Susan Raven
Ms Carol Reay
Mrs Alexis Redmond BA ACA
Ms Sharon Reed
Ms Marie Restori BSc MSC
Ms Judith Rich
Ms Joy Richardson
Mrs Jo Rickard
Miss Mary Riddell
Mrs Louise Riley Smith
Miss Angela Rippon
Dr Janet Ritterman BMus MMus PhD
    FTCL DSCM FRSA
Dr Caroline Roberts PhD
Mrs Pat Roberts Carins
Lieutenant Melanie Robinson

The Hon Lady Roche
Ms Tamara Rojo
Ms Susan Rozsnyai BA
Ms Anne Rumble
Professor Janette Rutterford
Ms Jane Ryan
Ms Martine Ryan
Ms Daniele Ryman
The Lady Sainsbury
Mrs Nousha Pakpour Samari
Professor Naomi Sargeant BA
Mrs Agnes Sassoon
Ms Margaret Anne Savage
Dr Julia Schofield MBE BSc PhD FRSA
    MBCS
Ms Lucie Scott
Ms Hilary Sears BSc MBA
Ms Ana Selby
Mrs Fiona Shackleton LLB
Mrs Susan Shaw MSI
Mrs Yasmin Sheikh
Sr Margaret Shepherd NDS BA MTA
Dr Janet Silver OBE DSc MPhil
    FBCOpton
Det Chief Inspector Debbie Simpson
Ms Maureen Skevington
Mrs Marie Skinner
Mrs Dottie Smalley MBE
Ms Amy Smith
Ms Eileen Smith
Miss Sally Elizabeth Smith QC
Samantha Smith
Mrs Valerie Smith
Mrs Cilla Snowball BA
Ms Sally Soames
Dr Jane Somerville MD FRCP
Ms Margaret Sparshott
Miss Barbara Speake ARAD MISTD
    MIDTA
Ms Lisa Spiro
Ms Clare Spottiswoode MA MPhil
Professor Margaret Spufford OBE DLitt
    FBA
The Countess of St Andrews BA MA
Mrs Suzanne Storer
Ms Moira Stuart
Ms Gillian Switalski
Mrs Barbara Switzer
Mrs Maxine Tabak
Miss Marion Tait OBE
Mrs Judy Tarlo BA
Alvina Benjamin Taylor
Miss Cynthia L Taylor
Ms Elly Taylor
Ms Joyce Taylor

Mrs Susan Taylor
Ms Dianne Thompson
Ms Yvonne Thompson
Ms Desrie Thomson
Miss Vivian Tierney
Mrs Lynda Till
Ms Gill Tishler
Ms Sandi Toksvig MA
Dr Joan Trowell
The Rt Hon The Baroness Trumpington
Ms Sylvia I M Tutt FCIS
Ms Susan Tyman MSc
Mrs Jenny Tzaig
Ms Yvette Vanson
Ms Deirdre Vine BA
Judy Wade
Mrs Sheila Wallis BEd FRSA
Mrs Grace Walmsley
Councillor Betty Walshe
Mrs Elizabeth Ward OBE
Ms Marina Warner FRSL DLitt
Mrs Perween Warsi
Julia Watson
Ms Tina Weaver
Lady Weir OBE
Mrs C D West
Ms Cindy West
Lady Mary Westenholz BA
Ms Nicola White
Ms Myrna Whiteson JP
Ms Sarah Whitley MA
Ms Helen Wilkinson
Ms Juliet Williams
Hazel Scotland Williamson
Mrs Janet Williamson
The Lady Wilson of Rievaulx
Mrs Precious Wilson
Ms Lorna Winstanley
Ms Caroline Wiseman
Mrs Marion Woodard DipCST FETC
Ms Jacqueline Wright RGN Dip Nursing
Ms Karen Wright MA MBA
Ms Dianna Marilyne Yach
The Hon Diane Zitcer JP

Monday 11th October 1999
THEME: HUMAN RIGHTS

Mary Able
Mrs Gurdev Abrol
Ms Niki Akhurst
Ms Clare Alexander
Dr Jean Alexander
Ms Ann Allen

Tamsin Allen
The Baroness Valerie Amos
Rachael Anderson
Mrs Eleanor Angel
Ms Carmel Angrave
Miss Joan Armatrading
Miss Val Arnison
Mrs Romi Arora
Miss Joyce Arram
Mrs Jenny Arwas
Anne Ashby
Ms Helen Ashton
Mrs Liz Attenborough
Penny Avis
Ms Zeinab Badawi
Ms Sally Baffour
Jan Bailey
Angela Baker
Julia Balfour-Lynn
Beryl Bamforth
Angela Banfield
Mrs Carol Banfield
Mrs Margaret Barbour
Mrs Belinda Barnes
Dr Susan Barnes
Miss Ann Barr
Mrs Joan Barrell
Mrs Helen Barton
Merry Baskin
Coral Bayley
Dawn Baynes
Mrs Joan Belcher
Judith Bell
Susan Bell
Ms Lynda Bellingham
Ms Sarah Benioff
Mrs Veronica Benjamin
Gill Bennett
Ms Margaret Bennett
Ms Pascale Bernard
Amanda Berry
Dr Mary Berry
Joey Bieber
Mrs Joan Bingley
Hilary Birt
Professor Carol Black
Ms Elizabeth Blackburn
Ms Kate Bleasdale
The Baroness May Blood
Mrs Irene Bloor
Mrs Janet Boateng
Jennie Bond
Trisha Booth
Trudy Boyce
Margo Boye-Anawoma

Ms Jenny Bradley
Ms Barbara Braithwaite
Jennifer Brown JP
Helen Browning
Ms Tanya Bruce-Lockhart
Mrs Janie Burford
Ms Rosemary Burnett
Ms Diane Burrell
Miss Maggie Butler
Dr Maria Calloni
Lady Cecil Cameron
Ms Nina Campbell
Paddy Campbell
Ms Sonia Campbell
Ms Diane Canady
Ms Janet Canetty-Clarke
Pat Cantrill
Ms Gill Carrick
Rosemary Carter
Ms Sally Cartwright
Miss Caroline Cassels
Ms Maureen Castens
Mrs Kate Cawley
Ms Caroline Charles
Dr Miriam Chung
Miss Lindka Cierach
Christine Clancy
Miss Felicity Clark
Pauline Clarke
Ms Jacqueline Clifton
Blondel Cluff
Ms Pamela Colbourne
Dr Beverly-Jane Collett
Ms Carole Collins
Mrs June Collins
Ms Lynn Collins
Ms Marion Colomb Kermanshahchi
Mrs Shirley Conran
Frances Cook
Ms Ann Copeland
Mrs Adine Copeman
Lindsey Coulson
Ms Ros Coward
Baroness Crawley
Ms Katy Cropper
Julie Crow
Baroness Cumberledge of Newick
Edwina Currie
The Countess of Dalkeith
Ms Isabel Davies
Hilary Davis
Joanna De la Force
The Countess Carolyn de Salis
Mrs Ruth Deech
Helen Dent

Lady Ann Dholakia
Ms Rita Donaghy
Ms Joyce D'Silva
Mrs Julia Duffield
Jennifer Duguid
Ms Heather Du Quesnay
Lady Eames
Belinda Earl
Dr Joy Edelman
Fiona Edward-Stuart
Miss Tracy Edwards
Ros Edwards
Ms Judith Elderkin
Mrs Sue Ellen
Ms Wendy Elsdon
Fiona Elworthy
The Countess of Euston
Miss Maria Ewing
Mrs Audrey Eyton
Mrs Sue Farr
Ms Lynda Farran
Rosalyn Fawcett
Josephine Fawkes
Amanda Feggetter
Ms Vanessa Feltz
Ms Penny Ferguson
Ann Field
Pamela Finn
Susanna Fitzgerald
Miss Emily Fitzroy
Miss Louise Fitzroy
Ms Jo Foley
Nicky Forrest
Miss Ann Foster
Mrs Vivien Fowle
Ms Sue Fox
Miss Wendy Franks
Ms Helen Fraser
Henny Frazer
Dr Theresa Freeman-Wang
Lady Jill Freud
Anne Fuller
Chloe Gardner
Sonja Garsvo
Mrs Janet Gaymer
Ms Pat George
Maggie Getfield
Ms Frances Gibb
Liz Gill
Virginia Glastonbury
Christine Glenn
Dr Vivette Glover
The Hon Lady Goodhart
Mrs Doreen Goodman
Donna Gordon

Mrs Jane Gordon-Clark
Helen Gordon-Smith
Ms Janice Graham
Ms Jacquie Granditer
Ms Rosamund Grant
Ms Anne Gray
Lynne Green
Anna Greening
Miss Patricia Gregory
Barbara Grundy
Joanne Gubbay
Mrs Angela Guillaume
Elizabeth Anne Gumbel
Mrs Olwyn Gunn
Ms Ursula Guy
Mrs Lois Hainsworth
Miss Jennie Halsall
Ms Susan Hardwick
Ms Belinda Harley
Miss Barbara Harmer
Sharon Harriott-Kerr
Mrs Colleen Harris
Kate Harris
Ruth Harris
Waveney Harris
Sue Harvey
Bernadette Hawkes
Miss Linda Haye
Mrs Eileen Hayes
Julia Head
Mrs Sandra Hepburn
Carole Hepworth
Mrs Maria Herron
Mrs Norma Heyman
Dr Rowan Hillson
Commodore Muriel Hocking
Lady Hollick
Mrs Joyce Hopkirk
Ms Simonetta Hornby
Ms Barbara Hosking
Baroness St Davids Howells
Professor Celia Hoyles
Miss Ella Hughes
Captain Sarah Hulm
Ms Sally Hunter
Emma Hurd
Margaret Hyde
Mrs Judy Ironside
Dr Jean Irvine
Ms Totlyn Jackson
Professor Lisa Jardine
Ms Jasmine Jayham
Miss Eva Jiricna
Ms Carolyn Jones
Ms Helen Jones

Ms Patricia Jones
Miss Sarah Jones
Patricia Jordan Evans
Liz Kaye
Mrs Lucy Keaveney
Ms Lorraine Kelly
Miss Linda Key
Dr Cay Kielty
Ms Diana Kingdon
Lynne Knowles
Ms Maggie Koumi
Ms Dorothy Kuya
Miss Sue Laing
Ms Anne Lambert
Carolyn Lambert
Dr Nancy Lane
Julia Langdon
Ms Claire Lavin
Mrs Doreen Lawrence
The Hon Mrs Carole Lawson
Ms Helen Lederer
Pamela Lee
Ms Lynda Lee-Potter
Miss Victoria Legge-Bourke
Ms Amanda Levete
Maureen Lipman
Moyra Livesey
Ms Dorothy Livingston
Claer Lloyd-Jones
Lynda Logan
Deborah Loudon
Mary Loveday
Professor Valerie Lund
Shena Macdonald
Ms Yvette Mahon
The Hon Diana Makgill
Ms Margaret Manley
Ms Bernadette Marjoram
Julie Marron
Ms Jayne Marsden
Mrs Ilana Martin
Corporal Karen Martin
Anne Marx
Ginny Mayall
Ms Mary McAnally
Margaret McCabe
Carolyn McCall
Helen McDermott
Joan McDermott
Caroline McDevitt
Rita McGeown
Professor Jacqueline McGlade
Ms Judy McGuire
Miss Julia McKenzie
Isobel McKenzie-Price

Miss Judy McKnight
Mrs Patricia McLean
Mrs Eileen Meadmore
Mrs Janice Meek
Rebecca Mehrabian
Ms Leonie Mellinger
Miss June Mendoza
Gill Middleburgh MVO
Mrs Lesley Millar
Dame Barbara Mills
Mrs Dawn Mitchell
Ms Anna Moffatt
Ms Alison Moore
Anne Moore
Edwina Moreton
Ms Margaret Morgan
Lady Morris of Kenwood
Ms Roz Morris
Gayle Morrison
Mrs Anne Moss
Mrs Lorna Muirhead
Ms Ann Murray Chatterton
Ms Nina Myskow
Mrs Louise Naftalin
Mrs Minna Nathoo
Dr Elizabeth Nelson OBE
Catherine Nelson-Piercy
Dr Elizabeth Neville
Dame Pauline Neville-Jones
Mrs Christina Noble
Ms Linda Norris
Bernadette O'Connell
Mary O'Flaherty
Miss Deborah Oliver
Nicky Oppenheimer
Rita O'Regan
Sandy Owen
Ms Ursula Owen
Mrs Jane Packer
Ms Diana Parker
Vigdis Parkins
Mrs Betty Parsons
Dr June Paterson-Brown
Ms Sara Paterson-Brown
Professor Catherine Peckham
Mary Pedlow
Lady Penn
Ann Phillips
Mrs Carole Phillips
Caroline Phillips
Ms Fiona Phillips
Dr Mary Phillips
Ms Penny Phipps
Mrs Sybil Phoenix
Ms Sylvie Pierce

Julia Pilau
Ms Anne-Marie Piper
Ms Jane Platt
Ms Eve Pollard
Nicola Poulston
Mrs Julia Prescot
Mrs Rosalind Preston
Mrs Joan Price
Pauline Prior-Pitt
Mrs Margaret Prosser
Ms Geraldine Proudler
Mrs Kailash Puri
Miss Jane Rabagliati
Miss Esther Rantzen
Ms Carol Reay
Ms Gail Rebuck
Mrs Alexis Redmond
Novette Rennie
Ms Marie Restori
Fiona Reynolds
Charlotte Rhodes
Miss Mary Riddell
Mrs Louise Riley-Smith
Miss Angela Rippon
Dr Janet Ritterman
The Hon Elizabeth Robins
Lieutenant Melanie Robinson
Sue Robinson
Zoe Robinson
Glynis Ronald
Jane Rothery
Ms Susan Rozsnyai
Ms Joan Ruddock
Ms Jane Ryan
Mrs Martine Ryan
Eunice Salmond
Mrs Nousha Pakpour Samar
Rita Sammons
Lee Samuel
Ms Annemarie Sand
Professor Naomi Sargant
Sandra Sayers
Ms Anna Scher
Dr Julia Schofield
Baroness Scotland
Gail Seal
Gil Sharp
Mrs Susan Shaw
Alison Shepherd
Ms Alexandra Shulman
Ms Mary Ann Sieghart
Ruth Silver CBE
Joan Simpson
Ms Jill Sinclair
Mrs Marie Skinner

Samantha Smith
Sarah Smith
Mrs Valerie Smith
Mrs Cilla Snowball
Ms Emma Soames
Ms Sally Soames
Professor Jane Somerville
Ms Margaret Sparshott
Miss Barbara Speake
Lady Jane Spencer-Churchill
Professor Margaret Spufford
Angela Squire
The Countess of St Andrews
Ann Steward
Tricia Stewart
Sue Stockdale
Helen Stone
Ms Moira Stuart
Her Excellency Dame Veronica
   Sutherland DBE CMG
Baroness Symons of Vernham Dean
Mrs Maxine Tabak
Liba Taub
Ms Elleanor Taylor
Kate Thirwall
Ms Dianne Thompson
Shelley Thompson
Ms Yvonne Thompson
Alice Thomson
Sister Bridget Tighe
Mrs Lynda Till
Jean Tomlin
Carole Tongue MEP
Ms Jill Tookey
Rita Turner

Ms Eileen Tyler
Mrs Jenny Tzaig
Caroline Van Den Brul
Ms Elizabeth Varlow
Mrs Beryl Vertue
Mrs Penny Vincenzi
Ms Deirdre Vine
Parminder Vir
Mrs Elizabeth Virgo
Ms Virginia Wade
Mrs Sheila Wallis
Mrs Grace Walmsley
Fiona Walsh
Barbara Ward
Dorotta Warren
Deirdre Watson
Maureen Watson
Mrs Grace Wedekind
Ms Molly Weir
Ms Nicola White
Ms Myrna Whiteson
Ms Beverley Whyte
Helen Williams
Jackie Williams
Ms Juliet Williams
Mrs Russell Willis-Taylor
Shirley Winter
Jane Withers
Joanna Womack
Ms Andrea Wonfor
Mrs Marion Woodard
Squadron Leader Helen Wray
Ms Karen Wright
Ms Dianna Yach

Bibliography

Benjamin, Floella *Coming to England* (Pavilion Books, 1995)

Boccaccio, Giovanni *Concerning Famous Women* (Rutgers University Press, 1963)

Buxton, Jayne *Ending the Mother War: Starting the Workplace Revolution* (Macmillan, 1998)

Campbell, Beatrix and Coote, Anna *Sweet Freedom: The Struggle for Women's Liberation* (Picador, 1982)

Chang, Jung *Wild Swans* (Flamingo, 1993)

Lothian, A *Valentina: First Woman in Space* (Pentland Press, 1997)

Marwick, Arthur *Women at War 1914–1918* (Fontana, 1977)

Mackenzie, Midge *Shoulder to Shoulder: A Documentary History of the Militant Suffragettes* (Penguin Books, 1975)

Nixon, Edna *Mary Wollstonecraft: Her Life and Times* (JM Dent & Sons, 1971)

O'Faolain, Sean *Constance Markievicz* (Sphere Books, 1967)

Rowbotham, Sheila *A Century of Women* (Penguin Books, 1999)

— *Woman's Consciousness, Man's World* (Pelican, 1974)

— *Women, Resistance and Revolution* (Pelican, 1975)

— *Hidden from History* (Pluto Press, 1974)